CONTRACTS

A Transactional Approach

ASPEN COURSEBOOK SERIES

CONTRACTS

A Transactional Approach

DAVID ZARFES

Associate Dean and Schwartz Lecturer in Law
The University of Chicago Law School

MICHAEL L. BLOOM

Lecturer in Law
The University of Chicago Law School

Law & Business

AUSTIN   BOSTON   CHICAGO   NEW YORK   THE NETHERLANDS

Aspen Publishers
Attn: Permissions Department
76 Ninth Avenue, 7th Floor
New York, NY 10011-5201

To contact Customer Care, e-mail customer.service@aspenpublishers.com,
call 1-800-234-1660, fax 1-800-901-9075, or mail correspondence to:

Aspen Publishers
Attn: Order Department
PO Box 990
Frederick, MD 21705

Printed in the United States of America.

1 2 3 4 5 6 7 8 9 0

ISBN 978-0-7355-1046-3

Library of Congress Cataloging-in-Publication Data

Zarfes, David.
  Contracts : a transactional approach / David Zarfes, Michael L. Bloom. — 1st ed.
    p. cm. — (Aspen casebook series)
  Includes index.
  ISBN 978-0-7355-1046-3
1. Contracts—United States—Cases.   2. Contracts—United States—Language.
I. Bloom, Michael L.   II. Title.
  KF801.A7Z37 2011
  346.7302—dc22

                                                                    2010049399

About Wolters Kluwer Law & Business

Wolters Kluwer Law & Business is a leading provider of research information and workflow solutions in key specialty areas. The strengths of the individual brands of Aspen Publishers, CCH, Kluwer Law International and Loislaw are aligned within Wolters Kluwer Law & Business to provide comprehensive, in-depth solutions and expert-authored content for the legal, professional and education markets.

CCH was founded in 1913 and has served more than four generations of business professionals and their clients. The CCH products in the Wolters Kluwer Law & Business group are highly regarded electronic and print resources for legal, securities, antitrust and trade regulation, government contracting, banking, pension, payroll, employment and labor, and healthcare reimbursement and compliance professionals.

Aspen Publishers is a leading information provider for attorneys, business professionals and law students. Written by preeminent authorities, Aspen products offer analytical and practical information in a range of specialty practice areas from securities law and intellectual property to mergers and acquisitions and pension/benefits. Aspen's trusted legal education resources provide professors and students with high-quality, up-to-date and effective resources for successful instruction and study in all areas of the law.

Kluwer Law International supplies the global business community with comprehensive English-language international legal information. Legal practitioners, corporate counsel and business executives around the world rely on the Kluwer Law International journals, loose-leafs, books and electronic products for authoritative information in many areas of international legal practice.

Loislaw is a premier provider of digitized legal content to small law firm practitioners of various specializations. Loislaw provides attorneys with the ability to quickly and efficiently find the necessary legal information they need, when and where they need it, by facilitating access to primary law as well as state-specific law, records, forms and treatises.

Wolters Kluwer Law & Business, a unit of Wolters Kluwer, is headquartered in New York and Riverwoods, Illinois. Wolters Kluwer is a leading multinational publisher and information services company.

To my father with gratitude. To my mother in loving memory. To Alan for his guidance and so much more. To Michael with thanks.

—D.Z.

To my parents for never asking—but always expecting—much of me.

—M.L.B.

· SUMMARY OF CONTENTS ·

· CONTENTS ·

Contents

· CONTRIBUTIONS ·

· ACKNOWLEDGMENTS ·

We owe a tremendous debt to the numerous friends, colleagues, and benevolent strangers (whom we hope we may now count among our friends and colleagues) who made this book possible. We are eternally grateful to the many people who took time out of their very busy schedules to contribute their observations, knowledge, and expertise. Their invaluable contributions make this book more rich and useful than it would have been otherwise. All errors and omissions are ours alone. (Contributor names are listed in the order in which their pieces appear in the book.)

For their comments on the state of legal education and the profession, we thank: Thomas A. Cole, Martin Lipton, Stephen L. Ritchie, Robert A. Helman, Keith C. Wetmore, and Evan R. Chesler.

For their thoughts and comments on legal education and their law firm experiences thus far, we thank: Bradley P. Humphreys, Cadence A. Mertz, Jaime E. Ramirez, Ian N. Bushner, Garrett Ordower, and Sean Z. Kramer.

For providing "A Practitioner Perspective" on various complicated issues, we thank: William L. Horton, Jr., Neal Stern, John Levi, Michael Delikat, Nancy Laben, Michel Gahard, Alan A. D'Ambrosio, Steven Barnett, Jack Bierig, Paul Roy, Jeffrey S. Rothstein, and Timothy M. Swan. We are also grateful to Michael Delikat and Neal Stern for providing us with their thoughts, ideas, suggestions, and critiques of various sections of the book.

We thank Professor Richard A. Epstein and Professor Douglas Baird for sharing their esteemed wisdom in their respective commentary pieces.

We are grateful to the many students who provided us with their indefatigable assistance. For providing research assistance, we thank: Joseph Mueller, Jeffery Lula, Jeanette Stecker, Alex Roitman, Michael Eber, and Salen Churi. For assisting with the development of materials for the teacher's manual, we thank Alex Roitman, Salen Churi, and Azi Lowenthal. For providing "focus group" feedback, we thank Oren Lund, Kathryn Hines, and Sean Z. Kramer. For source and citation assistance, we owe a great debt to the following students, all of whom found time between their school work and Law Review obligations to help with this project: Molly Grovak, Daniel Rosengard, and Kevin Swartz, and those who helped them, including Diana Watral, Chris Hagale, Kristen Mann, and David Didion.

Finally, we would like to extend a special "thank you" to The University of Chicago Law School and to Sidley Austin LLP for their support throughout this project.

· PREFACE ·

Background

Before one can hope to draft a contract with any deftness or comfort, one must understand how to read a contract; one must understand the "language of contracts"—their provisions, their conventions, and their structure. We hope that, through this book, the reader will gain a certain facility and familiarity with contracts as found in the "real world."

We stumbled upon the idea for this book while teaching an introductory transactions course at The University of Chicago Law School. David taught contractual documents, drawing upon his fifteen years' worth of experience as a general counsel at a major corporation. Michael taught contractual provisions, as treated by U.S. courts, drawing upon his research. We decided to expand this formula in published form—to teach contracts from the married perspectives of experience and judicial treatment and to reach out to a field of expert practitioners and esteemed academics to provide additional insight and expertise. This book is one attempt to fill some of the space between traditional law school education (with its classically heavy orientation toward litigation) and transactional practice, whether in a solo-shop, corporate-legal-department, or law-firm setting.

We were encouraged by the great enthusiasm and support we discovered for the teaching of transactional matters in law school, in general, and for our idea, in particular. For one, there are the widely cited institutional positions strongly in favor of the teaching of practical courses in law school, such as the Carnegie Report's call for an emphasis on practical legal education[1] and the Association of American Law Schools' requirement that law schools offer professional skills courses.[2] In addition, throughout the process of distilling and executing the idea for this book, we asked a few distinguished practitioners

---

1. WILLIAM M. SULLIVAN ET AL., EDUCATING LAWYERS: PREPARATION FOR THE PROFESSION OF LAW (2007).

2. Bylaws AALS—The Association of American Law Schools, at § 6-7(c), *available at* http://www.aals.org/about_handbook_bylaws.php. The 2009-10 ABA Standards and Rules of Procedure for Approval of Law Schools also require that law school curriculum include substantial instruction in "professional skills generally regarded as necessary for effective and responsible participation in the legal profession." AMERICAN BAR ASSOCIATION, PROGRAM OF LEGAL EDUCATION std. 302 (2009), *available at* http://www.abanet.org/legaled/standards/2009-2010%20StandardsWebContent/Chapter3.pdf.

who sit atop the legal profession to share their thoughts with us on the topic. We also asked a few former students (of David's and/or Michael's) to share their experiences in law firms, having had benefited from some version of the instruction encapsulated in this book. Their responses follow in the order in which they were received.

Comments from Distinguished Lawyers in Practice

Whether a student will ultimately become a transactions lawyer, a regulatory lawyer or a litigator, a good grounding in all forms of corporate transactions provides a critical window into the business milieu within which he or she will practice. A study of transactions and the agreements by which they are documented also illustrates to the student how different elements of substantive law, together with accounting and tax considerations, meld together in the real world. An earlier appreciation of these considerations is something that clients, and thus law firms, are demanding of the young lawyers who serve them. While many firms provide excellent in-house training, that often comes several months after a new associate has arrived on the scene. Thus, the young lawyer who has received a grounding while still in law school may be able to hit the ground running—even in a summer program—and create the positive first impression that can be so important at the start of a career.

Thomas A. Cole, Partner
Sidley Austin LLP

Mr. Cole serves as Chair of the Firm's Executive Committee.

———————————

A casebook on transactional law has long been desired. Transactional law is a hybrid— part contracts, part securities, part antitrust, part tax, part litigation and part other areas too numerous to name. To properly advise on a transaction, it is necessary to bring all the relevant aspects into focus and craft a transaction designed to combine all into an organized transaction that accomplishes the parties' objectives.

The ability to combine multiple disciplines is critical to a transaction lawyer. Having a law school course with a well organized casebook will be greatly appreciated by students who intend to become transaction lawyers. And I'm sure will be a factor in placement with business law firms.

Martin Lipton
Founding Partner
Wachtell, Lipton, Rosen & Katz

———————————

One of the most common complaints we receive from new corporate associates is that law school has not adequately prepared them for transactional practice in a law firm and, in particular, for what that practice requires of them in their first few years. This is not a new development; I experienced similar challenges when I was a new associate a little more than 20 years ago. Although law schools have certainly made some strides in this area since that time, introducing courses that bring more real-world situations into the classroom, a discrepancy remains between what even the finest law schools teach and what the transactional practice requires. As a result, we devote substantial resources to training our new lawyers for the tasks that they will perform as associates in the transactional practice, including drafting contracts. Our training focuses not on issues highlighted in traditional casebooks but instead on how contracts are actually drafted, how certain provisions can be varied to favor one party over another, how various provisions work together (or may be at odds with one another), and how mistakes can be made if one is not careful in drafting a contract. One can only appreciate these issues by working with—reading, analyzing and drafting—actual contracts.

As a result, law schools would perform a valuable service if they offered "hands-on" courses that focused on the contracts themselves rather than on cases involving those contracts. Of course, case study will always be important in teaching law students key legal principles and, more importantly, how to "think like a lawyer." However, I am confident that law firms would be pleased to welcome new associates who were better prepared for the demands of corporate practice and better able to make a more immediate contribution upon their arrival at the firm.

Stephen L. Ritchie, Partner
Kirkland & Ellis LLP

Mr. Ritchie serves on the Firm's global Management Committee, is Chairman of the Firm's Nonshare Partner and Associate Compensation Committee, and serves on the Firm's Administrative Committee.

I've been asked, as someone who has had a general corporate law practice for 54 years, and chaired Mayer Brown LLP from 1984-98, whether it is important for a law school graduate to have a basic knowledge of how the legal, business and public policy aspects of common and somewhat complex business transactions are reduced to writing, and the related question of whether it is important for the leading law schools to provide the education that leads to that knowledge. My answer to both questions is an unequivocal "yes!" There are some obvious but limited exceptions: if a student "knows" that he or she will have a specialized practice totally unrelated to business, e.g., criminal law of the non-white collar variety or public international law, a transactional law knowledge base would be ornamental but not essential. (However, no one can foresee the future with certainty.) For the rest, whether pointing toward a law firm, a law department, a legal aid program, the government or a career in business, this book meets an important and unmet need.

It is my belief in this practical aspect of legal education that led me to encourage Dean David Zarfes and Professor Michael Bloom's plan to undertake the preparation of this book.

My experience as a lecturer at the University of Chicago Law School has sharpened my ideas about legal education at the leading law schools, which justifiably think of themselves institutionally as being involved primarily in providing an intellectual foundation in the U.S. legal system for their students. Often, but not always, this leads to a certain disdain for problem-solving and clinical courses—"we are not a trade school" is the refrain. I believe that attitude is mistaken: an intellectual foundation is not valuable, except for certain scholars, unless the law school experience connects it to the solving of problems—that is what lawyers are called upon to do. And this book, born of lawyers' experience, with its suggested forms and commentary, will help students (and I daresay many practitioners) learn to do just that. Intellectual understanding and its application to the world of law practice are not, and should not be, mutually exclusive.

(A relevant personal experience: My first-year contracts class at Northwestern was taught by Dean Harold Havighurst, a stimulating teacher and a scholar. I enjoyed it immensely and learned a lot, but we were all surprised and dismayed when, after a full year course, the principal final exam topic described a "real world" business transaction and told us to draft and annotate, as appropriate, an agreement to reflect the apparent meeting of the minds. Except for extracts from contracts in the judicial opinions in Dean Havighurst's casebook, I had never read, let alone drafted, a business contract. Well, under the pressure of an unanticipated exam question, I learned; but I also learned the importance of connecting an understanding of doctrine to practice. This book makes that connection, and that is why it is important.)

Robert A. Helman, Partner
Mayer Brown LLP

Mr. Helman was Chairman of the Firm's Management Committee from 1984 to 1998.

———————————•———————————

Sophisticated contractual drafting reflects a mathematical elegance. All possible events in a commercial relationship—default in payment on a loan, failure of perform-ance by an employee, impossibility of delivery of goods, decline in stock value, increase in stock value, no change in stock value—are usually intended to be addressed within the agreement, with specified consequences for all events. The darkest hours in a trans-actional lawyer's life are those spent looking through last year's documents for the provi-sions that address this year's circumstance that no one anticipated.

Sophisticated contractual drafting requires careful, sometimes artful, use of words. Real world outcomes vary, and dollars change hands, based upon the drafter's use of "or" versus "and" or "before" versus "before and during."

Sophisticated contractual drafting follows custom and practice. Counsel for multina-tional corporations expect banking documents to follow the format and terminology used by banks globally. Sales warranties resemble each other, except to the extent the parties choose quite noticeably to vary them. That consistency simplifies commerce and allows high confidence in the meaning of many words and clauses, through repeated judicial interpretation and broad commercial understanding.

These hallmarks of sophisticated contractual drafting cannot be learned from review-ing cases, which usually address one flawed phrase in a contract. They are learned by reading the contracts themselves, and writing them yourself, and having your contracts edited by more experienced lawyers, and negotiating those contracts with opposing coun-sel, and disagreeing with opposing counsel a year later on the meaning of your own words. Nothing in law school can provide all of that—that's what careers are made of—but this course book is a great start.

Keith C. Wetmore, Chair
Morrison & Foerster LLP

———————————•———————————

There are few skills that are more important for a young lawyer to possess than a familiarity with the law, logic and sense of contracts and the transactions they represent.

So much of what lawyers do centers around the relationships in which their clients are involved. Those relationships, and the transactions that arise from them, typically involve contracts. A level of comfort and facility with contracts is, therefore, critical to a solid foundation as a practicing lawyer.

Evan R. Chesler
Presiding Partner
Cravath, Swaine & Moore LLP

Comments from Former Students

Law school courses, especially those taught in the first year, are unquestionably geared toward litigation. But for those considering a career in transactional law, there are few opportunities to understand what might lie ahead. As one of Dean Zarfes's former students, I benefited tremendously from a hands-on learning experience, and gained confidence critiquing and improving upon real-world corporate contracts. It's an experience I would recommend for all students with an open mind as to where their careers will take them.

This book offers some of the same concrete examples, along with many others, which will prepare students to hit the ground running when they graduate. Just as first-year classes teach students to grapple with the foreign language of legal vocabulary and the peculiarities of judicial opinions, these materials will introduce those students interested in transactional law to a similarly eye-opening experience.

Bradley P. Humphreys
The University of Chicago, J.D. 2009

Dry as desert sand and every bit as apparently identical as one grain from the other. That is, until the contract lands on your desk and you have to either get out of it or make it stick. All of a sudden every italicization, word, comma, semi-colon outside the quotation mark or inside the quotation mark is going to mean the difference between indemnity or not, liability or not, insurance coverage or not. You simply cannot appreciate this until you've held that contract in your hands, heard the counterargument and applied the words on the page in front of you in the service of your client's position.

Cases are helpful. Has the Eleventh Circuit already decided that an insurance clause identically worded to the one now in front of you means what your opponent wants it to mean? Has the Supreme Court defined the term of art you're now staring cross-eyed at? These are benchmarks; you cannot ignore them. But re-read your contract. There's a comma in your paragraph A.4(d) that isn't in the contract they interpreted. In a separate provision, your contract defines a word left undefined in the contract on which those cases were decided. Every contract is different. You learn this from considering each one individually. And, it takes practice to spot those differences. More, to know which ones really matter, which ones you can exploit. A contracts textbook that confines you to the learning of case law ignores this principle. It will teach you the basics, but it won't make you fluent. To get there you need to handle the documents, read them, defend them, enforce them, argue them. Having the real documents to consider from the first day of your first contracts class will ensure you get there well before your opponent.

Cadence A. Mertz, Associate
Williams & Connolly LLP
The University of Chicago, J.D. 2008

For those law students hoping to enter the world of corporate law, it's sometimes difficult to imagine how traditional law school classes fit into a future role as an advocate in a negotiation. It's only following graduation and well into your practice as a new lawyer that you begin to fully comprehend how the law contributes to and in many instances shapes commercial decisions in a contract negotiation.

Professor Zarfes' teaching method has always combined the Socratic method and traditional law school techniques with a refreshing and helpful combination of real-world negotiating exercises. Consistent with this method, this new textbook will undoubtedly serve to bridge the divide between theory and practice for an aspiring corporate attorney. Furthermore, this textbook will provide a much needed supplement to the traditional legal curriculum and a helpful introduction into the art of negotiating commercial agreements.

Jaime E. Ramirez, Associate
Sullivan & Cromwell LLP
The University of Chicago, J.D. 2007

Based upon my study of transactional law with attorneys (they are as much lawyers as professors) David Zarfes and Michael Bloom at The University of Chicago Law School, I can assure you that their combination of real world experience and academic depth is unparalleled in most of legal academia. Their students not only learn about the law, but more importantly they learn how to be lawyers. I benefited greatly from their method, and so will you.

Like most law students, I entered law school with little idea about what lawyers really do. At best, many of us had sentimental notions drawn from courtroom dramas, novels extolling the honest attorney, and history books describing landmark litigation. While the traditional law school curriculum, through civil procedure and intensive case law analysis, does give lawyers to-be some exposure to a litigator's tools, most students remain ignorant about transactional practice. As a result, many young transactional lawyers face a steep learning curve and, relative to their peers in litigation, have far more catching up to do before they can be effective. Long overdue, this book will serve to remedy these shortfalls and minimize the lag time before young lawyers can deliver real value to their clients.

Many law students graduate without ever having analyzed, much less drafted, complex contracts. Even in most contracts classes, students only read cases about contracts and do not review the agreements themselves. This is a mistake. Every young transactional lawyer has seen or heard the same story: he or she is pulled into a partner's office, given a basic overview of the deal, handed a document to use "as precedent" (often a contract between parties not involved in the current deal), and told to turn a draft of some agreement they have never heard of. The terror felt by these lawyers, and the ensuing frustration of the partners, is real, and so too is the bill footed by the client.

However, if during law school a student can get exposure to a range of transactional matters, gain familiarity with a variety of agreements, practice drafting in a deal context, and start developing their negotiating skills, the situation is reversed. A young lawyer with this legal education is ready to hit the ground running. He or she can understand a partner's instructions and ask appropriate, insightful questions regarding the assignment. The partner is freed to focus on strategy and client-specific concerns while skipping rudimentary instruction. Perhaps the clients receive the greatest benefit, for they no longer must subsidize on-the-clock basic transactional education.

Additionally, the transactional perspective presented in this book emphasizes client needs. Law is a service industry, and no lawyer can survive without the appropriate attention to client service. Unfortunately, reading cases, while necessary, will not itself expose students to the client side of practice. Working with contracts, on the other hand, forces students to ask several important questions. What is a client's specific objective in this transaction? How does this relate to its broader business plan? What is the relationship between the client and the counterparty? What is the industry standard? Over time, students who have studied from a transactional perspective can develop an intuition regarding client concerns. Young lawyers who develop this client-centered attitude will be far ahead of their peers who continue analyzing legal problems in the theoretical, Socratic vacuum they encountered in the law school classroom.

In the end, transactional lawyers must eventually learn these skills somewhere. They might as well learn them in law school where students can make mistakes in an environment which, relative to actual practice, is low pressure and consequence free. What's more, transactional lawyers will be learning the basics on their own dime, instead of the client's. After studying this book and putting forth required effort to develop their transactional skills in law school, young lawyers will be ahead of their peers and will enter the practice of law ready to benefit themselves, their firms, and their clients. Everybody wins.

Ian N. Bushner, Associate
Jenner & Block LLP
The University of Chicago, J.D. 2009

The moment any law student enters the real world, they will quickly realize that their 1L "Contracts" class was a bit of a misnomer—rarely, if ever, will they have actually examined a real contract or learned how a contract affects the parties to a transaction—this book aims to fill that gap.

Dean Zarfes is the rare law school professor who knows both the classroom and the boardroom, and in this book, as in his classes, he bridges the significant divide between the two using interesting, understandable, and, most importantly, relevant examples that illustrate the transactional practice students will be facing before they know it.

Zarfes and Bloom's students—both those who learn from this book or have either of them in class—will be uniquely prepared to handle real-world work the minute they walk in the door of a law firm or business, and these lessons will stay with them throughout their careers. Today, more than ever, that type of preparation is an asset that could mean the difference between success and failure.

Garrett Ordower, Editor-in-Chief
The University of Chicago Law Review
The University of Chicago, J.D. 2010

Simply put, there is much more to the practice of law, and, thus, to legal education, than litigation and the traditional case method of law school. Not only does the historical method—when used exclusively—fail young litigators, but it leaves the myriad law students who go into transactional fields completely unprepared.

Although I enjoyed most every aspect of law school and reveled in extrapolating complicated legal principles from seminal case law, I was surprised to finish the first year and select transactional-based classes, only to find that such courses were taught in the same way as the core classes: by analyzing fact-specific litigations.

I was always left wanting to combine the intellectual pursuit of the case method with the practical means of examining and drafting actual contracts; it seemed obvious that applying the legal principles—gleaned from the cases—to actual contracts, would more fully concrete one's knowledge of the concepts.

It was not until David Zarfes and Michael Bloom's courses on contract interpretation and negotiation and complex business transactions that I found the practical (yet still academic) teaching style that I had been looking for. After taking these courses and reading early versions of this book, the advantage that I had over my (highly qualified) colleagues in my summer associate program was obvious, and, throughout the summer, I received strong praise from partners for my understanding of the interplay between complicated contractual terms.

Zarfes and Bloom's book—and their teaching methodology—should be mandatory for any law student going into a transactional area of the law. The casebook makes complex concepts easy to understand and will leave students asking themselves something that law professors and practitioners take for granted due to their years of experience: How can students learn the language of contracts necessary to understand business relationships in the real world?

The answer lies in this book.

Sean Z. Kramer, Associate
Kirkland & Ellis LLP
The University of Chicago, J.D. 2010

What This Book Is, What It Is Not, and How to Use It

We took great stock of the above comments, as they came from people well positioned to speak to what many in the legal profession value in young lawyers as well as to what young lawyers have found to be valuable in their legal careers. We also realized we cannot be all things to all people and that, while the comments above call for a plethora of fantastic things, we had to pick a focus for this book. This book's mission is simple: to familiarize law students with the basic "language of contracts," with some of the basic and commonly found provisions found in "real-world" contracts, and with how those provisions act and interact to serve a party's position and interest. We will consider it no minor victory if the readers of this book no longer view contracts as strange, foreign creatures written in a strange, foreign language.

Accordingly, this book is intended to be "of this world," which means, for instance, that the contracts used in this book were contracts used by real-life parties in real-life transactions. These contracts are drawn from the Security and Exchange Commission's Electronic Data Gathering, Analysis, and Retrieval ("EDGAR") system, which is a database of documents that public companies have filed with the SEC. This also means that these agreements have their flaws. <u>We do not hold this book's agreements out as model documents</u>. On the contrary, we see these documents as teaching tools and as exemplars of the type and quality of documents a lawyer is likely to encounter in practice—as a precedent document used to draft a contract for a new transaction, as a document first drafted by opposing counsel, as a document reviewed at the behest of a client, etc. We consciously decided not to break up the agreements in this book because we think a great part of our mission is to "force" students to read whole contracts—much as other courses instill in students the skillful habit of reading cases and statutes.

We also note that, in this book, we do not consciously adhere to or adopt any particular style or school of drafting; for instance, the "plain language" school of drafting may have its admirable tenets, but we do not hold this book or (certainly) its agreements out to be in compliance with the "plain language" school's scriptures. Indeed, this book is not a "contract drafting" manual or guide, at all. We see this book as serving a very different purpose. To reiterate, the focus of this book is to introduce law students to contractual documents and their parts, in the context of actual contractual documents and transactions. Along the way, we offer some drafting notes here and there, but this book is not intended to be a comprehensive guide to contract drafting, grammar, style, or clarity.

This book is also not a practitioner's guide, and it is not a fifty-state survey. That is, in the United States, most of contract law is state law, and states may vary in their treatment of certain provisions or issues that arise in contracts. Of course, this book cannot comprehensively survey how every state addresses every issue. Necessarily, we have to speak at a certain level of generality, in terms of "majority" and "minority" rules, and, where we have not been able to discern a particular trend, we can only say that certain courts have taken a certain approach and others, another. This operates to flag some of the issues for the reader, but, of course, one cannot practice directly from this book, and one must research the law that will govern a particular contract. In addition, this book takes as its core focus U.S. domestic law but also attempts to include global perspectives to enrich this focus and broaden the scope of discussion.

A thematic lesson running throughout this book is the importance of understanding the intended purpose and the likely effect of a contract. One must understand and appreciate a contract's target audience—there may be several—in understanding the purpose of a contract. Inasmuch as a contract is intended to be enforceable in court (or arbitration), one should draft with an appreciation for how a future court (or arbitrator) might read and enforce the contract. Cases provide a source of information for how courts have treated contracts and some evidence for how they might treat them going forward.

This can be highly instructive for the contract drafter or reviewer, but the inquiry should not end there. Contracts may be enforced in ways that do not involve formal dispute resolution, including by the threat or in the shadow of litigation (the so-called "in terrorem" effect of contracts) and through a concern for business reputation. What is the dynamic between the contracting parties? Is this a "once-off" contract or is this a "repeat-game" scenario where the parties expect or hope to do business together going forward? Process may also be important; as an illustration, in a particular negotiation, a party may wish to keep contentiousness to a minimum and to draft accordingly, perhaps avoiding harsh-sounding language or picking and choosing which changes to suggest to the other party's offered draft. Contractual parties may understand a contract as a code of conduct or as a manual that documents their expected behavior throughout the course of a relationship or undertaking. These parties may conform their behavior to their written bargain without a consideration for overt enforcement mechanisms (again, perhaps with a concern for business reputation and perhaps even due to a more basic normative instinct to behave as promised). The reader is encouraged to reconsider these concerns on a consistent basis throughout this book. As you read, ask yourself: What is the drafter trying to accomplish here, and is the drafter going about this in the best way?

The premise of this book is that a student will acquire a meaningful set of skills and a certain level of facility through reading contracts, through slogging through their seemingly foreign text, and through wrestling with their meaning, purpose, and effect. Before (or at least in addition to) learning how to write contracts through acquiring finely tuned grammatical and stylistic tools for drafting an unambiguous sentence, students should learn how to understand whole agreements, to understand their basic provisions and their interaction, to understand what parties might want to accomplish through contracts, and to understand how contracts can (and cannot) go about accomplishing these objectives.

David Zarfes
Michael L. Boom

Chicago, IL
December 2010

CONTRACTS

A TRANSACTIONAL APPROACH

· CHAPTER ONE ·

Non-Disclosure and Confidentiality Agreements

Williams, who was employed by the Coca-Cola Company as an executive assistant to a high level Coca-Cola employee, approached co-defendant Edmund Duhaney in November 2005 at a family Thanksgiving dinner and told him that they needed to discuss a private matter. Afterward, Williams began calling and sending text messages to Duhaney about the matter. In late December 2005, Duhaney met with Williams at her apartment in Norcross, Georgia. Williams told Duhaney that she had copies of confidential Coca-Cola documents that were worth money to some competitors.

Specifically, Williams told Duhaney that she had memory sticks containing information, and she showed him confidential Coca-Cola marketing documents and a product sample. Although Williams was angry with Coca-Cola because she felt she was not "treated right," she told Duhaney that she had signed a nondisclosure confidentiality agreement with Coca-Cola and was therefore unable to do anything with the confidential materials. She wanted Duhaney to determine if someone could use the confidential information to obtain money from another company.

About one week later, Williams contacted Duhaney to ask about his progress with the Coca-Cola documents. . . . In February [2006], Duhaney contacted a friend of his, Dimson, who was interested in the documents because he realized they were worth money. Dimson agreed to travel to Georgia to review the documents. . . .

While Williams explained the documents to Dimson, Duhaney listened and then began thumbing through a magazine. During the meeting, Williams stated that this happens all the time in corporate America and Pepsi would be interested in this type of information. Dimson and Duhaney then decided to travel to a nearby Wal-Mart store to purchase a black roller bag and plastic folders for the documents.

United States v. Williams, 526 F.3d 1312, 1316 (11th Cir. 2008).

Unfortunately, situations of this sort occur often in corporate America.[1] Given this reality, how do corporations protect sensitive and confidential information from disclosure? This chapter addresses this question through examination of non-disclosure agreements.

Non-disclosure agreements, often referred to as NDAs, frequently arise in commercial and employment contexts and operate to prevent the wrongful disclosure (whether negligent or intentional) of confidential information. These agreements may impose confidentiality obligations on one or both (or several) parties. The basic purpose of an NDA is to obtain a legally binding promise from someone (natural person or company) before giving that someone access to information one wishes to keep secret. As we will observe in many instances throughout this book, obligations of confidentiality often arise in provisions within larger, more complex contracts.

At what point in a commercial transaction does it become advisable to issue or exchange NDAs? In the employment context, employers will require those employees who are likely to have access to sensitive company information to execute[2] NDAs protecting this information prior to, and as a condition of, the start of employment. Indeed, as we will discuss further, courts sometimes treat the promise of new, future employment as the consideration that supports these contracts. In some cases, employers may include confidentiality obligations as part of a comprehensive employment agreement, outlining the complete terms of the relationship. In the commercial context, parties will typically seek to protect the disclosure of confidential information at an early stage, prior to entering into sales or other commercial discussions and certainly well before they put pen to paper on a contract containing the full terms of their relationship. The NDA is used to protect the information one or both parties will need to evaluate the proposed relationship.[3] To amplify this discussion, we asked a seasoned practitioner to discuss the use and importance of NDAs in the "real world."

---

1. Joya Williams was found guilty of conspiracy to steal trade secrets and received a sentence of eight years. *United States v. Williams*, 526 F.3d 1312, 1316 (11th Cir. 2008).

2. Throughout this book, unless otherwise specified, we use "to execute" and the "execution" of a contract interchangeably with "to sign" and the "signing" of a contract, respectively. Note that there is some confusion as to whether execution refers to the *signing* or the *performance* of a contract. *See, e.g., Missouri-Indiana Inv. Group v. Shaw*, 699 F.2d 952, 954 (8th Cir. 1983) (Missouri law) ("Although the Supreme Court of Missouri has defined an 'executed contract' as one where nothing remains to be done, it did so in distinguishing an executed from an executory contract. In other contexts the Missouri court has equated execution of a contract with signing and delivery. Whatever the range of definitions of the verb 'to execute,' Missouri cases recognize that in popular speech, 'execute' is often used to refer merely to the act of signing a written contract.") (internal citations omitted).

3. For example, in the context of a sales transaction, one may wish to keep confidential the price and scope of the deal along with the underlying products to be delivered or services to be performed; or, in the mergers-and-acquisition context, one may wish to keep confidential information such as employee lists, intellectual property portfolios, and corporate assets.

A Practitioner Perspective: The Use and Purpose of NDAs

Non-disclosure agreements, also called "NDAs" or confidentiality agreements, play a very important role in modern commercial relationships. In order to develop complex technical products, provide broad-based client services and engage in activities that cross industry lines, companies and individuals frequently are required to work closely with and share proprietary, competitive information with unaffiliated third parties. NDAs provide the contractual basis on which this information is exchanged and give the participants the comfort they require in order to share their business strategies, financial information and competitive data with others outside their organizations.

NDAs serve myriad purposes in a corporate context. They are used by entrepreneurs who are seeking early-stage financing from angel investors in order to maintain the confidentiality of a new business idea. When a company sells itself or one of its businesses, prospective purchasers will not be permitted to see any of the company's financial or operating information prior to signing an NDA. Commercial agreements frequently include confidentiality requirements, sometimes limiting the disclosure of the existence of the commercial arrangement itself. In the employment context, a company may ask employees who are assigned to work on a particularly sensitive matter to execute NDAs related to that matter as a supplement to their general confidentiality obligations contained in the company's broad-based employment policies.

This last example of an employee signing a supplemental NDA highlights some of the essential features of all NDAs. One is that the NDA defines the information or topics that are considered confidential or proprietary and highlights the fact that those items are to remain confidential. The second feature is that such an NDA is a formal, written agreement to keep information confidential that the employee personally signs. This characteristic of NDAs is important because it relates to the incentives parties have to comply with their obligations under the agreements. People seem to give greater weight to, and may be less inclined to violate, an agreement they have signed than an oral agreement. In addition, individuals frequently see a general benefit in being perceived as someone whose word can be trusted. Similarly, in the corporate context, companies who are repeat players in a field, such as providing merger advisory services, typically believe it is important to the success of their businesses to be trusted by others with confidential information.

The seriousness with which a party takes an NDA is particularly important due to some of the inherent weaknesses of NDAs, which are different from other contracts. These weaknesses relate to enforceability of the contract itself—particularly the ability to prove a violation of the contract and to recover any damages. If two companies are parties to an NDA related to merger discussions and word of the discussions leaks to the press, it may be very difficult to prove that one or the other company (or any of their respective financial advisors, financing sources, attorneys or accountants) violated their obligations under the NDA, because the leaked information is known to so many people within each organization. The difficulty of proving a violation can also be seen in the context of a company that is trying to sell a business and permits a competitor who may be an interested purchaser to review the operating information for the business under an NDA. If the competitor does not purchase the business but in the future adopts operating strategies or solicits customers of that business, it may not be possible to demonstrate that the competitor is taking those actions in violation of the NDA as opposed to as a result of its own strategic thinking and business acumen.

The second weakness that can apply to NDAs relates to recovering damages. Even if a company can demonstrate that another breached its obligations under an NDA, in many cases the initial breach of the agreement is effectively irreparable. Once the market, or a competitor, hears the confidential information, the damage to the aggrieved party is done but the amount of damage to that company may be highly speculative and therefore very difficult to recover. As a result of these characteristics, depending on the circumstances surrounding the NDA, the parties may see little practical financial risk to breaching the agreement.

NDAs are essential to corporate and commercial relationships in our increasingly interdependent economy. However, for the reasons described above, when entering into a confidential relationship with a third party, a company needs to be mindful of the nature of the NDA relationship and its inherent limitations. In order to determine whether the company's confidential information is likely to be reasonably secure, it is important for practitioners to carefully assess all of the counterparty's incentives and motivations related to the relationship, not just the contractual obligation contained in the NDA.

> William L. Horton, Jr., Senior Vice President,
> Deputy General Counsel, and Corporate Secretary
> Verizon Communications Inc.

A. NON-DISCLOSURE AGREEMENT IN THE EMPLOYMENT CONTEXT

The following agreement sets forth the rights and obligations between an employer and its new employee.

Things to Consider...

As you read through the following agreement, please consider these items. You will want to return to the agreement, as you study the substantive discussion that follows.

> **Parties, Rights, and Obligations.** Who are (and who are not) the "parties" (i.e., the persons manifesting assent) to this agreement? Consider

who has the obligation to do what and, on the flipside, who has the right to benefit, under this agreement.

> **Prefatory Provisions.** Before it imposes obligations or rights on either party, the agreement contains language ("In consideration of…"). The provisions prior to the substance of an agreement are often called "recitals." Consider what purposes this language serves in this agreement and what purposes the inclusion of introductory text may serve in contracts generally. Similarly, what purposes may provisions like those contained in Section 2 ("Acknowledgement") in the agreement serve in the context of an agreement (whether they exist among an agreement's recitals or substantive terms)?

> **"Confidential Information" and Definitions.** Consider how this agreement defines "Confidential Information" and how the agreement uses this definition throughout. Taking the perspective of both parties in turn, does this definition strike you as particularly broad or narrow, given the circumstances of this relationship (from what you can tell from the agreement)?

AGREEMENT ON CONFIDENTIALITY, NON-COMPETITION AND NON-SOLICITATION[4]

In consideration of my continued employment by The Coca-Cola Company, a Delaware corporation, I agree with The Coca-Cola Company as follows:

1. Definitions. For the purposes of this Agreement, the following definitions apply:

(a) "Confidential Information" means any data or information, other than Trade Secrets, that is valuable to The Coca-Cola Company and/or its subsidiaries and affiliates (collectively "the Company") and not generally known to competitors of the Company or other outsiders, regardless of whether the information is in print, written, or electronic form, retained in my memory, or has been compiled or created by me, including, but not limited to, technical, financial, personnel, staffing, payroll, computer systems, marketing, advertising, merchandising, product, vendor, or customer data, or other information similar to the foregoing;

(b) "Trade Secret" means any information, including a formula, pattern, compilation, program, device, method, technique, or process,

---

4. Coca Cola Co., Agreement on Confidentiality, Non-Competition and Non-Solicitation (Form 10-K), at Exhibit 10.47 (Feb. 26, 2010), *available at* http://www.sec.gov/Archives/edgar/data/21344/000104746910001476/a2195739zex-10_47.htm.

that (i) derives independent economic value, actual or potential, from not being generally known to, and not being readily ascertainable by proper means by, other persons who can derive economic value from its disclosure or use and (ii) is the subject of efforts that are reasonable under the circumstances to maintain its secrecy; and

(c) "Customer" means anyone who (i) is or was a customer of the Company during my employment with The Coca-Cola Company, or (ii) is a prospective customer of the Company to whom the Company has made a presentation (or similar offering of services) within the one-year period immediately preceding the termination of my employment with The Coca-Cola Company or, if my employment has not terminated, the one-year period immediately preceding any alleged violation of this Agreement.

2. **Acknowledgement.** My services for The Coca-Cola Company are of a special, unique, extraordinary, and intellectual character, and are performed on behalf of the Company throughout the world. My position as a high-level executive of The Coca-Cola Company places me in a position of confidence and trust with the Customers and employees of the Company. So long as I shall remain in the employ of The Coca-Cola Company, I shall devote my whole time and ability to the service of the Company in such capacity as The Coca-Cola Company shall from time to time direct, and I shall perform my duties faithfully and diligently.

I acknowledge that the rendering of services to the Company's Customers necessarily requires the disclosure of the Company's Confidential Information and Trade Secrets to me. In addition, in the course of my employment with The Coca-Cola Company, I will develop a personal acquaintanceship and relationship with certain of the Company's Customers, and a knowledge of those Customers' affairs and requirements, which may constitute a significant contact between the Company and such Customers. Finally, the Customers with whom I will have business dealings on behalf of the Company are located throughout the world.

I further acknowledge that the provisions in this Agreement, including, but not limited to, the restrictive covenants and the governing law and forum selection provisions, are fair and reasonable, that enforcement of the provisions of this Agreement will not cause me undue hardship, and that the provisions of this Agreement are necessary and commensurate with the need to protect the Company's established goodwill and proprietary information from irreparable harm. In the event that I breach, I threaten in any way to breach, or it is inevitable that I will breach any of the provisions of this Agreement, damages shall be an inadequate remedy and The Coca-Cola Company shall be entitled, without bond, to injunctive or other equitable relief. The Coca-Cola Company's rights in this respect are in addition to all rights otherwise available at law or in equity.

3. **Non-Competition and Non-Solicitation.** [Omitted]

4. **Confidential Information and Trade Secrets.**

(a) During my employment with The Coca-Cola Company, I will acquire and have access to the Company's Confidential Information. I agree that while I am in The Coca-Cola Company's employ and for two years after the termination of my employment with The Coca-Cola Company for any reason whatsoever, I shall hold in confidence all Confidential Information of the Company and will not disclose, publish, or make use of such Confidential Information, directly or indirectly, unless compelled by law and then only after providing written notice to The Coca-Cola Company. If I have any questions regarding what data or information would be considered by the Company to be Confidential Information, I agree to contact the appropriate person(s) at the Company for written clarification; and

(b) During my employment with The Coca-Cola Company, I will also acquire and have access to the Company's Trade Secrets. I acknowledge that the Company has made and will continue to make reasonable efforts under the circumstances to maintain the secrecy of its Trade Secrets. I agree to hold in confidence all Trade Secrets of the Company that come into my knowledge during my employment with The Coca-Cola Company and shall not directly or indirectly disclose, publish, or make use of at any time such Trade Secrets for so long as the information remains a Trade Secret. If I have any questions regarding what data or information constitutes a Trade Secret, I agree to contact the appropriate person(s) at the Company for written clarification. Nothing in this provision shall be interpreted to diminish the protections afforded trade secrets under applicable law.

5. **Company Property.** Upon leaving the employ of The Coca-Cola Company, I shall not take with me any written, printed, or electronically stored Trade Secrets, Confidential Information, or any other property of the Company obtained by me as a result of my employment, or any reproductions thereof. All such Company property and all copies thereof shall be surrendered by me to the Company on my termination or at any time upon request of the Company.

6. **Inventions, Discoveries, and Authorship.** [Omitted]

7. **Governing Law.** This Agreement shall be construed, interpreted, and applied in accordance with the laws of the State of Delaware, without giving effect to the choice-of-law provisions thereof.

8. Mandatory Forum Selection. The Company and I hereby irrevocably submit any dispute arising out of, in connection with, or relating to this Agreement, including with respect to my employment by The Coca-Cola Company or the termination of such employment, to the exclusive concurrent jurisdiction of the state and federal courts located in the State of Delaware. The Company and I also both irrevocably waive, to the fullest extent permitted by applicable law, any objection either may now or hereafter have to the laying of venue of any such dispute brought in such court or any defense of inconvenient forum for the maintenance of such dispute. Finally, I waive formal service of process and agree to accept service of process worldwide.

9. Severability. In the event that any provision of this Agreement is found to be invalid or unenforceable by a court of law or other appropriate authority, the invalidity or unenforceability of such provision shall not affect the other provisions of this Agreement, which shall remain in full force and effect, and that court or other appropriate authority shall modify the provisions found to be unenforceable or invalid so as to make them enforceable, taking into account the purposes of this Agreement and the nationwide and international scope of the Company's business.

10. Waiver. No waiver of any provision of this Agreement shall be effective unless pursuant to a writing signed by me and the Company, and such waiver shall be effective only in the specific instance and for the specific purpose stated in the writing.

11. [Omitted]

12. Assignment. This Agreement shall inure to the benefit of the Company, allied companies, successors and assigns, or nominees of the Company, and I specifically agree to execute any and all documents considered convenient or necessary to assign transfer, sustain and maintain inventions, discoveries, copyrightable material, applications, and patents, both in this and foreign countries, to and on behalf of the Company.
[Signature Page Omitted]

1. Recitals and Acknowledgments

The Agreement begins with a recital (sometimes called a "whereas clause," as oftentimes each clause will begin with "WHEREAS"), which is a clause that appears at the very beginning of a contract. While the recital in the above Agreement is very thin (just a basic recital of consideration), recitals may be several paragraphs, as you will see in the agreements throughout this book, typically depending on the complexity of the transaction and the relationship for which the recitals provide context.

A recital purports not to state substantive terms of the contract but rather to suggest the motivation or purpose of undertaking the relationship. As a general rule, a recital does not create legally binding contractual obligations,[5] and other evidence may controvert a fact stated in a recital, even if the recital is part of a completely integrated document.[6] Despite that the substantive terms of a contract control, courts may read recitals in order to discern the parties' intent and to inform the reading and construction of the contract.[7] You will notice that Section 2 of the Agreement explains the underlying relationship between the parties and the motivation for entering the Agreement and contains the sort of language that sometimes may be found in a recitals section to frame and precede the main body of a non-disclosure agreement. For example, in an agreement similar to the one above, it would not be surprising to find the following at the top of the document:

> WHEREAS, my services for The Coca-Cola Company are of a special, unique, extraordinary, and intellectual character, and are performed on behalf of the Company throughout the world;
>
> WHEREAS, my position as a high-level executive of The Coca-Cola Company places me in a position of confidence and trust with the Customers and employees of the Company;
>
> WHEREAS, the rendering of services to the Company's Customers necessarily requires the disclosure of the Company's Confidential Information and Trade Secrets to me;
>
> NOW, THEREFORE, in consideration of my continued employment by The Coca-Cola Company, a Delaware corporation, I agree with The Coca-Cola Company as follows:....

In addition, a party to a contract may be estopped from denying the truth of a specific fact asserted by a recital, if the recital is relied upon in good faith and such reliance would prove unjustly detrimental should the truth of the recital be denied.[8] As an example, a party may be estopped from challenging a contract for lack of consideration, where the contract contains a recital that consideration was received (a recital of consideration is commonly found in contracts, including this Agreement).[9] Even if estoppel is

---

5. *See, e.g., Fab-Tech, Inc. v. E.I. DuPont De Nemours and Co.*, 311 F. App'x 443, 446 (2d Cir. 2009) (Vermont law) ("While introductory recitals in a contract may shed light on the motives behind forming the contract, they are not strictly a part of the contract....") (internal citations and quotation marks omitted).

6. *See* RESTATEMENT (SECOND) OF CONTRACTS § 218(1) cmt. b (1981); *see, e.g., Fulton v. L & N Consultants, Inc.*, 715 F.2d 1413, 1419 (10th Cir. 1982). Please see below for a discussion of "integration" and "integration clauses."

7. *See, e.g., Aramony v. United Way of Am.*, 254 F.3d 403, 413 (2d Cir. 2001).

8. *See* JOHN J. DVORSKE ET AL., 31 C.J.S. ESTOPPEL AND WAIVER § 73 (West 2009).

9. *See, e.g., Keller v. Bass Pro Shops, Inc.*, 15 F.3d 122, 124 (8th Cir. 1994) (holding that the plaintiff could not challenge the patent assignment for lack of consideration because consideration was recited in the

not appropriate, recitals of consideration are sometimes given at least some weight in determining whether a contract is supported by consideration.[10] Estoppel may also be available where a party "acknowledges" a fact in an agreement — whether in the recitals or body of an agreement.[11] Estoppel premised on a recital or acknowledgment in a contract is generally only proper in an action founded on that contract; that is, with respect to a claim that does not arise from a contract, one will not be estopped from denying the truth of a recital made in that contract.[12]

As a matter of drafting prudence, a party should avoid agreeing to recitals that express the other party's desired outcomes of the contract (e.g., saving costs) or that make additional promises the party does not wish to be bound to perform, even if the recital states that these unperformed promises were already performed. This avoids the potentiality of the other party, desiring an outcome or performance, later arguing that the recitals warranted or promised such.

2. Consideration in "Unilateral" Non-Disclosure Agreements

As discussed later in this chapter,[13] the consideration in exchange for the obligations assumed by an employee in an NDA is sometimes found in the promise or performance of future employment.[14] While a non-disclosure agreement itself may be "unilateral" in that it only imposes obligations on the employee,[15] an NDA in the employment context is ancillary to an employment agreement or relationship with, ideally, consideration flowing both ways. With this in mind, while this Agreement is designed to impose confidentiality obligations on only the employee, it may be supported by consideration found in the greater employment relationship—for example, in the employer's promise of continued employment.

---

contract); *Carroll Touch, Inc. v. Electro Mech. Sys., Inc.*, 15 F.3d 1573, 1581 (Fed. Cir. 1993) (noting that the party was estopped from claiming he did not receive consideration). *But see* RESTATEMENT (SECOND) OF CONTRACTS § 218 cmt. e (1981) ("An incorrect statement of a consideration does not prevent proof either that there was no consideration or that there was a consideration different from that stated. In some such cases the recital may imply a promise not explicitly stated.").

10. *See* RICHARD A. LORD, 3 WILLISTON ON CONTRACTS § 7:23 (West 4th ed. 2009) ("[T]he solution of the law has been generally to entitle the recital to some weight, but to permit the introduction of contrary evidence except in a few narrowly defined areas.")

11. *See, e.g.*, *Two Men and a Truck/Int'l Inc. v. Two Men and a Truck/Kalamazoo, Inc.*, 949 F. Supp. 500, 508 (W.D. Mich. 1996) ("Defendants entered into valid franchise agreements acknowledging the fact that plaintiff owned the 'Two Men and a Truck' name and mark; thus, defendants are estopped from claiming that the plaintiff's name and mark are invalid.").

12. *Bank of Am. v. Banks*, 101 U.S. 240 (1879); *see also* JOHN J. DVORSKE ET AL., 31 C.J.S. ESTOPPEL AND WAIVER § 73 (citing *Popplewell v. Stevenson*, 176 F.2d 362 (10th Cir. 1949)).

13. See *infra* the discussion of consideration in the context of NDAs.

14. In addition, as previously discussed, a recital of consideration will help satisfy some courts not to invalidate a contract for lack of consideration.

15. Note that the distinction drawn between "unilateral" and "bilateral" NDAs, which focuses on whether the underlying non-disclosure obligations are unidirectional or reciprocal, is not intended to mirror the distinction between "unilateral" and "bilateral" contracts, which are terms of art with specific meanings.

3. Tortious Interference: Legally Reaching a Third Party

"Tortious interference with contract" refers to a third party's intentional and improper act that causes a party not to perform under a contract, where such nonperformance proximately results in actual damages or losses.[16] In the NDA context, tortious interference provides a legal theory for holding third parties—that is, persons not party to the NDA—liable for causing a party to the NDA to breach her contractual confidentiality obligations.[17] For example, suppose an employer requires an employee to sign an NDA, and the employee then leaves to work for another company. At the new company, the employee discloses the original employer's confidential information in con-travention of the NDA. If the new company improperly acted with an inten-tion of causing the employee to breach her NDA, the new company may be liable to the original employer for tortious interference with the NDA.[18]

On the issue of tortious interference in the context of non-disclosure agreements, we invited a seasoned practitioner to share some practical insight.

A Practitioner Perspective: Tortious Interference and NDAs

In industries such as IT and finance, newly hired employees may arrive with vestiges from their previous employers in the form of nondisclosure agreements. How should the new employer address this possibility? In no event can the new employer turn a blind eye. The business risk is too great—an employee who vio-lates an NDA may expose himself and his new employer to serious legal risks. Additionally, the employee may be enjoined from working for his new employer.

One approach is for the prospective new employer to require a candidate for employment to provide a copy of his NDA for the new employer's review. While this course gives the new employer the opportunity to assess fully the candidate's obligations to his former employer and to determine whether the candidate will be able to fulfill the requirements of the new position without violating the NDA, it also enhances the likelihood of a successful tortious interference claim by the former employer should the new employer hire the candidate regardless of the terms of the NDA. The new employer's review of the NDA would serve as compelling evidence that the new employer had knowledge

---

16. *See* RESTATEMENT (SECOND) OF TORTS § 766 (1979); *see also Nova Consulting Group, Inc. v. Eng'g Consulting Servs., Ltd.*, 290 F. App'x. 727, 737 (5th Cir. 2008). For a list of factors important in determining whether an interference is improper, please see RESTATEMENT (SECOND) OF TORTS § 767 (1979).

17. *See, e.g., Nova*, 290 F. App'x at 738 (finding new employer liable for tortious interference with non-disclosure agreement).

18. As an illustration, in *Nova*, the court explained, "The evidence supports a reasonable jury's find-ing that ECS was aware of the agreements; yet, in contravention of them, and ignoring the warning from Nova lawyers that the agreements would be enforced through legal action if necessary, continued to require former Nova managers to load their client information into the ECS database." 290 F. App'x at 739.

of the contract and obligations owed to the former employer, critical elements of a tortious interference claim.

Another approach is to ask the candidate to make a written representation as to whether he is subject to any restrictions that would preclude him from working for and performing all of his contemplated duties with the prospective new employer. If the candidate answers no, then the new employer can take some comfort in the fact that it has no knowledge of any NDA (or non-compete) restrictions. Of course, absent review of all agreements between the candidate and the prior employer, the new employer will not have certainty. To manage this risk, the new employer may wish to seek an indemnification agreement by which the candidate would compensate the new employer for any losses it suffers because the candidate failed to disclose a nondisclosure obligation (although the value of such an agreement may be ephemeral if the candidate does not have deep pockets). If the candidate answers that he is subject to post-employment restrictions, the new employer would then request the relevant agreements for review.

Neal Stern
Assistant General Counsel
National Basketball Association

4. Employee's Duty of Confidentiality

Employees often have a duty of confidentiality to keep secret the confidential information of their employers. Indeed, as one commentator explains, "a relationship of confidence and trust inheres in most employment relationships," and "[an employment relationship] imposes a duty upon the employee not to use or disclose the employer's confidential information to the employer's detriment."[19] However, given that a court may characterize a relationship as not of the kind that imposes a duty of confidentiality, NDAs can be useful: They direct a court to find the relationship to be a confidential one, which avoids the vagaries of a court's fact-and-circumstances inquiry.[20] In light of this discussion, why else might NDAs be useful in the employment context?[21]

5. Trade Secrets

The Coca-Cola NDA above excludes "Trade Secrets" from the definition of Confidential Information and separately imposes obligations on the employee

---

19. MILGRIM ON TRADE SECRETS § 5.02(1) (2009); *see also Eaton Corp. v. Giere*, 971 F.2d 136, 141 (8th Cir. 1992) (Minnesota law); RESTATEMENT (THIRD) OF AGENCY § 8.05 (2006) (discussing agent's duty not to use or communicate principal's confidential information).

20. *See* MILGRIM ON TRADE SECRETS § 4.02(1)(b) (2009).

21. For a partial answer to this question, please see this chapter's discussion of trade secrets.

regarding Trade Secrets in § 4(b). What is a trade secret? Under the Uniform Trade Secrets Act ("UTSA") (and, not by coincidence, under the Agreement's definition, as well), a "trade secret" is information that:

> (i) derives independent economic value, actual or potential, from not being generally known to, and not being readily ascertainable by proper means by, other persons who obtain economic value from its disclosure or use, and
> (ii) is the subject of efforts that are reasonable under the circumstances to maintain its secrecy.[22]

Non-disclosure agreements are important in the context of trade secrets for at least two reasons. First, NDAs can help ensure one *has* a trade secret. As the UTSA provides, for information to be a trade secret, the "owner" of the information must make efforts to maintain its secrecy.[23] Requiring those who come into contact with the information to sign an NDA protecting that information is such an effort.[24] This matters when trying to recover from a party for misappropriation of a trade secret: If the would-be trade secret has been freely shared, it may fail to qualify as a trade secret in the first place. Note, however, that an NDA that expressly limits confidentiality obligations to a certain term has been held to place an express time limit on the trade-secret *status* of the underlying information.[25] Accordingly, an NDA may also work to *limit* trade-secrets rights that might exist absent the NDA.[26] How does the above NDA address this concern?

Second, NDAs can provide one with a claim under trade-secrets law. Trade-secrets law works to prohibit "misappropriation" of trade secrets.[27] The performance of various "improper means" may qualify as misappropriation of another's trade secret, and the disclosure or use of a trade secret in violation of a confidentiality agreement is one type of misappropriation actionable under the UTSA.[28] Moreover, trade-secrets law allows one to reach even persons who are not party to an NDA. Under the UTSA, a trade-secrets owner may recover for misappropriation against a third party who (1) acquires a trade secret by inducing a party to breach her NDA; or (2) uses or discloses a trade secret knowing (or with reason to know) that they (the third party) acquired

---

22. UNIFORM TRADE SECRETS ACT § 1(4) (1985).

23. *Id.* § 1(4)(ii).

24. *See, e.g., Tom James Co. v. Hudgins*, 261 F. Supp. 2d 636, 641-42 (S.D. Miss. 2003) (Miss. UTSA); *Liberty Am. Ins. Group, Inc. v. WestPoint Underwriters, LLC*, 199 F. Supp. 2d 1271, 1286 (M.D. Fla. 2001) (Fla. UTSA).

25. *See* CALLMANN ON UNFAIR COMPETITION, TR. & MONO. § 14:6 (West 4th ed. 2009); *see also infra* note 67 and accompanying text. *But see Wilson Mfg. Co. v. Fusco*, 258 S.W.3d 841, 847-48 (Mo. App. 2008) (explaining that misappropriation claim under Missouri UTSA could be brought after termination of NDA).

26. *See supra* note 25. Absent an NDA, a recipient of information may still be subject to a duty of confidentiality. On this, please see this chapter's discussion on an employee's duty of confidentiality for further discussion.

27. Please see UNIFORM TRADE SECRETS ACT § 1(2) (1985) for more on what may qualify as misappropriation.

28. UNIFORM TRADE SECRETS ACT § 1(2)(ii)(B)(II) (1985).

the trade secret from a party to an NDA.[29] This gives a trade-secrets owner a cause of action — potentially in addition to tortious interference, which can be a difficult-to-prove claim — for reaching third parties.

However, an NDA is unlikely to make a trade secret out of otherwise non-trade-secret information. Often, in non-disclosure agreements (as is the case in §§ 2 and 4(b) of this Agreement), a recipient of information will "acknowledge" that the recipient has received information that qualifies as a trade secret. These acknowledgments are of limited effect.[30] Indeed, despite having acknowledged the trade-secret status of information, a party is unlikely to be estopped from arguing that such information is not a trade secret because, for an acknowledgment to give rise to estoppel, "the party to be estopped must know the true facts and intend that its conduct be acted upon by the party asserting the defense."[31] Accordingly, the recipient's mere contractual acknowledgment of the trade-secret status of the discloser's information likely neither makes the information a trade secret nor denies a recipient the right to argue that such information is not a trade secret. Still, a contractual acknowledgment of trade-secret status is likely to give at least some weight and persuasive bite to the argument that the underlying information is a trade secret.[32]

Not only are NDAs important for the work they do in buttressing trade secrets, but also they may provide additional protection where trade-secrets law stops short. For instance, as discussed above, trade-secrets law generally only protects information that is valuable for being secret and which the putative owner takes steps to protect. However, an NDA may protect information that fails to qualify as a trade secret but that a party would still like to keep confidential.[33] On this point, consider the above Agreement's definition of "Confidential Information" and that it excludes "Trade Secrets." Section 4(a) of the Agreement imposes confidentiality obligations on the employee with respect to confidential, *non*-trade-secret information.

---

29. *Id.* §§ 1(2)(i), 1(2)(ii)(A), 1(2)(ii)(B)(III). Under the UTSA, "improper means" includes "breach or inducement of breach of a duty to maintain secrecy" in its definition. *Id.* § 1(1).

30. *See, e.g., Vincit Enters., Inc. v. Zimmerman*, No. 1:06-CV-57, 2006 WL 1319515, at *6 (E.D. Tenn. Mar. 12, 2006) (explaining recital that trade secrets are "valuable" is insufficient to allege trade secrets had "independent economic value" under the Tennessee UTSA; *Iroquois Indus. Corp. v. Popik*, 415 N.E.2d 4, 6 (Ill. App. 1980) (explaining recital that certain information was confidential was insufficient to give rise to trade-secrets interest, where information was not actually confidential); *Follmer, Rudzewicz & Co., P.C. v. Kosco*, 362 N.W.2d 676, 683 n.16 (Mich. 1984) ("[T]he mere fact that the employer puts self-serving statements in the 'Whereas' clause of an employment contract to the effect that many trade secrets will be disclosed cannot itself determine the existence of such secrets in the absence of hard proof."); Milgrim on Trade Secrets § 15.01(1)(a)(v) (2009).

31. *Computer Assocs. Int'l, Inc. v. Am. Fundware, Inc.*, 831 F. Supp. 1516, 1530 (D. Colo. 1993) (denying motion to estop a party who signed a contract acknowledging trade secrets) (internal citations omitted).

32. *See, e.g., Pre-Paid Legal Servs., Inc. v. Harrell*, No. CIV-06–019-JHP, 2008 WL 111319, at *11 (E.D. Okla. Jan. 8, 2008) (explaining contractual acknowledgment of trade-secret status provides evidence of efforts to maintain secrecy).

33. *See, e.g., AMP Inc. v. Fleischhacker*, 823 F.2d 1199, 1201 (7th Cir. 1987). For more on protecting non-trade-secret information, please see the discussion of the enforceability and reasonableness of NDAs below.

B. NON-DISCLOSURE AGREEMENT IN THE COMMERCIAL CONTEXT

The following agreement sets forth the obligations between two parties planning to enter into a commercial relationship.

Things to Consider…

As you read through the following agreement, please consider these items. You will want to return to the agreement, as you study the substantive discussion that follows.

> *Parties and Third Parties.* Who are (and who are not) the parties to *this* agreement? Consider who has the obligation to do what and, on the flip-side, who has the right to benefit, under this agreement. What is the right and power of a party to transfer its rights and its obligations under this agreement to a nonparty?

> *"Confidential Information" and Definitions.* Consider how *this* agreement defines "Confidential Information" and how the agreement uses this definition throughout. Taking the perspective of both parties in turn, does this definition strike you as particularly broad or narrow, given the circumstances of this relationship? Compare this to the previous agreement's definition and use of "Confidential Information."

> *Remedies and Redress.* Where may (and may not) a party bring suit for an action related to the agreement? What type of remedies and relief may the party obtain? How deferential do you think a court will be to the agreement's specification of these matters?

MICROSOFT CORPORATION NON-DISCLOSURE AGREEMENT (STANDARD RECIPROCAL)[34]

This Non-Disclosure Agreement (the "Agreement") is made and entered into as of the later of the two signature dates below by and between MICROSOFT CORPORATION, a Washington corporation ("Microsoft"), and Electronic Arts [Inc.], a Delaware corporation ("Company").

IN CONSIDERATION OF THE MUTUAL PROMISES AND COVENANTS CONTAINED IN THIS AGREEMENT AND THE MUTUAL DISCLOSURE OF CONFIDENTIAL INFORMATION, THE PARTIES HERETO AGREE AS FOLLOWS:

---

34. Electronic Arts Inc., Microsoft Corporation Non-Disclosure Agreement (Standard Reciprocal) (Form 10-Q), at Exhibit 10.6 (Nov. 10, 2009), *available at* http://www.sec.gov/Archives/edgar/data/712515/000119312509230789/dex106.htm.

1. Definition of Confidential Information and Exclusions

(a) "Confidential Information" means nonpublic information that a party to this Agreement ("Disclosing Party") designates as being confidential to the party that receives such information ("Receiving Party") or which, under the circumstances surrounding disclosure ought to be treated as confidential by the Receiving Party. "Confidential Information" includes, without limitation, information in tangible or intangible form relating to and/or including released or unreleased Disclosing Party software or hardware products, the marketing or promotion of any Disclosing Party product, Disclosing Party's business policies or practices, and information received from others that Disclosing Party is obligated to treat as confidential. Except as otherwise indicated in this Agreement, the term "Disclosing Party" also includes all Affiliates of the Disclosing Party and, except as otherwise indicated, the term "Receiving Party" also includes all Affiliates of the Receiving Party. An "Affiliate" means any person, partnership, joint venture, corporation or other form of enterprise, domestic or foreign, including but not limited to subsidiaries, that directly or indirectly, control, are controlled by, or are under common control with a party. Prior to the time that any Confidential Information is shared with an Affiliate who has not signed this Agreement, the Receiving Party that executed this Agreement below (the "Undersigned Receiving Party") shall have entered into an appropriate written agreement with that Affiliate sufficient to enable the Disclosing Party and/or the Undersigned Receiving Party to enforce all of the provisions of this Agreement against such Affiliate.

(b) Confidential Information shall not include any information, however designated, that: (i) is or subsequently becomes publicly available without Receiving Party's breach of any obligation owed Disclosing Party; (ii) became known to Receiving Party prior to Disclosing Party's disclosure of such information to Receiving Party pursuant to the terms of this Agreement; (iii) became known to Receiving Party from a source other than Disclosing Party other than by the breach of an obligation of confidentiality owed to Disclosing Party; (iv) is independently developed by Receiving Party; or (v) constitutes Feedback (as defined in Section 5 of this Agreement [Omitted]).

2. Obligations Regarding Confidential Information

(a) Receiving Party shall:

(i) Refrain from disclosing any Confidential Information of the Disclosing Party to third parties for five (5) years following the date that Disclosing Party first discloses such Confidential Information to Receiving Party, except as expressly provided in Sections 2(b) and 2(c) of this Agreement;

(ii) Take reasonable security precautions, at least as great as the precautions it takes to protect its own confidential information, but no less than reasonable care, to keep confidential the Confidential Information of the Disclosing Party;

(iii) Refrain from disclosing, reproducing, summarizing and/or distributing Confidential Information of the Disclosing Party except in pursuance of Receiving Party's business relationship with Disclosing Party, and only as otherwise provided hereunder; and

(iv) Refrain from reverse engineering, decompiling or disassembling any software code and/or pre-release hardware devices disclosed by Disclosing Party to Receiving Party under the terms of this Agreement, except as expressly permitted by applicable law.

(b) Receiving Party may disclose Confidential Information of Disclosing Party in accordance with a judicial or other governmental order, provided that Receiving Party either (i) gives the undersigned Disclosing Party reasonable notice prior to such disclosure to allow Disclosing Party a reasonable opportunity to seek a protective order or equivalent, or (ii) obtains written assurance from the applicable judicial or governmental entity that it will afford the Confidential Information the highest level of protection afforded under applicable law or regulation. Notwithstanding the foregoing, the Receiving Party shall not disclose any computer source code that contains Confidential Information of the Disclosing Party in accordance with a judicial or other governmental order unless it complies with the requirement set forth in sub-section (i) of this Section 2(b).

(c) The undersigned Receiving Party may disclose Confidential Information only to Receiving Party's employees and consultants on a need-to-know basis. The Receiving Party will have executed or shall execute appropriate written agreements with its employees and consultants sufficient to enable Receiving Party to enforce all the provisions of this Agreement.

(d) Receiving Party shall notify the undersigned Disclosing Party immediately upon discovery of any unauthorized use or disclosure of Confidential Information or any other breach of this Agreement by Receiving Party and its employees and consultants, and will cooperate with Disclosing Party in every reasonable way to help Disclosing Party regain possession of the Confidential Information and prevent its further unauthorized use or disclosure.

(e) Receiving Party shall, at Disclosing Party's request, return all originals, copies, reproductions and summaries of Confidential Information and all other tangible materials and devices provided to the Receiving Party as Confidential Information, or at Disclosing Party's option, certify destruction of the same.

3. Remedies

The parties acknowledge that monetary damages may not be a sufficient remedy for unauthorized disclosure of Confidential Information and that Disclosing Party shall be entitled, without waiving any other rights or remedies, to such injunctive or equitable relief as may be deemed proper by a court of competent jurisdiction.

4. Miscellaneous

(a) All Confidential Information is and shall remain the property of Disclosing Party. By disclosing Confidential Information to Receiving Party, Disclosing Party does not grant any express or implied right to Receiving Party to or under any patents, copyrights, trademarks, or trade secret information except as otherwise provided herein. Disclosing Party reserves without prejudice the ability to protect its rights under any such patents, copyrights, trademarks, or trade secrets except as otherwise provided herein.

(b) In the event that the Disclosing Party provides any computer software and/or hardware to the Receiving Party as Confidential Information under the terms of this Agreement, such computer software and/or hardware may only be used by the Receiving Party for evaluation and providing Feedback (as defined in Section 5 of this Agreement) to the Disclosing Party. Unless otherwise agreed by the Disclosing Party and the Receiving Party, all such computer software and/or hardware is provided "AS IS" without warranty of any kind, and Receiving Party agrees that neither Disclosing Party nor its suppliers shall be liable for any damages whatsoever arising from or relating to Receiving Party's use of or inability to use such software and/or hardware.

(c) The parties agree to comply with all applicable international and national laws that apply to (i) any Confidential Information, or (ii) any product (or any part thereof), process or service that is the direct product of the Confidential Information, including the U.S. Export Administration Regulations, as well as end-user, end-use and destination restrictions issued by U.S. and other governments. For additional information on exporting Microsoft products, see http://www.microsoft.com/exporting/.

(d) The terms of confidentiality under this Agreement shall not be construed to limit either the Disclosing Party or the Receiving Party's right to independently develop or acquire products without use of the other party's Confidential Information. Further, the Receiving Party shall be free to use for any purpose the residuals resulting from access to or work with the Confidential Information of the Disclosing Party, provided that the Receiving Party shall not disclose the Confidential Information except as expressly permitted pursuant to the terms of this Agreement. The term "residuals" means information in intangible form, which is retained in memory by persons who have had access to the Confidential Information, including ideas, concepts, know-how or techniques contained therein. The Receiving Party shall not have any obligation to limit or restrict the assignment of such persons or to pay royalties for any work resulting from the use of residuals. However, this sub-paragraph shall not be deemed to grant to the Receiving Party a license under the Disclosing Party's copyrights or patents.

(e) This Agreement constitutes the entire agreement between the parties with respect to the subject matter hereof. It shall not be modified except by written agreement dated subsequent to the date of this Agreement and signed by both parties. None of the provisions of this Agreement shall be deemed to have been waived by any act or acquiescence on the part of Disclosing Party, the Receiving Party, their agents, or employees, but only by an instrument in writing signed by an authorized employee of Disclosing Party and the Receiving Party. No waiver of any provision of this Agreement shall constitute a waiver of any other provision(s) or of the same provision on another occasion.

(f) If either Disclosing Party or the Receiving Party employs attorneys to enforce any rights arising out of or relating to this Agreement, the prevailing party shall be entitled to recover reasonable attorneys' fees and costs. This Agreement shall be construed and controlled by the laws of the State of Washington, and the parties further consent to exclusive jurisdiction and venue in the federal courts sitting in King County, Washington, unless no federal subject matter jurisdiction exists, in which case the parties consent to the exclusive jurisdiction and venue in the Superior Court of King County, Washington. Company waives all defenses of lack of personal jurisdiction and forum non conveniens. Process may be served on either party in the manner authorized by applicable law or court rule.

(g) This Agreement shall be binding upon and inure to the benefit of each party's respective successors and lawful assigns; provided, however, that neither party may assign this Agreement (whether by operation of law, sale of securities or assets, merger or otherwise), in whole or in part, without the prior written approval of the other party. Any attempted assignment in violation of this Section shall be void.

(h) If any provision of this Agreement shall be held by a court of competent jurisdiction to be illegal, invalid or unenforceable, the remaining provisions shall remain in full force and effect.

(i) Either party may terminate this Agreement with or without cause upon ninety (90) days prior written notice to the other party. All sections of this Agreement [relating] to the right and obligations of

the parties concerning Confidential Information disclosed during the term of the Agreement shall survive any such termination....
[Section 5 Omitted]
[Signature Line Omitted]

---

1. Integration and Merger Clauses

Under the parol evidence rule, an "integrated" contractual document prevents evidence of additional terms of agreement not found within the document from being admitted to *contradict* the document's terms.[35] A contractual document is considered integrated if it is the *final* expression of an agreement between the parties. A contractual document is considered "completely" integrated, if it is the complete expression of an agreement's terms, in which case the parol evidence rule bars even *consistent* additional terms. Where a contractual document contains final terms that make up only *part* of an agreement and, so, is only "partially integrated," consistent (but not contradictory) additional terms may be introduced as part of the agreement. Even if a contract is integrated (completely or partially), extrinsic evidence might still be admitted in order to resolve an ambiguity in the contract.[36] Also, notice that the parol evidence rule does not speak to whether the parties may vary (or have varied) an integrated agreement after contracting.[37]

A court will look to the intent of the contractual parties and to the face of a contractual document to determine if the document is the final (i.e., integrated) and complete expression of the agreement.[38] For this reason, subsection 4(e) of the above Microsoft Agreement provides that the Agreement "constitutes the entire agreement between the parties." Commonly called an "integration" or "merger" clause, this type of provision serves as a manifestation of party intent and operates as evidence to render a contract integrated (although query whether this Agreement's integration clause expressly evidences the *final* integration of the document). To determine whether a document is integrated, a court may also look to extrinsic evidence, as the parol evidence rule generally will not bar evidence as to whether a contract is actually integrated in the first

---

35. *See* RESTATEMENT (SECOND) OF CONTRACTS § 215 (1981).

36. *See, e.g., Kripp v. Kripp*, 849 A.2d 1159, 1161-62 (Pa. 2004) (finding a contractual term ambiguous and admitting extrinsic evidence to discern the parties' intended meaning). The Supreme Court of Pennsylvania in *Kripp* explained, "A contract is ambiguous if it is reasonably susceptible of different constructions and capable of being understood in more than one sense." *Id.* at 1163 (citation omitted).

37. Please see Chapter 2 for a discussion of "modification" and "no-oral-modification" provisions.

38. *See, e.g., Metoyer v. Chassman*, 504 F.3d 919, 935 (9th Cir. 2007); *Naimie v. Cytozyme Labs., Inc.*, 174 F.3d 1104, 1112 (10th Cir. 1999); RESTATEMENT (SECOND) OF CONTRACTS § 210 cmt. c (1981).

place.[39] An integration clause, while evidence of integration, is not dispositive of the issue.[40]

In whose interest is it that the Agreement be considered integrated? Is this Agreement's integration clause well drafted? Would you draft the clause any differently to communicate to a court that the document is integrated (i.e., the final expression of the parties' agreement) and supersedes any prior negotiations or agreements between the parties? Does this integration clause suggest that the Agreement is *partially* or *completely* integrated?

2. Severability Clauses

Should a court decide not to enforce a particular provision in the Agreement, subsection 4(h) attempts to "sever" the unenforceable provision in order to save the rest of the Agreement. This type of provision is called a "severability" clause.[41] In deciding whether or not to sever an unenforceable term, courts will look to whether or not the parties intended this.[42] To this end, courts will generally honor a severability clause — as evidencing party intent — and enforce the rest of the contract pursuant to the terms of the severability clause.[43] However, this is not without its limits. For instance, a severability clause will not save a contract from a finding of procedural unconscionability (where a contract is the product of unfair bargaining).[44] Likewise, where a contract would be incoherent or left without an essential part if devoid of an invalid provision, courts are unlikely to sever the invalid provision — severability clause or not.[45] Accordingly, in these situations, the entire contract fails. This is consistent with the general proposition that,

---

39. *See* RESTATEMENT (SECOND) OF CONTRACTS § 210(3) (1981); *see also id.* cmt. b, c.

40. *See, e.g., Jarvis v. K2 Inc.*, 486 F.3d 526, 536 (9th Cir. 2007) (Washington law); *LaHaye v. Goodneuz Group, LLC*, 172 F. App'x 733, 735 (9th Cir. 2006) (California law); *see also* RESTATEMENT (SECOND) OF CONTRACTS § 210 cmt. b, e (1981).

41. This section discusses "severability" clauses and not "savings" clauses, inasmuch as the former instructs a court to sever whole provisions or language and the latter instructs a court to interpret or modify the language of a provision so as to maintain its enforceability. In practice, the terms "severability clause" and "savings clause" are often used interchangeably. For the willingness of courts to modify provisions so as to make them reasonable (and enforceable), please see the discussion of judicial tailoring in Chapter 2.

42. *See, e.g., Jackson v. Cintas Corp.*, 425 F.3d 1313, 1317 (11th Cir. 2005) (Georgia law); *Booker v. Robert Half Int'l., Inc.*, 413 F.3d 77, 84 (D.C. Cir. 2005).

43. *See, e.g., Anders v. Hometown Mortg. Servs., Inc.*, 346 F.3d 1024 (11th Cir. 2003) (Alabama law); *Pilato v. Edge Investors, L.P.*, 609 F. Supp 2d 1301, 1309 (S.D. Fla. 2009) (Florida law); *Kraisinger v. Kraisinger*, 928 A.2d 333, 341 (Pa. Super. 2007) ("A court is bound by the clear language of a contract as to severability.") (internal citations omitted).

44. *See Sosa v. Paulos*, 924 P.2d 357, 364-65 (Utah 1996).

45. *See, e.g., Hill v. Names & Addresses, Inc.*, 571 N.E.2d 1085, 1100 (Ill. App. 1991) ("[C]lear and unmistakable specific provisions, which plainly exalt the invalid provisions of the restrictive covenant as 'essential' to the agreement, necessarily overcome the general and all-encompassing severability clause....").

while it is the province of the courts to give effect to party intent, it is not their role to rewrite contracts.[46]

3. Third-Party Rights and Duties: Assignment and Third-Party Beneficiaries

a. Assignment: Transferring Rights and Duties to a Third Party

"Assignment" refers to the transfer of a party's rights (and, as the term is often used, obligations) under a contract to another person or entity. The effect of an assignment is that the "assignee" (the party to whom the contract is assigned) steps into the shoes of the "assignor" (the party assigning the contract) and enjoys the rights that the assignor would have enjoyed under the contract going forward. Traditionally, assignment refers only to the transfer of contractual *rights*, whereas "delegation" refers to the transfer of contractual *duties*. When a third party agrees to take on the duties of a contract, she is bound to perform those duties, but this does not relieve the original party (i.e., the "delegating party") of her obligations under that contract.[47] Because parties often use terms of assignment to refer to the transfer of both rights and duties, courts are likely to presume that broad language of assignment conveys both the rights and the unperformed duties of a contract, absent contractual language or evidence to the contrary.[48]

Rights and obligations under a contract are generally transferable,[49] and, accordingly, contractual provisions allowing parties to assign their rights and to delegate their obligations under an NDA are generally enforceable.[50] However, subsection 4(g) of the NDA provides explicitly that neither party has the right to assign the Agreement, without the other party's prior written consent.

---

46. *See, e.g., Booker*, 413 F.3d at 84-85 ("If illegality pervades…such that only a disintegrated fragment would remain after hacking away the unenforceable parts, the judicial effort begins to look more like rewriting the contract than fulfilling the intent of the parties.").

47. Whereas an assignor loses those rights she assigns, a delegating party is *not* relieved "of the ultimate responsibility to see that the obligation is performed." *Contemporary Mission, Inc. v. Famous Music Corp.*, 557 F.2d 918, 925 (2d Cir. 1977).

48. *See Am. Flint Glass Workers Union v. Anchor Resolution Corp.*, 197 F.3d 76, 81 (3d Cir. 1999); RESTATEMENT (SECOND) OF CONTRACTS § 328 (1981) ("[A]n assignment in…general terms is an assignment of the assignor's rights and a delegation of his unperformed duties under the contract."); U.C.C. § 2-210(4) (2003).

49. *See Physical Distrib. Servs., Inc. v. R.R. Donnelley & Sons Co.*, 561 F.3d 792, 794-95 (8th Cir. 2009) (explaining that contracts rights are generally transferrable); *Contemporary Mission*, 557 F.2d at 924 (explaining that contract obligations are generally delegable, unless performance will vary materially); *see also* RESTATEMENT (SECOND) OF CONTRACTS § 317 (1981). However, some rights are not generally transferrable; notably licensed intellectual property rights (e.g., patent, copyright, trademark) are not transferable absent language in the license that expressly provides that the rights are transferrable. *See Cincom Sys., Inc. v. Novelis Corp.*, 581 F.3d 431, 436 (6th Cir. 2009).

50. *See, e.g., Chemetall GMBH v. Zr Energy, Inc.*, No. 99 C 4334, 2000 WL 1808568, at *2-4 (N.D. Ill. Dec. 6, 2000), *aff'd*, 320 F.3d 714 (7th Cir. 2003).

Sometimes called an "anti-assignment clause," these provisions are also generally enforceable.[51]

However, note that, as a matter of construction, a court is likely to read a provision that *prohibits* assignment of "the contract" only to prohibit the delegation of *duties* and not the assignment of *rights*.[52] Still, as the Sixth Circuit explains, "These rules of interpretation do not override express statements of the will of the parties. If the contract shows an intent by the parties to limit both delegations of duties and assignment of rights..., then the interpretive default rules are inapplicable."[53] Accordingly, an express prohibition of the assignment of *rights* under the contract would not implicate the interpretive rule and would express the parties' intent to prohibit the assignment of rights.

Here, the Microsoft Agreement prohibits assignment of "this Agreement" (without the other party's consent). How is a court likely to construe the clause? To effect a prohibition of the assignment of *rights* and, thereby, to avoid this rule of construction, how would you draft this provision? Do note that, "[g]iven the importance of free assignability,...antiassignment clauses are construed narrowly whenever possible,"[54] and that, despite a drafter's best efforts, a court may still decide not to enforce an anti-assignment clause in certain circumstances.[55]

Furthermore, subsection 4(g) specifies that assignment includes assignment "by operation of law, sale of securities or assets, merger or otherwise." Why do you suppose the parties included this language? A party may transfer her rights under a contract by means other than an ordinary "assignment," namely when another entity acquires the party or merges with the party. Accordingly, subsection 4(g) attempts to protect a party against the nonconsensual transfer of duties (and perhaps rights) no matter the name or form of the transaction that accomplishes the transfer (or something tantamount to a transfer).

Assuming an anti-assignment provision is effective to prohibit the assignment of rights, what remedies does a contracting party have if the other party breaches an anti-assignment provision and assigns her rights under an agreement? Most courts will distinguish between the *right* to assign and the *power* to assign.[56] Under this view, an enforceable anti-assignment provision that bars

---

51. *See, e.g., Physical Distrib. Servs.,* 561 F.3d at 794-95; *Travertine Corp. v. Lexington-Silverwood,* 683 N.W.2d 267, 273 (Minn. 2004); *Rumbin v. Utica Mut. Ins. Co.,* 757 A.2d 526 (Conn. 2000).

52. *See* RESTATEMENT (SECOND) OF CONTRACTS § 322(1) (1981); *see also* U.C.C. § 2-210(4) (2003). *See, e.g., Cedar Point Apartments, Ltd. v. Cedar Point Inv. Corp.,* 693 F.2d 748, 753 (8th Cir. 1982); *Charles L. Bowman & Co. v. Erwin,* 468 F.2d 1293, 1297-98 (5th Cir. 1972).

53. *Riley v. Hewlett-Packard Co.,* 36 F. App'x 194, 196 (6th Cir. 2002) (Michigan law) (internal citations omitted).

54. *Rumbin,* 757 A.2d at 531.

55. *See, e.g., Seaboard Constr. Co. v. The Weitz Co.,* No. CV208-105, 2009 WL 3855185, at *5 (S.D. Ga. Nov. 17, 2009) ("[O]nce a party to a contract performs its obligations under a contract, its right to enforce the other party's liability for payment under the contract may be assigned without the other party's consent, even if the contract contains an anti-assignment clause."); RESTATEMENT (SECOND) OF CONTRACTS § 322 cmt. b (1981) (explaining that certain anti-assignment provisions will not be effective).

56. *See Rumbin,* 757 A.2d at 531 ("In interpreting antiassignment clauses, the majority of jurisdictions now distinguish between the assignor's 'right' to assign and the 'power' to assign....").

the assignment of contractual rights only withholds a party's *right* to assign her contractual rights.[57] Accordingly, if a party assigns her rights in contravention of the enforceable anti-assignment provision, the party *will* have breached the contract, but the non-breaching party will only be entitled to damages for the breach.[58] On the other hand, an anti-assignment provision that explicitly provides that an assignment is "void" — or that the putative assigning party otherwise has no power to assign her rights under the contract — will likely be found to have withheld a party's *power* (in addition to her right) to assign.[59] Such a provision, if enforced, renders the assignment itself void, as if the transfer to the third party never occurred at all.[60]

b. Binding Third Parties

Note that subsection 4(g) contains an extremely common provision that attempts to make the Agreement binding on successors and assigns — a successor, being the legal entity that exists after a party merges or is acquired, and an assign, being the party to whom a party transfers its rights under the Agreement. It is a basic proposition of contract law that a party must manifest assent to (i.e., accept) a contract before she can be legally bound by that contract.[61] Accordingly, query the work done by section 4(g) itself and whether the Agreement may actually bind — that is *impose duties* on — third parties, not party to the Agreement. Likewise, subsection 1(a) defines "Affiliate" and imposes a duty on the Receiving Party, before sharing Confidential Information with an Affiliate, to have the Affiliate sign an agreement, binding her to the terms of this Agreement. Under this Agreement alone, could the Disclosing Party have a claim against an Affiliate for breach of the Agreement?

c. Benefitting Third Parties

Conversely, a contract between two parties may *give rights* to persons not party to that contract. Such persons are called "third-party beneficiaries." Whether a third party is a beneficiary of a contract generally turns on the intent of the parties to the contract.[62] Because this Agreement is silent about third-party beneficiaries, it is unlikely that a court would characterize

---

57. *See id.* at 528; *Pravin Banker Assocs., Ltd. v. Banco Popular Del Peru*, 109 F.3d 850 (2d Cir. 1997).
58. *See Rumbin*, 757 A.2d at 534; *Bel-Ray Co. v. Chemrite (Pty) Ltd.*, 181 F.3d 435, 442 (3d Cir. 1999).
59. *See Rumbin*, 757 A.2d at 531; *Pravin Banker*, 109 F.3d at 856 ("To reveal the intent necessary to preclude the power to assign, or cause an assignment violative of contractual provisions to be wholly void, [a contractual] clause must contain express provisions that any assignment shall be void or invalid if not made in a certain specified way.") (internal citations and quotation marks omitted).
60. *See supra* note 59.
61. *See* RESTATEMENT (SECOND) OF CONTRACTS § 17 (1981).
62. *See, e.g., Robins Dry Dock & Repair Co. v. Flint*, 275 U.S. 303, 307 (1927); *Cooper Power Sys., Inc. v. Union Carbide Chems. & Plastics Co.*, 123 F.3d 675, 680 (7th Cir. 1997); *McCarthy v. Azure*, 22 F.3d 351, 362 (1st Cir. 1994).

a third party as having rights under the Agreement, absent evidence other-wise to suggest that the parties intended to benefit the third party.[63] To this end, agreements will often contain prophylactic provisions that expressly state that the parties did not intend to benefit any third parties whatsoever. These provisions are generally enforceable. However, when a separate provision specifically states an intention to benefit a third party, the specific provision granting third-party rights will be effective despite a blanket provision in the same agreement that disclaims any third-party benefit. For example, a contract, that included the following provision (section 10.5), was held still to create third-party beneficiaries:

> This Agreement, the exhibits and schedules hereto, the Surviving Intercompany Contracts and the Confidentiality Agreement . . . are not intended to confer upon any Person other than the parties hereto, the Company, the Company Subsidiaries, the Purchaser Indemnified Persons and the Seller Indemnified Persons any rights or remedies hereunder.[64]

This is because that same contract included, by amendment, the following provision (section 6 of the amendment):

> (a) Purchaser [GTG] agrees that neither Purchaser nor the Company [VeriFone] nor any Company Subsidiary will terminate any U.S. employees of the Company or its affiliates (the 'U.S. VeriFone Employees') during the first sixty (60) days after Closing.
>
> (b) Purchaser agrees that the Equivalent-Severance Policy (as defined below) for U.S. VeriFone Employees that it would otherwise apply in the first ninety (90) days of its ownership of the Company will instead apply in the ninety (90) days beginning sixty-one (61) days after the Closing. In other words, if Purchaser concludes that it will terminate any U.S. VeriFone Employees at any time through one hundred fifty (150) days after Closing, any U.S. VeriFone Employees who are notified within that time that they will lose their jobs will receive severance benefits from Purchaser or the Company or a Company Subsidiary that are approximately equivalent to the cash compensation element of the Seller's [Hewlett-Packard's] unassigned pool benefits for the Seller's U.S. employees which the parties agree shall be no less than six months base salary (the 'Equivalent Severance Policy').[65]

The California Court of Appeals explained:

> Applying the law of third party beneficiaries to the language of the contract discloses GTG and Hewlett-Packard expressly intended to grant plaintiffs the promises contained in section 6 of the amendment. Indeed, section 6 is a classic third party provision. . . . The provision expressly benefits them, and only them. . . .

---

63. *See, e.g., Fleetwood Enters., Inc. v. Gaskamp*, 280 F.3d 1069, 1075-76 (5th Cir. 2002) (under Texas law, "the intent to make someone a third-party beneficiary must be clearly written or evidenced in the contract").

64. *Prouty v. Gores Tech. Group*, 18 Cal. Rptr. 3d 178, 180 n.1 (Cal. Ct. App. 2004).

65. *Id.* at 180 n.2.

GTG disagrees with our conclusion, asserting section 10.5 precludes plaintiffs from becoming third party beneficiaries.... If GTG and Hewlett-Packard had not wanted to benefit plaintiffs, they would not have written section 6....

Section 6 of the amendment does conflict with section 10.5 of the stock purchase agreement, and as incorporated into the amendment by section 8(b) of the amendment. Under rules of contract construction, however, the mere existence of sections 10.5 and 8(b) does not end this matter. The latter two provisions cannot be harmonized with section 6. Sections 10.5 and 8(b) state generally no rights or remedies exist under the contract to third persons; section 6 expressly grants rights to specific third persons regarding their employment with GTG. In this circumstance, under well established principles of contract interpretation, when a general and a particular provision are inconsistent, the particular and specific provision is paramount to the general provision. Section 6 of the amendment thus is an exception to section 10.5 of the original contract and section 8(b) of the amendment, and the plaintiffs can enforce it.[66]

4. Termination and Survival

Notice that subsection 4(i) of the NDA provides that either party may terminate the Agreement with or without cause (that is, for any or no reason at all), after providing 90 days notice. However, subsection 4(i) further provides that the parties' confidentiality obligations survive the termination of the Agreement. "Survival" works much as you might expect: The "termination" of an agreement means that the contract no longer imposes rights or obligations on any of the parties thereto; however, "survival" of some or all of an agreement's terms means that the rights and obligations imposed by those terms still apply with legally binding force, beyond termination. Is it clear to you from the NDA which provisions are to survive termination? Note that contracts will commonly list which specific provisions are to survive.

In the context of NDAs, survival of confidentiality obligations is important, as neither trade-secrets law nor the common law is likely to step in to continue any obligations of non-disclosure.[67]

5. Choice of Law and Forum

Subsection 4(f) of the Microsoft NDA contains a "choice-of-law" provision, which specifies that the Agreement should be interpreted and enforced in

---

66. *Id.* at 184-86 (internal citations omitted).

67. *See* CALLMANN ON UNFAIR COMPETITION, TR. & MONO. § 14:6 (West 4th ed. 2009); *see also supra* note 25. That is, trade-secrets law only forbids misappropriation of trade secrets, and it may not be misappropriation to use what was another's trade secret, when such trade secret is acquired pursuant to a confidentiality agreement, after the confidentiality agreement expires by its own terms.

accordance with the laws of the State of Washington. Choice-of-law provisions are very common in commercial agreements.

As seen in the Coca-Cola NDA at the beginning of this chapter, choice-of-law provisions will often provide that a certain state's law governs the contract *without regard for the state's choice-of-law principles*. The purpose of this language is to preempt the forum court (the court where the action is brought) from engaging in its own choice-of-law analysis. That is, this language instructs the court to disregard its own choice-of-law principles and to defer to the parties' specification of governing law. Courts are often unwilling to abide by such instructions and will still engage in their own choice-of-law analysis.[68]

Still, courts are likely to arrive at the same ends, as, in applying their own choice-of-law rules, courts generally give great deference to the parties' contractually specified choice of governing law.[69] Indeed, a court may even defer to a contractual designation of governing law with regard to a *tort* action between contractual parties (at least where the tort action is incidental to the contract), where the language of the contractual choice-of-law provision is sufficiently broad to apply to the relevant tort.[70] Generally, courts will defer to choice-of-law provisions so long as there is either some reasonable basis for the parties' choice of law or some substantial relationship between the parties (or their contract) and the state of the chosen law.[71] To illustrate, the official comment to the Restatement (Second) of Conflict of Laws explains:

> When the state of the chosen law has some substantial relationship to the parties or the contract, the parties will be held to have had a reasonable basis for their choice. This will be the case, for example, when this state is that where performance by one of the parties is to take place or where one of the parties is domiciled or has his principal place of business. The same will also be the case when this state is the place of contracting except, perhaps, in the unusual situation where this place is wholly fortuitous and bears no real relation either to the contract or to the parties. These situations are mentioned only for purposes of example. There are undoubtedly still other situations where the state of the chosen law will have a sufficiently close relationship to the parties and the contract to make the parties' choice reasonable.
>
> The parties to a multistate contract may have a reasonable basis for choosing a state with which the contract has no substantial relationship. For example, when contracting in countries whose legal systems are strange to them as

---

68. *See, e.g., Lynch Group v. Pohlman, Inc.*, No. 06-13501, 2007 WL 118937, at *3 (E.D. Mich. 2007); *Airtel Wireless, LLC v. Montana Elecs. Co.*, 393 F. Supp 2d 777, 783-84 (D. Minn. 2005).

69. *See Cook v. Little Caesar Enters., Inc.*, 210 F.3d 653, 656 (6th Cir. 2000); *Herring Gas Co. v. Magee*, 22 F.3d 604, 605 (5th Cir. 1994).

70. *See, e.g., Hitachi Credit Am. Corp. v. Signet Bank*, 166 F.3d 614, 628 (4th Cir. 1999) (Virginia law) (citing *In re Allegheny Int'l, Inc.*, 954 F.2d 167, 178 (3d Cir. 1992); *Moses v. Bus. Card Express, Inc.*, 929 F.2d 1131, 1139 (6th Cir. 1991)).

71. *See* RESTATEMENT (SECOND) OF CONFLICT OF LAWS § 187(2) (1971); *see also, e.g., Tschira v. Willingham*, 135 F.3d 1077, 1083 (6th Cir. 1998) (Tennessee law).

well as relatively immature, the parties should be able to choose a law on the ground that they know it well and that it is sufficiently developed. For only in this way can they be sure of knowing accurately the extent of their rights and duties under the contract....[72]

Note that New York and Delaware have passed statutes that provide that parties to certain contracts (in the case of New York, involving consideration of $250,000 or more; in the case of Delaware, involving $100,000 or more) may contractually select New York law or Delaware law, respectively, regardless of whether a reasonable relationship exists.[73]

On the other hand, a court may refuse to honor a choice-of-law provision where the application of the chosen law would contradict a fundamental public policy of the forum state.[74] For example, a court in California has refused to enforce a choice-of-law provision (selecting the law of a non-California state) with respect to a non-competition covenant because non-competition covenants are unenforceable under, and contrary to a fundamental public policy of, California law.[75]

Subsection 4(f) of the Microsoft NDA further contains a "forum-selection" clause, which is a provision that specifies an exclusive (as in this case) or non-exclusive jurisdiction and venue for disputes to be adjudicated between the parties. Here, the clause provides that the parties may only bring an action in federal or state court in King County, Washington. While once viewed with disfavor by American courts, forum-selection provisions are now generally viewed as presumptively valid.[76] Absent a showing of some compelling reason (e.g., fraud, undue influence, unfair bargaining) *not* to enforce a forum-selection clause, they are likely to be honored.[77] Notice, then, that selecting, say, New York as an exclusive forum allows parties to take advantage of the New York statute that honors the selection of New York law, in certain contracts, even absent a reasonable relationship to New York. Also, of interest, a court in California has honored an exclusive forum-selection clause, even where doing so meant an action regarding a non-competition covenant would be heard in a forum willing to enforce non-competition covenants.[78]

---

72. RESTATEMENT (SECOND) OF CONFLICTS § 187 cmt. f (1971); *see also, e.g., McBride v. Mkt. St. Mortgage,* No. 07-804, 2010 WL 2180608, at *6 (10th Cir. 2010) (Wyoming law); *Armarine Brokerage, Inc. v. OneBeacon Ins. Co.,* 307 F. App'x 562, 564-65 (2d Cir. 2009) (New York law).

73. N.Y. GEN. OBLIG. § 5-1401 (Consol. 1984); DEL. CODE. ANN. tit. 6 § 2708 (2005).

74. *See Dykes v. DePuy,* Inc., 140 F.3d 31, 39 (1st Cir. 1998).

75. *See, e.g., In re Gault S. Bay Litig.,* No. C 07-04659 JW, 2008 WL 4065843, at *5 (N.D. Cal. Aug. 27, 2008). Please see Chapter 2 for more on non-competition covenants.

76. *See* RESTATEMENT (SECOND) OF CONFLICTS § 80 (1971); *Nat'l Equip. Rental, Ltd. v. Szukhent,* 375 U.S. 311, 315–16 (1964); *see also M/S Bremen v. Zapata Off-Shore Co.,* 407 U.S. 1, 15 (1972); *Hugel v. Corp. of Lloyd's,* 999 F.2d 206, 210 (7th Cir.1993).

77. *See supra* note 76.

78. *See, e.g., Whipple Indus., Inc. v. Opcon AB,* No. CV-F-05-0902 REC SMS, 2005 WL 2175871, at *9-10 (E.D. Cal. Sep. 7, 2005).

Drafting Note: Forum-Selection Clauses; Exclusivity and Courts

In reading or writing a forum-selection clause, a couple basic questions are whether the provision specifies a permissive (i.e., non-exclusive) or mandatory (i.e., exclusive) forum, as discussed above, and to which courts the provision refers.

For example, specifying that parties "may" bring suit in certain courts generally has a permissive and non-exclusive effect; this means that the non-moving party has consented to jurisdiction and venue in the specified courts. Alternatively, parties may specify that jurisdiction is mandatory and exclusive by providing that the parties "may only" bring suit in certain courts or by stating plainly that the parties agree to "exclusive jurisdiction" in certain courts, as the parties did in Section 4(f) in the above Microsoft NDA. While this linguistic distinction may appear basic, this very issue is a common feature of litigation, and a prudent party will be careful to specify precisely whether the parties agree to permissive or mandatory jurisdiction and venue.

Another issue involves the specification of the courts with regard to which the parties are consenting to jurisdiction. Unclear drafting has led to litigation over the meaning of "of"—namely, whether a federal court sitting in a state constitutes a court "of" that state.[79] Put simply, the answer is "no."[80] If a party wishes to include federal courts among those specified for jurisdiction, the party should refer to the courts "*in*" (and not "of") a desired state. Or, more to the point, a party wishing to select federal courts may wish to specify "federal" courts expressly by name. We see the parties did just this in Section 4(f) of the Microsoft NDA, selecting exclusive jurisdiction in the "federal courts sitting in King County, Washington," and providing that, should there be no federal subject matter jurisdiction, the parties agree to exclusive jurisdiction and venue in the state courts in that same location.

---

6. Stipulating Remedies by Contract

a. *Stipulating Equitable Relief by Contract*

Section 3 ("Remedies") of the Microsoft NDA attempts to bolster a party's ability to obtain injunctive or other equitable relief. In general, before issuing a preliminary or permanent injunction, courts typically require a showing that the moving party will suffer irreparable harm should an injunction not issue and that remedies at law (e.g., monetary damages) will not provide the plaintiff with an adequate remedy, such that a remedy in equity is necessary. In section 3, both parties acknowledge that there would be an inadequate remedy

---

79. *See, e.g., Am. Soda, LLP v. Filter Wastewater Group, Inc.*, 428 F.3d 921, 926 (10th Cir. 2005); *Dixon v. TSE Int'l Inc.*, 330 F.3d 396, 398 (5th Cir. 2003).

80. *See supra* note 79.

at law (i.e., "monetary damages may not be a sufficient remedy") in the event of a breach of the NDA and that each party is entitled to seek injunctive relief. Parties also commonly stipulate in a contract that a breach of the contract may or will cause irreparable harm. In general, while these provisions may be persuasive or given some weight by courts,[81] they do not control whether equitable relief is appropriate or will be awarded.[82]

A court is only one of several potential audiences for a contract, and, as discussed further in Chapter 2, parties may find themselves before an arbitrator, attempting to enforce their contractual rights. An arbitrator may have the power to award injunctive or other equitable relief—and courts are likely to enforce such an arbitral decree—if the parties intended for the arbitrator to have these powers.[83] Accordingly, while a contractual provision that stipulates that injunctive relief is available may give some weight to a party's argument for injunctive relief for breach of contract,[84] this provision is also helpful for *empowering* an arbitrator to award injunctive relief.[85] However, this is not to suggest that a provision stipulating equitable relief will determine the matter of whether a court or arbitrator will award equitable relief.

b. Stipulating Monetary Damages by Contract: Liquidated Damages

As parties may attempt to provide by contract that equitable relief will be available upon breach, they may also attempt to establish an amount of monetary damages by contract. Given that damages for breach of contract are often difficult to prove or calculate, a party may wish to negotiate for a "liquidated-damages" provision in her contract. A liquidated-damages provision sets by contract the amount of damages a party will be due in the event of a specified breach of the contract. Such clauses may specify damages as a fixed sum or with a formula or schedule that calculates damages based on certain inputs. What makes damages liquidated is not that they are a fixed sum but that their measurement is determined by contract.

(1) The "Reasonableness" of Liquidated-Damages Provisions

Courts respect the intent of contractual parties to agree upfront and freely to contract about what damages a party should recover in the event of a breach

---

81. *See, e.g., Ticor Title Ins. Co. v. Cohen*, 173 F.3d 63, 69 (2d Cir. 1999) (New York law).

82. *See, e.g., Dominion Video Satellite, Inc. v. EchoStar Satellite Corp.*, 356 F.3d 1256, 1266 (10th Cir. 2004).

83. *See* Thomas H. Oehmke, 3 Commercial Arbitration § 119:1 (2010).

84. *See, e.g., Ticor Title*, 173 F.3d at 69 (New York law) ("In fact, the employment contract sought to be enforced concedes that in the event of Cohen's breach of the post-employment competition provision, Ticor shall be entitled to injunctive relief, because it would cause irreparable injury. Such, we think, might arguably be viewed as an admission by Cohen that plaintiff will suffer irreparable harm were he to breach the contract's non-compete provision.").

85. *See supra* note 83. Please see the discussion of arbitration in Chapter 2.

of the contract. However, it is a fundamental principle of contracts that contract law compensates and does not punish.[86] Accordingly, courts will only enforce a liquidated-damages provision that does not amount to a "penalty." So, the question is: What qualifies as an enforceable liquidated-damages provision and what qualifies as an unenforceable penalty?

While courts historically viewed liquidated damages with skepticism and favored a construction of the provisions as penalties, the law of liquidated damages is "chastened by an emerging presumption against interpreting liquidated-damages clauses as penalty clauses."[87] The test for whether a liquidated-damages provision is enforceable varies from state to state. The basic formulation requires that the provision be "reasonable" and that actual damages be difficult to estimate.

In general, before enforcing a liquidated-damages provision, a court will require that the contractual determination of damages bear a reasonable relationship to the actual damages that would result from the breach. Under the Restatement approach, a provision may be "reasonable," if the contractually determined amount of damages either: (1) "approximates the actual loss that has resulted from the particular breach, even though it may not approximate the loss that might have been anticipated under other possible breaches"; or (2) "approximates the loss anticipated at the time of the making of the contract, even though it may not approximate the actual loss."[88] Accordingly, that actual damages *turn out* to be disproportionate vis-à-vis a liquidated amount is generally not enough to make a liquidated-damages provision a penalty.[89] However, courts vary in their approaches to liquidated damages; for example, some courts *will* invalidate a provision as a penalty if the liquidated-damages amount turns out to be disproportionate to the actual damages, at the time of breach, without considering whether the amount approximated the loss anticipated at the time of contracting.[90]

---

86. *See* RESTATEMENT (SECOND) OF CONTRACTS § 355 cmt. a (1981) ("The purposes of awarding contract damages is to compensate the injured party.... For this reason, courts in contract cases do not award damages to punish the party in breach or to serve as an example to others unless the conduct constituting the breach is also a tort for which punitive damages are recoverable.").

87. *XCO Int'l Inc. v. Pac. Scientific Co.*, 369 F.3d 998, 1003 (7th Cir. 2004).

88. RESTATEMENT (SECOND) OF CONTRACTS § 356 cmt. b (1981).

89. *See, e.g., Choice Hotels Int'l, Inc. v. Chewl's Hospitality, Inc.*, 91 F. App'x 810, 817 (4th Cir. 2003) (Maryland law) ("The fact that actual damages turn out to be less than those stipulated in the liquidated damages provision does not characterize or stamp the stipulation as a penalty.") (internal citations and quotation marks omitted); *Yockey v. Horn*, 880 F.2d 945, 953 (7th Cir. 1989) ("As we have noted, the Restatement provides that the reasonableness of the amount set in a liquidated damages clause is to be looked at as of the time of contracting and at the time of actual breach. If at *either* time the estimate is reasonable, the clause will be enforced. Illinois law seems to conform to this model.") (internal citations omitted).

90. *See, e.g., In re Dow Corning Corp.*, 419 F.3d 543, 549-50 (6th Cir. 2005) (Texas law) ("In addition,... liquidated damages must not be disproportionate to actual damages, as measured at the time of the breach. Thus, if the liquidated damages are disproportionate to the actual damages, the clause will not be enforced and recovery will be limited to the actual damages proven.") (internal citations and quotation marks omitted).

As an illustration, the Seventh Circuit found the following provision to include an unenforceable penalty:

> In consideration of the special equipment [i.e., the new bagging system] to be acquired and furnished by LAKE-RIVER for handling the product, CARBORUNDUM shall, during the initial three-year term of this Agreement, ship to LAKE-RIVER for bagging a minimum quantity of [22,500 tons]. If, at the end of the three-year term, this minimum quantity shall not have been shipped, LAKE-RIVER shall invoice CARBORUNDUM at the then prevailing rates for the difference between the quantity bagged and the minimum guaranteed.[91]

This was because, as Judge Posner explained, the provision would liquidate damages at an amount greater than actual damages in all possible worlds.[92] The actual damages calculation would require reducing any damages award by the amount Lake River saved due to Carborundum's breach. However, the liquidated-damages provision in this case did not take into account expenses avoided due to breach. Instead, the clause required that Carborundum pay Lake River the same price it would have had Carborundum met its minimum quantity obligations. Accordingly, under the provision, Lake River would receive all of the benefit it would have received if Carborundum had fully performed the contract, with none of the additional costs.

In addition to requiring a reasonable estimation, courts also generally require that actual damages were speculative or difficult to estimate at the time of contracting.[93] Moreover, the more speculative and uncertain actual damages are, the more latitude parties may receive in determining what amounts to a reasonable estimate at the time of contracting.[94] For example, in contracts involving intellectual property (in particular, trade secrets), damages may be particularly difficult to calculate and a liquidated-damages provision may be appropriate.[95]

---

91. *Lake River Corp. v. Carborundum Co.*, 769 F.2d 1284, 1286 (7th Cir. 1985).

92. *Id.* at 1291.

93. *See, e.g., Ladco Props. XVII v. Jefferson-Pilot Life Ins. Co.*, 531 F.3d 718, 720 (8th Cir. 2008) ("Under North Carolina law, a liquidated damages provision is enforceable and will not be considered a penalty where (1) damages are speculative or difficult to ascertain, and (2) the amount stipulated is a reasonable estimate of probable damages or the amount stipulated is reasonably proportionate to the damages actually caused by the breach."); *Barrie School v. Patch*, 933 A.2d 382 (Md. 2007) ("Maryland courts will uphold a liquidated damages clause as valid, and not a penalty, if it satisfies two primary requirements. First, the clause must provide a fair estimate of potential damages at the time the parties entered into the contract. Second, the damages must have been incapable of estimation, or very difficult to estimate, at the time of contracting.") (internal citations and quotation marks omitted).

94. *See* RESTATEMENT (SECOND) OF CONTRACTS § 356 cmt. b (1981) ("The greater the difficulty either of proving that loss has occurred or of establishing its amount with the requisite certainty…, the easier it is to show that the amount fixed is reasonable. To the extent that there is uncertainty as to the harm, the estimate of the court or jury may not accord with the principle of compensation any more than does the advance estimate of the parties.").

95. *See, e.g., Midwest Oilseeds, Inc. v. Limagrain Genetics Corp.*, 387 F.3d 705, 717 (8th Cir. 2004) ("Because the breach involves the release of MO's intellectual property to its competitors, damages are extremely difficult to determine in this case.").

Furthermore, some states include additional requirements for the enforcement of liquidated-damages provisions. For example, in Illinois, courts at least sometimes have required that the parties agree to a liquidated-damages provision with the intent to settle in advance future damages under the contract.[96] In addition, many courts state as a separate requirement that the parties intend the provision "solely to compensate the nonbreaching party and not as a penalty for breach or as an incentive to perform."[97]

Drafting Note: Specifying Relevant Breaches in Liquidated-Damages Clauses

Contracts are often complex documents imposing all sorts of obligations on the parties thereto. Accordingly, not all failures to perform an obligation are equal, and, therefore, not all breaches of a contract will necessarily result in the same amount of damages. A liquidated-damages provision may be reasonable vis-à-vis certain breaches and wholly disproportionate vis-à-vis others. (Indeed, the Federal Circuit went so far as to find a liquidated-damages clause unenforceable under Missouri law because actual damages would have been easy to estimate for a hypothetical breach of just one of the contract's provisions![98]) For this reason, some courts will read liquidated-damages provisions—that do not provide otherwise—to apply only to material breaches of the contract and will evaluate their enforceability based on this presumption.[99] More importantly, for this reason, a prudent party should specify to which breaches of which contract provisions a liquidated-damages clause applies. Indeed, the Supreme Judicial Court of Massachusetts has counseled:

> Failing to provide any recognition for the type, or timing, of the default, while by no means determinative, tends to indicate that the provision's intended purpose was not to estimate the different types of damages that might arise from a future default, but to penalize for any failure, however immaterial.[100]

If a provision is found to operate as a penalty, then the provision will be ignored, and the court will award actual damages, as if the contract does not

---

96. *Energy Plus Consulting, LLC v. Illinois Fuel Co.*, 371 F.3d 907, 909 n.2 (7th Cir. 2004).

97. *See, e.g., Renaudette v. Barrett Trucking Co.*, 712 A.2d 387, 388 (Vt. 1998) (internal citation omitted); *see also* RICHARD A. LORD, 24 WILLISTON ON CONTRACTS § 65:3 (4th ed. 2009).

98. *Monsanto Co. v. McFarling*, 363 F.3d 1336, 1348 (Fed. Cir. 2004) ("[A] liquidated damages clause is invalid if even one breach covered by the clause fails to qualify for enforceability as liquidated damages."). However, please note that the Federal Circuit did not evaluate whether this rule would apply when the damages amount called for by the liquidated damages provision turns out to be reasonable vis-à-vis the actual damages resulting from the breach that actually occurred. *See id.*

99. *See, e.g., JMD Holding Corp. v. Cong. Fin. Corp.*, 828 N.E.2d 604, 612 (N.Y. 2005) (citing *United Air Lines, Inc. v. Austin Travel Corp.*, 867 F.2d 737, 741 (2d Cir. 1989)).

100. *TAL Fin. Corp. v. CSC Consulting, Inc.*, 844 N.E.2d 1085, 1093 (Mass. 2006).

contain the liquidated-damages provision.[101] If a liquidated-damages provision is enforceable, then "the measure of damages for a breach will be the sum in the clause, no more, no less."[102]

(2) "Optional" Liquidated-Damages Provisions

A classic liquidated-damages clause provides the exclusive monetary remedy available to a contractual party for a specified breach of the contract. In this way, a liquidated-damages clause provides both an upper and lower bound—located at the same amount—on the liability available for breach of contract. In contrast, as we discuss in Chapter 3, a contract may include a limitation-of-liability provision, which imposes only an upper limit on liability.

A variation of the classic, an "optional" liquidated-damages provision specifies that, in the event of a breach, a non-breaching party may either obtain the contractually specified damages *or* sue for actual damages. Notice that a "rational" party will invoke this type of liquidated-damages provision only if actual damages (minus any additional costs associated with suing for actual damages) turn out to be less than those provided by the liquidated-damages provision and will opt not to invoke the provision if actual damages promise richer spoils. In effect, then, an optional liquidated-damages provision provides only a lower bound on liability.

Some jurisdictions refuse to enforce such optional liquidated-damages provisions. For example, in a jurisdiction requiring that liquidated-damages provisions reflect a "settlement" of prospective damages, a court has held that an optional provision, leaving open the potential for actual damages, does not evince an actual settlement of future actual damages.[103] However, some courts have been willing to enforce optional liquidated-damages provisions, especially as between sophisticated parties.[104]

(3) "Alternative-Performance" Contracts

Note that liquidated-damages provisions operate to stipulate a damages amount in the event that a party *breaches* a contract—that is, in the event that

---

101. *See JMD Holding Corp.*, 828 N.E.2d at 609 ("If the clause is rejected as being a penalty, the recovery is limited to actual damages proven.") (internal citations and quotation marks omitted).

102. *Id.*

103. *Grossinger Motorcorp, Inc. v. Am. Nat'l Bank and Trust Co.*, 607 N.E.2d 1337, 1346 (Ill. App. Ct. 1992) ("[T]he optional nature of the liquidated damages clause shows that the parties never intended to establish a specific sum to constitute damages in the event of a breach."); *see also, e.g., Jefferson Randolph Corp. v. Progressive Data Sys., Inc.*, 553 S.E.2d 304 (Ga. Ct. App. 2001), *rev'd on other grounds*, 568 S.E.2d 474 (Ga. 2002).

104. *See, e.g., Nw. Airlines, Inc. v. Flight Trails*, 3 F.3d 292, 294-95 (8th Cir. 1993); *Avery v. Hughes*, Civil No. 09-cv-265-JD, 2010 WL 338092, at *3-4 (D.N.H. Jan. 20, 2010) (finding optional liquidated damages provision to be enforceable); *McMaster v. McIlroy Bank*, 654 S.W.2d 591 (Ark. Ct. App. 1983) (finding optional liquidated damages provision to be enforceable); *Noble v. Ogborn*, 717 P.2d 285, 287 (Wash. Ct. App. 1986) ("A liquidated damages clause does not preclude a party from suing for actual damages if that right is preserved in the contract between the parties.") (internal citation omitted).

a party fails to perform in accordance with a contract. When a contract provides that a party may satisfy an obligation under the contract by one of several means, on its face at least, the contract states an "alternative-performance" provision—and not a liquidated-damages provision. Accordingly, a contract may provide that a party has a duty to perform by doing X or by paying Y dollars, where paying Y dollars is simply one of several performance alternatives available to a party. Query the functional difference between an "alternative-performance" and a "liquidated-damages" arrangement. Is the difference in form alone? Is the payment of damages (actual or stipulated) not always an "alternative" performance?

Courts often state that whether a contract contains a liquidated-damages provision is a question of substance and not form.[105] Indeed, courts often give short rhetorical shrift to whether the parties call a provision a "liquidated-damages" provision, in considering whether a provision is for liquidated damages or a penalty.[106] Still, in practice, some courts have given some weight to the language used by parties in their contract, for instance, where parties have labeled a provision "liquidated damages" or a "penalty."[107] Similarly, courts recite that determining whether a provision is for alternative performance or stipulated damages is a question of substance and not form. The Restatement advises:

> Sometimes parties attempt to disguise a provision for a penalty by using language that purports to make payment of the amount an alternative performance under the contract, that purports to offer a discount for prompt performance, or that purports to place a valuation on property to be delivered. Although the parties may in good faith contract for alternative performances and fix discounts or valuations, a court will look to the substance of the agreement to determine whether this is the case or whether the parties have attempted to disguise a provision for a penalty that is unenforceable under this Section. In determining whether a contract is one for alternative performances, the relative value of the alternatives may be decisive.[108]

Courts have frequently found a contract to involve an "alternative-performance" arrangement and not a liquidated-damages provision, side-stepping the law of liquidated damages and its penalty inquiries. For example, in the case of prepayment fees, courts have often found that a borrower that

---

105. *See, e.g., JKC Holding Co. v. Washington Sports Ventures, Inc.*, 265 F.3d 459, 468 (4th Cir. 2001) (New York law) ("In interpreting a provision fixing damages, it is immaterial what the parties choose to call the provision."); *In re Graham Square, Inc.*, 126 F.3d 823, 829 (6th Cir. 1997) (Ohio law) ("Neither the parties' actual intention as to its validity nor their characterization of the term as one for liquidated damages or a penalty is significant in determining whether the term is valid.") (internal citations and quotation marks omitted).

106. *See supra* note 105.

107. *See, e.g., Kalenka v. Taylor*, 896 P.2d 222, 229 (Alaska 1995) (noting that the court was "inclined to disallow the 'penalties' sought by the Kalenkas based on their moniker alone"); *Equity Enters., Inc. v. Milosch*, 633 N.W.2d 662, 672 (Wis. Ct. App. 2001) ("In short, the label the parties apply to the clause, which might indicate their intent, does have some evidentiary value, but it is not conclusive.").

108. RESTATEMENT (SECOND) OF CONTRACTS § 356 cmt. c (1981).

opts to prepay her loan in accordance with a prepayment provision in her contract is merely performing alternatively and that the prepayment provision does not operate as a stipulation of "damages," as there has been no breach.[109] In addition, courts have found "take-or-pay" gas contracts, where a buyer agrees either to purchase a certain quantity of gas or to pay a sum for such gas,[110] and "early termination fee" provisions, where a party agrees to continue to receive services under a contract or to pay a fee to terminate the contract,[111] to be alternative-performance contracts and not to involve liquidated damages.

In contrast, the Tenth Circuit found a provision that required a party to pay a sum "as liquidated damages" in the event the party failed to meet a minimum-volume requirement to be a liquidated-damages provision and not an alternative-performance provision.[112] The court further explained, "PSO's commitment to ship 2,600,000 tons of coal annually via BN was not set forth in the Agreement as one of the two alternative performances to be given by PSO."[113] Accordingly, while the test for whether a provision operates as liquidated damages or an alternative performance turns on the substance of the arrangement, courts may still look to the language and structure of the contract to determine this substance. That is, courts will look to the contract to determine whether the parties intended to create a provision as a remedy for a breach or to provide one of several ways to satisfy a performance obligation. As Professor Corbin is oft-cited for explaining, "If, upon a proper interpretation of the contract, it is found that the parties have agreed that either one of the two alternative performances is to be given by the promisor and received by the promisee as the agreed exchange and equivalent for the return performance rendered by the promisee, the contract is a true alternative contract."[114] A party wishing to create a "true" alternative performance contract, then, should be clear in structuring her agreement to specify several performances, each of which the promisor may elect in satisfaction of a contractual obligation.

---

109. *See, e.g., Great Plains Real Estate Dev., LLC v. Union Cent. Life Ins. Co.*, 536 F.3d 939, 945 (8th Cir. 2008) (Iowa law) ("Here, the Note gave GPR the choice of paying according to the Note's terms or prepaying the Note in full and paying the PPP. When GPR elected to prepay, GPR was not breaching the contract but was in fact acting in accordance with an express option provided under the contract."); *Carlyle Apartments Joint Venture v. AIG Life Ins. Co.*, 635 A.2d 366, 373 (Md. 1994) ("We have matched the contract against the facts and find no breach. Absent any breach by the borrower, there is no occasion to consider damages or to look for a liquidated damages clause in disguise....").

110. *See, e.g., Prenalta Corp. v. Colorado Interstate Gas Co.*, 944 F.2d 677, 689 (10th Cir. 1991) (Wyoming law) (noting that "a take-or-pay contract provides for performance in the alternative" and that "courts have distinguished the 'pay' provision from a liquidated damages provision").

111. *See, e.g., Hutchison v. AT & T Internet Servs., Inc.*, No. CV07-3674 SVW (JCx), 2009 WL 1726344 (C.D. Cal. May 5, 2009).

112. *Pub. Serv. Co. v. Burlington N. R.R.*, 53 F.3d 1090, 1099 (10th Cir. 1995) (Oklahoma law).

113. *Id.* (internal quotation marks omitted).

114. 11-58 CORBIN ON CONTRACTS § 58.18 (2010).

C. THE ENFORCEABILITY AND LIMITS OF NDAS

When will courts enforce or not enforce a non-disclosure agreement? Are there limits to what may be included or to how long the confidentiality obligations persist? Consider the following case.

Coady v. Harpo, Inc.

Appellate Court of Illinois, First District, Fifth Division, 1999.
719 N.E.2d 244.

Justice GREIMAN delivered the opinion of the court:

Plaintiff Elizabeth Coady appeals the dismissal of her cause of action seeking a declaratory judgment that a confidentiality policy established by defendant Harpo, Inc., was unenforceable against plaintiff, a former employee of defendant....

In her complaint, plaintiff stated that from November 1993 to March 1998 she was employed by defendant in a number of positions, most recently as a "senior associate producer" for defendant's television series, "The Oprah Winfrey Show." Plaintiff alleged that for some time prior to March 26, 1998, defendant engaged in a course of conduct designed to force plaintiff from her employment and defendant's treatment of plaintiff became so intolerable as to amount to constructive termination. On March 26, 1998, plaintiff notified defendant by letter from her attorney that she resigned effectively immediately.

Paragraph 16 of plaintiff's complaint states that she, "a trained journalist, intends to write or otherwise report about her experiences as an employee of defendant, matters of legitimate public interest and concern." Plaintiff further alleged that her intention to exercise her rights of free speech and free press was not prohibited by a confidentiality policy, which was entitled "Business Ethics, Objectivity, and Confidentiality Policy" and contained in defendant's September 1996 employee manual. Plaintiff maintained that the purported restrictions of the confidentiality policy, as stated in the employee manual, were unenforceable for one or more of eight enumerated reasons.

In a letter dated April 24, 1998, and attached to plaintiff's complaint, defendant "reminded" plaintiff that she had signed a document entitled "Business Ethics, Objectivity and Confidentiality Policy" on March 12, 1995, and provided her a copy of the agreement in the letter. Defendant's letter further stated that in the March 12, 1995, agreement, plaintiff "agreed (among other things) to keep confidential, during her employment and thereafter, all information about the Company, Ms. Winfrey, her private life, and Harpo's business activities which she acquired during or by virtue of her employment with Harpo." Defendant further stated that it intended to enforce and ensure compliance with the confidentiality agreement....

Both the independent document entitled "Business Ethics, Objectivity and Confidentiality Policy" (hereinafter the 1995 agreement) and the portion of the employee manual with the same title (hereinafter the 1996 employee manual) include a section entitled "Confidentiality Assurances," which provides in pertinent part as follows:

"1. During your employment or business relationship with Harpo, and thereafter, to the fullest extent permitted by law, you are obligated to keep confidential and never disclose, use, misappropriate, or confirm or deny the veracity of, any statement or comment concerning Oprah Winfrey, Harpo (which, as used herein, included all entities related to Harpo, Inc., including Harpo Productions, Inc., Harpo Films, Inc.) or any of her/its Confidential Information. The phrase 'Confidential Information' as used in this policy, includes but is not limited to, any and all information which is not generally known to the public, related to or concerning: (a) Ms. Winfrey and/or her business or private life; (b) the business activities, dealings or interests of Harpo and/or its officers, directors, affiliates, employees or contractors; and/or (c) Harpo's employment practices or policies applicable to its employees and/or contractors.

2. During your employment or business relationship with Harpo, and thereafter, you are obligated to refrain from giving or participating in any interview(s) regarding or related to Ms. Winfrey, Harpo, your employment or business relationship with Harpo and/or amy [sic] matter which concerns, relates to or involves any Confidential Information."

...The relevant documents also provide that commitment to the stated policies is required as a condition of employment: "Your commitment to the guidelines set forth in this policy is a condition of your employment or business relationship with Harpo."

In addition, defendant's motion to dismiss attached a copy of plaintiff's acknowledgment of the employee manual, which she signed upon the commencement of her employment at defendant in 1993. The acknowledgment signed by plaintiff states in relevant part:

"I acknowledge and understand that I may not use any confidential or proprietary information of HARPO for my own purposes either during or after my employment with HARPO, and I understand that I am prohibited from removing, disclosing or otherwise misappropriating any of HARPO's confidential or proprietary information for any reason."

...[P]laintiff asserts that the confidentiality policy is not enforceable, primarily arguing that it is overly broad and not reasonably necessary to protect defendant's legitimate business interests. Defendant, however, contends that the confidentiality agreement is enforceable because it does not violate any public policy, was supported by adequate consideration, was not an adhesion contract and properly protected defendant's legitimate business interests.

Until the filing of her appellate reply brief, plaintiff relied on the 1996 employee manual to support her cause of action, contending that the confidentiality policy contained therein was not enforceable because the 1996 employee manual included a contract disclaimer, *i.e.,*"[t]his manual is not a contract." Plaintiff relied on case law that addressed whether an employee handbook creates contractual rights.

In light of the facts in the present case, the employee-handbook analysis is unnecessary because defendant attached the 1995 agreement to its...motion to dismiss as the affirmative matter refuting plaintiff's crucial conclusions of law based on the 1996 employee manual and the language in both documents is identical. As acknowledged by plaintiff in her appellate reply brief, "[t]he covenant in the manual contains precisely the same language and terms as the confidentiality agreement which plaintiff signed on March 12, 1995." Plaintiff further stated that her arguments as to the enforceability of the restrictive covenant remain the same regardless of which version is considered. Accordingly, we will not unnecessarily elongate this opinion by conducting a pointless exercise to determine whether the 1996 employee manual created a contract. Instead, we consider the identical language contained in the 1995 agreement to determine its validity.

"A postemployment restrictive covenant will be enforced if its terms are reasonable." To determine the reasonableness of a restrictive covenant, "it is necessary to consider whether enforcement of the covenant will injure the public, whether enforcement will cause undue hardship to the promisor and whether the restraint imposed by the covenant is greater than is necessary to protect the interests of the employer."

The reasonableness of some types of restrictive covenants, such as nonsolicitation agreements, also is evaluated by the time limitation and geographical scope stated in the covenant. However, a confidentiality agreement will not be deemed unenforceable for lack of durational or geographic limitations where trade secrets and confidential information are involved.

Postemployment restrictive covenants typically involve agreements by a past employee not to compete with the business of her former employer, not to solicit clients or customers of her former employer, and not to disseminate trade secrets of her former employer. The covenants in these typical cases are carefully scrutinized because Illinois courts abhor restraints on trade.

Although restraint of trade is a significant concern, "[a]n equally important public policy in Illinois is the freedom to contract." Furthermore, postemployment restrictive covenants "have a social utility in that they protect an employer from the unwarranted erosion of confidential information."

Unlike the traditional line of restrictive covenant cases, the confidentiality agreement at issue in the instant case does not impose any of the typical restrictions commonly adjudicated in restrictive covenant cases. Defendant does not seek to restrain plaintiff's future career. Plaintiff is free to choose her future occupation, the locale in which she may choose to work, and the time when she can commence her new career. Defendant does not object to plaintiff becoming a journalist, competing with defendant in the same venue and in any locale, including Chicago, and in beginning her new venture immediately. The confidentiality agreement does not restrict commerce and does not restrict plaintiff's ability to work in any chosen career field, at any time. Instead, the 1995 confidentiality agreement restricts plaintiff's ability to disseminate confidential information that she obtained or learned while in defendant's employ. Most certainly, plaintiff had no problem with keeping confidences as long as she was a senior associate producer and continued her work with defendant.

Moreover, we find unpersuasive plaintiff's argument that the confidentiality agreement is too broad because it remains effective for all time and with no geographical boundaries. Whether for better or for worse, interest in a celebrity figure and his or her attendant business and personal ventures somehow seems to continue endlessly, even long after death, and often, as in the present case, extends over an international domain.

Under the facts of this case and the terms of the restrictive covenant at issue, we find that the 1995 confidentiality agreement is reasonable and enforceable. Accordingly, we affirm the trial court's order dismissing plaintiff's cause of action as stated in count I of her complaint....

---

1. The Limits of NDAs: Reasonableness, etc.

The central question concerning the enforceability of an NDA is whether or not the restrictive covenant is "reasonable."[115] Whether or not a non-disclosure covenant is reasonable turns on "if it (1) is no greater than required for the protection of the employer, (2) does not impose undue hardship on the employee and (3) is not injurious to the public."[116] In *Coady*, the court found the confidentiality agreement in question to be reasonable, explaining that the NDA in question need not contain time or geographic limitations to be enforceable. Courts are split as to whether an NDA must be limited by time and/or geography in order to be reasonable and enforceable.[117]

---

115. *See, e.g., 1st Am. Sys., Inc. v. Rezatto*, 311 N.W.2d 51, 57 (S.D. 1981); *Eden Hannon & Co. v. Sumitomo Trust & Bank Co.*, 914 F.2d 556, 560-61 (4th Cir. 1990) (Virginia law).

116. *1st Am.*, 311 N.W.2d at 59. It would seem that a similar "reasonableness" test would generally inform the enforceability of NDAs in the commercial context; however, the case law on this issue is surprisingly lacking. Note that at least one court has explained that NDAs are presumptively valid and, accordingly, do not require a "reasonableness" inquiry to be enforced. *See Zep Mfg. Co. v. Harthcock*, 824 S.W.2d 654, 663 (Tex. App. 1992).

117. *Compare, e.g., Synergetics, Inc. v. Hurst*, 477 F.3d 949, 958-59 (8th Cir. 2007) (holding that under Missouri law, confidentiality agreements need not contain time or geographic restrictions), *Everett J. Prescott, Inc. v. Ross*, 390 F. Supp 2d 44, 46 & n.3 (D. Me. 2005), *Wang Labs., Inc. v. CFR Assocs., Inc.*, 125 F.R.D. 10, 13 (D. Mass. 1989), *Revere Transducers, Inc. v. Deere & Co.*, 595 N.W.2d 751, 762 (Iowa 1999), *and Zep Mfg. Co. v. Harthcock*, 824 S.W.2d 654, 663 (Tex. App. 1992), *with Nalco Chem. Co. v. Hydro Techs., Inc.*, 984 F.2d 801, 803 (7th Cir. 1993) (holding that under Wisconsin law, a non-disclosure clause without a time limit is void

Generally, an NDA may impose confidentiality obligations pertaining to any information, whether or not such information constitutes a "trade secret."[118] However, some courts have been reluctant to enforce an NDA as to information that is not at least actually confidential.[119] Courts are not uniform on this matter, as some have explained that a confidentiality obligation is enforceable according to its bargained-for terms, irrespective of whether or not the underlying information is publicly known.[120]

There is one — at least partial — solution that addresses the concern that a court may find an NDA unreasonable and, so, unenforceable: the "savings" clause.[121] A savings clause can work as a stopgap measure to float an otherwise overbroad and unenforceable agreement down to the level of reasonableness. That is, the clause instructs the court to ignore the unreasonable aspects of the NDA and to enforce the remaining enforceable parts. On this measure, courts may obey; however, a prudent party who wishes later to enforce an NDA will attempt to draft a provision no more restrictive than reasonable.[122] Of course, a savings clause does nothing to save, or to bolster the enforceability of, the "unreasonable" aspects of the confidentiality obligations.

2. Consideration and Employee Non-Disclosure Agreements

Given that the employee in this case began work for Harpo in 1993, was there consideration to support either of the 1995 Agreement or the 1996 Agreement? Courts take divergent views on this issue, with some treating "substantial continued employment" after the execution of an NDA as sufficient consideration

---

unless the underlying information is a trade secret, as statute provides that no time limit is required for trade-secret restrictions), *and Opteum Fin. Servs., LLC v. Spain*, 406 F. Supp. 2d 1378, 1381 (N.D. Ga. 2005).

118. *See, e.g., Eaton Corp. v. Giere*, 971 F.2d 136, 141 (8th Cir. 1992) (Minnesota law); *Cincinnati Tool Steel Co. v. Breed*, 482 N.E.2d 170, 174 (Ill. App. 1985) ("[A]n enforceable restrictive covenant may protect material which does not constitute a trade secret."); *1st Am. Sys.*, 311 N.W.2d at 58.

119. *See, e.g., Rivendell Forest Prods., Ltd. v. Georgia-Pacific Corp.*, 824 F. Supp. 961, 968 (D. Colo. 1993), *rev'd on other grounds*, 28 F.3d 1042, 1046 (10th Cir. 1994); *Durham v. Stand-By Labor of Georgia, Inc.*, 198 S.E.2d 145, 149-50 (Ga. 1973).

120. *See, e.g., Health Alliance Network, Inc. v. Cont'l Cas. Co.*, 354 F. Supp. 2d 411, 422 (S.D.N.Y. 2005); *Forest Labs., Inc. v. Lowey*, 218 U.S.P.Q. (BNA) 646, 658 (N.Y. Sup. 1982).

121. A "severability clause," which is discussed earlier in the chapter, is similar to a "savings clause." This book uses "severability clause" to refer to clauses that instruct a court to "sever" any unenforceable provisions in order to enforce the remaining portions of the contract and "savings clause" to refer to clauses that instruct a court to interpret or modify a provision in order to render the provision enforceable. However, please note that in practice the terms are often used interchangeably and that the distinction is a blurry one.

122. Please see the discussion of judicial tailoring in Chapter 2, which details the various approaches that states take to modifying overly restrictive covenants. Note that not all courts are willing to modify provisions. *See, e.g., Rollins Protective Servs. Co. v. Palermo*, 287 S.E.2d 546, 549 (Ga. 1982) (holding, in the employment context, that if any portion of a restrictive covenant is invalid, the entire covenant must fail). However, under Georgia law, "a severability clause will allow a court to excise the *entire* restrictive covenant so as to preserve the other covenants in the contract." *Johnstone v. Tom's Amusement Co.*, 491 S.E.2d 394, 397 (Ga. Ct. App. 1997) (emphasis in original).

and with others finding an NDA void for lack of consideration, where the NDA is executed after an employee begins the underlying employment.[123]

3. The Distinction Between Non-Disclosure and Non-Compete Obligations

The distinction between non-disclosure and non-competition obligations is significant.[124] Non-disclosure obligations impose a duty to refrain from sharing confidential information, whereas non-competition obligations impose a duty not to work for competitors, as defined by the agreement. The distinction is important because courts are more suspicious of covenants not to compete, requiring that they meet a more stringent standard to be enforced.[125] Why? Covenants not to compete are considered "restraints of trade" (or, "restraints on trade"), which serve to impede the freedom of the marketplace by restricting labor and business activity.[126] Non-disclosure obli-

---

123. *Compare Curtis 1000, Inc. v. Suess*, 24 F.3d 941, 945 (7th Cir. 1994), *Dixie Homecrafters, Inc. v. Homecrafters of Am., LLC*, No. 1:08-CV-0649-JOF, 2009 WL 596009, at *6 (N.D. Ga. Mar. 5, 2009) (noting that, under Georgia law, continued employment is sufficient consideration for non-disclosure agreement, where employment was otherwise at will), *and Woodfield Group, Inc. v. DeLisle*, 693 N.E.2d 464, 469 (Ill. App. 1998), *with Rivendell Forest Prods.*, 824 F. Supp. at 968 (finding that an employee confidentiality agreement signed after the start of employment is void for lack of consideration), *rev'd on other grounds*, 28 F.3d 1042 (10th Cir. 1994), *and Jostens, Inc. v. Nat'l Computer Sys., Inc.*, 318 N.W.2d 691, 703 (Minn. 1982) (noting that continuation of employment is insufficient consideration to support a confidentiality agreement). *See also SFX USA, Inc. v. Bjerkness*, 636 F. Supp 2d 696, 709-10 (N.D. Ill. 2009) (finding that a restrictive covenant was supported by consideration, where agreement recited adequate consideration and there may have been continued substantial employment had employee not voluntarily resigned); *Picker Int'l., Inc. v. Blanton*, 756 F. Supp. 971, 982 (N.D. Tex. 1990) ("Special training or knowledge acquired by an employee during employment may constitute independent valuable consideration."); *Mann Frankfort Stein & Lipp Advisors, Inc. v. Fielding*, 289 S.W.3d 844, 850-52 (Tex. 2009) (finding consideration for non-disclosure and non-compete agreement in employer's "implied promise" to disclose confidential information to employee). For a thoughtful discussion on the various approaches taken by courts to assess consideration in restrictive covenant agreements in the employment context, *see McGough v. Nalco Co.*, 496 F. Supp 2d 729, 744-52 (N.D. W. Va. 2007) (finding continued employment to be valid consideration, under Alabama law, for a non-disclosure agreement entered into after employment began).

124. Courts sometimes mistakenly conflate an analysis of non-disclosure covenants with that of non-compete covenants. *See, e.g., Guy Carpenter & Co., Inc. v. Provenzale*, 334 F.3d 459, 465-66 (5th Cir. 2003) (Texas law) (concluding that the district court made a faulty assumption that statute governing restraint of trade informed merits of non-disclosure claim); *Perman v. ArcVentures, Inc.*, 554 N.E.2d 982, 986 (Ill. App. 1990); *1st Am. Sys.*, 311 N.W.2d at 56 (noting that the "trial court erred because the contract was divisible and a nondisclosure agreement differs from a noncompetition agreement").

125. *See, e.g., Guy Carpenter*, 334 F.3d at 465; *Revere Transducers, Inc. v. Deere & Co.*, 595 N.W.2d 751, 761 (Iowa 1999).

126. *See* Terry Morehead Dworkin & Elletta Sangrey Callahan, *Buying Silence*, 36 Am. Bus. L.J. 151, 156 (1998) ("Anti-competition covenants are legally disfavored because they restrain trade by inhibiting promisors' freedom of movement among employment opportunities. Accordingly, these agreements are limited or prohibited by statute in some states, and are closely examined in others. Confidentiality agreements, in contrast, are enforceable even in states in which anti-competition clauses are prohibited. Concerns regarding restraint of trade are much less directly implicated in this context; restrictions on access to information, rather than employee movement, are involved. Thus, the policy in favor of freedom of contract is given precedence.").

gations are generally not considered restraints of trade and, accordingly, are unlikely to be subjected to the higher degree of scrutiny,[127] unless such provisions operate, in effect, as obligations not to compete.[128]

---

127. *See, e.g., Guy Carpenter*, 334 F.3d at 465; *Lear Siegler, Inc. v. Ark-Ell Springs, Inc.*, 569 F.2d 286, 289 (5th Cir. 1978) (Mississippi law); *Papa John's Int'l, Inc. v. Pizza Magia Int'l, LLC*, No. CIV.A. 3:00CV-548-H, 2001 WL 1789379, at *4 (W.D. Ky. May 10, 2001); *Revere Transducers*, 595 N.W.2d at 761. *But see Central Monitoring Serv. v. Zakinski*, 553 N.W.2d 513, 515-16 (S.D. 1996) (noting that non-disclosure agreements are restraints of trade).

128. *See, e.g., Quixote Transp. Safety, Inc. v. Cooper*, No. 03 C 1401, 2004 WL 528011 (N.D. Ill. Mar. 12, 2004) ("[I]f we accept that [one] can establish a violation of this particular non-disclosure agreement by showing [recipient] will inevitably use the confidential information if employed by a competitor, then the non-disclosure agreement as written effectively becomes a permanent non-compete agreement. The Illinois courts have long rejected the reasonableness of such restrictions; the agreement cannot be enforced if it does not place reasonable limitations on the duration of the restriction.").

· CHAPTER TWO ·

EMPLOYMENT AGREEMENTS

———————————————●———————————————

This action asserting breach of contract and related tort claims arises out of a September 8, 2004 broadcast that plaintiff Dan Rather narrated on the CBS 60 Minutes II television program about then President George W. Bush's service in the Texas Air National Guard. Rather alleges that CBS disavowed the broadcast after it was attacked by Bush supporters, and fraudulently induced him to apologize personally for the broadcast on national television as well as to remain silent as to his belief that the broadcast was true. Rather alleges that, following President Bush's re-election, CBS informed him that he would be removed as anchor of the CBS Evening News. Rather claims that although his employment agreement required that, in the event he was removed as anchor, CBS would make him a regular correspondent on 60 Minutes or immediately pay all amounts due under the agreement and release him to work elsewhere, CBS kept him on the payroll while denying him the opportunity to cover important news stories until May 2006 when it terminated his contract, effective June 2006. . . .

Contractually, CBS was under no obligation to "use [Rather's] services or to broadcast any program" so long as it continued to pay him the applicable compensation. This "pay or play" provision of the original 1979 employment agreement was specifically reaffirmed in the 2002 Amendment to the employment agreement.

Rather v. CBS Corp., 886 N.Y.S.2d 121, 123–24 (N.Y. App. Div. 2009).

As with most relationships, a prudent party enters an employment agreement with hopes for the best and plans for the worst. Here, a New York court found that CBS owed its anchor of four decades only that which the employment agreement between the two parties required.[1] Indeed, as the court explained,

---

1. *Rather v. CBS Corp.*, 886 N.Y.S.2d 121, 125 (N.Y. App. Div. 2009).

Rather "negotiated a contract that was extensively amended several times, that paid Rather a lucrative salary, and that detailed, in 50 pages, everything from his assignments and on-air work at CBS Evening News to requirements that he attend rehearsals and join the union."[2] Accordingly, CBS was able to terminate the services its employee in accordance with the terms of its negotiated employment agreement, without being liable to its employee for anything more.

In this chapter, we discuss the rights and obligations of employers and employees as allocated by employment agreements.

Subject to limited exceptions,[3] in the absence of a written agreement providing for a fixed term of employment, employment is considered to be "at will." This means employment can be terminated by the employer or the employee for any reason or no reason absent unlawful discrimination. One of these aforementioned exceptions is where the employer has recognized a union and is party to a collective bargaining agreement. While labor law and collective bargains are outside the scope of this chapter, in order to provide context, we asked a seasoned practitioner with expertise in the area to explain the history and difference between labor and employment law.

A Practitioner Perspective: The Emergence of Employment Law

Forty-five years ago, a law firm department specializing in U.S labor and employment law would have dealt almost exclusively with what we now refer to as traditional labor law. "Labor law" as we in the practice think of it, involves the relationship between employers and their unionized employees or their employees being unionized. The legal framework for this field of law is primarily set forth in the National Labor Relations Act (which includes the Taft-Hartley Act), although a number of other acts such as the Labor Management Reporting and Disclosure Act, the Davis Bacon Act and the Railway Labor Act also impact the field. The relationship between an employer and a union representing its employees is usually set forth in a collective bargaining agreement (CBA), which establishes for a period of years the pay, benefits and other terms of employment to be provided to employees in the bargaining unit. In addition, a CBA typically contains a method for handling employee performance issues (i.e., progressive discipline) and provides for the ultimate resolution, through a final, binding arbitration process, of any dispute between the union and the employer. As a part of this dispute-resolution system, the CBA would also likely contain a no-strike, no-lockout provision for the duration

---

2. *See id.* at 125-26.

3. The principal exceptions exist in public policy and implied contract, or where the employer has recognized a union and belongs to a collective bargain.

of the agreement. Labor law, as a field, also involves the rights of individual union members to receive fair representation from their union.

As a part of, and following, the Civil Rights movement of the 1960's, workers in non-union and unionized workplaces acquired numerous individual rights through federal and state law protections, primarily in the discrimination area, and with this legislation, the modern field of employment law emerged. Workers acquired these rights from a variety of sources including the Civil Rights Act of 1964, the Age Discrimination in Employment Act, the Employee Retirement Income Security Act, the American with Disabilities Act, the Consolidated Omnibus Budget Reconciliation Act, the Family Medical Leave Act, the Worker Adjustment and Retraining Notification Act, and the Occupational Safety and Health Act, as well as countless related state laws and local ordinances. These laws substantively govern the employer/employee relationship and give significant rights to non-unionized (as well as unionized) employees. Furthermore, state laws and local ordinances mirroring the federal laws gave rise to the creation of state and municipal departments overseeing employee rights, which in turn incentivized companies to institute significant internal departments of human resources to ensure compliance.

Employment law, as a field, has thus developed around these statutes and various common law rights affecting the workplace, including such matters as discrimination, wrongful termination, workplace safety, harassment, rights of whistleblowers, family leave, health care coverage, pay for overtime, etc. Because of the many issues that may arise in the workplace, employers frequently create employee manuals setting forth company policies and those polices are often the subject of legal review and scrutiny. Employment law also includes the law governing individual agreements between employers and employees establishing the significant terms of employment, or those agreements prepared in connection with an employee's separation from employment. These agreements, when involving executives, typically contain post-employment restrictive covenants involving non-solicitation of customers or employees and non-competition clauses. Over the past 45 years, the field of employment law has developed into one that affects most of the U.S. workforce and occupies a prominent place in many U.S. law firms.

John Levi, Partner
Sidley Austin LLP

The terms of employment contained in an employment agreement extend beyond just duration or term of employment. They typically include scope of employment and employment responsibilities, whether the work is full- or part-time, compensation and frequency of payment, employee position and reporting relationship, work location, benefits (including medical and dental coverage, sick leave, vacation days, and participation in an employer-sponsored retirement plan), restrictive covenants (most often limiting use of confidential materials and preventing work for competitors), severance rights, and dispute resolution procedures.

The employment agreement may also incorporate by reference the employer's code of conduct as well as specific policies and procedures pertaining to travel and expense reimbursement, pre- and post-employment background checks, drug testing, surveillance of employee communications, and other privacy rights. In some cases, an employee handbook or a code of conduct may add to the rights and obligations specifically contained in the employment agreement and provided by applicable law.[4] Consider, for example, a handbook which American Colloid Company distributed, entitled "For the New Employee of American Colloid Company," which provided, in part:

> *Probation*
> All new employees are automatically on a probationary period at the beginning of their employment. During this period, their abilities and work performance are closely evaluated by their supervisor. If for any reason, on or before the end of this period, it is determined that an employee is not suited for the job for which he was hired, his employment may be terminated. At the completion of the probationary period, you will become a permanent employee.[5]

As a result of this company policy, the Supreme Court of Wyoming found that a former American Colloid employee had an "enforceable right to be discharged only for cause" or, in other words, that the employee, after the probationary period, was no longer an at-will employee.[6]

Employment agreements for executives may or may not provide for a specific term of employment but are likely to distinguish between "for cause" and "for convenience" termination and address the payments the executive will receive in the event of termination on each of these grounds. They are also likely to contain elaborate provisions addressing payments to the executive in the event the corporate employer experiences a change in control or ownership.

---

4. *See, e.g., Weiner v. McGraw-Hill, Inc.*, 457 N.Y.S.2d 193 (N.Y. 1982); *Leithead v. Am. Colloid Co.*, 721 P.2d 1059, 1062-63 (Wyo. 1986). In addition, in cases where an employee manual is contractually binding, some courts find that an employer may make unilateral changes to the handbook and that these changes will be binding upon the employee who continues to work at the company, as long as the employee is given proper notice of the changes. In contrast, other courts require something more (e.g., a new benefit to the employee or a new detriment to the employer) to provide adequate consideration for the modification. *Compare Browning v. 24 Hour Fitness, Inc.*, No. C05-5732RBL, 2006 WL 151933, at *2 (W.D. Wash 2006) (consideration for modification found in continued work), *with Doyle v. Holy Cross Hosp.*, 708 N.E.2d 1140, 1144 (Ill. 1999) (holding that a unilateral modification of a contractually binding employee handbook failed for lack of consideration and that the employee's continued work did not constitute the requisite consideration).

5. *Leithead*, 721 P.2d at 1061.

6. *Id.* at 1063. *But see Stedillie v. Am. Colloid Co.*, 967 F.2d 274 (8th Cir. 1992) (holding that, under South Dakota law, employee of American Colloid given the same handbook was still an at-will employee subject to termination at any time).

A Practitioner Perspective: Negotiating the More Challenging Terms of Employment and Separation Agreements

Although the vast majority of American workers are employed "at-will" and the number of unionized workers covered by collective bargaining agreements has declined, an increasing number of employees, especially at the executive level, are entering into employment contracts covering the terms and conditions of their employment. And with many employees, including those who do not have a written employment agreement, the use of a separation and release agreement has become common when the employee leaves the employer and receives additional consideration above and beyond what they were otherwise entitled to receive. Employment lawyers play an increasingly important role in the drafting of these agreements and the interpretation and enforcement of them when disputes arise.

The most heavily negotiated and carefully drafted provisions of employment agreements generally involve compensation and benefits, grounds for termination, severance payments and post-employment restrictions. While the "base salary" terms are simply a matter of negotiation, the lure of many agreements will be the incentive or bonus compensation provisions. Whether bonuses are guaranteed, tied to the achievement of performance targets or completely discretionary, whether they are paid in cash, deferred compensation or equity and whether or not such compensation can be forfeited or "clawed back" for competition or negative performance in the future are some of the most intensely negotiated provisions of these agreements. Another extremely important provision involves the definition of termination for cause by the employer and termination for "good reason" by the employee. Interpretation and application of these provisions are typically at the center of most disputes when the employment contract is terminated before its natural expiration date. Careful attention needs to be paid to the precise reasons for termination, whether any notice needs to be given and whether or not there are cure periods for reasons that could eventually justify a termination. Post-employment restrictions range from notice or garden leave provisions to full-blown covenants not to compete, with intermediate restrictions like customer non-solicitation and employee non-solicitation.

The most heavily negotiated terms of separation and release agreements typically involve consideration to be paid for the release of claims, the scope and breadth of the release, confidentiality with respect to the terms of the separation, non-disparagement, the type of reference the employer will give, whether the individual can apply for re-hire and the tax treatment of the consideration being paid. If claims under federal statutes like the Age Discrimination in Employment Act are being released, a bevy of additional requirements under the Older Workers Benefit Protection Act apply to the terms of the release including a requirement that the agreement be in plain English, that the employee be given up to 21 days to consider the proposed release and then 7 days to revoke any acceptance. In the event of layoffs where at least two individual employees

> are involved, additional requirements govern the enforceability of the release. It is critical that the employment lawyer carefully draft the release to ensure its ultimate enforceability.
>
> Michael Delikat, Partner and Global
> Chair, Employment Practice Group
> Orrick, Herrington & Sutcliffe LLP

A. EXECUTIVE EMPLOYMENT AGREEMENT

The following agreement sets forth the rights and obligations of a corporate employer and a high-level executive.

Things to Consider...

As you read through the following agreement, please consider these items. You will want to return to the agreement, as you study the substantive discussion that follows.

> **Rights and Obligations.** What is the Executive getting, and what is the Executive giving under this Agreement? Specifically, what are the various forms of the Executive's compensation, and what are the Executive's responsibilities?

> **Termination.** What is the term of this Agreement? What allows each party to terminate the Agreement prior to its expiration? What are the consequences of the various types of termination under this Agreement? What provisions will continue to be in effect despite the expiration or termination of the Agreement?

> **Restrictive Covenants.** What purpose is served by the restrictive covenants (e.g., not to disclose, not to compete) found in this Agreement? Are these overbroad or reasonable given the relationship at issue? How does the Agreement attempt to ensure their enforceability?

EMPLOYMENT AGREEMENT[7]

EMPLOYMENT AGREEMENT, dated as of July 28, 2009 (this "Agreement"), between SIRIUS XM RADIO INC., a Delaware corporation (the "Company"), and SCOTT A. GREENSTEIN (the "Executive").

---

7. Sirius XM Radio Inc., Employment Agreement (Form 8-K), at Exhibit 10.1 (July 29, 2009), *available at* http://www.sec.gov/Archives/edgar/data/908937/000093041309003897/c58358_ex10-1.htm.

In consideration of the mutual covenants and conditions set forth herein, the Company and the Executive agree as follows:

1. **Employment.** Subject to the terms and conditions of this Agreement, the Company hereby employs the Executive, and the Executive hereby agrees to continue his employment with the Company.

2. **Duties and Reporting Relationship.** (a) The Executive shall be employed in the capacity of President and Chief Content Officer of the Company. In such capacity, the Executive shall be responsible for management of all aspects of the Company's programming and corporate brand marketing functions and all personnel working in such areas shall report to the Executive. During the Term (as defined below), the Executive shall, on a full-time basis and consistent with the needs of the Company, use his skills and render services to the best of his ability. The Executive shall perform such activities and duties consistent with his position as the Chief Executive Officer of the Company shall from time to time reasonably specify and direct. During the Term, the Executive shall not perform any consulting services for, or engage in any other business enterprises with, any third parties without the express written consent of the Chief Executive Officer of the Company or the General Counsel of the Company, other than passive investments.

(b) The Executive shall generally perform his duties and conduct his business at the principal offices of the Company in New York, New York.

(c) The Executive shall report solely to the Chief Executive Officer of the Company.

3. **Term.** The term of this Agreement shall commence on July 28, 2009 (the "Effective Date") and end on July 27, 2013, unless terminated earlier pursuant to the provisions of Section 6 (the "Term").

4. **Compensation.** (a) During the Term, the Executive shall be paid an annual base salary of $850,000; provided that on (i) January 1, 2010 such annual base salary shall be increased to no less than $925,000, (ii) January 1, 2011 such annual base salary shall be increased to no less than $1,000,000, (iii) January 1, 2012 such annual base salary shall be increased to no less than $1,100,000, (iv) January 1, 2013 such annual base salary shall be increased to no less than $1,250,000, and (v) thereafter may be subject to increase from time to time by recommendation of the Chief Executive Officer of the Company to, and approval by, the Board of Directors of the Company (the "Board") (such amount, as increased, the "Base Salary"). All amounts paid to the Executive under this Agreement shall be in U.S. dollars. The Base Salary shall be paid at least monthly and, at the option of the Company, may be paid more frequently.

(b) On the date hereof, the Company shall grant to the Executive an option to purchase 27,768,136 shares of the Company's common stock, par value $.001 per share (the "Common Stock"), at an exercise price of $0.43 per share, the closing price of the Common Stock on the Nasdaq Global Select Market on the date hereof. Such options shall be subject to the terms and conditions set forth in the Option Agreement attached to this Agreement as Exhibit A.

(c) All compensation paid to the Executive hereunder shall be subject to any payroll and withholding deductions required by applicable law, including, as and where applicable, federal, New York state and New York City income tax withholding, federal unemployment tax and social security (FICA).

5. **Additional Compensation; Expenses and Benefits.** (a) During the Term, the Company shall reimburse the Executive for all reasonable and necessary business expenses incurred and advanced by him in carrying out his duties under this Agreement. The Executive shall present to the Company an itemized account of all expenses in such form as may be required by the Company from time to time.

(b) During the Term, the Executive shall be entitled to participate fully in any other benefit plans, programs, policies and fringe benefits which may be made available to the executive officers of the Company generally, including, without limitation, disability, medical, dental and life insurance and benefits under the Company's 401(k) savings plan.

(c) During the Term, the Executive shall be entitled to participate in any bonus plans generally offered to executive officers of the Company. Bonuses may be subject to the Executive's individual performance and satisfaction of objectives established by the Board or the compensation committee thereof (the "Compensation Committee"). Bonuses may be paid in the form of cash, stock options, restricted stock, restricted stock units or other securities of the Company.

6. **Termination.** The date upon which the Executive's employment with the Company under this Agreement is deemed to be terminated in accordance with any of the provisions of this Section 6 is referred to herein as the "Termination Date." A termination of employment shall not be deemed to have occurred for purposes of any provision of this Agreement providing for the payment of any amounts or benefits upon or following a termination of employment unless such termination also constitutes a "separation from service" within the meaning of Section 409A ("Section 409A") of the Internal Revenue Code of 1986, as amended (the "Code"), and the regulations thereunder (a "Separation from Service"), and notwithstanding anything contained herein to the

contrary, the date on which a Separation from Service takes place shall be the Termination Date.

(a) The Company has the right and may elect to terminate this Agreement for Cause at any time. For purposes of this Agreement, "Cause" means the occurrence or existence of any of the following:

(i) (A) a material breach by the Executive of the terms of this Agreement, (B) a material breach by the Executive of the Executive's duty not to engage in any transaction that represents, directly or indirectly, self-dealing with the Company or any of its affiliates (which, for purposes hereof, shall mean any individual, corporation, partnership, association, limited liability company, trust, estate, or other entity or organization directly or indirectly controlling, controlled by, or under direct or indirect common control with the Company) which has not been approved by a majority of the disinterested directors of the Board, or (C) the Executive's violation of the Company's Code of Ethics which is demonstrably and materially injurious to the Company, if any such material breach or violation described in clauses (A), (B) or (C), to the extent curable, remains uncured after 15 days have elapsed following the date on which the Company gives the Executive written notice of such material breach or violation;

(ii) the Executive's act of dishonesty, misappropriation, embezzlement, intentional fraud, or similar intentional misconduct by the Executive involving the Company or any of its affiliates;

(iii) the Executive's conviction or the plea of *nolo contendere* or the equivalent in respect of a felony;

(iv) any damage of a material nature to any property of the Company or any of its affiliates caused by the Executive's willful misconduct or gross negligence;

(v) the repeated nonprescription use of any controlled substance or the repeated use of alcohol or any other non-controlled substance that, in the reasonable good faith opinion of the Board, renders the Executive unfit to serve as an officer of the Company or its affiliates;

(vi) the Executive's failure to comply with the Chief Executive Officer's reasonable written instructions on a material matter within 5 days; or

(vii) conduct by the Executive that in the reasonable good faith written determination of the Board demonstrates unfitness to serve as an officer of the Company or its affiliates, including a finding by the Board or any judicial or regulatory authority that the Executive committed acts of unlawful harassment or violated any other state, federal or local law or ordinance prohibiting discrimination in employment.

Termination of the Executive for Cause pursuant to this Section 6(a) shall be communicated by a Notice of Termination for Cause. For purposes of this Agreement, a "Notice of Termination for Cause" shall mean delivery to the Executive of a copy of a resolution or resolutions duly adopted by the affirmative vote of not less than a majority of the directors (other than the Executive, if the Executive is then serving on the Board) present (in person or by teleconference) and voting at a meeting of the Board called and held for that purpose after 15 days' notice to the Executive (which notice the Company shall use reasonable efforts to confirm that Executive has actually received and which notice for purposes of this Section 6(a) may be delivered, in addition to the requirements set forth in Section 17, through the use of electronic mail) and a reasonable opportunity for the Executive, together with the Executive's counsel, to be heard before the Board prior to such vote, finding that in the good faith opinion of the Board, the Executive was guilty of conduct set forth in any of clauses (i) through (vii) of this Section 6(a) and specifying the particulars thereof in reasonable detail. For purposes of this Section 6(a), this Agreement shall terminate on the date specified by the Board in the Notice of Termination for Cause.

(b) (i) This Agreement and the Executive's employment shall terminate upon the death of the Executive.

(ii) If the Executive is unable to perform the essential duties and functions of his position because of a disability, even with a reasonable accommodation, for one hundred eighty days within any three hundred sixty-five day period ("Disability"), the Company shall have the right and may elect to terminate the services of the Executive by a Notice of Disability Termination. The Executive shall not be terminated following a Disability except pursuant to this Section 6(b)(ii). For purposes of this Agreement, a "Notice of Disability Termination" shall mean a written notice that sets forth in reasonable detail the facts and circumstances claimed to provide a basis for termination of the Executive's employment under this Section 6(b)(ii). For purposes of this Agreement, no such purported termination shall be effective without such Notice of Disability Termination. This Agreement shall terminate on the day such Notice of Disability Termination is received by the Executive.

(c) The Executive shall have the absolute right to terminate his employment at any time with or without Good Reason. Should the Executive wish to resign from his position with the Company during the Term, for other than Good Reason (as defined below), the Executive shall give at least fourteen days prior written notice to the Company. This Agreement shall terminate on the effective date of the resignation set forth in the notice of resignation, however, the Company may, at its sole discretion, instruct that the Executive perform no job responsibilities and cease his active employment immediately upon receipt of the notice from the Executive.

(d) The Company shall have the absolute right to terminate the Executive's employment without Cause at any time. This Agreement shall terminate one day following receipt of such notice by the Executive, however, the Company may, at its sole discretion, instruct that the Executive cease active employment and perform no more job duties immediately upon provision of such notice to the Executive.

(e) Should the Executive wish to resign from his position with the Company for Good Reason during the Term, the Executive shall give seven days prior written notice to the Company. This Agreement shall terminate on the date specified in such notice, however, the Company may, at its sole discretion, instruct that the Executive cease active employment and perform no more job duties immediately upon receipt of such notice from the Executive.

For purposes of this Agreement, "Good Reason" shall mean the continuance of any of the following events (without the Executive's prior written consent) for a period of thirty days after delivery to the Company by the Executive of a notice of the occurrence of such event:

(i) the assignment to the Executive by the Company of duties not reasonably consistent with the Executive's positions, duties, responsibilities, titles or offices at the commencement of the Term, any material reduction in the Executive's duties or responsibilities as described in Section 2 or any removal of the Executive from or any failure to re-elect the Executive to any of such positions or the Executive not being the most senior executive, other than the Company's Chief Executive Officer, who is responsible for all programming and corporate brand marketing activities and personnel (except in connection with the termination of the Executive's employment for Cause, Disability or as a result of the Executive's death or by the Executive other than for Good Reason); or

(ii) the Executive ceasing to report directly to the Chief Executive Officer of the Company; or

(iii) any requirement that the Executive report for work to a location more than 25 miles from the Company's current headquarters for more than 30 days in any calendar year, excluding any requirement that results from the damage or destruction of the Company's current headquarters as a result of natural disasters, terrorism, acts of war or acts of God; or

(iv) any reduction in the Base Salary; or

(v) the Company's failure to make a *bona fide* offer in writing to renew this Agreement, for an additional one-year term, on the terms and conditions set forth in this Agreement (including the Base Salary set forth in Section 4(a), but excluding any equity–based compensation set forth in Section 4(b)), at least 90 days prior to (x) the fourth anniversary of the Effective Date and (y) each subsequent anniversary of the Effective Date following the fourth anniversary of the Effective Date; provided that (for purposes of this clause (y) only) this Agreement has been renewed on the previous anniversary of the Effective Date; or

(vi) any material breach by the Company of this Agreement.

(f) (i) If the employment of the Executive is terminated by the Company for Cause, by the Executive other than for Good Reason or due to death or Disability, the Executive shall, in lieu of any future payments or benefits under this Agreement, be entitled to (A) any earned but unpaid Base Salary and any business expenses incurred but not reimbursed, in each case, prior to the Termination Date and (B) any other vested benefits under any other benefit plans or programs in accordance with the terms of such plans and programs (collectively, the "Accrued Payments and Benefits").

(ii) If the employment of the Executive is terminated without Cause or the Executive terminates his employment for Good Reason, then the Executive shall have an absolute and unconditional right to receive, and the Company shall pay to the Executive without setoff, counterclaim or other withholding, except as set forth in Section 4(c), (A) the Accrued Payments and Benefits, (B) a lump sum amount equal to the sum of (x) the Executive's annualized Base Salary then in effect and (y) an amount in cash equal to the bonus, whether denominated as an annual, performance, incentive, retention or other bonus, last paid (or due and payable) to the Executive in respect of the fiscal year immediately preceding the year in which the Termination Date occurs, and (C) the continuation, at the Company's expense (by direct payment, not reimbursement to the Executive) of (1) medical and dental benefits in a manner that will not be taxable to the Executive and (2) life insurance benefits, on the same terms as provided by the Company for active employees for one year following the Termination Date. The lump sum amount contemplated by clause (B) above shall be paid on the 60th day following the Termination Date.

(g) The Company's obligations under Section 6(f)(ii) shall be conditioned upon the Executive executing, delivering, and not revoking during the seven day revocation period a waiver and release of claims against the Company, substantially in the form attached as Exhibit B (the "Release") within 60 days following the Termination Date; provided that the Executive shall have no obligation to execute such Release in order to receive the payments and benefits under Section 6(f)(ii) in the event that a Release executed by the Company has not been delivered by the Company to the Executive within five days following the Termination Date.

(h) Notwithstanding any provisions of this Agreement to the contrary, if the Executive is a "specified employee" (within the meaning of Section 409A and determined pursuant to policies adopted by the Company) at the time of his Separation from Service and if any portion of the payments or benefits to be received by the Executive upon Separation from Service would be considered deferred compensation under Section 409A ("Nonqualified Deferred Compensation"), amounts that would otherwise be payable pursuant to this Agreement during the six-month period immediately following the Executive's Separation from Service that constitute Nonqualified Deferred Compensation and benefits that would otherwise be provided pursuant to this Agreement during the six-month period immediately following the Executive's Separation from Service that constitute Nonqualified Deferred Compensation will instead be paid or made available on the earlier of (x) the first business day of the seventh month following the date of the Executive's Separation from Service and (y) the Executive's death.

7. Nondisclosure of Confidential Information. (a) The Executive acknowledges that in the course of his employment he will occupy a position of trust and confidence. The Executive shall not, except in connection with the performance of his functions or as required by applicable law, disclose to others or use, directly or indirectly, any Confidential Information.

(b) "Confidential Information" shall mean information about the Company's business and operations that is not disclosed by the Company for financial reporting purposes and that was learned by the Executive in the course of his employment by the Company, including, without limitation, any business plans, product plans, strategy, budget information, proprietary knowledge, patents, trade secrets, data, formulae, sketches, notebooks, blueprints, information and client and customer lists and all papers and records (including computer records) of the documents containing such Confidential Information, other than information that is publicly disclosed by the Company in writing. The Executive acknowledges that such Confidential Information is specialized, unique in nature and of great value to the Company, and that such information gives the Company a competitive advantage. The Executive agrees to deliver or return to the Company, at the Company's request at any time or upon termination or expiration of his employment or as soon as possible thereafter, all documents, computer tapes and disks, records, lists, data, drawings, prints, notes and written information (and all copies thereof) furnished by or on behalf of the Company or prepared by the Executive in the course of his employment by the Company, provided that the Executive will be able to keep his cell phones, blackberries, personal computers, personal rolodex and the like so long as any Confidential Information is removed from such items.

(c) The provisions of this Section 7 shall survive indefinitely.

8. Covenant Not to Compete. During the Restricted Period (as defined below), the Executive shall not, directly or indirectly, enter into the employment of, render services to, or acquire any interest whatsoever in (whether for his own account as an individual proprietor, or as a partner, associate, stockholder, officer, director, consultant, trustee or otherwise), or otherwise assist, any person or entity engaged in any operations in North America involving the transmission of radio entertainment programming, the production of radio entertainment programming, the syndication of radio entertainment programming, the promotion of radio entertainment programming or the marketing of radio entertainment programming, in each case, in competition with the Company (each, a "Competitive Activity"); provided that nothing in this Agreement shall prevent the purchase or ownership by the Executive by way of investment of less than 5 percent of the shares or equity interest of any corporation or other entity. Without limiting the generality of the foregoing, the Executive agrees that during the Restricted Period, the Executive shall not call on or otherwise solicit business or assist others to solicit business from any of the customers of the Company as to any product or service described above that competes with any product or service provided or marketed by the Company on the date of the Executive's termination of employment with the Company during the Term (as such Term may be extended in accordance with Section 6(e)(5) of the Agreement) (the "Milestone Date"). The Executive agrees that during the Restricted Period he will not solicit or assist others to solicit the employment of or hire any employee of the Company without the prior written consent of the Company. For purposes of this Agreement, the "Restricted Period" shall mean the period of one year following the Milestone Date. For purposes of this Agreement, the term "radio" shall mean terrestrial radio, satellite radio, HD radio, internet radio and other audio delivered terrestrially, by satellite, HD or the internet (which audio is not coupled with moving visual elements, such as television, movies, or other moving visual images delivered via the internet or otherwise). Notwithstanding anything to the contrary in this Section 8, it shall not be a violation of this Section 8 for the Executive to join a division or business line of a commercial enterprise with multiple divisions or business lines if such division or business line is not engaged in a Competitive Activity; provided that the Executive performs services solely for such non-competitive division or business line.

9. Change in Control Provisions. If the Executive is, in the opinion of a nationally recognized accounting firm jointly selected by the Executive and the Company, required to pay an excise tax on "excess parachute payments" (as defined in Section 280G(b) of the Code) under Section 4999 of the Code as a result of an acceleration of the vesting of stock options or otherwise, the Company shall have an absolute and unconditional obligation to pay the Executive in accordance with the terms of this Section 9 the amount of such taxes. In addition, the Company shall have an absolute and unconditional obligation to pay the Executive such additional amounts as are necessary to place the Executive in the exact same financial position that he would have been in if he had not incurred any tax liability under Section 4999 of the Code. The determination of the exact amount, if any, of any "excess parachute payments" and any tax liability under Section 4999 of the Code shall be made by a nationally-recognized independent accounting firm selected by the Executive and the Company. The fees and expenses of such accounting firm shall be paid by the Company. The determination of such accounting firm shall be final and binding on the parties. The Company irrevocably agrees to pay to the Executive, in immediately available funds to an account designated in writing by the Executive, any amounts to be paid under this Section 9 within two business days after receipt by the Company of written notice from the accounting firm which sets forth such accounting firm's determination. In addition, in the event that such payments are not sufficient to pay all excise taxes on "excess parachute payments" under Section 4999 of the Code as a result of an acceleration of the vesting of options or for any other reason and to place the Executive in the exact same financial position that he would have been in if he had not incurred any tax liability under Section 4999 of the Code, then the Company shall have an absolute and unconditional obligation to pay the Executive such additional amounts as may be necessary to pay such excise taxes and place the Executive in the exact same financial position that he would have been had he not incurred any tax liability as a result of a change in control under the Code. Notwithstanding the foregoing, in the event that a written ruling (whether public or private) of the Internal Revenue Service ("IRS") is obtained by or on behalf of the Company or the Executive, which ruling expressly provides that the Executive is not required to pay, or is entitled to a refund with respect to, all or any portion of such excise taxes or additional amounts, the Executive shall promptly reimburse the Company in an amount equal to all amounts paid to the Executive pursuant to this Section 9 less any excise taxes or additional amounts which remain payable by, or are not refunded to, the Executive after giving effect to such IRS ruling. Each of the Company and the Executive agrees to promptly notify the other party if it receives any such IRS ruling. The payments contemplated by this Section 9 shall in all events be paid no later than the end of the Executive's taxable year next following the Executive's taxable year in which the excise tax (and any income or other related tax or interest or penalties thereon) on a payment is remitted to IRS or any other applicable taxing authority; or, in the case of amounts relating to any claim by IRS or any other taxing authority that does not result in the remittance of any federal, state, local and foreign income, excise, social security and other taxes, the calendar year in which the claim is finally settled or otherwise resolved. Any amounts required to be repaid to the Company pursuant to this Section 9 will be repaid to the Company within five business days of the Executive's receipt of any refund with respect to any excise tax.

10. Remedies. The Executive and Company agree that damages for breach of any of the covenants under Sections 7 and 8 will be difficult to determine and inadequate to remedy the harm which may be caused thereby, and therefore consent that these covenants may be enforced by temporary or permanent injunction without the necessity of bond. The Executive believes, as of the date of this Agreement, that the provisions of this Agreement are reasonable and that the Executive is capable of gainful employment without breaching this Agreement. However, should any court or arbitrator decline to enforce any provision of Section 7 or 8 of this Agreement, this Agreement shall, to the extent applicable in the circumstances before such court or arbitrator, be deemed to be modified to restrict the Executive's competition with the Company to the maximum extent of time, scope and geography which the court or arbitrator shall find enforceable, and such provisions shall be so enforced.

11. Indemnification. The Company shall indemnify the Executive to the full extent provided in the Company's Amended and Restated Certificate of Incorporation and Amended and Restated Bylaws and the law of the State of Delaware in connection with his activities as an officer of the Company.

12. Entire Agreement. The provisions contained herein constitute the entire agreement between the parties with respect to the subject matter hereof and supersede any and all prior agreements, understandings and communications between the parties, oral or written, with respect to such subject matter, including the Employment Agreement between the Executive and the Company dated May 5, 2004, as amended, but excluding any equity award agreements between the Executive and the Company.

13. Modification. Any waiver, alteration, amendment or modification of any provisions of this Agreement shall not be valid unless in writing and signed by both the Executive and the Company.

14. Severability. If any provision of this Agreement shall be declared to be invalid or unenforceable, in whole or in part, such invalidity or unenforceability shall not affect the remaining provisions hereof, which shall remain in full force and effect.

15. Assignment. The Executive may not assign any of his rights or delegate any of his duties hereunder without the prior written consent of the Company. The Company may not assign any of its rights or delegate any of its obligations hereunder without the prior written consent of the Executive, except that any successor to the Company by merger or purchase of all or substantially all of the Company's assets shall assume this Agreement.

16. Binding Effect. This Agreement shall be binding upon and inure to the benefit of the successors in interest of the Executive and the Company.

17. Notices. All notices and other communications required or permitted hereunder shall be made in writing and shall be deemed effective when delivered personally or transmitted by facsimile transmission, one business day after deposit with a nationally recognized overnight courier (with next day delivery specified) and five days after mailing by registered or certified mail:

if to the Company:
[Company Notice Information Omitted]
if to the Executive:
[Executive Notice Information Omitted]
with a copy to:
[Law Firm Notice Information Omitted]

or to such other person or address as either party shall furnish in writing to the other party from time to time.

18. Governing Law. This Agreement shall be governed by and construed in accordance with the laws of the State of New York applicable to contracts made and to be performed entirely within the State of New York.

19. Non-Mitigation. The Executive shall not be required to mitigate damages or seek other employment in order to receive compensation or benefits under Section 6 of this Agreement; nor shall the amount of any benefit or payment provided for under Section 6 of this Agreement be reduced by any compensation earned by the Executive as the result of employment by another employer.

20. Arbitration. (a) The Executive and the Company agree that if a dispute arises concerning or relating to the Executive's employment with the Company, or the termination of the Executive's employment, such dispute shall be submitted to binding arbitration under the rules of the

American Arbitration Association regarding resolution of employment disputes in effect at the time such dispute arises. The arbitration shall take place in New York, New York, before a single experienced arbitrator licensed to practice law in New York and selected in accordance with the American Arbitration Association rules and procedures. Except as provided below, the Executive and the Company agree that this arbitration procedure will be the exclusive means of redress for any disputes relating to or arising from the Executive's employment with the Company or his termination, including disputes over rights provided by federal, state, or local statutes, regulations, ordinances, and common law, including all laws that prohibit discrimination based on any protected classification. **The parties expressly waive the right to a jury trial, and agree that the arbitrator's award shall be final and binding on both parties, and shall not be appealable.** The arbitrator shall have discretion to award monetary and other damages, and any other relief that the arbitrator deems appropriate and is allowed by law. The arbitrator shall have the discretion to award the prevailing party reasonable costs and attorneys' fees incurred in bringing or defending an action, and shall award such costs and fees to the Executive in the event the Executive prevails on the merits of any action brought hereunder.

(b) The Company shall pay the cost of any arbitration proceedings under this Agreement if the Executive prevails in such arbitration on at least one substantive issue.

(c) The Company and the Executive agree that the sole dispute that is excepted from Section 20(a) is an action seeking injunctive relief from a court of competent jurisdiction regarding enforcement and application of Sections 7, 8 or 10 of this Agreement, which action may be brought in addition to, or in place of, an arbitration proceeding in accordance with Section 20(a).

21. Compliance with Section 409A. (a) To the extent applicable, it is intended that the compensation arrangements under this Agreement be in full compliance with Section 409A (it being understood that certain compensation arrangements under this Agreement are intended not to be subject to Section 409A). The Agreement shall be construed, to the maximum extent permitted, in a manner to give effect to such intention. Notwithstanding anything in this Agreement to the contrary, distributions upon termination of the Executive's employment may only be made upon a Separation from Service. Neither the Company nor any of its affiliates shall have any obligation to indemnify or otherwise hold the Executive harmless from any or all such taxes, interest or penalties, or liability for any damages related thereto. The Executive acknowledges that he has been advised to obtain independent legal, tax or other counsel in connection with Section 409A.

(b) With respect to any amount of expenses eligible for reimbursement under this Agreement, such expenses will be reimbursed by the Company within thirty (30) days following the date on which the Company receives the applicable invoice from the Executive in accordance with the Company's expense reimbursement policies, but in no event later than the last day of the Executive's taxable year following the taxable year in which the Executive incurs the related expenses. In no event will the reimbursements or in-kind benefits to be provided by the Company in one taxable year affect the amount of reimbursements or in-kind benefits to be provided in any other taxable year, nor will the Executive's right to reimbursement or in-kind benefits be subject to liquidation or exchange for another benefit.

(c) Each payment under this Agreement shall be regarded as a "separate payment" and not of a series of payments for purposes of Section 409A.

22. Counterparts. This Agreement may be executed in counterparts, all of which shall be considered one and the same agreement, and shall become effective when one or more counterparts have been signed by each of the parties and delivered to the other party.

23. Executive's Representation. The Executive hereby represents and warrants to Company that he is not now under any contractual or other obligation that is inconsistent with or in conflict with this Agreement or that would prevent, limit, or impair the Executive's performance of his obligations under this Agreement.

24. Survivorship. Upon the expiration or other termination of this Agreement or the Executive's employment with the Company, the respective rights and obligations of the parties hereto shall survive to the extent necessary to carry out the intentions of the parties under this Agreement.

[Signature Page Omitted]
[Exhibits Omitted]

---

1. Familiarity Breeds Fluency: A Review

Prior to this Agreement, you had not encountered an employment agreement in this book. Yet, hopefully you found much of the Agreement to be somewhat familiar.

- Section 7 of this Agreement imposes confidentiality obligations. Why do you suppose confidentiality obligations are important in the context of this relationship? Are these obligations mutual or unilateral? How does § 7(b) define "Confidential Information"? How does this definition compare to the definitions found in the two NDAs in Chapter 1? What is the effect of the Executive's acknowledgments in § 7(b)? (See Chapter 1.)

- Section 10 provides that both parties agree that equitable relief is appropriate and that damages would be an inadequate remedy. What effect is this provision likely to have in court? What are some reasons one or both parties may wish to include this type of provision? (See Chapter 1.)

- Section 12 contains an integration clause. What is the effect of integration clauses? Are they dispositive of the question of integration? Does this clause purport that the Agreement is *completely* or *partially* integrated? (See Chapter 1.)

- Section 14 contains a severability clause. What is the effect of severability clauses? (See Chapter 1.)

- Section 15 contains an anti-assignment provision. Does this provision srohibit the assignment of rights and duties, or is it likely that a court will read this provision only to prohibit the delegation of duties? Does this provision render a prohibited assignment void? (See Chapter 1.)

- What law likely governs this Agreement? How do you know? (See Chapter 1.)

- Section 6 provides the mechanisms by which the Agreement may be terminated, which we discuss at greater length below. Section 24 further provides a vague statement that the parties' rights and obligations shall survive "to the extent necessary to carry out the intentions of the parties under this Agreement." To make clear at least one of those intentions, note that § 7(c) provides that section 7 ("Nondisclosure of Confidential Information") shall survive termination indefinitely. (See Chapter 1.)

2. No-Oral-Modification Provisions

In Chapter 1, we discussed integration and the application of the parol evidence rule. There we saw that the parol evidence rule helps determine what actually were the terms of agreement at the time of contracting (i.e., whether a contractual document contains the final terms of agreement). However, integration and the parol evidence rule do not apply to prevent *future* terms from becoming part of a contract. That is, a contractual document may indeed be completely integrated and contain the universe of an agreement's final terms, but the parties may "modify" this agreement going forward. Given this, the parties may attempt to provide by contract how modification of that contract may or may not be effective.

Section 13 ("Modification") provides that modifying any aspect of the Agreement is only valid if certain conditions—that the modification is in writing and signed by both the Executive and the Company—are satisfied. Can a contract control how it may be modified? Provided that there is consideration sufficient to support a later contract,[8] can an earlier contract stop parties from entering into a later contract that effectively alters the parties' contractual relationship?

The general, common-law rule is that an earlier contract cannot bind a later contract, and that a contract purporting to limit the power of the parties to modify that contract has no effect.[9] Some states—notably New York and California—have attempted by statute to alter the common-law rule and to give bite to no-oral-modification provisions.[10] Still, courts (and the statutes themselves) have narrowed the effect of these statutory incursions on the right of parties to modify their contracts. For example, a New York court has held that a party may be equitably estopped from barring proof of oral modification, notwithstanding the New York statute, where such party "has induced another's significant and substantial reliance upon an oral modification," and where such "conduct relied upon to establish estoppel [is] not otherwise...compatible with the agreement as written."[11]

As with acknowledgments of trade-secret status (as discussed in Chapter 1) and of reasonableness (as discussed below), it may still make sense to include a no-oral-modification provision despite that a court might not give effect to it. Are contracts only as useful as courts will enforce them? Consider that business reputation may animate contractual compliance and that parties may understand their contract as a manual of conduct.

3. Implied Waiver and No-Waiver Provisions

Section 13 of the Agreement, in addition to speaking to modification, provides that any "waiver" of any provision of the Agreement must be in writing to be effective. Waiver refers to the voluntary, intentional surrendering of a known right.[12] One may voluntarily and intentionally waive a right either by words

---

8. Additional consideration is not necessary for the modification of contracts governed by Article 2 of the U.C.C. Please see Chapter 4 for further discussion of this.

9. *See, e.g., Cambridgeport Sav. Bank v. Boersner*, 597 N.E.2d 1017, 1022 (Mass. 1992); *Quality Prods. & Concepts Co. v. Nagel Precision, Inc.*, 666 N.W.2d 251, 253 (Mich. 2003).

10. N.Y. GEN. OBLIG. LAW § 15-301 (Consol. 2001); CAL. CIV. CODE § 1698 (West 1985); *see also* U.C.C. § 2-209(2) (2003).

11. *Rosa v. Spa Realty Assocs.*, 366 N.E.2d 1279, 1283 (N.Y. 1977); *see also MacIsaac & Menke Co. v. Cardox Corp.*, 14 Cal. Rptr. 523, 528 (Cal. Ct. App. 1961); *Nutrisoya Foods, Inc. v. Sunrich LLC*, 626 F. Supp. 2d 985, 990 (D. Minn. 2009); CAL. CIV. CODE § 1698(b) (West 2009); U.C.C. § 2-209(4) (2003). Note that the statute of frauds may require a modification to be in writing in order to be an effective contract. The general rule is that the modification must be in writing if the resultant contract, given the modification, must be in writing under the statute of frauds. *See, e.g.,* CAL. CIV. CODE § 1698(c) (West 2009).

12. *Delta Consulting Group, Inc. v. R. Randle Constr., Inc.*, 554 F.3d 1133, 1140 (7th Cir. 2009); *Bott v. J.F. Shea Co., Inc.*, 388 F.3d 530, 533 (5th Cir. 2004) ("Under Texas law waiver is an intentional relinquishment of a known right or intentional conduct inconsistent with claiming that right.") (internal quotations omitted).

that expressly waive the right or by deeds (which may also be words) that impliedly waive the right.[13] What deeds may rise to the level of an implied waiver? "An implied waiver may arise where a person against whom the waiver is asserted has pursued such a course of conduct as to sufficiently evidence an intention to waive a right or where his conduct is inconsistent with any other intention than to waive it."[14] The burden of showing evidence sufficient to show an intention of waiver is high—indeed, finding an implied waiver requires inferring that a party has given up a right. The more valuable this right, the greater the evidence generally must be to ensure that waiver of the right was intended.[15] In general, to find a waiver of a right, the waiver must be evidenced by "a clear, unequivocal, and decisive act of the party showing such purpose."[16]

Jurisdictions vary in their treatment of so-called "no-waiver clauses." In some states, courts enforce these provisions by their terms to prevent certain acts (e.g., acceptance of less than full performance) or failures to act from constituting a waiver of a right to damages and/or a waiver of a right to demand full performance in the future.[17] Still, even these courts are unlikely to find that a no-waiver provision operates to nullify an express waiver.[18] Some jurisdictions will regard no-waiver clauses as only one piece of evidence in discerning whether or not a party has intended to waive a right.[19] In addition, some

---

13. *Delta Consulting*, 554 F.3d at 1140.

14. *Id.; see also S. Colorado MRI, Ltd. v. Med-Alliance, Inc.*, 166 F.3d 1094, 1100 (10th Cir. 1999) ("[A]n implied waiver of a contractual right must be free from ambiguity and clearly manifest the intention not to assert the benefit.") (internal quotation marks omitted); *Little Beaver Enters. v. Humphreys Ry., Inc.*, 719 F.3d 75, 79 (4th Cir. 1983) ("Generally, this implied waiver is most often recognized where the party's conduct is inconsistent with any other intention than the waiver of contract rights or where the party accepts alternative performance which provides roughly the same protections as strict performance would have provided.").

15. *See, e.g., Groves v. Prickett*, 420 F.2d 1119, 1126 (9th Cir. 1970) ("As minimum requirements to constitute an 'implied waiver' of substantial rights, the conduct relied upon must be clear, decisive and unequivocal of a purpose to waive the legal rights involved. Otherwise, there is no waiver."); *Bank of Boston v. Haufler*, 482 N.E.2d 542, 547 n.9 (Mass. App. 1985) ("Unless required by some rule of law, waiver of valuable rights should not be lightly inferred.").

16. *Barnes v. Bradley County Mem'l Hosp.*, 161 F. App'x 555, 559 (6th Cir. 2006) (Tennessee law) (citation and internal quotation marks omitted); *see also Bott*, 388 F.3d at 533 (5th Cir. 2004) (Texas law) ("Waiver is largely a matter of intent, and for implied waiver to be found through a party's actions, intent must be clearly demonstrated by the facts and circumstances.").

17. *See, e.g., Wis. Elec. Power Co. v. Union Pac. R.R.*, 557 F.3d 504, 508 (7th Cir. 2009) (under Wisconsin law, no-waiver provisions are enforceable); *Cornus Corp. v. GEAC Enter. Solutions, Inc.*, 356 F. App'x 993, 995 (9th Cir. 2009) ("Non-waiver provisions are enforceable under Oregon law, at least so long as a party is alleged to have waived a right by a failure to act rather than by an affirmative act."); *America's Collectibles Network, Inc. v. MIG Broad. Group, Inc.*, 330 F. App'x 81, 88 (6th Cir. 2009) (Tennessee law) ("The Agreement's no-waiver clause also renders defendants' argument unavailing."); *MAFCO Elec. Contractors, Inc. v. Turner Constr. Co.*, 357 F. App'x 395, 398 (2d Cir. 2009) (Connecticut law) ("Because of the subcontract's non-waiver provision and its incorporation by reference in the change order form, MAFCO must offer written evidence that Turner expressly waived its contractual rights and not simply that it engaged in some alleged course of dealing."); *Long Island Sav. Bank, FSB v. United States*, 503 F.3d 1234, 1252-53 (Fed. Cir. 2007) (non-waiver clause sufficient to prove no implied waiver of right occurred). *But see Republic Ins. Co. v. PAICO Receivables, LLC*, 383 F.3d 341, 348-49 (5th Cir. 2004) (citing *Cos. of Kingston v. Latona Trucking Inc.*, 159 F.3d 80, 85 (2d Cir. 1998)) (no-waiver clause of no effect when a party otherwise waives its right to arbitration).

18. *See supra* note 17.

19. *See, e.g., A LoPresti & Sons, Inc. v. General Car & Truck Leasing Sys., Inc.*, 79 F. App'x 764 (6th Cir. 2003) (Ohio law); *Bott*, 388 F.3d at 534 ("Texas courts consider a contract's non-waiver clause to be some evidence

courts will find that no-waiver clauses themselves may be waived.[20] Still, a waiver of a no-waiver clause requires proof "by clear and convincing evidence" (a high evidentiary threshold) and must be proven as any other waiver.[21]

Contracts sometimes will also include "no-continuing-waiver" language, which does not speak to whether a particular act or omission rises to the level of a waiver of a right under the contract, but, rather, takes up the situation once there *is* a waiver of a contractual right and specifies that a single waiver of a right does not waive this right for all time.[22] These provisions are likely to give at least some weight to a finding that a single waiver or omission did not waive that right for all time.[23]

4. Arbitration and Dispute Resolution

Section 20 ("Arbitration") in the Agreement provides for exclusive, non-appealable, and binding arbitration for any dispute relating to the Executive's employment. Arbitration is classically understood as beneficial, vis-à-vis traditional adjudication, for its increased speed and efficiency and reduced costs of process.[24] In addition, arbitration decisions may be kept private, unlike court decisions. However, arbitration is not without its downsides and detractors, who contend that society loses out when cases move from public adjudication to private settlement.[25] Moreover, a common complaint is that arbitrators are more apt to deliver "split the baby" decisions that attempt to strike a middle ground than to rule "correctly."

Exclusive (or mandatory) arbitration means that the movant may only proceed with his action through the arbitral process — and not, say, in state or federal court. In contrast, arbitration may be permissive. However, despite a

---

of non-waiver, but not a substantive bar to finding that a particular provision was indeed waived.") (citation and internal quotation marks omitted); *Perry Eng'g Co. v. AT & T Commc'ns, Inc.*, No. 92-2050, 998 F.2d 1010, at *5 (4th Cir. 1993) (Virginia law) ("Although the contract's 'no waiver' clause provides evidence of AT & T's intent, it does not necessarily control. Like all contractual rights, the rights under the 'no waiver' clause are themselves subject to waiver.").

20. *See, e.g., Wis. Elec. Power Co.*, 557 F.3d at 508-09 (7th Cir. 2009); *A. LoPresti & Sons, Inc.*, 79 F. App'x at 769 ("[N]on-waiver clauses notwithstanding, parties that have acted in contradiction of their contractual rights have been held to have waived them.").

21. *Wis. Elec. Power Co.*, 557 F.3d at 508-09; *PPM Fin., Inc. v. Norandal USA, Inc.*, 297 F. Supp. 2d 1072, 1087 (N.D. Ill. 2004) ("[No-waiver clauses] are strictly enforceable under Illinois law, though they may be waived by [the] words and deeds of the parties, so long as the waiver is proved by clear and convincing evidence.") (quotation marks omitted).

22. *See, e.g., Perry v. Wolaver*, 506 F.3d 48, 54 (1st Cir. 2007) ("Perry's reliance on the 'non-waiver' provision is misdirected. Under the Note, a forbearance by Perry regarding a default does not waive Perry's right to any remedy under the Note during any *continuing* or *subsequent* default. That, however, is beside the point. The real issue is whether Perry could choose to excuse a specific default and waive the penalty for that specific default.") (emphasis added).

23. *See, e.g., N. Helex Co. v. United States*, 455 F.2d 546, 554 (Fed. Cl. 1972) ("With this provision in the contract it is very hard to infer a continuing waiver."); *Chapman v. VLM Entm't Group, Inc.*, No. 00 C 7791, 2002 WL 1610970, at *5 (N.D. Ill. July 22, 2002).

24. *See* Richard A. Bales, *Normative Consideration of Employment Arbitration at Gilmer's Quinceañera*, 81 TUL. L. REV. 331 (2006).

25. *See, e.g.*, Owen M. Fiss, *Against Settlement*, 93 YALE L.J. 1073 (1984); Kathryn A. Sabbeth & David C. Vladeck, *Contracting (Out) Rights*, 36 FORDHAM URB. L.J. 803 (2009).

contract's mandatory arbitration clause, a party generally need not submit to arbitration those questions that go to the existence or enforceability of the arbitration agreement itself.[26] This makes good axiomatic sense, as before an arbitration agreement can be enforced, there must be an enforceable agreement to arbitrate. Furthermore, that the Agreement qualifies arbitration as *non-appealable* means that an arbitrator's rendering of the claim may not be appealed to state or federal court (or anywhere else for that matter). Similarly, the Agreement specifies that arbitration is *binding* so as to make clear that the resulting decision is not mere recommendation but is rather a binding, final resolution of the issue. Contractually providing for these arbitration features is commonplace, and one can generally expect an arbitration provision to be respected by courts,[27] with an exception for any statutory claims for which "Congress itself has evinced an intention to preclude a waiver of judicial remedies...."[28] In general, courts are extremely deferential to arbitrator decisions.[29] As the Supreme Court has said in the context of a collective-bargaining agreement, "Courts...do not sit to hear claims of factual or legal error by an arbitrator as an appellate court does in reviewing decisions of lower courts."[30] The Court went on to say, "[A]s long as the arbitrator is even arguably construing or applying the contract and acting within the scope of his authority, that a court is convinced he committed serious error does not suffice to overturn his

---

26. *See AT&T Techs. v. Commc'ns Workers of Am.*, 475 U.S. 643 (1986); *Janiga v. Questar Capital Corp.*, 615 F.3d 735 (7th Cir. 2010); *Spahr v. Secco*, 330 F.3d 1266, 1272-73 (10th Cir. 2003). A challenge to an agreement that contains an exclusive agreement to arbitrate such issues must be brought in arbitration in accordance with the arbitration provision; however, if the arbitration provision itself is challenged as unenforceable, then a court is the proper forum to resolve this dispute. *See Rent-A-Center, W., Inc. v. Jackson*, 130 S. Ct. 2772, 2778-79 (2010) (holding that where a contract contains an agreement to arbitrate questions of enforceability of the contract, a challenge to the contracts' enforceability but not specifically to the severable arbitration provision must be submitted to arbitration).

27. *See Circuit City Stores, Inc. v. Adams*, 532 U.S. 105, 119 (2001) (holding that a clause requiring an employee to submit to exclusive, final, and binding arbitration is enforceable under the Federal Arbitration Act); *Gilmer v. Interstate/Johnson Lane*, 500 U.S. 20, 35 (1991) (holding that the ADEA does not preclude arbitration of age discrimination actions).

28. *Mitsubishi Motors Corp. v. Soler Chrysler-Plymouth, Inc.*, 473 U.S. 615, 628 (1985); *see also Gilmer*, 500 U.S. at 23 (agreement to arbitrate claims under the Age Discrimination in Employment Act held enforceable); *Rodriguez de Quijas v. Shearson/Am. Exp., Inc.*, 490 U.S. 477, 479-80 (1989) (agreement to arbitrate claims under the Securities Act of 1933 held enforceable); *Shearson/Am. Exp., Inc. v. McMahon*, 482 U.S. 220, 242 (1987) (agreement to arbitrate claims under the Securities Exchange Act of 1934 and the Racketeer Influenced and Corrupt Organizations Act enforceable); *E.E.O.C. v. Luce, Forward, Hamilton & Scripps*, 345 F.3d 742, 744-45 (9th Cir. 2003) (agreement to arbitrate claims under Title VII held enforceable). Courts have found that certain statutory claims, at least under certain circumstances, may not be subjected to arbitration, despite an agreement to arbitrate. *See, e.g., Cunningham v. Fleetwood Homes of Georgia, Inc.*, 253 F.3d 611, 617-24 (11th Cir. 2001) (claims under federal Magnuson-Moss Warranty Act, 15 U.S.C. §§ 2301-12, may be arbitrated but, under the statute, agreement to arbitrate must be disclosed clearly in the same document as all relevant terms of warranty); *Greenwood v. Compucredit Corp.*, 617 F. Supp. 2d 980, 986-87 (N.D. Cal. 2009) (the right to bring suit for claims under the Credit Repair Organization Act is non-waivable and arbitration cannot be compelled).

29. *See, e.g., Gupta v. Cisco Sys., Inc.*, 274 F.3d 1, 3 (1st Cir. 2001) ("Our review of an arbitrator's decision is extremely narrow and exceedingly deferential.") (internal citation and quotation marks omitted); *El Dorado School Dist. No. 15 v. Cont'l Cas. Co.*, 247 F.3d 843, 847 (8th Cir. 2001); *Gingiss Int'l, Inc. v. Bormet*, 58 F.3d 328, 333 (7th Cir. 1995).

30. *United Paperworkers Int'l Union, AFL-CIO v. Misco, Inc.*, 484 U.S. 29, 38 (1987).

decision."[31] In very limited cases, an arbitral award may be subject to review in court for certain defects (e.g., fraud).[32]

Mediation is another common form of dispute resolution but differs from arbitration in that it involves facilitating agreement, rather than resolving disputes, and does not result in a legally binding ruling. Given a varied array of dispute resolution options, companies often institute an internal process of resolving grievances through gradual escalation, involving increasingly senior levels of management until the dispute is resolved. For example, a company and employee might agree upfront to a procedure, where an aggrieved employee first is to notify a supervisor of a concern before notifying a grievance committee, before engaging in informal, internal mediation, before participating in formal, external mediation, and before, then, finally resolving the matter in arbitration. Why might a company wish to institute a gradual-escalation mechanism for dispute resolution?[33]

Under the Agreement, what disputes must be submitted to binding arbitration? Consider the text of section 20, which provides that any dispute that "arises concerning or relating to the Executive's employment" must be submitted to arbitration. Federal and state courts alike routinely recite that arbitration, in general, enjoys a "favored status" and that "an agreement to arbitration should be read liberally in favor of arbitration."[34] Accordingly, courts will generally read language broadly to include most any claim arguably captured.[35]

Drafting Note: Arbitration Provisions; "Arising out of" and "Related to"

This general rule of broad construction is not without its limits. For instance, "courts distinguish 'narrow' arbitration clauses that only require arbitration of disputes 'arising out of' the contract from broad arbitration clauses governing disputes that 'relate to' or 'are connected with' the contract."[36] Claims that "arise out of" a contract are those claims that are *based* on the contract (e.g., breach of the

---

31. *Id.*

32. For example, under the Federal Arbitration Act, a U.S. district court may vacate an arbitral award for various failings of the arbitral process (e.g., corruption, fraud, arbitrator misconduct). 9 U.S.C. § 10(a) (2009). *See also United Paperworkers*, 484 U.S. at 38 ("Of course, decisions procured by the parties through fraud or through the arbitrator's dishonesty need not be enforced. But there is nothing of that sort involved in this case."). Under various state laws, an arbitral award may be similarly reviewed. *See, e.g.,* MINN. STAT. § 572.19 (2006); UNIFORM ARBITRATION ACT § 23 (2000). For further discussion on the judicial review of arbitration awards in the employment context, see Michael H. LeRoy, *Do Courts Create Moral Hazard?: When Judges Nullify Employer Liability in Arbitrations*, 93 MINN. L. REV. 998 (2009).

33. Indeed, grievance arbitration is a hallmark mechanism of dispute resolution in labor contracts.

34. *Garfinkel v. Morristown Obstetrics & Gynecology Associates, P.A.*, 773 A.2d 665, 670 (N.J. 2001); *see also Moses H. Cone Mem'l Hosp. v. Mercury Constr. Corp.*, 460 U.S. 1, 24-25 (1983).

35. *See, e.g., Pers. Sec. & Safety Sys. Inc. v. Motorola Inc.*, 297 F.3d 388, 392 (5th Cir. 2002) ("[A] valid agreement to arbitrate applies unless it can be said with positive assurance that the arbitration clause is not susceptible of an interpretation which would cover the dispute at issue.") (internal citations and quotations omitted).

36. *Pennzoil Exploration and Prod. Co. v. Ramco Energy Ltd.*, 139 F.3d 1061, 1067 (5th Cir. 1998).

contract), whereas claims that "relate to" or "are connected with" a specified contract are those that—while not necessarily based on the contract—at least "touch" the contract.[37] As an illustration, the Fifth Circuit found a claim of sexual assault against a former employer and co-workers to be outside the scope of an arbitration clause that required all claims "related to" the employment to be arbitrated.[38]

If a party desires a broad arbitration provision, should the party attempt to define the scope of the claims to be submitted to arbitration as those that (i) "arise under" *or* "relate to" (ii) the "employment contract" *or* the "employment"? What are the differences?[39]

Why might the Company prefer arbitration? What risks and benefits does arbitration pose to the Executive? Given your answers to the foregoing, how might each party wish to draft the arbitration provision in the Agreement differently?

How does the "carve-out" found in subsection 20(c) work with the rest of section 20? What is the purpose and function of this provision? Does it favor the interests of the Company or the Executive (or does it serve both)? Note that, inasmuch as parties intend by contract to empower an arbitrator to award injunctive relief, specific performance, or other equitable remedies, the arbitrator generally will be so empowered, and courts will generally stand behind such an arbitral decree.[40]

5. Waiving the Right to a Jury Trial

Notice that section 20 on arbitration further provides that both "parties expressly waive the right to a jury trial," as agreeing to arbitration as an exclusive

---

37. *See, e.g., Mitsubishi Motors Corp. v. Soler Chrysler-Plymouth Inc.*, 473 U.S. 614, 625 (1985) (claim under the Sherman Act subject to arbitration because the claim at least "touched" matters covered by the contract); *JLM Indus., Inc. v. Stolt-Nielsen SA*, 387 F.3d 163, 172-73 (2d Cir. 2004) (allegations that price-fixing conspiracy undermined legitimate contractual relations between contractual parties "touched" the contract and were subject to arbitration under contractual provision); *see also Pennzoil Exploration*, 139 F.3d at 1067 (concluding that for matters to be within the scope of an arbitration clause that provided that all claims "related to" the contract must be arbitrated, such matters must have a "significant relationship" to the contract).

38. *Jones v. Halliburton Co.*, 583 F.3d 228, 239 (5th Cir. 2009) (holding that a sexual assault claim did not "relate to" employment because it did not bear a "significant relationship" to the employment); *see also Smith ex rel. Smith v. Captain D's, LLC*, 963 So.2d 1116 (Miss. 2007). *But see Forbes v. A.G. Edwards & Sons, Inc.*, No. 08 Civ. 552(TPG), 2009 WL 424146, at *8 (S.D.N.Y. 2009) ("Because the relevant arbitration agreements clearly require arbitration of 'matters related to or arising from' plaintiff's employment, plaintiff's claims of assault and battery must be submitted to arbitration.").

39. Consider, for example, *Forbes*, 2009 WL 424146, at *8 ("The arbitration clauses at issue here did not limit mandatory arbitration to disputes arising from the employment *contracts;* rather, they explicitly required arbitration of matters related to or arising from plaintiff's employment. The language requires arbitration of tort as well as contract claims.") (emphasis in original); *Martindale v. Sandvik, Inc.*, 800 A.2d 87, 883-84 (N.J. 2002) (unlike agreement in previous case that pertained only to claims concerning the *agreement*, the agreement here covered "all disputes relating to…employment…or termination thereof").

40. Please see Chapter 1 on this topic.

means of dispute resolution involves waiving one's right to a jury trial. While the Seventh Amendment to the U.S. Constitution preserves the right to a jury trial in federal courts where the amount in controversy exceeds 20 dollars, this right generally may be waived by contract.[41] Such waiver must be done "knowingly and intentionally" to be effective.[42] Why, then, do you suppose that this clause is bolded in the Agreement? Generally and in addition to other requirements, for a jury-trial waiver to be "knowing and intentional," an agreement should emphasize the provision by, for example, giving the waiver its own paragraph and bolding or enlarging its text.[43] Despite that some commentators have argued that mandatory arbitration provisions should be analyzed as, and held to the standard of, waivers of the right to a jury trial,[44] courts generally have not done so and instead have enforced arbitration provisions regardless of whether they satisfy a "knowing and intentional" standard.[45]

6. Indemnifying a Corporate Officer

Section 11 ("Indemnification") provides that the Company will indemnify the Executive as provided for in the Company's articles of incorporation and bylaws and as provided by Delaware law. "Indemnification" refers to an obligation to pay another person (or, on the other side of the coin, the right of that other person to be paid) for certain damages or losses suffered — in this case, as is provided by the articles of incorporation, the bylaws, and the laws of Delaware.[46] "Articles of incorporation" (sometimes called a "charter" or "certificate of incorporation") refer to the document filed with the state by the organizers of a corporation that forms, and lays out the fundamental governing aspects of, a corporation. "Bylaws" provide a second level of governing provisions that generally need not be filed with the state and that further specify the rules governing the corporation.

Section 145 of Delaware General Corporation Law provides for the indemnification of officers, directors, and employees.[47] Under the provision, a Delaware corporation *may* indemnify any person made party to an action in his capacity as an officer, director, or employee of the corporation for reasonable

---

41. *See, e.g., Leasing Serv. Corp. v. Crane*, 804 F.2d 828, 832-33 (4th Cir. 1986). Various state constitutions generally also provide for a right to a jury trial, which may be waived.

42. *See supra* note 41.

43. *See, e.g., RDO Fin. Servs. Co. v. Powell*, 191 F. Supp. 2d 811, 814 (N.D. Tex. 2002) (finding a waiver of a jury trial not to be knowingly and intentionally made, where it was "buried in the middle of a lengthy paragraph, not set off from the rest of the text through differential bold, larger print, italics, or any other form of emphasis or distinction").

44. *See, e.g.,* Jean R. Sternlight, *The Rise and Spread of Mandatory Arbitration as a Substitute for the Jury Trial*, 38 U.S.F. L. REV. 17 (2003).

45. *Id.* at 22-23.

46. We revisit indemnification in much greater depth in Chapter 3, where we discuss contractual tools for shifting risk more generally.

47. 8 DEL. CODE ANN. tit. 8, § 145 (2009).

expenses, fines, judgments, and settlements, as long as that person (1) acted in good faith; (2) in a manner he reasonably believed not to disserve the best interests of the company; and (3), regarding a criminal action, had no reasonable cause to believe his criminal conduct was unlawful.[48] Furthermore, Delaware law provides that a corporation *shall* indemnify an officer or director for any expenses (including attorneys' fees) actually and reasonably incurred by such person in *successfully defending* against any action brought against the person as officer or director of the corporation.[49]

Drafting Note: Incorporating Outside Sources of Obligations

Companies will commonly offer to indemnify officers, directors, and certain high-level employees in order to attract the best talent to the posts. This is because these positions become far less attractive when coupled with the potential for significant personal liability. With this in mind, consider whether section 11 provides adequate assurances to the Executive. Does section 11 require anything of the Company more than what the Company either has already agreed (or will agree) to do under its articles and bylaws or must do as required by law? If Delaware law permits the Company to indemnify the Executive, does section 11 by its terms require the Company to do so?

These questions turn on the meaning of "provided" as used in section 11, and, from the section, it is not clear if "provided" means "allowed" (which would yield a broader indemnity) or "required" (which would yield a narrower indemnity). What do you think the parties intended by this provision, and how would you draft this provision more clearly to express this intent? Also, consider that corporate articles and bylaws can be amended (although to do so may be difficult and generally requires shareholder approval) and that the Company's indemnification obligations under section 11, as provided by the Company's articles and bylaws, may be subject to change.

---

7. Terminating the Employment Relationship

Subsection (a) of section 6 ("Termination") gives *the Company* the right to terminate the Agreement at any time, as long as any of the several, enumerated events and conditions constituting "Cause" occurs and the Company provides the proper notice of, and undergoes the proper procedure for, termination. Similarly, subsection (e) gives *the Executive* the right to terminate for "Good Reason," listing several events that—if uncorrected for 30 days—constitute "Good Reason." Under the Agreement, what is the significance of "Cause" or

---

48. *Id.* § 145(a).
49. *Id.* § 145(c).

"Good Reason"? After all, subsections 6(c) and (d) provide that the Executive and the Company, respectively, each have the right to terminate the Agreement *with or without* Good Reason or Cause.

Much of the answer lies in subsection 6(f): If the Company terminates for Cause, or if the Executive terminates *without* Good Reason, then the Executive is only entitled to receive that which he is already due (e.g., earned but unpaid salary, vested benefits). However, if the Company terminates *without* Cause (sometimes referred to as "termination for convenience"), or if the Executive terminates with Good Reason, then the Executive is entitled to receive not only that which is already due but also a lump sum amount and a continuation of benefits. This bundle of pay and benefits due upon termination of employment is commonly called a "severance package."

a. Severance and Release

Subsection 6(g) conditions the Executive's right to severance payment on his executing a waiver and release of claims against the Company. This means that the Executive must agree not to bring suit against the Company for certain claims before the Executive may receive his severance package. Often, at the time of termination, an employer will present an employee with a severance package in exchange for the employee's execution of a waiver of all claims against the employer.[50] This waiver, given by the employee in exchange for severance pay, is likely to be enforced as any other contract (i.e., subject to the classic failings of contracts, e.g., fraud, failure of consideration, duress, unconscionability, mutual mistake).[51] The general rule is that "[o]rdinarily, public policy does not prohibit an otherwise valid release from acting as a waiver of a federal statutory cause of action."[52] However, various federal laws intersect with freedom of contract to prevent waiver of certain claims or to impose certain requirements for such waivers to be effective as to such claims. Note that merely because a waiver fails to satisfy the requirements for waiver of claims under a certain federal statute does not necessarily mean that the waiver fails entirely or as to other claims.[53]

Examples of such federal laws in the employment context include the Employee Retirement Income Security Act (ERISA), the Fair Labor Standards

---

50. Note the distinction between the two scenarios: In the Agreement, the Executive is given the option—at the time of *employment*—to receive severance pay upon termination without Cause or for Good Reason, if he later signs a waiver of claims. Separately, employers commonly present such offers (whether or not *previously* granting the employee an option) at the time of termination. The Executive's option to *compel* severance pay by presenting a waiver of claims may operate as an optional liquidated damages provision. Please see Chapter 1 for more on liquidated damages.

51. *See, e.g., Skirchak v. Dynamics Research Corp.*, 508 F.3d 49, 59-60 (1st Cir. 2007) (finding a class action waiver in employment agreement to be unconscionable); *Shaheen v. B.F. Goodrich Co.*, 873 F.2d 105, 107 (6th Cir. 1989) ("[W]e will examine waivers of employee rights under normal contract principles.").

52. *Shaheen*, 873 F.2d at 107 (citing *Rogers v. Gen. Elec. Co.*, 781 F.2d 452, 454 (5th Cir. 1986)).

53. *See, e.g., Madrid v. Phelps Dodge Corp*, 211 F. App'x 676, 680 (10th Cir. 2006).

Act (FLSA), the Family and Medical Leave Act (FMLA), the Age Discrimination in Employment Act (ADEA), the Workers Adjustment and Retraining Notification Act (WARN), and the American with Disabilities Act (ADA). For example, ERISA regulates employee benefit plans. Claims arising under ERISA *can* be waived, but such waiver must be "knowing and voluntary."[54] Whether a release of ERISA claims is "knowing and voluntary" is a "totality of the circumstances" inquiry that includes the following factors:

(1) the clarity and specificity of the release language; (2) the plaintiff's education and business experience; (3) the amount of time plaintiff had for deliberation about the release before signing it; (4) whether plaintiff knew or should have known his rights upon execution of the release; (5) whether plaintiff was encouraged to seek, or in fact received benefit of counsel; (6) whether there was an opportunity for negotiation of the terms of the Agreement; and (7) whether the consideration given in exchange for the waiver and accepted by the employee exceeds the benefits to which the employee was already entitled by contract or law.[55]

As an additional illustration, the ADEA forbids employment discrimination against employees who are at least 40 years old. As with ERISA, an employee may waive his ADEA rights, but the waiver must be "knowing and voluntary" to be enforceable.[56] For a waiver of ADEA rights to be "knowing and voluntary," the following criteria must be satisfied:

(A) the waiver is part of an agreement between the individual and the employer that is written in a manner calculated to be understood by such individual, or by the average individual eligible to participate;

(B) the waiver specifically refers to rights or claims arising under this chapter;

(C) the individual does not waive rights or claims that may arise after the date the waiver is executed;

(D) the individual waives rights or claims only in exchange for consideration in addition to anything of value to which the individual already is entitled;

(E) the individual is advised in writing to consult with an attorney prior to executing the agreement;

(F) (i) the individual is given a period of at least 21 days within which to consider the agreement; or

(ii) if a waiver is requested in connection with an exit incentive or other employment termination program offered to a group or class of employees, the individual is given a period of at least 45 days within which to consider the agreement;

(G) the agreement provides that for a period of at least 7 days following the execution of such agreement, the individual may revoke the agreement, and the

---

54. *See Washington v. Bert Bell/Pete Rozelle NFL Ret. Plan*, 504 F.3d 818, 824-25 (9th Cir. 2007).

55. *Madrid*, 211 F. App'x at 679 (internal citation and quotation marks omitted); *see also, e.g., Frommert v. Conkright*, 535 F.3d 111, 121 (2d Cir. 2008).

56. *See Am. Airlines, Inc. v. Cardoza-Rodriguez*, 133 F.3d 111, 117 (1st Cir. 1998).

agreement shall not become effective or enforceable until the revocation period has expired;

(H) if a waiver is requested in connection with an exit incentive or other employment termination program offered to a group or class of employees, the employer (at the commencement of the period specified in subparagraph (F)) informs the individual in writing in a manner calculated to be understood by the average individual eligible to participate, as to—

(i) any class, unit, or group of individuals covered by such program, any eligibility factors for such program, and any time limits applicable to such program; and

(ii) the job titles and ages of all individuals eligible or selected for the program, and the ages of all individuals in the same job classification or organizational unit who are not eligible or selected for the program.[57]

Notice that subsection 6(g) of the Agreement contemplates the requirements for waiving rights under the ADEA, as 6(g) references the seven-day revocation period required by the statute reproduced above.

b. Material Breach (and Substantial Performance)

Section 6(a)(i) provides, among other things, that a "material breach" of the Agreement by the Executive means that the Company has the right to terminate the Agreement for "Cause." Likewise, section 6(e)(iv) provides that a "material breach" by the Company allows the Executive to terminate the Agreement for "Good Reason."

If parties to an employment agreement do not define what constitutes "cause," then a court may find "cause" in any act constituting "material breach" of the agreement.[58] Accordingly, the Agreement defines "cause" more broadly than this judicial inference, as the Agreement includes several enumerated occurrences in addition to material breach.

What qualifies as a material breach? How does a material breach differ from an immaterial breach? The question of whether a breach is material is necessarily an amorphous, "facts and circumstances" inquiry. Courts generally recite some variety of the following standard for what "material" means: "A breach is material if it destroys the essential object of the agreement or deprives the non-breaching party of a benefit that the party reasonably expected."[59] The

---

57. 29 U.S.C. § 626(f) (2009); *see also Am. Airlines, Inc.,* 133 F.3d at 117. For further discussion of waiver and federal employment statutes, see *Copeland v. ABB, Inc.,* 521 F.3d 1010, 1014 (8th Cir. 2008) (rights under the FLSA cannot be waived except by payment in full of due wages under the supervision of the Secretary of Labor); 29 C.F.R. § 825.220(d) (2009) (retrospective rights may be waived under the FMLA); *Int'l Ass'n of Machinists and Aerospace Workers, AFL-CIO v. Compania Mexicana de Aviacion, S.A. de C.V.,* 199 F.3d 796, 799 (5th Cir. 2000) (claims under the WARN Act validly waived); *Rivera-Flores v. Bristol-Myers Squibb Caribbean,* 112 F.3d 9, 10 (1st Cir. 1997) (explaining the "knowing and voluntary" standard under the ADA).

58. *See, e.g., Gresham v. Lumbermen's Mut. Cas. Co.,* 404 F.3d 253, 260 (4th Cir. 2005).

59. *Int'l Prod. Specialists, Inc. v. Schwing Am., Inc.,* 580 F.3d 587, 595 (7th Cir. 2009); *see also Rano v. Sipa Press, Inc.,* 987 F.2d 580, 586 (9th Cir. 1993).

Second Restatement of Contracts lists several factors to serve as guideposts.[60] In light of this factor-laden inquiry, parties can gain some certainty by specifying in the contract how a court will understand material breach of the contract, as a court is likely to find a breach to be material if the parties so contractually specify.[61] A common example is where parties specify that "time is of the essence," which generally makes the failure to perform a contract in a timely manner (as contractually specified) a material breach under the contract.[62]

Examples of a material breach of an employment agreement have included an employer reducing an employee's base salary,[63] an employee's failure "to perform with the customary level of professionalism and competence that is standard in virtually any industry," including recurrent failure to comply with assigned tasks and complicity in altering documents,[64] and an employee violating a non-compete restrictive covenant.[65]

A material breach is significant not only because it may contractually trigger certain rights and obligations (as it does in the Agreement) but also because material breach generally may give the non-breaching party the right not to perform under, and to terminate, the contract.[66] Notice that the mirror image of material breach is "substantial performance." For example, a party has substantially performed its contractual obligations and is due payment under the contract, even when the party mistakenly installs a brand of pipe equal in quality but different from that specified in the contract.[67] Realize also what this does not mean. Anything short of a full and complete performance is still a breach — just perhaps not a *material* breach. The non-breaching party is still entitled to damages that proximately result from the less-than-full performance.[68]

---

60. RESTATEMENT (SECOND) OF CONTRACTS § 241 (1981) (In determining whether a failure to render or to offer performance is material, the following circumstances are significant: (a) the extent to which the injured party will be deprived of the benefit which he reasonably expected; (b) the extent to which the injured party can be adequately compensated for the part of that benefit of which he will be deprived; (c) the extent to which the party failing to perform or to offer to perform will suffer forfeiture; (d) the likelihood that the party failing to perform or to offer to perform will cure his failure, taking account of all the circumstances including any reasonable assurances; (e) the extent to which the behavior of the party failing to perform or to offer to perform comports with standards of good faith and fair dealing.)

61. *See, e.g., Finova Capital Corp. v. Richard A. Arledge, Inc.*, No. 07-16384, 2009 WL 166933, at *1 (9th Cir. Jan. 9, 2009); *Dunkin' Donuts of Am., Inc. v. Middletown Donut Corp.*, 495 A.2d 66, 75 (N.J. 1985).

62. *See, e.g., Retrofit Partners I, L.P. v. Lucas Indus., Inc.*, 201 F.3d 155, 160 (2d Cir. 2000).

63. *See, e.g., E.E.O.C. v. R.J. Gallagher Co.*, 181 F.3d 645, 651 (5th Cir. 1999).

64. *See, e.g., Carco Group, Inc. v. Maconachy*, 644 F. Supp. 2d 218, 233 (E.D.N.Y. 2009).

65. *See, e.g., NCMIC Fin. Corp. v. Artino*, 638 F. Supp. 2d 1042, 1069-70 (S.D. Iowa 2009).

66. *See* RESTATEMENT (SECOND) OF CONTRACTS § 237 (1981); *Comedy Club, Inc. v. Improv W. Assocs.*, 553 F.3d 1277, 1289 n.12 (9th Cir. 2009).

67. *Jacob & Youngs v. Kent*, 230 N.Y. 239, 241 (1921) (Cardozo, J.). However, if the party less-than-fully performs in *bad faith*, then the doctrine of substantial performance is unlikely to save him, and this breach — while perhaps less than material — *will* excuse the other party's performance. *See Moore's Builder and Contractor, Inc. v. Hoffman*, 409 N.W.2d 191, 192 (Iowa App. 1987).

68. *See Matador Drilling Co., v. Post*, 662 F.2d 1190, 1195 (5th Cir. 1981); *Jacob & Youngs*, 230 N.Y. at 247.

c. Constructive Termination

If an employee were to quit, then he may forego many of the benefits he would have received had his employer instead terminated the employment relationship. For instance, in this Agreement, the Executive is better off if the Company were to terminate his employment without Cause than if the Executive were to quit without Good Reason. Indeed, many employment agreements do not include a "Good Reason" provision, and, under these agreements, the employee is likely better off to be fired without cause than to quit *for any reason*. On the flipside, for this reason, an employer generally would rather an employee quit than the employer have to fire him. Accordingly, an employer that wants to terminate an employee might take measures to "motivate" an employee to quit. What is an employee to do should his employer, say, reduce his responsibilities considerably or significantly reduce his pay or assign him to work in an isolated, desert office?

He could quit. If he were afforded the protection of the Good Reason provisions of this Agreement, he would be entitled to a severance package, provided that these occurrences amounted to Good Reason. But what if the employee's agreement contained no such provisions, or what if the employer made the employee's work life intolerable in ways that somehow did not constitute Good Reason? Seemingly, the employee would face the choice of quitting and not receiving a heightened severance package or carrying on despite unsavory conditions.

To provide an employee with some recourse, courts have developed the doctrine of "constructive termination" (or "constructive discharge"). Constructive termination generally occurs when working conditions and arrangements become such that a reasonable employee would be compelled to resign and the employer at least knows of these conditions.[69] "In general, single, trivial, or isolated acts of misconduct are insufficient to support a constructive discharge claim."[70] As an example, one court found constructive termination when an employee was taken off an account he spent eight years obtaining, was forced to report his sales activity on a daily basis, and had his monthly take-home pay reduced from $8,000 to $3,000.[71] Another court refused to find constructive termination when an employee's status was changed to at-will, his managerial responsibilities reduced, and his base salary reduced from $235,000 to $175,000.[72]

"[A] constructive discharge is legally regarded as a firing rather than a resignation."[73] Accordingly, all that follows from being fired—rather than

---

69. *See, e.g., Moisant v. Air Midwest, Inc.,* 291 F.3d 1028, 1032 (8th Cir. 2002); *King v. AC & R Adver.,* 65 F.3d 765, 767 (9th Cir. 1995).

70. *Turner v. Anheuser-Busch, Inc.,* 7 Cal. 4th 1238, 1247 (Cal. 1994).

71. *Gower v. IKON Office Solutions, Inc.,* 177 F. Supp. 2d 1224, 1233 (D. Kan. 2001).

72. *King,* 65 F.3d at 766.

73. *Turner,* 7 Cal. 4th at 1245.

quitting—follows from a constructive termination, including any contractual rights and benefits.

B. POST-EMPLOYMENT RESTRICTIVE COVENANTS AND THEIR ENFORCEABILITY

1. Covenants, Generally

Generally speaking, a covenant is any promise to perform under a contract. Covenants may be affirmative or negative—that is, a party may covenant *to do* something and a party may covenant *not to do* something. A covenant differs from a representation and from a warranty (each of which we will discuss in greater length in Chapter 3) in that a covenant promises some action—or lack of action. In contrast, a representation is a statement of fact and a warranty is a promise that a statement is true, for the duration of the warranty.[74] While a warranty may incentivize the performance (or non-performance) of an action—as the warrantor may wish to ensure that the warranty remains true so as to avoid breach—a covenant states directly an obligation to perform (or not to perform) an action. For example, if A wishes to hire B to paint A's house, A may pay B for a promise that A's house will be painted—a warranty—but, more to the point, A is likely to pay B for a promise to paint A's house. That is, A will pay B for a covenant to paint A's house. Of course, A may demand additional representations and warranties from B. For example, B may represent that he is licensed and qualified to paint houses and warrant that inclement weather will not damage the paint job.

2. Restrictive Covenants: Obligations Not to Compete, Solicit, or Hire

Section 8 ("Covenant Not to Compete") provides that the Executive will not compete with the Company. There are three principal aspects of the provision: (1) the provision restricts Competitive Activities, listing several acts (e.g., becoming employed, rendering services, acquiring an interest, otherwise assisting) and defining each as a prohibited Competitive Activity when performed for a certain entity (e.g., those engaged in operations involving the transmission, production, syndication, promotion, or marketing of radio entertainment programming); (2) the provision contains a geographic restriction, defining Competitive Activities as only those that assist competitors in North America;

---

74. As we discuss in greater detail in Chapter 3, note that some attorneys doubt whether "representation" and "warranty" are meaningfully distinct.

and (3) the provision contains a durational restriction, only imposing the non-competition obligation on the Executive during the Restricted Period, which extends one year from the date the Executive's employment terminates.

In addition, section 8 contains two covenants not to solicit: (1) the Executive may not solicit *business* from the Company's customers for products or services that compete with those of the Company; and (2) the Executive may not solicit the *employment* of the Company's employees. Note that these covenants, too, only restrict the Executive during the Restricted Period but are not limited in geographical scope. This is likely because competition may pose a threat to a company only in certain geographical areas, whereas solicitation of the Company's customers and employees is dangerous no matter where this solicitation occurs. Might it be difficult to prove who solicited whom? For this reason, an employer may attempt to include a covenant not to employ—along with a covenant not to solicit—the employer's employees in order to provide the company with a more provable breach; the competing concern is that this type of provision is more restrictive.

A Practitioner Perspective: Retaining Employees and Post-Employment Restrictions

Despite the financial crisis that began in 2007 and the resulting unemployment it has created, the protection of human capital and valuable company trade secrets remains a number one priority for many employers. To succeed in these extraordinarily competitive times, companies face the daunting tasks of creating innovative products and services; developing and maintaining a customer base; recruiting and training an expert and efficient work force; and keeping all of their innovations—and all of their customers and employees—from falling into the hands of their competitors.

These tasks are especially difficult because the most valuable, knowledgeable and highly skilled employees are also the most mobile. When such employees leave their jobs and move on to work for a competitor—or to start their own competitive company—they present an unparalleled risk to their former employer. This risk is further exacerbated by the fact that in the electronic age sensitive data can be misappropriated in milliseconds with unprecedented ease. A departing employee can export important documents and company secrets to external storage devices, PDA's, portable hard drives, and cell phones in mere seconds. Unless the employer does a careful forensic examination of the departing employee's electronic devices, such misappropriation will often go unnoticed.

The employment lawyer plays an important role in helping the company protect itself proactively and then helping the employer to take appropriate steps to move quickly to minimize the damage of the departing employee. Most important to this process are the drafting of enforceable trade secret protections and post-employment restrictions.

Employers frequently attempt to prevent their employees from unfairly competing with them upon termination of their employment by having them covenant, as part of an employment agreement, that they will not compete with their employer after their employment ends. Although many of these disputes end up in federal court under diversity jurisdiction, the enforceability of such agreements is a matter of state common law and statutory law. Many states, including New York, follow the general rule that such agreements are enforceable, provided they are necessary to protect a legitimate interest of the employer and are reasonably limited in time, geography, and the restrictions they place on the employee in pursuing his or her profession.

Other states, including California, Montana, North Dakota, and Oklahoma, do not follow the general rule. For example, California Business & Professions Code section 16600 provides that "every contract by which anyone is restrained from engaging in a lawful profession, trade or business of any kind is to that extent void." California courts have rigorously applied this provision in the employment context and have routinely invalidated agreements purporting to preclude employees (expressly or implicitly through penalties) from working for competitors upon completion of their employment.

Other post-employment restrictions include non-solicitation of employees and customers, and of course, non-retention and non-use of confidential employer information. Employers who want to be proactive about retaining their employees will craft employment and other compensation agreements that create substantial monetary disincentives for employees to leave before certain dates. In some jurisdictions, enforceability of these types of agreements is subject to a similar analysis as the enforceability of non-competes. In other jurisdictions, if an employee resigns his or her employment voluntarily, these kinds of forfeiture provisions may be enforced as ordinary contracts under the "employee choice doctrine."

Michael Delikat, Partner and Global
Chair, Employment Practice Group
Orrick, Herrington & Sutcliffe LLP

Why might a company (or, the Company) want to impose these restrictive covenants on an employee (or, the Executive)? Companies often invest substantial resources in the training and development of employees. In this way, an employee is similar to any of a company's assets. A company may invest hundreds of thousands of dollars in the development of a piece of heavy machinery. If that machinery could pick itself up, dust itself off, and walk out, straight to a competitor (or into the ocean, for that matter), the company's investment would be largely for naught. Indeed, a company might be hesitant to invest large sums in these assets—at least not without bolting the machinery to the company floor. Of course, the awkwardness of this analogy reveals how we treat and think of human beings and machines differently. Our society may wish to incent companies to invest in labor, and a prospective employee may wish a company to invest heavily in him; however, this desire to motivate companies to invest *ex ante* must be balanced against *ex post* (i) a person's right not to work (under the Thirteenth Amendment) and (ii) a person's right to work elsewhere, in addition to society's need for that person's work.

As for a person's right not to work, a party may not compel another to perform labor: If an employee does not perform under an employment agreement, the company cannot specifically enforce the agreement; a court will not force a person to work.[75] If a company cannot compel performance, then a next-best alternative may be *preventing* the employee from performing for any competitors and/or from taking any company business or competitors—not to mention secrets—with him. Enforcing these covenants may involve requesting a court to issue an injunction so as to stop the employee from working for a competitor or soliciting company customers or employees—but does not involve coercing the employee to act affirmatively. Accordingly, the same Thirteenth Amendment concerns are not at play. Will courts, then, enforce post-employment restrictive convents not to compete, solicit, or hire? The answer lies in the second balancing act: the company's legitimate interest in restricting the future employment of the employee as against the employee's right to work elsewhere, while also considering the public interest at stake.

a. Requirement of Reasonableness

Courts are generally suspicious of "restraints of trade" (e.g., non-competition covenants), as we saw in Chapter 1, and, for this reason, may construe them strictly against the employer.[76] To be valid and enforceable, a restrictive covenant not to compete (or to solicit or to hire) must be reasonable.[77] While the exact requirements vary state to state,[78] in general, the question of unreasonableness turns on two independent balancing inquiries: (1) whether the restraint is broader in scope than necessary to protect an employer's legitimate interest; and (2) whether the restraint imposes a hardship on the employee and a likely injury on the public that, together, outweigh the employer's needs for the restraint.[79] That is, the first inquiry asks whether a restraint as written is

---

75. *See* RESTATEMENT (SECOND) OF CONTRACTS § 367 (1981); *Beverly Glen Music, Inc. v. Warner Commc'ns, Inc.*, 224 Cal. Rptr. 260, 261 (Cal. Ct. App. 1986).

76. *See, e.g., Grant v. Carotek, Inc.*, 737 F.2d 410, 412 (4th Cir. 1984).

77. *See* RESTATEMENT (SECOND) OF CONTRACTS § 186(1) (1981) ("A promise is unenforceable on grounds of public policy if it is unreasonably in restraint of trade.").

78. A poignant example is California, which, by statute, does not enforce non-competition agreements in the employment context: "Except as provided in this chapter, every contract by which anyone is restrained from engaging in a lawful profession, trade, or business of any kind is to that extent void." CAL. BUS. & PROF. CODE § 16600 (2008). However, California does not prohibit non-competition agreements with geographic limitations that are ancillary to a sale of a business or among dissociating partners. CAL. BUS. & PROF. CODE §§ 16601, 16602, 16602.5 (2008).

79. *See* RESTATEMENT (SECOND) OF CONTRACTS § 188(1) (1981); *see also Lampman v. DeWolff Boberg & Assocs.*, 319 F. App'x 293, 299-300 (4th Cir. 2009); *Certified Restoration Dry Cleaning Network, LLC v. Tenke Corp.*, 511 F.3d 535, 545-47 (6th Cir. 2007); *Victaulic Co. v. Tieman*, 499 F.3d 227, 235 (3d Cir. 2007).

more restrictive than necessary to serve a legitimate interest of the employer — even if the employer's interest is more important than the harm a narrowly drawn restraint would impose on the employee and the public. By contrast, the second inquiry asks whether a restraint — even if neatly tailored to the employer's interest, under the first prong — imposes an unreasonable burden on the employee and the public.

As for the first inquiry, the breadth of a restrictive covenant is commonly analyzed along three dimensions: geography, duration, and restricted activity.[80] Courts will generally consider these qualifications in the context of each other (e.g., a covenant appropriately narrow in activity and duration might not need to be bounded by geography).[81] Whether a restrictive covenant is appropriately tuned to the legitimate needs of an employer necessarily turns on the particularities of each case.

As for the second inquiry, a post-employment obligation not to compete may also be invalid if it causes the employee undue hardship and/or if it is likely to cause the public injury, either (or the combination) of which outweighs the employer's needs for the restriction. A classic example of a restrictive covenant causing an employee to suffer undue hardship is where the restraint prevents the employee from earning gainful employment elsewhere.[82] The likelihood of injury to the public may outweigh the employer's needs if the employee's not working in a particular trade causes the public substantial harm. For example, where a town had only two doctors and a covenant prevented one from providing his services there, the covenant was held to be unenforceable.[83]

Outside of the employment context, restrictive covenants are also commonly used alongside the sale of a business. Courts are generally more lenient in this business-to-business context, when construing the meaning and assessing the reasonableness of a restrictive covenant, than in the employment context.[84]

---

80. *See* RESTATEMENT (SECOND) OF CONTRACTS § 188 cmt. d (1981); *see, e.g., Lampman*, 319 F. App'x at 302; *Certified Restoration Dry Cleaning Network*, 511 F.3d at 545-47; *Victaulic Co.*, 499 F.3d at 235.

81. *See, e.g., Victaulic Co.*, 499 F.3d at 238; *Simmons v. Miller*, 544 S.E.2d 666, 678 (Va. 2001).

82. *See* RESTATEMENT (SECOND) OF CONTRACTS § 188 cmt. c (1981); *see also, e.g., Lampman*, F. App'x at 299-300.

83. *See, e.g., Iredell Digestive Disease Clinic, P.A. v. Petrozza*, 373 S.E.2d 449, 455 (N.C. Ct. App. 1988), *aff'd*, 377 S.E.2d 750 (N.C. 1989) (holding an otherwise reasonable non-compete covenant unenforceable where it would jeopardize public health because it would leave only one gastroenterologist within a forty-five-mile radius of town). In measuring harm to the public welfare, how important is it that the restricted doctor provides "medically necessary" services? Consider *Weber v. Tillman*, 913 P.2d 84, 95-96 (Kan. 1996) (explaining that the public welfare is not harmed if residents of the town have to travel further for dermatology services). Consider this decision in light of a popular episode of *Seinfeld*, in which Jerry asserts that a dermatologist is not a "life saver" doctor, only to realize that he neglected to consider skin cancer.

84. *See, e.g., Zimmer Melia & Assocs., Inc. v. Stallings*, No. 3:08-0663, 2008 WL 3887664, at *5 (M.D. Tenn. Aug. 21, 2008); *Centorr-Vacuum Indus., Inc. v. Lavoie*, 609 A.2d 1213, 1215 (N.H. 1992). As an extreme example, California, which does not enforce non-compete covenants at all in the employment context, will enforce reasonable non-compete agreements that are ancillary to the sale of an entity or division. CAL. BUS. & PROF. CODE § 16601 (2008).

Note the recitation in section 10 of this chapter's Agreement of the Executive's belief in the reasonableness of the restrictive covenants found in the Agreement and that "the Executive is capable of gainful employment without breaching this Agreement." Similar to the acknowledgment we saw with regard to trade secrets in Chapter 1, an otherwise unreasonable restrictive covenant is not made reasonable merely because the parties characterize it so in their agreement.[85] Contractual recitations of reasonableness may be given some weight, but a court still may inquire into the actual facts and perform the same analysis regarding the reasonableness of a restrictive covenant.[86] Still, that these recitations of reasonableness may be given any weight and that they may persuasively frame a narrative for a future reader and decision-maker may be reason enough to push for inclusion.

b. Lawyer's Agreement Not to Compete

In order to protect the freedom of clients to choose their lawyers,[87] the American Bar Association's Model Rules of Professional Conduct include Rule 5.6:

> A lawyer shall not participate in offering or making:
>
> (a) a partnership, shareholders, operating, employment, or other similar type of agreement that restricts the right of a lawyer to practice after termination of the relationship, except an agreement concerning benefits upon retirement; or
>
> (b) an agreement in which a restriction on the lawyer's right to practice is part of the settlement of a client controversy.[88]

Accordingly, non-competition agreements for lawyers are per se unenforceable in those states that have adopted Rule 5.6.[89] This rule has its limits; for instance, the rule against lawyer non-competition agreements does not apply

---

85. *See, e.g., Poole v. U.S. Money Reserve, Inc.*, No. 09-08-137CV, 2008 WL 4735602, at *8 (Tex. App. Oct. 30, 2008); *Jackson Hewitt Inc. v. Childress*, No. 06-CV-0909 (DMC), 2008 WL 834386 (D.N.J. Mar. 27, 2008).

86. *See supra* note 85.

87. MODEL RULES OF PROF'L CONDUCT R. 5.6 cmt. 1 (2010).

88. *Id.* at R. 5.6.

89. As of August 15, 2010, every state but California has adopted some version of the Model Rules. *See* Dates of Adoption of the Model Rules of Professional Conduct, http://www.abanet.org/cpr/mrpc/alpha_states.html (last visited Aug. 15, 2010). California has an analog to Model Rule 5.6 in its Rules of Professional Conduct Rule 1-500, which provides:

> (A) A member shall not be a party to or participate in offering or making an agreement, whether in connection with the settlement of a lawsuit or otherwise, if the agreement restricts the right of a member to practice law, except that this rule shall not prohibit such an agreement which:
>
> (1) Is a part of an employment, shareholders', or partnership agreement among members provided the restrictive agreement does not survive the termination of the employment, shareholder, or partnership relationship; or
>
> (2) Requires payments to a member upon the member's retirement from the practice of law; or
>
> (3) Is authorized by Business and professions Code sections 6092.5 subdivision (i), or 6093.
>
> (B) A member shall not be a party to or participate in offering or making an agreement which precludes the reporting of a violation of these rules.

to those agreements that are ancillary to a sale of a law practice.[90] In addition, the Supreme Court of California has held that an agreement "imposing a reasonable cost on departing partners who compete with the law firm in a limited geographical area" is not void.[91] However, the Supreme Judicial Court of Massachusetts has recognized, "The strong majority rule in this country is that a court will not give effect to an agreement that greatly penalizes a lawyer for competing with a former law firm…"[92] Furthermore, the prohibition on lawyer non-competition agreements does not extend to a condition on a lawyer's retirement benefits: A retiring lawyer's covenant not to compete with its law firm, given in exchange for retirement benefits, is not automatically void.[93]

c. An Employer's Protectable Interest

An employer's legitimate interest in a post-employment restriction usually involves preventing the employee from using or disclosing valuable confidential information, exploiting the company's goodwill,[94] or stealing the company's customers.[95] In addition, courts often look to whether the covenant reasonably protects the company's investment of specialized training in the employee or, instead, unreasonably prohibits the employee from using his general knowledge and skills elsewhere.[96] Without a legitimate interest at stake, the employer's restrictive covenant will fail.[97] How do courts determine whether such a legitimate interest is at stake? Consider the following case.

Nike, Inc. v. McCarthy
United States Court of Appeals, Ninth Circuit, 2004.
379 F.3d 576.

FISHER, Circuit Judge.

In this case we must determine the validity of a noncompete agreement under Oregon law. Eugene McCarthy left his position as director of sales for Nike's Brand Jordan division in June 2003 to become vice president of U.S.

---

90. MODEL RULES OF PROF'L CONDUCT R. 5.6 cmt. 3 (2010).

91. *Howard v. Babcock*, 863 P.2d 150, 160 (Cal. 1993).

92. *Pettingell v. Morrison, Mahoney & Miller*, 687 N.E.2d 1237, 1239 (Mass. 1997) (expressly disagreeing with the California Supreme Court in *Howard* and noting that most courts have taken a view contrary to that ruling).

93. *See* MODEL RULES OF PROF'L CONDUCT R. 5.6 cmt. 1 (2010); *Donnelly v. Brown, Winick, Graves, Gross, Baskerville, Schoenebaum, & Walker, P.L.C.*, 599 N.W.2d 677, 681 (Iowa 1999).

94. "Goodwill" generally refers to the good reputation and brand value a company enjoys. More technically, in accounting, "goodwill" refers to the amount an acquiring company pays to acquire a target company beyond the target company's book value.

95. RESTATEMENT (SECOND) OF CONTRACTS § 188 cmt. b (1981); *see, e.g., Certified Restoration Dry Cleaning Network*, 511 F.3d at 547; *Victaulic Co. v. Tieman*, 499 F.3d 227, 235 (3d Cir. 2007).

96. *See supra* note 95.

97. *See Victaulic Co.*, 499 F.3d at 235.

footwear sales and merchandising at Reebok, one of Nike's competitors. Nike sought a preliminary injunction to prevent McCarthy from working for Reebok for a year, invoking a noncompete agreement McCarthy had signed in 1997 when Nike had promoted him to his earlier position as a regional footwear sales manager.... We ... hold that Nike has a legitimate interest in enforcing the agreement, because there is a substantial risk that McCarthy—in shaping Reebok's product allocation, sales and pricing strategies—could enable Reebok to divert a significant amount of Nike's footwear sales given the highly confidential information McCarthy acquired at Nike. Thus, we affirm the district court's preliminary injunction enforcing the agreement.

I. FACTUAL AND PROCEDURAL BACKGROUND

McCarthy began working for Nike in 1993 and became a key account manager in 1995.[1] During the spring of 1997, Nike undertook a major, national reorganization. Out of this came McCarthy's promotion to eastern regional footwear sales manager—and the present dispute as to when that promotion actually occurred. On February 28, John Petersen, McCarthy's supervisor, called McCarthy and asked, "How would you like to be the regional footwear sales manager for the eastern region?" McCarthy answered, "Absolutely, yes." Petersen mentioned there would be an increase in pay but did not say what the salary would be.[2]

In the following weeks, McCarthy continued to perform some of his old duties while assuming some of the duties of his new position, including leading meetings and preparing a report. In order to perform these duties, McCarthy obtained confidential information he had not seen before that described the top-selling styles in the eastern region. During the week of March 10, Petersen announced to a group of employees that McCarthy was the new regional footwear sales manager. During the remainder of March, McCarthy took several business trips, which were expensed to the cost center for the regional footwear sales manager position.

On March 27, McCarthy received a letter from Petersen confirming the offer for the regional footwear sales manager position ("Offer Letter"). The letter indicated that the "start date" for the new position was April 1, 1997. According to several Nike executives, it is not unusual for an employee to begin to perform the duties of a new position prior to the start date, in order to ensure a smooth transition once he or she "officially" starts in the new position. The Offer Letter also specified that McCarthy's salary would be $110,000, which became effective April 1. Before that date, McCarthy's salary was charged to the cost center for the key account manager position.

---

1. McCarthy signed a covenant not to compete as part of his employment agreement for the key account manager position, but that is not the noncompete agreement at issue here.

2. Petersen testified that he did not have actual authority to offer McCarthy the position at that time but rather was calling to see if McCarthy would be interested in the position.

In addition, the Offer Letter required McCarthy to sign an attached covenant not to compete and nondisclosure agreement as a condition of acceptance of the offer. The covenant not to compete contained the "Competition Restriction" clause at issue here, stating in relevant part:

> During EMPLOYEE'S employment by NIKE...and for one (1) year thereafter, (the "Restriction Period"), EMPLOYEE will not directly or indirectly...be employed by, consult for, or be connected in any manner with, any business engaged anywhere in the world in the athletic footwear, athletic apparel or sports equipment and accessories business, or any other business which directly competes with NIKE or any of its subsidiaries or affiliated corporations.

McCarthy signed the agreement that day. It is this noncompete agreement that Nike now seeks to enforce.

Two years later, McCarthy was again promoted, this time to the position of director of sales for the Brand Jordan division, the position he held until he resigned from Nike in June 2003. He was not asked to sign a new noncompete agreement. During the spring of 2003, McCarthy accepted a position with Reebok as vice president of U.S. footwear sales and merchandising and tendered his resignation in June. McCarthy began working at Reebok on July 22, 2003.

On August 18, 2003, Nike filed suit in Oregon circuit court, claiming breach of contract and seeking a declaratory judgment that McCarthy's employment with Reebok violated the covenant not to compete. McCarthy removed the case to the United States District Court for the District of Oregon, which had jurisdiction pursuant to 28 U.S.C. § 1332. Nike then moved for a temporary restraining order, which the district court granted on August 26. After conducting an evidentiary hearing, the court granted Nike's motion for a preliminary injunction on September 24. Specifically, the court enjoined McCarthy from "engaging in any athletic footwear business, athletic apparel business, or any other business which directly competes with Nike or any of its subsidiaries or affiliated corporations," including Reebok, through August 25, 2004. McCarthy appeals the grant of the preliminary injunction....

B. Protectible interest

Even if the covenant not to compete is not void under [an Oregon statute], it is a contract in restraint of trade that must meet three requirements under Oregon common law to be enforceable:

> (1) it must be partial or restricted in its operation in respect either to time or place; (2) it must be on some good consideration; and (3) it must be reasonable, that is, it should afford only a fair protection to the interests of the party in whose favor it is made, and must not be so large in its operation as to interfere with the interests of the public.

To satisfy the reasonableness requirement, the employer must show as a predicate "that [it] has a 'legitimate interest' entitled to protection." McCarthy argues that Nike has failed to show such a legitimate interest in this case.

McCarthy's general skills in sales and product development as well as industry knowledge that he acquired while working for Nike is not a protectible interest of Nike's that would justify enforcement of a noncompete agreement. "It has been uniformly held that general knowledge, skill, or facility acquired through training or experience while working for an employer appertain exclusively to the employee. The fact that they were acquired or developed during the employment does not, by itself, give the employer a sufficient interest to support a restraining covenant, even though the on-the-job training has been extensive and costly."

Nonetheless, an employer has a protectible interest in "information pertaining especially to the employer's business."

Nike has shown that McCarthy acquired information pertaining especially to Nike's business during the course of his employment with Nike. As Brand Jordan's director of sales, McCarthy obtained knowledge of Nike's product launch dates, product allocation strategies, new product development, product orders six months in advance and strategic sales plans up to three years in the future. This information was not general knowledge in the industry. For instance, McCarthy was privy to information about launch dates—the date Nike plans to introduce a product in the marketplace—for Brand Jordan shoes up through the spring of 2004. According to the undisputed testimony of one of Nike's executives, if a company knew its competitor's launch dates, it could time the launch dates of its own products to disrupt the sales of its competitor.

Nevertheless, McCarthy argues that acquisition of confidential information alone is insufficient to justify enforcement of a noncompete agreement. He contends that Nike must show actual use or potential disclosure of confidential information before a noncompete agreement can be enforced. He attempts to distinguish [Oregon cases that find an employer's interest in protecting confidential information to be a protectable interest] as cases in which the employees actually used the confidential information, for example, to solicit the former employer's customers on behalf of the new employer. These cases do not suggest that actual use is required for a noncompete clause to be enforceable, however. For example, in [one case], the court stated:

> It is clear that if the nature of the employment is such as will bring the employee [i]n personal contact with the patrons or customers of the employer, or enable him to acquire valuable information as to the nature and character of the business and [t]he names and requirements of the patrons or customers, *enabling him...to take advantage of such knowledge* of [o]r acquaintance with the patrons or customers of his former employer, and thereby gain an unfair advantage, equity will interfere in behalf of the employer and restrain the breach of a negative covenant not to engage in such competing business....

Thus, the court recognized that an employee's mere ability to take advantage of the employer's confidential information and thereby gain an unfair advantage may be sufficient for equity to restrain the employee from engaging in a competing business.

An employee's knowledge of confidential information is sufficient to justify enforcement of the noncompete if there is a "substantial risk" that the employee will be able to divert all or part of the employer's business given his knowledge. Given the nature of the confidential information that McCarthy acquired at Nike and his new position with Reebok, there is a substantial risk that Reebok would be able to divert a significant part of Nike's business given McCarthy's knowledge. McCarthy had the highest access to confidential information concerning Nike's product allocation, product development and sales strategies. As vice president of U.S. footwear sales and merchandising for Reebok, McCarthy would be responsible for developing strategic sales plans, providing overall direction for product allocation and shaping product lines, including how products are priced. Thus, McCarthy could help choose product allocation, sales and pricing strategies for Reebok that could divert a substantial part of Nike's footwear sales to Reebok based on his knowledge of information confidential to Nike without explicitly disclosing this information to any of Reebok's employees. Accordingly, the potential use of confidential information by McCarthy in his new position with Reebok is sufficient to justify enforcing the noncompete agreement. We conclude that Nike has demonstrated a likelihood of success as to the enforceability of its noncompete agreement with McCarthy....

---

d. *Reasonably in Restraint of Trade: Ancillarity*

In addition, a restrictive covenant not to compete will be found unenforceable as an *unreasonable* restraint of trade (note that "restraints of trade" are not inherently unreasonable or unenforceable), if the covenant is not "ancillary" to a valid transaction or relationship.[98] The Restatement neatly explains how this requirement dovetails with the requirement of reasonableness for restraints of trade:

> In order for a promise to refrain from competition to be reasonable, the promisee must have an interest worthy of protection that can be balanced against the hardship on the promisor and the likely injury to the public. The restraint must, therefore, be subsidiary to an otherwise valid transaction or relationship that gives rise to such an interest. A restraint that is not so related to an otherwise valid transaction or relationship is necessarily unreasonable.[99]

Such a valid transaction or relationship is commonly found in an employment agreement to which the restrictive covenant is ancillary.[100] Likewise,

---

98. *See* RESTATEMENT (SECOND) OF CONTRACTS § 187 (1981).

99. RESTATEMENT (SECOND) OF CONTRACTS § 187 cmt. b (1981) (citations omitted).

100. *See, e.g., Ray Mart Inc. v. Stock Bldg. Supply of Texas LP*, 302 F. App'x 232, 238 (5th Cir. 2008) (applying Texas law); *Siech v. Hobbs Group, LLC*, 198 F. App'x 840, 842 (11th Cir. 2006) (applying Georgia law); *JAK Prods., Inc. v. Wiza*, 986 F.2d 1080, 1086-87 (7th Cir. 1993) (applying Indiana law).

restraints of trade are often found valid as ancillary to the sale of a business.[101] Courts have also treated a variety of other transactions or relationships as the legitimate basis to which a restraint of trade may be ancillary, including a landlord-tenant relationship,[102] a gift,[103] and a non-disclosure agreement.[104]

e. Judicial Response to Overly Restrictive Clauses

As with the judicial response to unreasonable non-disclosure covenants, there are three basic judicial approaches for treatment of unreasonably broad covenants not to compete: (1) do nothing; (2) "blue-pencil"; or (3) rewrite to be reasonable.

A few states are unwilling to alter unreasonable restrictive covenants at all, leaving them to fail and severing them from the remainder of the contract so long as appropriate.[105] These courts are unwilling to alter unreasonable restrictive covenants at all because to do so would incent the employer to write overbroad restrictions to later be reduced to reasonableness by a court, if need be.[106] However, these courts may still be willing to sever the unenforceable provision from the rest of the contract.[107]

Some courts are willing to "blue-pencil" an overbroad clause, which means they will enforce a restrictive covenant by *striking* any unreasonable language, provided that this results in a coherent, enforceable provision.[108] In so doing, these courts will not *add* to a restrictive covenant in order to make it valid.[109]

---

101. *See, e.g., National-Arnold Magnetics Co. v. Wood*, 46 F. App'x 416, 418 (9th Cir. 2002) (Illinois law); *LDDS Commc'ns, Inc. v. Automated Commc'ns, Inc.*, 35 F.3d 198, 199 (5th Cir. 1994) (Mississippi law).

102. *See, e.g., Red Sage Ltd. P'ship v. DESPA Deutsche Sparkassen Immobilien-Anlage-Gasellschaft mbH*, 254 F.3d 1120, 1132-33 (D.C. Cir. 2001).

103. *See, e.g., Liautaud v. Liautaud*, 221 F.3d 981, 986 (7th Cir. 2000).

104. *See, e.g., Picker Int'l, Inc. v. Blanton*, 756 F. Supp. 971, 982 (N.D. Tex. 1990).

105. *See, e.g., Lampman v. DeWolff Boberg & Assocs., Inc.*, 319 F. App'x 293, 300 (4th Cir. 2009) (South Carolina law); *Palmer & Cay, Inc. v. Marsh & McLennan Cos.*, 404 F.3d 1297, 1303-04 (11th Cir. 2005) (Georgia law); *Nalco Chem. Co. v. Hydro Techs., Inc.*, 984 F.2d 801, 806 (7th Cir. 1993) (Wisconsin law) (citing Wis. Stat. Ann. § 103.465). However, Georgia courts are willing to reform restrictive covenants in the context of the sale of a business. *See Palmer & Cay*, 404 F.3d at 1303.

106. *See, e.g., White v. Fletcher/Mayo/Assocs., Inc.*, 303 S.E.2d 746, 748 (Ga. 1983) (noting that courts altering an employment restrictive covenant to make it more reasonable gives employers the incentive to cast overbroad provisions, which is harmful given the "in terrorem" effects of countless employees abiding by such overbroad provisions without making a fuss).

107. *See, e.g., Lampman*, 319 F. App'x at 300 (4th Cir. 2009). Note that Georgia's approach means that "if an otherwise valid contract contains one overly broad non-solicitation or non-competition covenant, the other non-solicitation or non-competition covenants in the same agreement are automatically rendered unenforceable." *Palmer & Cay*, 404 F.3d at 1304 (internal citations omitted). Please see Chapter 1 for more on severability.

108. *See, e.g., JAK Prods., Inc. v. Wiza*, 986 F.2d 1080, 1087 (7th Cir. 1993) (noting that "[i]n Indiana, the blue pencil doctrine applies to a covenant not to compete that is severable in its terms" and finding that the blue pencil doctrine could save the restrictive covenants in this case); *Dearborn v. Everett J. Prescott, Inc.*, 486 F. Supp. 2d 802, 810 (S.D. Ind. 2007) (applying Indiana's blue-pencil rule to find that mere striking would not render the provision enforceable); *Tech. Partners, Inc. v. Hart*, 298 F. App'x 238, 243-44 (4th Cir. 2008) (applying North Carolina's blue-pencil rule to find that mere striking would not render the provision enforceable).

109. *See, e.g., Dearborn*, 486 F. Supp. 2d at 810.

Whether a court is of the do-nothing or the blue-pencil school, it is unlikely to do anything more to abide by a contractual provision like that found in section 10 ("Remedies") of the Agreement, instructing a court that the restrictive covenant "be deemed to be modified to restrict the Executive's competition with the Company to the maximum extent of time, scope and geography which the court or arbitrator shall find enforceable."[110] How might this inform the Company's inclusion and drafting of such a provision (and other relevant provisions) in the Agreement?

The modern trend is the more flexible "rule of reasonableness" (sometimes termed the "partial enforcement") approach.[111] Courts subscribing to this approach are willing to rewrite an unreasonable clause so as to make it reasonable and, thereby, enforceable.[112] Note, however, that this approach merely permits — and does not require — courts to modify restrictive covenants, and courts may opt not to modify a restrictive covenant.[113]

---

110. *See, e.g., Nalco Chem.*, 984 F.2d at 806 (ruling that, under Wisconsin law, a savings clause instructing a court to enforce a non-compete covenant inasmuch as reasonable is not effective); *Prod. Action Int'l, Inc. v. Mero*, 277 F. Supp. 2d 919, 928-29 (S.D. Ind. 2003) (ruling that, under Indiana law, a court will not add terms to make a provision enforceable even if the provision says "to the extent permitted by law").

111. *See, e.g., A.N. Deringer v. Strough*, 103 F.3d 243, 246 (2d Cir. 1996) (finding that the rule of reasonableness applies under Vermont law); *Ferrofluidics Corp. v. Advanced Vacuum Components, Inc.*, 968 F.2d 1463, 1469 (1st Cir. 1992) (finding that the rule of reasonableness applies under Massachusetts and New Hampshire law); *Raimonde v. Van Vlerah*, 325 N.E.2d 544, 546-47 (Ohio 1975) (noting that many states had abandoned the blue-pencil approach in favor of a rule of reasonableness and opting to do the same); *Ehlers v. Iowa Warehouse Co.*, 188 N.W.2d 368, 372 (Iowa 1971) (adopting the rule of reasonableness in Iowa); *Solari Indus., Inc. v. Malady*, 264 A.2d 53, 57-61 (N.J. 1970) (adopting the rule of reasonableness in New Jersey).

112. *See supra* note 111.

113. *See, e.g., Lamp v. Am. Prosthetics, Inc.*, 379 N.W.2d 909, 910-11 (Iowa 1986) (declining to modify an overly broad restrictive covenant, where it was not properly preserved for appeal, because the *Ehlers* decision does not *require* a court to modify an unreasonable provision).

· CHAPTER THREE ·

SERVICES AGREEMENTS

Telcove is an internet service provider ("ISP"), which purchases capacity from "upstream" providers of internet services and sells that capacity to smaller ISPs "downstream," like Asch. Telcove and Asch entered into a three-year agreement ("Agreement") under which Telcove agreed to provide internet services to Asch. Shortly after activating Asch's internet service in February 2004, Telcove began receiving complaints about emails sent from internet protocol ("IP") addresses associated with Asch. Telcove eventually received nearly fifteen hundred complaints about emails sent from these IP addresses.... On April 28, 2004, Telcove informed Asch by letter that it was terminating its internet service on April 30, 2004. The letter notified Asch that the Agreement was being terminated in accordance with sections (b) and (g) of the Acceptable Use Policy set forth in the Agreement. However, after a discussion between counsel, Telcove agreed to continue providing internet service to Asch so that it would have time to procure internet services from another provider. On June 10, 2004, Telcove stopped providing internet service to Asch.

Asch did not reach agreement with another internet provider and ceased operations. Asch then initiated this civil action against Telcove. Telcove moved for summary judgment on these claims, arguing that an exculpatory clause in the Agreement prevented Asch from recovering the damages it sought. The District Court granted summary judgment in favor of Telcove and subsequently denied Asch's motion for reconsideration. Asch filed a timely appeal....

In this litigation, Asch argued that Telcove's termination of the Agreement destroyed its business. Accordingly, as damages, it sought the fair market value of its business, allegedly $1.43 million, in consequential damages. If the exculpatory clause is enforceable, by its terms it relieves Telcove of any liability for the damages Asch seeks because Asch agreed to release Telcove from "all liability or responsibility for any direct, indirect, incidental or consequential damages... suffered by [Asch] in connection with [its] use of or inability to use the Telcove internet services."

Asch Webhosting, Inc. v. Adelphia Bus. Solutions,
362 F. App'x 310, 311-13 (3d Cir. 2010).

Before entering a services agreement—or any agreement—a party should take care to understand the risks posed by the relationship and the terms contemplated. After all, an agreement essentially consists of two components: potential costs and benefits. After considering the risky scenarios and deciding which potential costs a party wishes to avoid or to minimize, the party may try to structure the agreement to limit its exposure to these risks. As the above-excerpted case illustrates, a party can effectively limit its liability exposure under a services contract (as a party may in most any contract). In the case expected above, Telcove accomplished this by including a provision excluding so-called "consequential" damages (and, while the court did not decide the case on this issue, by including a provision allowing for termination upon violation of certain policies).[1] In this chapter, we discuss both the benefits and costs of service agreements and further explore ways in which parties may manage potential costs and shift risk.

We turn our attention in this chapter to agreements for the purchase and sale of services between sophisticated business entities.[2] These agreements include, *inter alia*, independent contractor, consulting, master services, and outsourcing agreements and at a minimum address scope and price of services, term, ownership of any specific goods or products ("deliverables") resulting from the services, and confidentiality undertakings. Most agreements also include pricing assumptions, procedures for determining and specifying changes in scope and for purchasing out-of-scope services, performance standards, warranties,

---

1. *Asch Webhosting, Inc. v. Adelphia Bus. Solutions*, 362 F. App'x 310, 313-14 (3d Cir. 2010) (affirming the district court's decision to enforce the exculpatory clause at issue). The exculpatory provision in full provided:

Warranties/Disclaimers

TELCOVE'S INTERNET SERVICE IS PROVIDED ON AN "AS IS, AS AVAILABLE" BASIS UNLESS STATED OTHERWISE IN THE TELCOVE'S SERVICE LEVEL AGREEMENT (SLA). NO WARRANTIES, EXPRESS OR IMPLIED, INCLUDING, BUT NOT LIMITED TO, THOSE OF MERCHANTABILITY OR FITNESS FOR A PARTICULAR PURPOSE, ARE MADE WITH RESPECT TO TELCOVE'S INTERNET SERVICE(S) OR ANY INFORMATION OR SOFTWARE THEREIN. CUSTOMER RELEASES TELCOVE FROM ALL LIABILITY OR RESPONSIBILITY FOR ANY DIRECT, INDIRECT, INCIDENTAL OR CONSEQUENTIAL DAMAGES, INCLUDING BUT NOT LIMITED TO DAMAGES DUE TO LOSS OF REVENUES OR LOSS OF BUSINESS, SUFFERED BY CUSTOMER IN CONNECTION WITH THEIR USE OF OR INABILITY TO USE THE TELCOVE INTERNET SERVICES. WITHOUT LIMITING THE GENERALITY OF THE FOREGOING, TELCOVE DISCLAIMS TO THE FULL EXTENT PERMITTED BY APPLICABLE LAW ANY RESPONSIBILITY FOR (AND UNDER NO CIRCUMSTANCES SHALL BE LIABLE FOR) ANY CONDUCT, CONTENT, GOODS AND SERVICES AVAILABLE ON OR THROUGH THE INTERNET OR TELCOVE SERVICES. IN NO EVENT SHALL TELCOVE'S AGGREGATE LIABILITY EXCEED THE AMOUNT PAID BY CUSTOMER TO TELCOVE FOR THE TELCOVE SERVICES. USE OF ANY INFORMATION OBTAINED VIA TELCOVE'S INTERNET SERVICE IS AT THE CUSTOMER'S OWN RISK. TELCOVE SPECIFICALLY DISCLAIMS ANY RESPONSIBILITY FOR THE ACCURACY OR QUALITY OF THE INFORMATION OBTAINED THROUGH ITS SERVICES.

Id. at 312 (emphasis in original; bold removed).

2. We do not address consumer services contracts, and, accordingly, the Magnuson-Moss Act and other consumer protection laws are outside the scope of this chapter.

remedies, limitations of liability, indemnifications, and rights around subcontracting and termination.

The particular service offerings and engagements covered by these agreements are of different forms and complexities. They range from relatively straightforward agreements for staff extension (temporary workers) services, to those for the development and installation of complex IT systems, to those for multi-year outsourcings (in which a service provider undertakes to operate one or more often critical areas of a client's business such as data management, customer relationship management, accounting, or payroll).

In this chapter, we examine a services agreement that involves the provision of services between two business entities. But, first, we turn the floor over to a seasoned practitioner, experienced in the negotiation of services agreements.

A Practitioner Perspective: The More Contentious Terms in Services Contracts

Each party to a services agreement starts the negotiations from a mutual desire to agree upon the services to be provided by the service provider and to provide a foundation that maximizes the potential for project success. From that point on each party wants to make sure that they will receive the benefit of the bargain. In addition, they are trying to balance the potential risks with the proposed reward. With that as background, I separate my discussion into two parts: (i) themes I am seeing in the market, and (ii) specific, heavily negotiated issues.

I am seeing a number of counsel advise clients the contract must be used to maintain leverage over the other party. This not only leads them to take aggressive positions in a number of areas; it ignores the notion that a contract should be a platform for resolving issues and challenges in delivery and should provide balanced incentives for each party to perform. An example of an issue I often see in this area is a clear and defined list of responsibilities that each party, including the customer, must perform as a part of making the project successful. Many buyer counsel take the position that the customer should avoid taking on clear accountability, and that the provider should not be given any excuse if the project is not delivered successfully. I understand the appeal of that argument. Unfortunately it ends up taking clear accountability off of the buyer's personnel for getting essential tasks like reviewing and accepting project deliverables in a timely manner. It is a leading cause of projects going off course, which is not good for the buyer or the provider.

There are a number of specific terms and conditions that tend to be contentious as they relate to allocation of risk between the parties. These terms include warranties, damages, indemnifications, and limits of liability. More recently, discussions regarding compliance obligations particularly in the areas of data protection and export compliance are starting to be difficult. While the same terms present issues for outsourcing contracts, given the long-term nature of an outsourcing transaction, economic terms including benchmarking and termination become heavily negotiated as well.

> Nancy Laben, Senior Vice President
> and General Counsel
> AECOM

Prior to publication, Ms. Laben left Accenture LLP, where she was Deputy General Counsel, to join AECOM.

A. MASTER SERVICES AGREEMENT

The following agreement sets forth the rights and obligations of two corporations, one to provide Internet services to the other.

Things to Consider...

As you read through the following agreement, please consider these items. You will want to return to the agreement, as you study the substantive discussion that follows.

> **Context of Relationship.** Notice how this agreement's recitals (i.e., the "whereas" clauses) explain the context and history of this transaction and the underlying relationship between the parties. What is the historical context and purpose of this agreement?

> **Master Structure.** This agreement is a "master" agreement, which is a framework agreement that provides high-level terms to govern a relationship and that contemplates the use of specific statements (i.e., "Service Orders") to provide a second level of terms to govern particular transactions to occur within the relationship. Consider what this master agreement opts to address and what it leaves to be decided by Service Orders.

> **Shifting Risk.** Consider the ways in which certain provisions in this agreement—including the representation and warranty provisions, the force majeure clause, the indemnification provisions, and the limitation-of-liability provisions—operate to allocate certain risks between the parties.

CONFIDENTIAL MASTER SERVICES AGREEMENT[3]

THIS MASTER SERVICES AGREEMENT (the "Agreement") is made and entered into on November 16, 2009 and effective as of December 1, 2009 (the "Effective Date"), between AOL Inc., a Delaware corporation

---

3. AOL Inc., Confidential Master Services Agreement (Form 10-12B/A), at Exhibit 10.73 (Nov. 16, 2009), *available at* http://www.sec.gov/Archives/edgar/data/1468516/000119312509235507/dex1073.htm.

with offices at 770 Broadway, New York, New York 10003 (together with its Subsidiaries hereinafter referred to as "AOL"), and Time Warner Inc., a Delaware corporation with offices at One Time Warner Center, New York, NY 10019 ("Time Warner").

WHEREAS, AOL and Time Warner are parties to that certain Separation and Distribution Agreement, dated November 16, 2009, whereby they have agreed that Time Warner shall distribute its entire interest in AOL as a stock dividend to the Time Warner common stockholders with the result that AOL and Time Warner will no longer be affiliated companies (the "Separation").

WHEREAS, prior to the Separation AOL's predecessor, AOL LLC and its Affiliates, have been providing certain Internet services to Time Warner and Time Warner's Affiliates (other than AOL) (each of Time Warner and Time Warner's Affiliates other than AOL, a "TW Company," and together, the "TW Companies") pursuant to a Master Services Agreement between AOL LLC and Turner Broadcasting System, Inc., dated November 1, 2006 and a Managed Hosting Agreement between AOL LLC and Time, Inc., dated October 22, 2008 ("Previous Agreements") and certain other service orders and arrangements.

WHEREAS Time Warner has requested and AOL has agreed to terminate the Previous Agreements and continue to provide such services to the TW Companies (including, for the avoidance of doubt, AOL LLC) pursuant to this Agreement. AOL and each participating TW Company may be referred to herein as a "Party" and collectively the "Parties") [sic].

NOW, THEREFORE, in consideration of the mutual promises set forth herein, AOL and Time Warner hereby agree as follows:

1. **Definitions.** Capitalized terms used but not defined in the body of this Agreement shall have the respective meanings given to such terms in Exhibit A attached hereto.

2. **Provision of Services.**

2.1 **Previous Agreements.** As of the date of this Agreement, the Parties shall terminate the Previous Agreements; provided, however that notwithstanding the termination of the Previous Agreements, the Service Orders issued thereunder, and attached as Exhibits E and F, shall remain in effect and shall be governed by this Agreement. Time Warner represents and warrants that it has the authority to terminate the Previous Agreements and enter into this Agreement on behalf of itself and the TW Companies.

2.2 **Service Orders.** The type and scope of the Services to be provided to each TW Company under the terms of this Agreement, including any of the additional Services described in the attached Exhibits, shall be specified in an applicable Service Order. The fees for the Services will be set forth in the Service Order. Notwithstanding anything in this Agreement to the contrary, neither party has any obligation to execute any Service Order, and no Service Order shall be effective (i.e. become a Service Order) unless executed by both Parties; provided, however, that AOL and TW Company shall negotiate all Service Orders in good faith to reach agreement.

2.3 <u>Additional Service Orders.</u> If a TW Company and AOL execute multiple Service Orders, unless otherwise stated in any additional Service Orders, each additional Service Order will supplement rather than replace any prior Service Orders. This will only apply when the Service Orders are for the same Service. For example, if a TW Company has licensed five Licensed Spaces at a particular Collocation Facility and AOL agrees to license four more Licensed Spaces to such TW Company at that Collocation Facility, the second Service Order will specify an order for four Licensed Spaces, and the invoice to TW Company as to that Collocation Facility will reflect that Customer now has licensed nine Licensed Spaces at that Collocation Facility (under two separate Service Orders). It would not apply, if a Service Order was currently in place for Licensed Spaces and a new Service Order was executed for the delivery of a completely different Service. In that case there would be no supplement between the two.

2.4 <u>Use of Services by Affiliates Parties.</u> AOL acknowledges that certain TW Companies are, as of the Effective Date, making the Services available to (i) other Affiliates of Time Warner and (ii) certain joint operations in which such TW Company or its subsidiary is a participant. Such TW Companies may continue to make such Services available to such parties during the term in accordance with this Agreement.

3. **AOL Responsibilities.** AOL will provide the Services in a manner and with the same level and degree of care from and after the Separation as it has been providing to the TW Companies prior to the Separation.

3.1 <u>Services.</u> AOL shall provide Services to each TW Company as detailed in one or more Exhibits and Service Orders attached to this Agreement setting forth the nature, scope and price of such Services, subject to the terms and conditions contained herein, including all payment obligations. The parties acknowledge and agree that the Exhibits and Service Orders attached hereto shall describe the nature, scope and price of the Services as they have been provided to each TW Company immediately prior to the Separation it being the intention of the Parties that AOL continue to provide such Services from and after the Separation pursuant to the terms hereof. AOL reserves the right not to provide Services to any Customer Site or Customer Domain that AOL determines, in its reasonable discretion, to misappropriate or infringe upon the intellectual property or other rights of AOL or any Third Parties, if a TW Company fails to cure such misappropriation or infringement within five (5) business days of AOL's written notice of such misappropriation or infringement. For avoidance of doubt, in the event of a ruling by a court or agency of competent jurisdiction that a Customer Site or Customer Domain misappropriates or infringes upon the intellectual property rights of AOL or any Third Parties, AOL shall have the right to immediately discontinue Services without further liability to AOL or without further contractual liability by AOL to the affected TW Company under this Agreement, except for amounts payable by the affected TW Company and accrued upon the date of discontinuance of Services.

3.2 <u>Equipment.</u> Each Service Order will set forth the servers, software infrastructure, switches, and associated hardware being provided by AOL to provide the Services. Equipment owned, licensed or leased by AOL and provided to Customer shall hereinafter be referred to as "Equipment". Equipment owned, licensed or leased by a TW Company, including routers on the Customer Site, and provided to AOL shall hereinafter be referred to as "Customer Equipment". As between AOL and the relevant TW Company, AOL shall retain all title, rights and interest in and to the Equipment. AOL shall maintain the Equipment in accordance with its routine maintenance schedule. AOL shall use its Commercially Reasonable Efforts to provide upgrades and patches to maintain the Equipment as necessary for the Equipment to perform its obligations under this Agreement. AOL reserves the right to maintain and/or substitute any Equipment for the Services, as AOL in its sole discretion, deems necessary or reasonable in light of future product releases, industry changes or other events, so long as the Services continue to function materially in accordance with the performance metrics set forth herein; provided that such Equipment is certified by any Third Party whose software is being used on the Host, if necessary.

3.3 <u>Technical Support.</u> AOL shall provide 7x24 technical support for the Services via a network operating center ("NOC") or similar entity. In addition, AOL shall provide technical support, as set forth in the Exhibits, SLAs and the applicable Service Orders attached hereto.

3.4 <u>SLA.</u> The service level agreements ("SLAs") applicable for the Services are attached hereto as Exhibit B.

3.5 <u>Documentation.</u> AOL shall provide Documentation as AOL, in its sole discretion, deems necessary relating to access and use of the Services. Any TW Company may reasonably request information regarding the access to and use of the Services, that may or may not be contained in Documentation, and AOL shall make commercially reasonable efforts to provide such information.

3.6 <u>Reports.</u> As identified in the Exhibits and Service Orders, AOL shall provide to each applicable TW Company reports identifying

AOL's service level compliance to such TW Company, any applicable credits due such TW Company in accordance with the SLA, and such TW Company's utilization and billing detail.

3.7 Additional Deliverables. In connection with or in addition to the Deliverables, a TW Company may request Additional Deliverables from AOL. If AOL agrees to provide such Additional Deliverable, the Parties shall mutually agree upon and execute an additional Service Order. Such Service Order shall be executed by both Parties and attached as an Exhibit to this Agreement and shall be deemed to be incorporated herein by this reference.

3.8 Designated Contact. AOL shall provide a designated contact person for each TW Company ordering Services hereunder in the same manner and with the same level of access during the Term as it provided prior to the Separation.

4. Intentionally Omitted.

5. Fees and Payments.

5.1 Payments. Each TW Company will be billed in arrears for monthly and non-monthly Fees and any applicable Taxes for the Services provisioned during the previous calendar month. AOL shall provide itemized billing and separately itemized charges for taxable and non-taxable property and Services. Pursuant to Section 5.4, TW Companies may provide allocation data to be used to determine the tax situs of the Services. The applicable TW Company will pay all amounts owed under the Agreement (including, without limitation, any amounts owed under a Service Order) within forty-five (45) days of the date of each AOL invoice. All payments will be made in U.S. dollars and by wire transfer at the account information specified by AOL. Notwithstanding the foregoing to the contrary, AOL shall maintain the same billing practices from and after the Separation with respect to each TW Company as it maintained prior to the Separation.

5.2 Late Payments. In addition to all due and outstanding amounts, AOL reserves the right to charge and collect a Service fee of one percent (1.0%) over the U.S. prime rate per month, or the highest lawful rate, whichever is less (the "Late Fee"), for all such amounts, whether or not disputed, not paid on or before any due dates set forth in this Agreement. The Late Fee will be computed pro rata for each day any payment is late. In the event that AOL incurs expenses in collecting delinquent amounts from Customer, including reasonable attorneys' fees and court costs, AOL will provide Customer notice and a description of such expenses incurred by AOL and Customer will reimburse AOL for all such documented expenses within thirty (30) days after receiving such notice.

5.3 <u>Disputed Payments.</u> If a TW Company legitimately disputes any invoice amount, such TW Company shall: (i) pay AOL any undisputed portion of the invoice; (ii) provide AOL with a detailed written description of the disputed amount and the basis for such TW Company's dispute concerning such amount; and (iii) cooperate with AOL in promptly resolving any disputed amounts pursuant to Section 12.7.

5.4 <u>Taxes.</u> All Fees required by this Agreement and under the Services Schedules are exclusive of all federal, state, municipal, local or other governmental excise, sales, and use taxes imposed on the sale of the Services provided, now in force or enacted in the future ("Taxes"). Taxes do not include any taxes that are preempted by any Federal law now in force or enacted in the future, including, but not limited to, the Internet Tax Freedom Act currently set forth in the notes to 47 U.S.C. § 151. TW Companies will have sole discretion with respect to the allocation of Services among taxing jurisdictions for purposes of determining tax situs. TW Companies will not be responsible for any taxes or fees not contained within the definition of Taxes, including gross receipts or similar taxes, such as, but not limited to, the Ohio Commercial Activity Tax and the Virginia Business Professional Occupational and License Taxes. TW Companies will tender all such tax payments and reimbursements hereunder to AOL in accordance with Section 5.1 unless otherwise provided by law, such as in the case of an applicable direct pay permit. In addition, if applicable, Customer Equipment, whether or not physically affixed to the Licensed Spaces, will not be construed to be fixtures, and each TW Company is responsible for preparing and filing any necessary ad valorem property tax return for, and paying, any and all taxes separately levied or assessed against the Customer Equipment.

5.5 <u>Changes to Rates, Fees and Charges.</u> AOL has the right to modify any of its rates, fees and charges at any time. Any such modification during the Term of this Agreement will not be effective as to any Service Orders executed by the Parties prior to the modification but will be effective as to any Service Orders (including amendments to Service Orders) executed on or after the date of the modification, unless otherwise stated in a Service Order. Any modification shall take place no later than ten (10) business days after written notice of any such modification.

5.6 <u>Fraudulent Use of Services.</u> Each TW Company is responsible for all charges attributable to such TW Company and incurred respecting Services provided to such TW Company, even if incurred as the result of fraudulent or unauthorized use of Service; except that no TW Company shall be responsible for fraudulent or unauthorized use by AOL or its employees.

5.7 <u>Records Maintenance.</u> AOL shall maintain information, records, and documentation relating to the Services and AOL's performance thereof, including any such records, information, and documentation: (a) required to be maintained under applicable laws and regulations; or (b) necessary to verify AOL's compliance with the SLAs; or (c) necessary and sufficient to document the Services and Fees paid or payable by any TW Company under this Agreement, in the same manner after the Separation as it has been maintaining prior to the Separation. AOL shall cooperate with the TW Companies to provide records as may be reasonably requested by them.

6. Proprietary Rights.

6.1 <u>Customer Data.</u> Each TW Company shall own any and all data collected from use of the Services the Customer Sites, the content and Customer Domains (collectively, the "Customer Data"). Each TW Company hereby grants AOL and its Affiliates, as applicable, a non-exclusive, limited, revocable, worldwide, royalty-free license to copy, transmit, modify and use the Customer Data solely as necessary to perform its obligations under this Agreement or, with prior written notice by the applicable WT [sic] Company, where practicable, as necessary to comply with applicable laws, regulations, and government orders or requests. Such Customer Data shall not be used by AOL for any marketing or commercial purpose whatsoever and AOL shall not use Customer Data to contact any user of any TW Company products or services without the prior written consent of the applicable TW Company.

6.2 <u>AOL Intellectual Property.</u> Each TW Company acknowledges that all rights to patents, copyrights, trademarks, trade secrets, AOL's name and trademarks, and all intellectual property or proprietary and Confidential Information of any kind or character inherent in or appurtenant to the Services under this Agreement (the "AOL Works") are the sole and exclusive property of AOL. Each TW Company agrees and acknowledges that it is not purchasing title to the AOL Works and that none of the AOL Works or Deliverables shall be considered "works made for hire" within the meaning of the United States Copyright Act. All rights, title and interest in the AOL Works and Services, and derivative works thereof, shall be deemed to vest and remain vested in AOL, including, but not limited to, patents, copyrights, trademarks, trade secrets and other intellectual property rights. All rights, title, and interest in and to the AOL Works not expressly granted herein are reserved to AOL. Notwithstanding the foregoing or any other provision of this Agreement, nothing contained herein shall be construed as granting AOL any right, title or interest in or to any of the TW Companies' intellectual property rights or Confidential Information. Further, the Parties mutually acknowledge that, in providing Services pursuant to this Agreement, AOL and its personnel and agents may become acquainted with certain general ideas, concepts, know-how, methods, techniques, processes, tools, or skills pertaining to the Services and retained in the unaided memory of such personnel and agents (the "Residual Knowledge"). Each TW Company acknowledges and agrees that, excluding such TW Company's intellectual property rights and Confidential Information, AOL may use such Residual Knowledge for any purpose.

7. Insurance.

7.1 <u>Time Warner Required Insurance and Certificates of Insurance.</u> At the TW Companies' expense, during the Term of this Agreement, and with respect to any claims-made policies, for a period of three years thereafter, the TW Companies will maintain in full force and effect with regard to the activities at, or relating to, each of the Collocation or Transit Facilities, (1) Commercial General Liability Insurance in an amount not less than Two Million U.S. Dollars ($2,000,000) per occurrence for bodily injury and property damage, products and completed operations and advertising liability, which policy will include a contractual liability coverage insuring the activities of the TW Companies contemplated by this Agreement; (2) Worker's Compensation and employer's liability insurance in an amount not less than that prescribed by statutory limits; (3) Commercial Automobile Liability Insurance (including owned, non-owned, leased and hired vehicles), which insurance will apply to bodily injury and property damage in a combined single limit of no less than One Million U.S. Dollars ($1,000,000) per accident, if applicable; and (4) Errors and Omissions Liability Insurance covering liability for loss or damage due to an act, error, omission or negligence with a minimum limit per event of Five Million U.S. Dollars ($5,000,000). The TW Companies will ensure that all of the foregoing insurance covers all periods in which this Agreement is in effect, regardless of whether the claims are made during the Term or after this Agreement expires or is earlier terminated. The TW Companies will furnish AOL with certificates of insurance evidencing the minimum levels of insurance set forth herein and shall name AOL as an additional insured on all such policies. Such certificates of insurance will provide that each additional insured must be given at least thirty (30) days prior written notice of any termination, non-renewal, or modification of insurance coverage. All policies shall be primary and non-contributory to any insurance coverage maintained by AOL. Policies shall be written with a licensed insurance company with a Best's Rating of no less than A-VIII. The TW Companies shall, or shall cause their insurance company(ies) to, provide the additional insured thirty (30) days prior written notice of cancellation and/or any material change in any such policy. In the event AOL is providing Services to a Divested Entity in accordance with Section 11.3, such Divested Entity shall obtain or maintain insurance coverage in order to comply with this Section 7.

7.2 <u>AOL Required Insurance and Certificates of Insurance.</u> During the term of this Agreement, and with respect to any claims-made policies, for a period of three years thereafter, AOL shall maintain in full force and effect the following insurance coverage: (i) Commercial General Liability insurance with limits of no less than $2 million per occurrence and $2 million as an annual aggregate, including but not limited to products and completed operations and advertising liability; (ii) Workers' Compensation insurance in compliance with all statutory requirements; (iii) Errors and Omissions liability insurance covering the types of products and services (including all technology products) as well as cyber-liability provided by AOL under this Agreement with limits of no less than $5 million per claim and $5 million as an annual aggregate; and (iv) Business Auto liability insurance with no less than $2 million combined single limit. Time Warner and its Affiliates, successors and assigns existing now or hereafter shall be named as additional insured on all such policies with the exception of workers compensation insurance, as applicable. All policies shall be primary and non-contributory to any insurance coverage maintained by Time Warner. Policies shall be written with a licensed insurance company with a Best's Rating of no less than A-VIII. AOL shall provide a certificate of insurance evidencing all such coverage and a renewal certificate fifteen (15) days prior to the renewal of any such policy. Supplier shall, or shall cause its insurance company(ies) to, provide the additional insured thirty (30) days prior written notice of cancellation and/or any material change in any such policy.

7.3 <u>Customer Waiver and Waiver of Subrogation.</u> Notwithstanding anything in this Agreement to the contrary, Time Warner and each TW Company waives and releases any and all claims and rights of recovery against the AOL Parties for liability or damages if such liability or damage is covered by such insurance policies then in force or the insurance policies required pursuant to this Agreement (whether or not the insurance required pursuant to this Agreement is then in force and effect), whichever is broader. The for[e]going waiver shall not be limited by the amount of insurance then carried by the TW Companies and any deductible shall be deemed to be included in the insurance coverage. The TW Companies will cause and ensure that each insurance policy covering the Customer Equipment, Customer Domain, Customer Site and occurrences thereon, and all other areas of property, or occurrences thereon, will provide that the underwriters waive all claims and rights of recovery by subrogation against the AOL

Parties in connection with any liability or damage covered by such insurance policies.

7.4 <u>AOL Waiver and Waiver of Subrogation.</u> Notwithstanding anything in this Agreement to the contrary, AOL waives and releases any and all claims and rights of recovery against the TW Company Parties for liability or damages if such liability or damage is covered by AOL's insurance policies then in force or the insurance policies AOL is required to obtain pursuant to this Agreement (whether or not the insurance AOL is required to obtain is then in force and effect), whichever is broader. AOL's waiver shall not be limited by the amount of insurance then carried by AOL and any deductible shall be deemed to be included in the insurance coverage. AOL will cause and ensure that each insurance policy of AOL covering the AOL Data Centers, AOL Stadium, AOL Works, Collocation Facility, Equipment, Inter-rack-Cabling, Licensed Spaces, Transit Facilities and occurrences thereon, and all other areas of property, or occurrences thereon, will provide that the underwriters waive all claims and rights of recovery by subrogation against the TW Company Parties in connection with any liability or damage covered by AOL's insurance policies.

8. Confidentiality; Data Security.

8.1 <u>Confidential Information.</u> Each Party acknowledges that Confidential Information may be disclosed to the other Party during the course of this Agreement. During the Term and for a period of three (3) years following expiration or termination of this Agreement, each Party shall use at least the same degree of care as it employs to avoid unauthorized disclosure of its own information, but in no event less than a commercially reasonable degree of care and in the same manner and with the same degree of care from and after the Separation as prior to the Separation, to prevent the duplication or disclosure of Confidential Information of the other Party, other than by or to (i) its employees and Permitted Agents who need to know such Confidential Information for the purpose of performing the receiving Party's obligations or exercising its rights under this Agreement and then only to the extent needed to do so, provided that each such employee or Permitted Agent shall agree to comply with confidentiality requirements no less restrictive than those contained in this paragraph and is informed by the receiving Party of the confidential nature of such Confidential Information; and (ii) independent third party auditors that agree in writing to comply with confidentiality requirements no less restrictive than those contained herein. If a disclosure would be deemed a breach of this Agreement if committed by the receiving Party itself, then the receiving Party shall be liable to the other Party for any such disclosure made by its employees or Permitted Agents to whom it has disclosed the other Party's Confidential Information. If a receiving Party is legally compelled to disclose any of the disclosing Party's Confidential Information, then, prior to such disclosure, the receiving Party will (i) assert the confidential nature of the Confidential Information and (ii) cooperate fully with the disclosing Party in protecting against any such disclosure and/or obtaining a protective order narrowing the scope of such disclosure and/or use of the Confidential Information. In the event such protection is not obtained, the receiving Party shall disclose the Confidential Information only to the extent necessary to comply with the applicable legal requirements.

8.2 **Reimbursement for Disclosures.** The applicable TW Company shall reimburse AOL for any costs incurred by AOL related to disclosures of Confidential Information of such TW Company made by AOL pursuant to a court order, subpoena, or government order, including but not limited to the clean up and repair of any impacted servers and the replacement cost of any affected machines or Equipment. AOL shall reimburse the applicable TW Company for any costs incurred by such TW Company related to disclosures of Confidential Information of AOL made by such TW Company pursuant to a court order, subpoena, or government order, including but not limited to the clean up and repair of any impacted servers and the replacement cost of any affected machines or Customer Equipment.

8.3 **Data Security.** In order to protect the Confidential Information, AOL shall maintain appropriate standard security measures with respect to the Confidential Information including without limitation, technical, physical and organizational controls, and shall maintain the confidentiality, integrity and availability thereto, in the same manner and with the same level and degree of care from and after the Separation as it has been providing with respect to the Services prior to the Separation. In the event that AOL's systems or property are compromised such that any Confidential Information owned by any TW Company or any employee or customer of a TW Company may have been acquired or is reasonably believed to have been, or is reasonably believed to be at risk of becoming, acquired by unauthorized parties (an "Information Breach"), AOL will, within forty-eight (48) hours of the time it becomes aware of such Information Breach, report any Information Breach to each affected TW Company at the contact information set forth in Schedule 8.3 attached hereto. In the event of an Information Breach, AOL shall cooperate with the applicable TW Company to meet any obligations of such TW Company to notify individuals whose personal information has been compromised as a result of an Information Breach; provided that in no event shall AOL serve any notice or otherwise publicize an Information Breach without the prior written consent of such TW Company.

9. Representations and Warranties.

Each Party represents and warrants to the other Party that: (a) such Party has the full corporate right, power and authority to enter into the Agreement, to grant the rights and licenses granted hereunder and to perform the acts required of it hereunder; (b) such Party shall comply with the provisions of all applicable federal, state, country and local laws, ordinances, regulations and codes; (c) the execution of the Agreement by such Party, and the performance by such Party of its obligations and duties hereunder, do not and will not violate any agreement to which such Party is a party or by which it is otherwise bound; (d) when executed and delivered by such Party, the Agreement will constitute the legal, valid and binding obligation of such Party, enforceable against such Party in accordance with its terms; and (e) such Party acknowledges that the other Party makes no representations, warranties or agreements related to the subject matter hereof that are not expressly provided for in the Agreement.

10. Indemnity and Limitation of Liability.

10.1 <u>Mutual Indemnification.</u> Each of AOL on the one hand and each TW Company on the other hand (the "Indemnifying Party") shall defend, indemnify, save and hold harmless the other and such other's Affiliates and each of its and their officers, directors, agents, affiliates, distributors, franchisees and employees (the "Indemnified Parties"), from any and all Third-Party claims, demands, liabilities, costs or expenses, including reasonable attorneys' fees ("Losses"), resulting from any Third Party claim, suit, action, or proceeding (each, an "Action") brought against one or more of the Indemnified Parties arising out of or resulting from (i) the Indemnifying Party's material breach of any obligation, representation, or warranty of this Agreement; (ii) any injury (including death) to any natural person or damages to tangible property or facilities thereof to the extent arising out of or resulting from the negligence or misconduct of the Indemnifying Party, its officers, employees, servants, affiliates, agents, contractors, licensees, invitees and vendors in connection with the performance by the Indemnifying Party of this Agreement; (iii) any violation by an Indemnifying Party of any regulation, rule, statute or court order of any governmental authority in connection with the performance by the Indemnifying Party of this Agreement.

10.2 <u>Intellectual Property Indemnification.</u> AOL shall defend, indemnify, save and hold harmless the TW Companies and each of their respective the officers, directors, agents, Affiliates, distributors, franchisees and Employees from and against any and all Losses arising out of or relating to any claim that the Services infringe a patent, trademark, trade name, trade secret, copyright or any other intellectual property right (an "Intellectual Property Infringement") of any

Third Party. In addition to any indemnification payable pursuant to this Agreement, in the event any Third Party claims an Intellectual Property Infringement and without prejudice to any rights of any TW Company, AOL may at its own expense and option either: (i) procure the right for the Services to continue to be used in the manner provided in the Agreement; (ii) make such alterations, modifications or adjustments to the Services so that they become non-infringing without incurring a material diminution in performance or function; or (iii) replace the Services with non-infringing substitutes provided that such substitutes do not produce a material diminution in performance or function, or (iv) if AOL determines that the for[e]going is not commercially practicable, then AOL may terminate the Services without further liability.

Each TW Company shall defend, indemnify, save and hold harmless AOL and its officers, directors, agents, Affiliates, distributors, franchisees and employees from and against any and all Losses arising out of or relating to (a) such TW Company's Customer Site or any Customer Domain (including, any claim by a customer or end-user of the Customer Site); (b) claims related to any authorizations, rights or licenses necessary to provide the Customer Site; (c) claims that the Customer Site, any Updates, the Customer Domain, the registration of the same, and the manner in which a TW Company uses or permits others to use such Customer Site or Customer Domain directly or indirectly, misappropriate or infringe any copyright, trade secret, or trademark or any Patent or other legal rights of any Third Party and (d) claims for reimbursement for any costs arising from or related to the subpoena of any Customer Data, or Customer connection, including but not limited to costs associated with the clean-up of any impacted servers and the replacement cost of any affected machines or Equipment.

10.3 <u>General Provisions.</u> If any Action arises as to which a right of indemnification provided in this Section 10 applies, the Indemnified Party shall promptly notify the Indemnifying Party thereof (provided that any failure to provide timely notice shall not relieve a Party of its obligations under this Section 10 except to the extent actually prejudiced), and allow the Indemnifying Party the opportunity to assume direction and control of the defense against such Action, at the Indemnifying Party's sole expense, including, the settlement thereof at the sole option of the Indemnifying Party to the extent that Indemnified Party's liability is not thereby invoked. The Indemnified Party shall cooperate with the indemnifying Party in the disposition of any such matter (at the Indemnifying Party's expense). The Indemnified Party shall have the right and option to participate in the defense of any Action as to which this Section 10 applies with separate counsel at the Indemnified Party's election and cost. If the Indemnifying Party fails or declines to assume the defense of any such Action within ten (10) days after notice thereof, the Indemnified Party may assume the defense thereof for the account and at the risk of the Indemnifying Party. The Indemnifying Party shall pay promptly to the Indemnified Party any Losses to which the indemnity under this Section 10 relates, as they are incurred.

10.4 <u>Limitation of Indemnity.</u> A Party's indemnity obligations shall be mitigated to the extent of the negligence, recklessness or intentional misconduct of the other Party or the other Party's Affiliates, directors, officers, employees, consultants or agent. The TW Companies agree and acknowledge that AOL shall be in no way responsible for, and each TW Company shall indemnify and hold AOL harmless for, any claims arising from the actions, policies or conduct of the users of the Customer Site of such TW Company. No TW Company shall be obligated under the indemnity provisions in Sections 10.1 or 10.2 for any Losses solely caused by or resulting from the acts or omissions of any other TW Company and AOL shall look only to the applicable TW Company for enforcement of such TW Company's indemnity obligations hereunder.

10.5 <u>SERVICE LEVELS.</u> UNDER NO CIRCUMSTANCES WILL A TW COMPANY RECEIVE A CREDIT FOR ANY NON-RECURRING CHARGES EVEN WHERE SUCH TW COMPANY IS ENTITLED TO A CREDIT FOR RECURRING CHARGES. NOTWITHSTANDING THE FOREGOING, ANY CLAIM BY A TW COMPANY FOR CREDITS WILL BE DEEMED CONCLUSIVELY WAIVED UNLESS, WITHIN THIRTY (30) DAYS AFTER THE DATE OF THE OCCURRENCE OF THE EVENT GIVING RISE TO THE CREDIT, THE APPLICABLE TW COMPANY NOTIFIES AOL THAT SUCH TW COMPANY IS SEEKING A CREDIT AND SPECIFYING THE BASIS FOR THE CLAIM. IN ADDITION, WITHOUT LIMITING THE FOREGOING, ALL OTHER CLAIMS BY A TW COMPANY OF WHATEVER NATURE AGAINST AOL WILL BE DEEMED CONCLUSIVELY TO HAVE BEEN WAIVED UNLESS SUCH TW COMPANY NOTIFIES AOL (SPECIFYING THE NATURE OF THE CLAIM) WITHIN SIX (6) MONTHS AFTER THE DATE OF THE OCCURRENCE GIVING RISE TO THE CLAIM.

10.6 <u>No Other Warranty.</u> EXCEPT AS EXPRESSLY PROVIDED IN THIS AGREEMENT, THE DELIVERABLES ARE PROVIDED ON AN "AS IS" BASIS, THE TW COMPANIES' USE OF THE DELIVERABLES IS AT ITS OWN RISK. EXCEPT AS EXPRESSLY SET FORTH HEREIN, NO PARTY MAKES, AND EACH HEREBY DISCLAIMS, ANY AND ALL EXPRESS AND/OR IMPLIED WARRANTIES, INCLUDING, BUT NOT LIMITED TO, WARRANTIES OF MERCHANTABILITY, FITNESS FOR A PARTICULAR PURPOSE, AND ANY WARRANTIES ARISING FROM

A COURSE OF DEALING, USAGE, OR TRADE PRACTICE. AOL DOES NOT WARRANT THAT THE DELIVERABLES SHALL BE UNINTERRUPTED, ERROR-FREE OR COMPLETELY SECURE.

10.7 <u>Disclaimer of Actions Caused by and/or Under the Control of Third Parties.</u> AOL DOES NOT AND CANNOT CONTROL THE FLOW OF DATA TO OR FROM AOL'S DATA CENTERS AND THE INTERNET. SUCH FLOW DEPENDS IN LARGE PART ON THE PERFORMANCE OF INTERNET SERVICES PROVIDED OR CONTROLLED BY THIRD PARTIES. AT TIMES, ACTIONS OR INACTIONS CAUSED BY THESE THIRD PARTIES CAN PRODUCE SITUATIONS IN WHICH A TW COMPANY'S CONNECTIONS TO THE INTERNET (OR PORTIONS THEREOF) MAY BE IMPAIRED OR DISRUPTED. ALTHOUGH AOL SHALL USE COMMERCIALLY REASONABLE EFFORTS TO TAKE ACTIONS IT DEEMS APPROPRIATE TO REMEDY AND AVOID SUCH EVENTS, AOL CANNOT GUARANTEE THAT THEY WILL NOT OCCUR. ACCORDINGLY, AOL DISCLAIMS ANY AND ALL LIABILITY RESULTING FROM OR RELATED TO SUCH EVENTS. AOL DISCLAIMS ANY AND ALL LIABILITY FOR ANY DAMAGES ARISING FROM OR RELATED TO ANY THIRD PARTY SOFTWARE USED BY AOL OR A TW COMPANY, WHETHER PROVIDED BY AOL OR A TW COMPANY, EXCEPT FOR AND LIMITED TO THE SERVICE LEVELS AND CREDITS SET FORTH IN EXHIBIT B.

10.8 <u>Exclusions.</u> EXCEPT AS EXPRESSLY PROVIDED HEREIN, AOL SHALL NOT BE LIABLE TO ANY TW COMPANY, ITS EMPLOYEES, ITS AUTHORIZED REPRESENTATIVES, OR ANY THIRD PARTY FOR ANY CLAIMS ARISING OUT OF OR RELATED TO THIS AGREEMENT, CUSTOMER SITE, CUSTOMER DATA, OR OTHERWISE. EXCEPT FOR (I) ACTS OF GROSS NEGLIGENCE OR WILLFUL MISCONDUCT, (II) BREACHES OF CONFIDENTIALITY OBLIGATIONS AND (II[I]) EACH PARTY'S INDEMNIFICATION OBLIGATIONS HEREUNDER, NO PARTY SHALL BE LIABLE TO ANY OTHER PARTY FOR ANY LOST REVENUE, LOST PROFIT, REPLACEMENT GOODS, LOSS OF TECHNOLOGY, RIGHTS OR SERVICES, INCIDENTAL, PUNITIVE, INDIRECT OR CONSEQUENTIAL DAMAGES, LOSS OF DATA, OR INTERRUPTION OR LOSS OF USE OF SERVICE OR OF ANY EQUIPMENT OR BUSINESS, EVEN IF ADVISED OF THE POSSIBILITY OF SUCH DAMAGE, WHETHER UNDER THEORY OF CONTRACT, TORT (INCLUDING NEGLIGENCE), STRICT LIABILITY OR OTHERWISE.

10.9 <u>Maximum Liability.</u> NOTWITHSTANDING ANYTHING TO THE CONTRARY IN THIS AGREEMENT, EXCEPT FOR (I) ACTS OF GROSS NEGLIGENCE OR WILLFUL MISCONDUCT, (II) BREACHES OF CONFIDENTIALITY OBLIGATIONS AND (II[I]) EACH PARTY'S INDEMNIFICATION OBLIGATIONS HEREUNDER, AS BETWEEN

AOL AND EACH TW COMPANY, EACH PARTY'S MAXIMUM AGGREGATE LIABILITY FOR ALL MATTERS RELATED TO, IN CONNECTION WITH, OR ARISING OUT OF, THIS AGREEMENT SHALL NOT EXCEED THE TOTAL AMOUNT PAID BY EACH TW COMPANY TO AOL HEREUNDER FOR THE PRIOR TWELVE (12) MONTH PERIOD.

10.10 Basis of the Bargain; Failure of Essential Purpose. Each TW Company acknowledges that AOL has established its Fees and entered into this Agreement in reliance upon the limitations of liability and the disclaimers of warranties and damages as set forth herein, and that the same form an essential basis of the bargain between the Parties. The Parties agree that the limitations and exclusions of liability and disclaimers specified in this Agreement shall survive and apply even if found to have failed of their essential purpose.

11. Term and Termination.

11.1 Term. The Agreement shall be in effect through the two year anniversary of the Effective Date (the "Term"; and the date of expiration, the "Expiration Date") unless terminated earlier in accordance with this Agreement. The Agreement cannot be renewed by any Party and all Services will cease on the Expiration Date. Each Service Order shall include a term for each Service (the "Service Term"). For the avoidance of doubt, and notwithstanding Section 12.9, in the event that the Service Term or Term of any Service Order conflicts with this Section 11.1, this Section 11.1 shall prevail (i.e., no Service Order shall extend beyond the Term of the Agreement for any reason).

11.2 Termination or Expiration.

11.2.1 For Cause. Either Party shall have the right to terminate this Agreement by giving notice of termination to the other Party, if: (i) the other breaches any material term or condition of this Agreement and fails to cure such breach within thirty (30) days after receipt of notice of the same (other than breaches addressed by Section 11.2.3 or Section 5.1 of Exhibit C); (ii) the other becomes the subject of a voluntary petition in bankruptcy or any voluntary proceeding relating to insolvency, receivership, liquidation, or composition for the benefit of creditors; or (iii) the other Party becomes the subject of an involuntary petition in bankruptcy or any involuntary proceeding relating to insolvency, receivership, liquidation, or composition for the benefit of creditors, if such petition or proceeding is not dismissed within sixty (60) days of filing.

11.2.2 Additional Grounds for Termination by AOL. AOL may terminate this Agreement or any Service Order as to any TW Company and discontinue Service without liability immediately (i) in the event of a ruling by a court or agency of competent jurisdiction that such TW Company violated any law, rule, regulation or policy of any government authority related to the Service; (ii) if such TW Company fails to cure its fraudulent use of the Services after fifteen (15) days' notice from AOL, provided that if such TW Company, in AOL's sole reasonable determination, has taken material steps to cure its fraudulent use of the Services, AOL may not terminate this Agreement or the applicable Service Order as to such TW Company pursuant to this provision of the Agreement; or (iii) if a court or other government authority prohibits AOL from furnishing the Services.

11.2.3 For Non-Payment by a TW Company. Notwithstanding Section 11.2.1, AOL shall have the right to terminate this Agreement (and thereby cease providing all Deliverables under this Agreement) as to a defaulting TW Company only by giving fifteen (15) days notice of non-payment to such defaulting TW Company if any of AOL's undisputed invoices to such TW Company remain unpaid for more than sixty (60) days after the due date indicated on such invoice. No TW Company shall be liable for the fees or charges incurred or payable by any other TW Company and AOL shall look only to the applicable TW Company for payment of such TW Company's invoices.

11.2.4 For Failure to Meet Service Levels. For the purposes of this Section 11.2.4, failure to meet any of the Service Levels in the SLA shall not be deemed a breach of this Agreement by AOL, unless otherwise defined as such in the SLA; provided, however, that if there is any dispute between the applicable Parties as to whether or not such a material breach as described above has in fact occurred, such dispute shall be referred to dispute resolution procedures in accordance with Section 12.7 and this Agreement shall remain in effect until such dispute is resolved in accordance therewith.

11.2.5 Effect of Expiration or Termination. Upon the effective date of expiration or termination of this Agreement or any one or more of the Services: (i) AOL shall cease providing the terminated Services (which may be some or all of the Services); (ii) the applicable TW Companies shall pay AOL (a) any Fees due for Services that have been rendered up to the effective termination/expiration date (provided, that in the event certain Services are terminated prior to others and the Fees for such Services are bundled with Fees for continuing Services, then the Fees shall be reduced pro rata to account for the reduction in Services) and (b) any Out-Of-Pocket Expenses incurred by AOL while providing the Services; and (iii) each Party shall return or destroy all Confidential Information of the other Party in its possession at the time of expiration or termination within forty-five (45) days after such expiration or termination, and shall not make or retain any copies of such Confidential Information except as required to comply with any applicable legal or accounting record-keeping requirement. Upon termination, AOL shall delete Customer Data from its production systems and shall make best efforts to delete or return Customer Data from all other systems and back-ups.

11.2.6 For Convenience. Subject to Section 11.2.5 above, prior to the Expiration Date, any TW Company may terminate this Agreement as to itself and/or any of its Service Orders for any one or more of the Services for any reason. The terminating TW Company shall provide AOL with sixty (60) days notice and shall provide AOL with a project plan for migration of the Services to another provider.

11.3 <u>Divestiture.</u> If Time Warner sells or divests an entity or assets (each, a "Divested Entity"), Time Warner shall inform AOL promptly upon the closing of the divestiture transaction. AOL shall make the Services available to any Divested Entity on the same terms and conditions as stated herein until the end of the Term.

11.4 <u>Transition.</u> Each TW Company shall be responsible for migrating off of all Services and obtaining services from another services provider prior to the expiration of the Term. During the Term, AOL shall cooperate with the TW Companies in the migration of all Services to another provider and shall provide that information and assistance in the transition process as the TW Companies may reasonably request.

12. Miscellaneous.

12.1 <u>Marketing.</u> Neither AOL on the one hand nor any TW Company on the other hand shall use the other Party's name(s), trademark(s), trade name(s) or logo(s), whether or not registered, in publicity releases, marketing materials, or other publicly-available documents (including publicly-available web pages) without securing the prior written approval of the other.

12.2 <u>Assignment.</u> Neither Party shall assign the Agreement or any right, interest or benefit under the Agreement without the prior written consent of the other, such consent not to be unreasonably withheld, conditioned or delayed. Notwithstanding the foregoing, either Party may assign or transfer its rights under this Agreement without the other's consent to: (a) any Subsidiary of such Party; or (b) another business entity in connection with a transaction pursuant to which the business entity acquires all or substantially all of the property or assets of AOL to which this Agreement relates. Subject to the foregoing, this Agreement shall bind and inure to the benefit of each Party's successors and permitted assigns.

12.3 <u>Subcontractors.</u> In providing any of the Deliverables under this Agreement, AOL may, in its sole discretion, subcontract for or otherwise use services provided by Third Parties or any AOL Affiliate, provided that AOL shall remain jointly and severally liable for the performance of such Third Party subcontractor and for all obligations under this Agreement.

12.4 <u>Injunctive Relief.</u> It is understood and agreed that, notwithstanding any other provisions of this Agreement, any breach or threatened breach of the provisions of this Agreement by either AOL on the one hand or any TW Company on the other hand may cause the other irreparable damage for which recovery of money damages would be inadequate and that each Party therefore may seek and obtain timely injunctive relief to protect its rights under this Agreement in addition to any and all other remedies available at law or in equity.

12.5 <u>Force Majeure.</u> No Party will have any liability for any failure or delay in its performance arising from, or relating to, the failure of power, equipment, systems, connections or services not under the control of such party, or the unavailability, inadequate, untimely or poor performance or non-performance of any facilities outside the control of such Party. Without limiting the foregoing, neither Party will be liable for any failure or delay in its performance under this Agreement due to any cause beyond its reasonable control, including, without limitation, national emergencies; acts of war or other civil commotion; acts of God; earthquakes; fires; flood; adverse weather conditions; explosions; other catastrophes; embargo; insurrections; riots; acts of terrorism, sabotage; strikes; lockouts; work stoppages or other labor difficulties; any law, order, regulation or other action of any governing authority or agency thereof; or failure of the Internet (each a "Force Majeure Event") provided that such Party has taken Commercially Reasonable Efforts to resolve or mitigate the effects of such Force Majeure Event. During any period in which Services to any one or more TW Company are reduced, suspended or terminated by AOL pursuant to this Section 12.5, the affected TW Company(ies) shall not be obligated to make payment of Fees with respect to the unfulfilled, suspended or terminated portion of Services until Services are fully resumed. In the event any Force Majeure event shall occur for more than fifteen (15) consecutive business days, the unaffected party shall have the right to terminate the affected Services, upon ten (10) business days written notice to the other party, provided that if an affected TW Company terminates this Agreement, such TW Company shall reimburse AOL for all of AOL's reasonable Out-Of-Pocket Expenses incurred through the date of termination.

12.6 <u>Survival.</u> The provisions of Sections 5, 6, 8, 10, 11.2.5, 12.4, 12.6, and 12.8 of this Agreement shall survive any expiration or termination of this Agreement. In addition, all provisions of this Agreement that can only be given proper effect if they survive the termination of this Agreement will survive the termination of this Agreement. This Agreement will be valid as to any obligation incurred prior to termination of this Agreement. Without limiting the foregoing, the TW Companies will pay all amounts owed to AOL under this Agreement, including, without limitation, any amounts that may become due after the expiration or earlier termination of this Agreement.

12.7 <u>Dispute Resolution.</u> All disputes arising under or relating to this Agreement, except for disputes relating to issues of proprietary rights, including but not limited to intellectual property and confidentiality, shall be governed by this Section 12.7. Any dispute subject to this Section 12.7 will be negotiated between the applicable Parties (at appropriate levels of senior management) commencing upon written notice from one Party to the other for a period of thirty (30) days. Settlement discussions and materials will be confidential and inadmissible in any subsequent proceeding without written consent from all applicable Parties. If the dispute is not resolved by negotiation within thirty (30) days following such notice, the affected Parties may seek remedies in equity or law.

12.8 <u>Legal Construction.</u> Subject to Section 12.7, this Agreement is made under and shall be governed by and construed in accordance with the laws of the State of New York (except that body of law controlling conflicts of law) and specifically excluding from application to this Agreement that law known as the United Nations Convention on the International Sale of Goods. Each Party irrevocably consents to the exclusive jurisdiction of the federal courts located in the Southern District of New York and the local courts located in Manhattan, New York, New York, USA. in connection with any action violating this Agreement. In the event of any conflict between these terms and conditions and those of any Service Order, the Service Order shall prevail.

12.9 <u>Entire Agreement; Counterparts.</u> This Agreement, including all Exhibits and Service Orders, but only as to the Parties to that Service Order, and documents incorporated herein by reference, constitutes the complete and exclusive agreement between the Parties with respect to the subject matter hereof, and supersedes and replaces any and all prior or contemporaneous discussions, negotiations, understandings and agreements, written and oral, regarding such subject matter. This Agreement may be executed in two or more counterparts, each of which shall be deemed an original, but all of which together shall constitute one and the same instrument. In the event of any conflict between the terms of this Agreement, and the terms of any Exhibit or Service Order, the documents shall control in the following order: (1) Service Order; (2) Exhibit; and (3) Agreement.

12.10 <u>Notice.</u> Any notice, approval, request, authorization, direction or other communication under this Agreement will be given in writing and will be deemed to have been delivered and given for all purposes (i) on the delivery date if delivered by confirmed facsimile to a then-valid facsimile number assigned exclusively to the intended recipient; (ii) on the delivery date if delivered personally to the Party to whom the same is directed; (iii) one business day after deposit with a commercial overnight carrier, with written verification of receipt; or (iv) five business days after the mailing date, whether or not actually received, if sent by U.S. mail, return receipt requested, postage and charges prepaid, or any other means of rapid mail delivery for which a receipt is available. In the case of AOL, such notice will be provided to the Deputy General Counsel ([omitted]), each at the address of AOL set forth in the first paragraph of this Agreement. In the case of Time Warner except as otherwise specified herein, the notice address shall be the address for Time Warner set forth in the first paragraph of this Agreement attention to the Vice President, Information Technology, with a copy to the General Counsel ([omitted]). If to any other TW Company, to the address set forth in the Service Order for such TW Company.

12.11 <u>Relationship of Parties.</u> This Agreement shall not constitute, create, or in any way be interpreted as a joint venture, partnership, subsidiary, or formal business organization of any kind. Neither AOL nor the TW Companies have the power to bind the other or incur obligations on the other's behalf without the other's prior written consent, except as otherwise expressly provided herein.

12.12 <u>Amendment and Waiver.</u> The provisions, terms, and covenants of this Agreement may not be amended nor modified and the observance of any provision of this Agreement may not be waived (either generally or in any particular instance and either retroactively or prospectively) without a writing signed by all Parties to which the amendment or modification is intended to apply. The failure of either Party to enforce its rights under this Agreement at any time for any period shall not be construed as a waiver of such rights.

12.13 <u>Severability.</u> In the event that any of the provisions of this Agreement are held unenforceable by a court or other tribunal of competent jurisdiction, the remainder of this Agreement shall remain in full force and effect.

12.14 <u>Non-Exclusivity.</u> Nothing herein shall limit either Party's ability to enter into any agreements with any Third Party for the provision of services similar to those provided and purchased hereunder.

[Signature Page Omitted.]

Exhibit A—Definitions

"Action" has the meaning set forth in Section 10.1 of the Agreement.

"Additional Deliverables" means any products, services, or documents beyond the Deliverables expressly to be provided by AOL pursuant to this Agreement or any Service Order hereunder.

"Affiliate" means, with respect to any Person, any other Person which, directly or indirectly, controls, is controlled by, or is under common control with, such other Person. A Person shall be deemed to "control" another Person if it owns, directly or indirectly, more than fifty percent (50%) of the outstanding voting securities, capital stock, or other comparable equity or ownership interest of such Person.

"Agreement" has the meaning set forth in the preamble.

"AOL" has the meaning set forth in the preamble.

"AOL Data Centers" means AOL owned or controlled facilities used to Host the Customer Site.

"AOL Employee" means, for the purposes of this Agreement only, any employee [or] contractor of AOL.

"AOL Stadium" (Trademark) is an infrastructure of routers, switches, servers and software required to operate the delivery of static Internet content and accompanying management services.

"AOL Works" has the meaning set forth in Section 6.2 of the Agreement.

"Backup Service Level" has the meaning set forth in Exhibit B—2.

"Business Day" means Monday, Tuesday, Wednesday, Thursday, or Friday, excluding holidays observed in the United States of America.

"Collocation Facility" means the building where Licensed Space is located as defined in a Service Order.

"Collocation Network Service" has the meaning set forth in Exhibit B—1.

"Collocation Service Order" means a request to collocate submitted by Customer in the form of Exhibit C-2.

"Commercially Reasonable Efforts" means that degree of skill, effort, expertise, and resources that a business entity's employees with ordinary skill, ability, and experience, under circumstances similar to those addressed herein, would reasonably use and otherwise apply with respect to fulfilling the obligations assumed hereunder.

"Confidential Information" means information relating to or disclosed in the course of the Agreement, which is or should be reasonably understood to be confidential or proprietary to the disclosing Party, including, but not limited to, the material terms of this Agreement, Customer Data, information about technical processes and formulas, source codes, product designs, sales, cost and other unpublished financial information, pricing, product and business plans, projections, and marketing data. Confidential Information shall not include information (a) already

lawfully known to or independently developed by the receiving Party, (b) disclosed in published materials, (c) generally known to the public, or (d) lawfully obtained by the receiving Party from any Third Party which lawfully was entitled to have and share the information. Notwithstanding anything herein to the contrary, personally identifiable information about a natural person shall be deemed to be Confidential Information for all purposes.

"*Connection Notice*" means written notice from AOL that the Transit Service ordered by a TW Company has been installed by AOL pursuant to the applicable Transit Service Order.

"*Content*" means the digital audio, video, data, text, animation, graphics, photographs, artwork, links, software, applications, other multimedia materials, and combinations of any or all of the foregoing presented in the Customer Site.

"*Customer Data*" has the meaning set forth in Section 6.1 of the Agreement.

"*Customer Domain*" means the domain names to be Hosted by AOL on behalf of a TW Company.

"*Customer Equipment*" has the meaning set forth in Section 3.2 of the Agreement.

"*Customer Notification*" means a communication from AOL to a TW Company informing such TW Company of AOL's acceptance of the Transit Service Order.

"*Customer Premises*" means the location or locations occupied by the TW Companies or its end users to which Transit Services are to be delivered.

"*Customer Site*" means all of the architecture and Content for each of the participating TW Company's website(s) to be located at the Customer Domains.

"*Deliverable*" means any part of the Services or Technical Support, Documentation, Equipment or any other products or services delivered or made available by AOL to any TW Company under this Agreement.

"*Divested Entity*" has the meaning set forth in Section 11.3 of the Agreement.

"*Documentation*" means specifications, descriptions and written instructions, including on-line instructions.

"*Dollar*" and the sign "*$*" mean the lawful money of the United States.

"*ENMP*" has the meaning set forth in section 3.2 of Exhibit B.

"*Effective Date*" has the meaning set forth in the preamble.

"*Employee*" means, for the purposes of this Agreement only, any employee or contractor of a TW Company.

"*Equipment*" has the meaning set forth in Section 3.2 of the Agreement.

"*Expiration Date*" has the meaning set forth in Section 11.1.

"Fees" means any fee, pricing, or payment of any type under the Agreement, excluding Taxes.

"Force Majeure Event" has the meaning set forth in Section 12.5.

"Host" means to provide the software and hardware infrastructure for and the maintenance, operation and administration of certain TW Companies' server software applications.

"Implement" means to acquire and install any applicable Equipment and other implementation services agreed upon by the applicable Parties. *"Implementation"* shall be construed accordingly.

"Include," *"includes"*, and *"including"*, whether or not capitalized, mean "include but are not limited to", "includes but is not limited to", and "including but not limited to", respectively.

"Indemnified Party" has the meaning set forth in Section 10.1 of the Agreement.

"Indemnifying Party" has the meaning set forth in Section 10.1 of the Agreement.

"Information Breach" has the meaning set forth in Section 8.3 of the Agreement.

"Intellectual Property Infringement" has the meaning set forth in Section 10.2 of the Agreement.

"Inter-rack Cabling" means cabling that connects Customer Equipment (i) to electric power sources designated by AOL; (ii) to AOL's routers and distribution network to the extent necessary as determined by AOL; and (iii) upon a TW Company's request, to other Customer Equipment located in separate Licensed Spaces in the same room.

"Late Fee" has the meaning set forth in Section 5.2 of the Agreement.

"Launch" means the date on which Implementation has been completed and the Customer Site is launched via the Services.

"Licensed Spaces" means the areas licensed by a TW Company under this Agreement as to the amount of spaces. AOL will determine the rooms and the location in the rooms where the Licensed Space(s) will be located, and AOL will notify the applicable TW Company of the locations.

"Local Loop" means the connection between Customer Premises and the AOL intercity backbone network.

"Losses" has the meaning set forth in Section 10.1 of the Agreement.

"NOC" means network operating center.

"Out-of-Pocket Expenses" means reasonable, verifiable and actual expenses incurred and paid by AOL to a Third Party, but excluding AOL's overhead costs (or allocations thereof), administrative expenses or other mark-ups and excluding expenses which could reasonably have been avoided or which could reasonably be recouped by AOL.

"Party" has the meaning set forth in the recitals.

"Permitted Agents" shall mean attorneys, accountants, auditors, lenders and contractors.

"Person" means any individual, corporation, partnership, joint venture, trust, unincorporated organization, government or other department or agency thereof or any other entity.

"PNMP" has the meaning set forth in Section 3.1 of Exhibit B.

"Residual Knowledge" has the meaning set forth in Section 6.2 of the Agreement.

"Service Level" has the meaning set forth in Exhibit B.

"Service Order" means the service orders executed by the Parties pursuant to the terms of this Agreement.

"Services" means the services, functions and responsibilities of AOL as described in the Agreement (including the Exhibits and Service Orders) as such services, functions and responsibilities may evolve during the Term and may be supplemented and enhanced in accordance with the Agreement.

"Service Outage" has the meaning set forth in Section [this is Mentioned but not defined in Section 3.2 of Exhibit B]

"Service Term" means the term for each Service included on each Service Order.

"SLA" has the meaning set forth in Exhibit B of the Agreement.

"Subsidiary" means an entity in which a Party holds over fifty percent (50%) of the equity or voting interest.

"Systems Service Level" has the meaning set forth in Exhibit B—3.

"Taxes" has the meaning set forth in Section 5.4 of the Agreement.

"Technical Specifications" means the technical specifications communicated by AOL to a TW Company as supported by the Services.

"Technical Support" has the meaning set forth in Section 3.3 of the Agreement.

"Term" has the meaning set forth in Section 11.1 of the Agreement.

"Third Party" means a Person other than an Employee, AOL Employee, AOL or any TW Company.

"Third Party Software" means software owned by Third Party vendors.

"Transit Facility" or *"Transit Facilities"* means property owned or leased by AOL and used to deliver the Transit Service, including without limitation terminal and other equipment, wires, lines, ports, routers, switches, channel service units, data service units, cabinets, racks, private rooms and the like.

"Transit Service" means Internet protocol (IP) transit service offered by AOL pursuant to a Transit Service Order. As part of this IP Transit Service, AOL will advertise all the Internet routes/prefixes which collectively form the Internet Routing Table.

"Transit Service Order" means a request for Transit Service submitted by Customer in the form of Exhibit D-1.

"Transit Service Term" means the term for Transit Service included on the Transit Service Order.

"*TW Company*" has the meaning set forth in the preamble to this Agreement.

"*Unauthorized Code*" shall mean (i) any virus, Trojan horse, worm, or other software routines designed to permit unauthorized access, or to disable, erase, modify, deactivate or otherwise harm software, hardware, or data or (ii) any back door, time bomb, drop dead device, protect codes, data destruct keys, or other software routines designed to disable a computer program automatically with the passage of time.

"*Update*" has the meaning set forth in Exhibit C to this Agreement.

"*Web Hosting Service Level Identifier*" has the meaning set forth in Exhibit B—8.

[Other Exhibits Omitted]

---

1. Familiarity Breeds Fluency: A Review

Prior to this Agreement, you had not encountered a services agreement in this book. Yet, hopefully you found much of the Agreement to be somewhat familiar.

- For instance, you should understand the purpose and the effect of the "whereas" (i.e., recital) clauses in this Agreement. What are recital clauses, and what are their purpose and effect? Do the recitals in this Agreement purport to impose any rights or obligations on AOL or TW? Would it be appropriate or wise for these clauses to do so? (See Chapter 1.)

- Subsection 8.1 imposes confidentiality obligations. Are these obligations unilateral or mutual? What is included and what is excluded from the meaning of "Confidential Information"? In whose interest—AOL's or TW's—is a broad definition of Confidential Information? What results if a Party's employee discloses Confidential Information? Why might a disclosing party still wish that a receiving party's employees and Permitted Agents still agree to confidentiality obligations at least as restrictive as the Agreement's? (See Chapter 1.)

- Subsection 10.10 provides that certain provisions (e.g., limitations of liability, disclaimers of warranty) are the essential basis of the bargain. If these provisions are found unenforceable, could they be severed from the rest of the Agreement? If these provisions are breached, is the breach likely to constitute a "material breach"? (See Chapters 1 and 2.)

- Subsection 12.12 contains no-oral-modification and no-waiver provisions. How are courts likely to treat these provisions? Is an oral modification likely to be effective? (What law governs this Agreement?) Is a waiver less likely to be found? (See Chapter 2.)

- Under § 11, what is the term, and how may each Party terminate the Agreement? May a Party terminate for convenience? According to § 12.6, what provisions survive the expiration or termination of this Agreement? Why do you think these provisions were selected for survival? (See Chapters 1 and 2.)

2. Master Agreements: Structure, Precedence, and Incorporation by Reference

As its title attests, this Agreement is a master services agreement (sometimes called an "MSA"). Like any services agreement, a master services agreement contemplates a services relationship and provides the terms that will govern that relationship. However, a master services agreement additionally contemplates that for specific services to be provided, the parties will issue a "Service Order" (sometimes called a "work order," a "purchase order," or a "statement of work," often referred to as an "SOW"), which provides the specifications and other details pertinent to the particular services to be performed under the order. For instance, section 2.2 of the Agreement provides, "The type and scope of the Services to be provided to each TW Company under the terms of this Agreement . . . shall be specified in an applicable Service Order. The fees for the Services will be set forth in the Service Order." Accordingly, a master services agreement acts as a global framework agreement, governing the entire services relationship and incorporating by reference (or being incorporated *into*) specific work orders to be issued (contemporaneously with, or subsequent to, the execution of the Agreement) as specific work is commissioned.

What is the legal force of service orders? What is the legal relationship between Service Orders and the Master Services Agreement? As foreshadowed in the previous paragraph, typically either a master services agreement will incorporate work orders into the agreement by reference, or a work order will incorporate a master services agreement into the work order.[4] For exam-

---

4. As a general rule, when two or more documents are executed and pertain to the same transaction, they are to be read and construed together, as a whole. RESTATEMENT (SECOND) OF CONTRACTS § 202(2) (1981) ("A writing is interpreted as a whole, and all writings that are part of the same transaction are interpreted together."); *W. United Life Assurance Co. v. Hayden*, 64 F.3d 833, 842 (3d Cir. 1995) ("Under Pennsylvania law, when two or more writings are executed at the same time and involve the same transaction, they should be construed as a whole. If the writings pertain to the same transaction, it does not matter that the parties to each writing are not the same. This general rule also applies where several agreements are made as part of one transaction even though they are executed at different times.") Accordingly, absent a finding that either of a master services agreement and a statement of work is fully integrated and excludes all other documents, a court may understand a statement of work and a master

ple, section 3.7 of the Agreement provides that if the Parties mutually agree and execute an additional Service Order, then the Service Order "shall be deemed to be incorporated herein by this reference." As the Third Circuit has explained, "As a matter of contract law, incorporation by reference is generally effective to accomplish its intended purpose where the provision to which reference is made has a reasonably clear and ascertainable meaning."[5] Moreover, for incorporation to be effective, the incorporating provision should clearly and specifically identify the document (or provision therein) it purports to incorporate.[6] On this, the Federal Circuit has advised:

> Our Circuit likewise does not require "magic words" of reference or of incorporation. However, we stress that parties...may easily avoid or at least minimize the risk of having to litigate this issue by simply adopting widely-used and judicially-approved language of incorporation, such as "is hereby incorporated by reference" or "is hereby incorporated as though fully set forth herein," and by including specific and sufficient information identifying a particular document, such as the title, date, parties to, and section headings of any document to be incorporated.[7]

For those among us who wish to "avoid or at least minimize the risk of having to litigate," take note. Is the above MSA likely to be found to have incorporated a particular Service Order?

Is there a concern where an agreement provides for the incorporation of a *future* document's terms—provisions of a document that does not exist when the original, incorporating agreement is executed? As a general rule, an agreement may incorporate by reference a provision that is to exist in the future.[8] However, there is some authority for just the opposite: "[W]hat is being incorporated must *actually exist at the time of the incorporation,*

---

services agreement, executed as part of a single transaction, together to be a single agreement to be read as a whole.

5. *Century Indem. Co. v. Certain Underwriters at Lloyd's, London, Subscribing to Retrocessional Agreement Nos. 950548, 950549, and 950646,* 584 F.3d 513, 534 (3d Cir. 2009) (Pennsylvania law) (internal citations omitted); *see also OBS Co., Inc. v. Pace Constr. Corp.,* 558 So. 2d 404 (Fla. 1990).

6. *See Northrop Grumman Info. Tech., Inc. v. United States,* 535 F.3d 1339, 1345 (Fed. Cir. 2008) ("[T]o incorporate extrinsic material by reference [the contract] must explicitly, or at least precisely, identify the written material being incorporated."); *PaineWebber Inc. v. Bybyk,* 81 F.3d 1193, 1201 (2d Cir. 1996) (under New York law, "a party will not be bound to the terms of any document unless it is clearly identified in the agreement").

7. *Northrop Grumman Info. Tech., Inc.,* 535 F.3d at 1346.

8. *See, e.g., Lamb v. Emhart Corp.,* 47 F.3d 551, 559 (2d Cir. 1995) (under Connecticut law, finding amended stock option agreements to be incorporated into termination agreement); *PB Group, Inc. v. Proform Thermal Sys., Inc.,* No. 06-CV-15755, 2008 WL 2714426 (E.D. Mich. July 8, 2008); *DVD Copy Control Ass'n v. Kaleidescape, Inc.,* 176 Cal. App. 4th 697 (Cal. App. 6th Dist. 2009); *Martinson v. Brooks Equip. Leasing, Inc.,* 36 Wis. 2d 209, 217 (Wis. 1967) ("[M]atters not presently in existence may nevertheless be made a part of a contract by reference."); *see also Grandis Family P'ship, Ltd. v. Hess Group,* 588 F. Supp. 2d 1319, 1328 (S.D. Fla. 2008) (finding that reference to non-contemporaneous purchase order was not sufficiently specific and direct to effect an incorporation by reference).

so the parties can know exactly what they are incorporating."[9] In those jurisdictions where a future provision may be incorporated by reference, for incorporation to be effective, at least one court has required that there be some ascertainable standard for the creation of the future terms "that can provide a substitute for a present knowledge of and assent to the subsequently adopted provisions."[10] For example, where a stock option plan to be incorporated could be modified only in accordance with certain restrictions, including shareholder approval, such future modification was found to be subject to an "ascertainable standard."[11] Another line of authority has required that to enforce a would-be incorporated future provision against a party, that party must have "adopted" the incorporated provision.[12] As an example, where a party performed in accordance with the specifications of a putatively incorporated document that came to exist after incorporation, the party was found to have "adopted" the document and incorporation of the future document was effective.[13] Notice that under sections 2.2 and 3.7, the Parties under this Agreement must both execute a future Service Order for the Agreement to incorporate that Service Order. Is a court likely to find this to satisfy either or both of the "ascertainable standard" and the "adoption" rules? Given that some courts are reluctant to enforce the incorporation by reference of a future provision at all, what might the Parties do to ensure that all the terms of their arrangement are enforceable? One solution is to incorporate the terms of the MSA into each Service Order. Incorporation by reference of the earlier-in-time MSA should pose none of the "future" issues presented by the incorporation of a future Service Order at the time of MSA execution. Do you see any drawbacks to this approach? Do you see any other solutions?

Could a Service Order ever stand on its own as a contract binding the parties thereto? The answer appears to be "yes."[14] Accordingly, could a work order alter a contractual relationship in contravention of a master services agree-

---

9. *Gilbert Street Developers, LLC v. La Quinta Homes, LLC*, 174 Cal. App. 4th 1185, 1194 (Cal. App. 4th Dist. 2009) (emphasis in original); *see also U.S. for use of Lighting and Power Services, Inc. v. Interface Constr. Corp.*, 553 F.3d 1150, 1155 (8th Cir. 2009) ("[U]nder Missouri law, a contract cannot incorporate by reference a second contract that is not yet in existence."); *Skouras v. Admiralty Enters. Inc.*, 386 A.2d 674, 678 n.3 (Del. Ch. 1978) ("[S]trict requirements for incorporating by reference an otherwise independent document are that such document be in existence when the incorporating document is executed.").

10. *Lamb*, 47 F.3d at 559 (Connecticut law) (citing *Housing Auth. of Hartford v. McKenzie*, 412 A.2d 1143, 1146 (Conn. Super. Ct. 1979)).

11. *Id.* at 559.

12. *Martinson*, 36 Wis. 2d at 217 ("[P]lans and specifications unagreed upon may [not] be incorporated without some form of adoption by the person sought to be charged with performance.").

13. *See id.* at 217-18.

14. *See, e.g., Pervel Indus., Inc. v. T.M. Wallcovering, Inc.*, 871 F.2d 7, 8 (2d Cir. 1989) (finding purchase orders to be contracts unto themselves); *Grandis Family P'ship*, 588 F. Supp. 2d at 1334-35 (discussing that a purchase order may be a contract unto itself but declining to find so on the facts of the case). Please also reference the discussion of contract modification in Chapter 2. While a master services agreement may control what it incorporates by reference, could such a master services agreement control what may

ment that purports to incorporate the work order? A party wishing not to bestow independent contractual force onto an SOW may wish to state as much in the SOW itself and specify its relationship to the master agreement. Please reference the discussion, in Chapter 2, of the modification of contractual rights by future contracts.

The effect of incorporating an external provision by reference is that the incorporated provision is treated as any other term of the agreement.[15] Accordingly, unless otherwise provided by contract, terms incorporated into an agreement by reference have no special favored or disfavored status vis-à-vis the other terms of the agreement. Indeed, just like the other terms of an agreement, the incorporated terms might create ambiguities within a contract and must be considered in determining whether or not a contract is ambiguous.[16] An agreement may specify which provisions (e.g., the provisions incorporated by reference, the agreement's original provisions) should take "precedence" over the other, should there be a conflict between terms. For example, master agreements will often provide that, in the event that a provision in an SOW contradicts a provision within the master agreement, the conflict should be resolved in accordance with the master agreement's terms. Courts will generally respect an order-of-precedence provision as a manifestation of party intent, inasmuch as the provision unambiguously guides the court to a coherent reading of the contract.[17] However, keep in mind that courts, where at all possible, will read contractual terms to be consistent and to avoid finding a conflict (and, so, the need to invoke a precedence provision).[18] Accordingly, an order-of-precedence provision can afford

---

constitute a future contract or whether a future contract may modify the rights and obligations provided by the master services agreement?

15. *See, e.g., Lamb*, 47 F.3d at 558; *Wilson v. Wilson*, 577 N.E.2d 1323, 1329 (Ill. App. Ct. 1991).

16. *See, e.g., J.E. Hathman, Inc. v. Sigma Alpha Epsilon Club*, 491 S.W.2d 261 (Mo. 1973).

17. *See, e.g., Cessna Aircraft Co. v. Dalton*, 126 F.3d 1442, 1454 (Fed. Cir. 1997). However, what would happen if both the MSA and the statement of work each included a precedence provision that contradicted each other (e.g., the MSA incorporated the SOW by reference, the MSA included a provision that the MSA trumped the SOW, and the SOW included a provision that the SOW trumped the MSA)? Here, there would be a contradiction between the very terms that explain how to resolve contradictions! For the purposes of reading the MSA as incorporating—or incorporated into—the SOW, the terms of the MSA and the SOW must be read as a whole and with equal weight, and neither can resolve the issue. Even if the agreement is fully integrated (see the discussion of integration clauses in Chapter 1), extrinsic evidence may be admitted to resolve this ambiguity.

18. *See, e.g., Pub. Serv. Co. of Oklahoma v. United States*, 88 Fed. Cl. 250, 255 n.5 (2009) ("The court does not, however, see any inconsistency here that requires application of the conflicts or order of precedence clauses of the contract."); *U.S. Fidelity and Guar. Co. v. Stanley Contracting, Inc.*, 396 F. Supp. 2d 1157, 1169 (D. Or. 2005); *CooperVision, Inc. v. Intek Integration Techs., Inc.*, 794 N.Y.S.2d 812, 818 (N.Y. Sup. 2005) ("Accordingly, the mere absence of a forum selection clause in the Implementation Agreement does not create a conflict as between it and the Software License Agreement sufficient to invoke the former's order of precedence clause."). In addition, inasmuch as an SOW may stand on its own as a contract between two parties, an order-of-precedence provision in a master agreement—while instructive for how to read the master agreement as incorporating the SOW—might not govern how to read the SOW as a later-in-time contract unto itself.

only so much comfort, and a party should not rely on such a provision in lieu of clear and consistent drafting.

As a matter of practice, some service providers will prefer a precedence provision that provides that the master service agreement governs, as the master agreement acts as the core document to govern the relationship and, accordingly, is often negotiated heavily and carefully.[19] By contrast, parties may wish statements of work to control so as to provide the flexibility necessary to tailor the contract for each project. Or, parties may draft a hybrid arrangement, providing, for example, a general precedence provision in the master agreement that the master agreement governs but including a phrase (e.g., "except as provided by a Service Order") in certain provisions indicating that such provisions are the default unless a statement of work provides otherwise.

3. Definitions Sections

Most sophisticated documents will define several terms. A contract may define terms either in a separate definitions section or as each term arises throughout the agreement. There are benefits and costs to each approach. Definitions sections provide a single repository of all defined terms, allowing a future reader of the contract (for instance, a judge or arbitrator) easy reference. However, definitions sections may add to the heft of an agreement, may make an agreement optically more formal (which may be a positive or a negative, depending on the context of the agreement), and do not necessarily make for intuitive reading. An alternative approach involves defining an agreement's meaningful terms as each appears initially in the document (sometimes called "in-line" definitions). This approach may make for relatively simpler reading the first time the definition is used (depending on the length of the definition), but how does a reader know where to find a particular definition again without searching through the many pages of the document? One hybrid approach involves defining terms as they first appear but also including an index of defined terms, preceding or following the rest of the agreement, that directs the reader to where each defined term is located in the agreement. Another hybrid approach is to define some terms the first time they appear and other terms in a separate section. As you can see, there are many approaches to defining terms, and certainly creative parties may devise other schemes still. Regardless of the approach taken, a contract will signify that a term is to be given a specific meaning throughout

---

19. This, of course, is certainly not to suggest that work orders are not or should not be carefully negotiated, as well.

the agreement by enclosing the term in quotation marks where the term is defined and by capitalizing the term each time such term is used as defined in the agreement.

Exhibit A of the Agreement is an example of a definitions section. Notice how each defined term is enclosed in quotation marks where the term is assigned a particular meaning. Also notice that, when the Agreement wishes to use a particular term as so contractually defined, the first letter of each word in the term is capitalized. Even Agreements that include a definitions section are likely to define some basic terms outside of the section. For example, this Agreement defines, *inter alia*, Agreement, Effective Date, and Parties within its first few paragraphs.

Why define terms? Words have several meanings, especially across different contexts. Definitions sections can help ensure that the *parties'* definitions—and only the parties' definitions—will govern the agreement by directing the potential, future reader (imagine an overburdened judge or arbitrator) to the parties' intended meaning for each particular term of importance.[20] However, opting out of Webster's is only one purpose of the definitions section. Sophisticated contractual documents can quickly grow highly technical and nuanced. The parties may be hard-pressed to define a particular term in fewer than 200 words. (For illustration, the Parties use 141 words to explain the meaning of Confidential Information in Exhibit A.) Rather than adding confusion and weight to an already potentially confusing and weighty document, parties may choose to define a term a single time so that they may incorporate that definition by reference throughout the document.

Parties may agree to certain imprecise definitions purposefully. There will be times where parties prefer to leave aspects of their bargain vague: Perhaps articulation with specificity is unduly difficult in the abstract or unduly contentious in negotiations. Parties may prefer to strike the deal with some imprecision, assuming the risk of an unfavorable interpretation down the line, than not to strike the deal at all.

Definitions sections are only one tool for attaining precision. In the context of services agreements, another place where precision may be desirable is in delineating what is and is not expected of the services provider—that is, the "scope" of the provider's obligations, an important part of services agreements as alluded to in an earlier practitioner comment. To discuss this issue of scope, we have called upon another seasoned practitioner to provide insight.

---

20. *See, e.g.*, Restatement (Second) of Contracts § 202(3) (1981) ("Unless a different intention is manifested, (a) where language has a generally prevailing meaning, it is interpreted in accordance with that meaning; (b) technical terms and words of art are given their technical meaning when used in a transaction within their technical field.").

A Practitioner Perspective: The Perils of "Scope Creep"

Scope creep is one of the top causes of failed services projects (a services project is failing if it either exceeds estimated budget or schedule by more than 25% or fails to deliver material functionality documented in the requirements). As a legal practitioner supporting a services project, it is important to understand what scope creep is, what causes it and what the lawyer can do to assist the project team to deliver the project successfully.

Scope creep occurs when the agreed-upon scope of work is increased without addressing the resulting impact to project schedule, budget and resources. Given the dynamic nature of many projects, scope change is inevitable. Successful project delivery requires project teams to embrace this reality; it is critical that project teams implement the necessary techniques, of which there are many, to properly manage it. Most projects suffer from scope creep for one (or more) of the following reasons:

1) project scope is poorly defined before project is initiated;
2) the duration of the project is long (more than a year);
3) management of project scope during delivery is inadequate;
4) project governance is ineffective; or
5) the project manager is inexperienced.

While the proper management of these five areas of risk rests largely with the project manager, sponsor and key stakeholders, the legal practitioner plays an important role as well.

The legal practitioner can help avoid scope creep by ensuring the project teams are properly focused and equipped to manage it. Below are four techniques a lawyer can employ to manage the potential problem of scope creep:

1) **Define scope before work.** Ensure project scope is clearly documented and understood by all parties. In addition, all key scope-related project assumptions and dependencies should be documented. All of these points should also be clearly identified in the contract between the parties. This is not easy, as the scope and related dependencies and assumptions are often stated in very technical language filled with acronyms. Do your best to keep it simple, using plain language to describe these items. This will require the lawyer to work closely with the project teams. If the teams are struggling to document the project's scope in sufficient detail, it is usually an indicator that more work is needed to better understand the scope. In these cases, an initial project focusing all parties on determining and documenting the scope is highly recommended before broader project work begins. Parties should avoid beginning work without properly defining scope, as the results are usually poor.

2) Employ shorter project schedule(s). The longer the project, the greater opportunity for change. As a result, a lawyer may encourage the team to reduce the project duration into smaller, more discrete working efforts when possible (no longer than a year is recommended). Using delivery methods that allow for manageable project timelines is strongly recommended.

3) Embrace and manage change. Change is inevitable, so plan for it and effectively manage it. To accomplish this, an effective change management process and committee of professionals must be implemented before work begins. There are many good examples of proven change management processes. Choose the one that is right for the project and its team members. Once it is established, it is equally important to test the process with a real (and insignificant) change to ensure it meets the needs of the project. The change management process should be clearly documented in the contract, together with a change management form noting any impacts to schedule, price and scope, as well as any changes in responsibilities and appropriate approval needed to make the change officially part of the new scope. Additionally, the lawyer should periodically review the change logs (it will reflect the change orders) and be part of the change management board to ensure the changes are carefully considered and documented consistent with the contract. *Note*: If change orders or changes are not reflected in the change logs (the document that records all change orders), it is usually not an indicator that there are no changes (remember change is inevitable); it is almost certainly an indicator that the change management process is not being followed and the project may be headed for trouble!

4) Ensure proper governance. Without effective governance from project teams, stakeholders and sponsors, chaos will infect the project making scope creep, among other project ailments, inevitable. Consequently, it is important to ensure the right people are involved in the project at the right levels, providing adequate representation of the project team, users, stakeholders and sponsor. Most governance structures include a sponsor, steering committee and project team, among others. Generally, a project manager is primarily responsible for managing project scope and change management, among many other things. For this reason, a project manager should have a proven track record of successfully delivering projects of similar size, complexity and domain area. Moreover, meeting frequency and communications (e.g. meeting notes, status reports) standards should be implemented as the project begins and rigorously adhered to throughout the life of the project. These elements should all be addressed in the contract—here, the more detail the better. Finally, the lawyer should be involved in the governance of the project and review regular status reports to address early warning signs of scope creep should it appear and to ensure the change management process is being followed.

Michel Gahard, General Manager
Microsoft Corporation
Lecturer in Law
The University of Chicago Law School

4. Service Levels and Credits

As we see in § 3.4, the AOL Agreement contemplates the use of "service levels" as agreed to in separate service level agreements.

One of the primary drivers of the decision to retain a service provider or to outsource one or more functional areas of a client's business is to increase the quality and reduce the associated costs to the client of performing the service itself. How one measures quality of performance and service is no small matter and often forms the basis of protracted contractual negotiations.

In what instances would a client seek to impose contractual requirements upon its service provider to meet particular levels of service? From the number of rings a call center takes to answer a call, to the number of matters a customer relations management (CRM) worker successfully handles, to the number of lines of data that can be properly processed in a particular time period, the quality and level of performance of services is of critical importance. Specifying service levels in this way can serve to add articulation and specificity to a perhaps vague "performance standard" (e.g., "best efforts," "commercially reasonable"), which we discuss further in Chapter 4.

Client and service provider alike frequently are concerned with establishing and delineating the particular levels of services required under the contract and with developing and implementing procedures and tools to measure and report the service provider's performance in meeting agreed-upon service levels. Service providers cannot deliver against a "moving target," and clients do not want to pay for deficient services.

As you read the excerpted service level provision below, consider the role service credits play in compensating the client for the service provider's failure to meet established service levels. Do service credits constitute an exclusive remedy (a concept we address later in this chapter) or does the contract permit the client to accept service credits and also sue to recover additional damages? Is benchmarking used to determine the cost of services? Is it necessary to consider service levels when exercising benchmarking rights? Do satisfaction surveys impose additional service level obligations upon the service provider and in this way constitute a "second bite of the apple" for the client?

SECTION 12. SERVICE LEVELS[21]

12.1. <u>Service Levels.</u> HP shall perform the Services with promptness and diligence, in a workmanlike manner and in accordance with the Service Levels set forth in Schedule B (and such other service levels as may be agreed upon for

---

21. Excerpted from Cowen Holdings, Inc. (formerly Cowen Group, Inc.), Services Agreement (Form S-1/A), at Exhibit 10.7 (May 17, 2006), *available at* http://www.sec.gov/Archives/edgar/data/1355007/000104746906007356/a2168660zex-10_7.htm.

those services) and the standards set forth in Section 4.1. HP shall be excused from its obligation to perform the Services in accordance with the applicable Service Levels if, and to the extent that, it cannot meet such Service Levels as a result of SG Cowen failing to perform any obligation hereunder for which the affected Services are dependent; provided that HP promptly notifies SG Cowen of any such failure of SG Cowen to perform an obligation which will or is likely to cause, or has caused, HP to fail to meet the applicable Service Levels.

12.2. Measurement and Monitoring Tools. As of the Services Commencement Date, HP shall implement and utilize the measurement and monitoring tools and procedures set forth in the SOW which are required to measure and report HP's performance of the Services against the Service Levels as specified in Schedule B (and such other service levels as may be agreed upon for those services). HP shall ensure that any measurement and monitoring tools are generally commercially available and that HP's use of such measurement and monitoring tools shall not adversely affect the performance of the Equipment and/or Systems, and will promptly replace any measurement and monitoring tool which degrades or otherwise negatively impacts the Equipment and/or Systems. HP shall further ensure that such measurement and monitoring tools shall permit reporting at a level of detail sufficient to verify compliance with the Service Levels, and HP acknowledges that such measurement and monitoring tools shall be subject to audit by SG Cowen. HP shall provide SG Cowen with information and access to all such measurement and monitoring tools and procedures upon request, for purposes of verification.

12.3. Reports. As part of the Base Services, HP shall provide monthly performance reports to SG Cowen as agreed upon by the Parties from time to time. As one such report, HP shall provide a monthly performance report, which shall be delivered to SG Cowen within seven (7) days after the end of each calendar month, describing HP's performance of the Services in the preceding month (the "Monthly Performance Report"). Such Monthly Performance Report shall:

(a) separately address HP's performance in each area of the Services;

(b) for each area of the Services, assess the degree to which HP has attained or failed to attain the pertinent objectives in that area as described in this Agreement, including with respect to the Service Levels;

(c) explain deviations from the Service Levels and other applicable performance standards and include a plan for corrective action for each such deviation;

(d) describe the status of problem resolution efforts, ongoing projects, and other initiatives, and the status of HP's performance with respect to change requests; and

(e) include such documentation and other information as SG Cowen may reasonably request for purposes of verifying compliance with, and meeting the objectives of, this Agreement.

12.4. SG Cowen Satisfaction Surveys. No less frequently than twice annually, HP shall perform customer satisfaction surveys acceptable to SG Cowen and shall share the results of those surveys with SG Cowen. All such results shall be deemed the property and Confidential Information of SG Cowen. HP and SG Cowen shall mutually agree upon the form and content of such surveys during Transition.

12.5. <u>Benchmarking.</u> SG Cowen reserves the right from time to time, at its discretion, beginning in the second year of this Agreement and with respect to a complete benchmark no more than once annually, to obtain the services of an independent third party (the "Benchmarker") to benchmark the charges for help-desk Services. The pool of potential benchmarkers shall consist of the following third party firms: (a) Gartner Group; (b) Compass; (c) Meta; and (d) Everest. Additional third parties may be added if one or more of the pre-approved benchmarkers is unavailable, so long as they are independent (i.e., not a competitor of HP or an outsourcing consultant to SG Cowen), are experienced in conducting benchmarking in the relevant industry and region, and possess the information necessary to arrive at an objective and proper result. If none of the pre-approved benchmark service providers is available to perform the benchmark services, then the parties will use best efforts to agree upon a third party qualified to perform the services. If the Parties do not agree within twenty (20) business days of SG Cowen's request, then the third party shall be designated by SG Cowen. SG Cowen will bear the costs and expenses of conducting the benchmark and all results of the benchmark and materials created pursuant to the Benchmark shall be SG Cowen's sole and exclusive property and Confidential Information. The Benchmarker shall perform the benchmarking in accordance with the Benchmarker's documented procedures which shall be provided to the Parties prior to the start of the benchmarking process and to which the Parties may comment prior to the benchmarking, as modified herein. The Benchmarker shall compare the costs, charges and/or performance of the Services under this Agreement, as appropriate, for the Services being benchmarked to the costs, charges, and/or performance in a representative sample of well-managed IT operations performing services similar to the Services. The Benchmarker shall select the representative sample from entities (x) identified by the Benchmarker, and (y) identified by a Party and approved by the Benchmarker. The following conditions apply to the representative sample: (i) it may include entities that have not outsourced IT operations, and (ii) it may include entities that are outsourcing customers of HP. The Benchmarker is to conduct a benchmarking as promptly as is prudent in the circumstances. In conducting the benchmarking, the Benchmarker shall normalize the data used to perform the benchmarking to accommodate, as appropriate, differences in volume of services, scope of services, service levels, financing or payment streams, and other pertinent factors. Each Party shall be provided a reasonable opportunity to review, comment on and request changes in the Benchmarker's proposed findings. Following such review and comment, the Benchmarker shall issue a final report of its findings and conclusions, which final report shall be the property and Confidential Information of SG Cowen. Based upon the final results of such benchmarking, including the aggregate results from the customer satisfaction surveys, HP shall cooperate with SG Cowen to investigate variances, if any, and to take corrective action to respond to any deficiencies; provided that, if such results show that the Fees paid by SG Cowen are higher than the midpoint of fees charged with respect to other well managed outsourcing organizations, HP shall have sixty (60) days to reduce the Fees charged hereunder accordingly. Any dispute as to such deficiencies, variances or reduction shall be resolved pursuant to Section 29.

12.6. <u>Failure to Perform.</u>

(a) **Service Level Credits.** HP recognizes that SG Cowen is paying HP to deliver the Services at specified Service Levels. Without limiting any other remedy which SG Cowen may have hereunder or otherwise, whether at law, in equity, or otherwise, if HP fails to meet any Service Level(s) (other than due to a Force Majeure event), then HP shall credit to SG Cowen the performance credits specified in Schedule B (the "Service Level Credits") in recognition of the diminished value of the Services resulting from HP's failure to meet the agreed upon level of performance. HP acknowledges and agrees that such Service Level Credits shall not be deemed a penalty.

(b) **Failure.** If HP fails to meet any Service Levels, HP shall promptly and in accordance with the Service Levels (i) investigate and report on the causes of the problem; (ii) advise SG Cowen, as and to the extent requested by SG Cowen, of the status of remedial efforts that will be and/ or are being undertaken with respect to such problems; (iii) correct the problem(s) that led to such failure, and begin meeting the Service Levels; and (iv) take appropriate preventive measures to ensure that the applicable problem(s) do not recur. The foregoing shall not be deemed to limit any other remedy to which SG Cowen may be entitled hereunder or otherwise, whether at law, in equity, or otherwise.

(c) **Root Cause Analysis.** Within twenty-four (24) hours of any Critical Service Level failure, HP shall: (i) perform a root cause analysis to identify the cause of such failure; (ii) provide SG Cowen with a report detailing the cause of, and procedure for correcting, such failure; and (iii) provide SG Cowen with assurances satisfactory to SG Cowen that such failure will not recur after the procedure has been completed.

(d) **Additional Termination Right.** In addition to, and without limiting any other rights or remedies of SG Cowen under this Agreement, whether at law, in equity or otherwise, SG Cowen shall have the right to terminate this Agreement, without payment of any termination fee or other liability, if, in any two (2) months in a consecutive three (3) month period, (i) HP fails to perform any Services in accordance with any of the Critical Service Levels, or (ii) HP fails to perform Services in accordance with four (4) or more of the Service Levels.

As you can see, service levels may be the subject of considerable and careful negotiation between parties to services contracts. This may serve the interest of both parties, as the service provider attains clarity as to how it must perform to satisfy its obligations, and the client attains comfort that it is purchasing a certain, measurable quality and type of services. For more on the importance of service levels in practice, we turn again to a seasoned practitioner.

A Practitioner Perspective: The Importance of Service Levels

Service levels are particularly important in services agreements, as they provide a reasonable mechanism to monitor the quality of an ongoing stream of services without having to resort to dispute resolution for small, day-to-day issues. An agreed service level serves to specify the obligations of both parties in a fair and transparent manner. The recipient of the services wants to make sure that the provider is focused on the right performance measures and will want to see some sort of financial payment in the event of a major failure. The service provider wants to be able to demonstrate in a clear fashion that the contractual obligations are being met and that the financial payments for failures are capped and reasonable. There are often two different kinds of service levels. A key service level is a measurement of performance of the services that does not result in financial penalties or credits. A critical service level is a measurement of performance of the base services that may result in financial penalties/credits. Service levels are either negotiated prior to the commencement of services or can be set based upon baselines generated once the service provider has started to provide the services. It is most important that the service levels are limited in number so they can be monitored cost-effectively and simple enough to be executed, agreed upon and transparent to all parties. They should be meaningful to the operation of the contract such that any failure to meet a service legal agreement would actually impact the business of the client.

Nancy Laben, Senior Vice President
and General Counsel
AECOM

Prior to publication, Ms. Laben left Accenture LLP, where she was Deputy General Counsel, to join AECOM.

---

5. Notice and Waiver of Claims; Contractual "Statute of Limitations"

The last sentence of section 10.5 of the AOL Agreement provides that "all other claims by a TW Company of whatever nature" will be waived unless Time Warner provides AOL with notice of the claim within six months of the accrual of the claim. Such a notice provision operates to give AOL an opportunity to remedy the claim or at least to contain the potential damages resulting from the event that gave rise to the claim. In addition, this type of notice provision also works to insulate AOL from liability for any claims where Time Warner, for one reason or another, fails to comply with the notice requirement.

These provisions are not uncommon, and courts are willing to honor them.[22] However, such provisions are generally ineffective where the time limitation is not "reasonable."[23] Similarly, a court will generally enforce a contractual "statute of limitations," where parties in their contract reduce a statute of limitations as applicable to the parties, so long as the contractual period is reasonable.[24] For both notice-requirement provisions and contractual statute-of-limitations provisions, the question of reasonableness turns on the facts and circumstances at issue. For example, a New York court has held that a 10-day period for a notice-requirement provision was unreasonable because, in that case, the party to give notice of a claim could not realistically know of the claim within the 10-day period.[25] However, note that at least one jurisdiction has opted no longer to follow this rule, explaining, "A mere judicial assessment of 'reasonableness' is an invalid basis upon which to refuse to enforce contractual provisions."[26]

In addition to a concern for the reasonableness of the time period, courts have looked to whether a contractual time-bar provision expressly sets forth the consequences of noncompliance.[27] For example, a notice-requirement provision is more likely to bar a claim, where the provision specifically states that the claim will be barred if the notice requirement is not met or that satisfaction of the notice requirement is a condition precedent to bringing such a claim.[28] Accordingly, do you think the penultimate and last sentences of section 10.5 are likely to be effective?

---

22. *See, e.g., Cameo Homes v. Kraus-Anderson Constr. Co.*, 394 F.3d 1084, 1088 (8th Cir. 2005) (Minnesota law); *Am. Mfrs. Mut. Ins. Co. v. Payton Lane Nursing Home, Inc.*, No. CV 05-5155(AKT), 2010 WL 144426, at *14 (E.D.N.Y. Jan. 11, 2010) ("Under New York law, courts regularly enforce notice requirements...where the relevant provision explicitly states that notice of such a claim is a condition precedent to bringing such a claim....").

23. *See, e.g., Landsman Packing Co., Inc. v. Continental Can Co., Inc.*, 864 F.2d 721, 730-31 (11th Cir. 1989) (New York law).

24. *See, e.g., Sarmiento v. Grange Mut. Cas. Co.*, 835 N.E.2d 692, 696 (Ohio 2005). However, under certain statutes, there may be limits to the extent to which the parties may vary the statute of limitations by agreement, if they may at all. *See, e.g.,* U.C.C. § 2-725(1) (2003) ("By the original agreement the parties may reduce the period of limitation to not less than one year but may not extend it. However, in a consumer contract, the period of limitation may not be reduced.").

25. *Weisz v. Parke-Bernet Galleries, Inc.*, 325 N.Y.S.2d 576, 582-83 (N.Y. Civ. Ct. 1971), *rev'd on other grounds,* 351 N.Y.S.2d 911 (N.Y. App. Term 1974).

26. *Rory v. Continental Ins. Co,* 703 N.W.2d 23, 31 (Mich. 2005).

27. *See, e.g., F.D.I.C. v. Kansas Bankers Sur. Co.*, 963 F.2d 289, 294 (10th Cir. 1992) (Oklahoma law).

28. *See, e.g., Smurfit Newsprint Corp. v. Se. Paper Mfg.*, 368 F.3d 944, 951-52 (7th Cir. 2004) (New York law) ("The general language that the obligation of SP to indemnify Smurfit is subject to other terms and conditions of [the Agreement] is not sufficiently precise to make prompt written notice an express condition precedent to indemnification.") (internal quotation marks omitted); *American Mfrs. Mut. Ins. Co. v. Payton Lane Nursing Home, Inc.*, No. CV 05-5155(AKT), 2010 WL 144426, at *15 (E.D.N.Y. 2010). For more on "conditions precedent," please see the discussion in Chapter 4.

Drafting Note: Broad Provisions in Specific Sections

Do you see any issues with placing the last sentence of § 10.5—that purports to apply to "all other claims"—in a section ostensibly about service levels? Imagining you are counsel for AOL in this transaction, might you recommend, as a matter of prudence, that such a provision deserving of conspicuous text might also be deserving of its own section, if the intention indeed is to impose a time limitation on all other claims? Notice that courts, as with the court in *Mobil* presented later in this chapter, may be reluctant to read a broadly worded provision—that affects meaningful or valuable rights—to apply to an entire agreement, where such a provision is tucked away in a section that appears narrow in scope.

---

6. Representations, Warranties, and Their Differences

Despite that representations and warranties are commonly spoken of and drafted together (as the AOL Agreement demonstrates) representations and warranties are different in their meanings and effects. A "representation" is a statement of fact as of a point in time, usually made to induce someone to enter into a contract.[29] If a representation proves false, then a party may sue the representation-making party for misrepresentation (a tort). On the other hand, a "warranty" is "[a]n express or implied promise that something in furtherance of the contract is guaranteed by one of the contracting parties."[30] If a warranty proves false, then the non-breaching party may sue the warranty-making party for breach of warranty. A contract will usually provide *both* representations and warranties to give a party the rights and benefits afforded by each. With all this said, parties in a complex agreement (e.g., lending, mergers and acquisitions, i.e., "M&A") often specify the universe of rights and remedies that follow from the representations and warranties made in the agreement (and will attempt to exclude those purportedly made outside the agreement), and, accordingly, a contractually designed edifice may wash away much of the significance of any differences in meaning. As we further explore the differences between representations and warranties, please consider the following case.

---

29. Black's Law Dictionary 1415 (9th ed. 2009).
30. *Id.* at 1725.

CBS Inc. v. Ziff-Davis Publ'g Co.

Court of Appeals of New York, 1990.

75 N.Y.2d 496.

HANCOCK, Judge.

A corporate buyer made a bid to purchase certain businesses based on financial information as to their profitability supplied by the seller. The bid was accepted and the parties entered into a binding bilateral contract for the sale which included, specifically, the seller's express warranties as to the truthfulness of the previously supplied financial information. Thereafter, pursuant to the purchase agreement, the buyer conducted its own investigation which led it to believe that the warranted information was untrue. The seller dismissed as meritless the buyer's expressions of disbelief in the validity of the financial information and insisted that the sale go through as agreed. The closing took place with the mutual understanding that it would not in any way affect the previously asserted position of either party. Did the buyer's manifested lack of belief in and reliance on the truth of the warranted information prior to the closing relieve the seller of its obligations under the warranties? This is the central question presented in the breach of express warranty claim brought by CBS Inc. (CBS) against Ziff-Davis Publishing Co. (Ziff-Davis).[1] The courts below concluded that CBS's lack of reliance on the warranted information was fatal to its breach of warranty claim and, accordingly, dismissed that cause of action on motion.... We granted leave to appeal and, for reasons stated hereinafter, disagree with this conclusion and hold that the warranty claim should be reinstated.

I

The essential facts pleaded—assumed to be true for the purpose of the dismissal motion—are these. In September 1984, Goldman Sachs & Co., acting as Ziff-Davis's investment banker and agent, solicited bids for the sale of the assets and businesses of 12 consumer magazines and 12 business publications. The offering circular, prepared by Goldman Sachs and Ziff-Davis, described Ziff-Davis's financial condition and included operating income statements for the fiscal year ending July 31, 1984 prepared by Ziff-Davis's accountant, Touche Ross & Co. Based on Ziff-Davis's representations in the offering circular, CBS, on November 9, 1984 submitted a bid limited to the purchase of the 12 consumer magazines in the amount of $362,500,000. This was the highest bid.

On November 19, 1984 CBS and Ziff-Davis entered into a binding bilateral purchase agreement for the sale of the consumer magazine businesses for the price of $362,500,000. Under section 3.5 of the purchase agreement, Ziff-Davis warranted that the audited income and expense report of the businesses for

---

1. Ziff-Davis is a privately held corporation and is a wholly owned subsidiary of defendant Ziff Corporation. Ziff Corp. is the guarantor of the purchase agreement at issue. For ease of reference, when addressing arguments raised by these defendants, I will refer to the defendants collectively as Ziff-Davis.

the 1984 fiscal year, which had been previously provided to CBS in the offering circular, had "been prepared in accordance with generally accepted accounting principles" (GAAP) and that the report "present[ed] fairly the items set forth". Ziff-Davis agreed to furnish an interim income and expense report (Stub Report) of the businesses covering the period after the end of the 1984 fiscal year, and it warranted under section 3.6 that from July 31, 1984 until the closing, there had "not been any material adverse change in Seller's business of publishing and distributing the Publications, taken as a whole". Section 6.1(a) provided that "all representations and warranties of Seller to Buyer shall be true and correct as of the time of the closing," and in section 8.1, the parties agreed that all "representations and warranties...shall survive the closing, notwithstanding any investigation made by or on behalf of the other party." In section 5.1 Ziff-Davis gave CBS permission to "make such investigation" of the magazine businesses being sold "as [it might] desire" and agreed to give CBS and its accountants reasonable access to the books and records pertaining thereto and to furnish such documents and information as might reasonably be requested.

Thereafter, on January 30, 1985 Ziff-Davis delivered the required Stub Report. In the interim, CBS, acting under section 5.1 of the purchase agreement, had performed its own "due diligence" examination of Ziff-Davis's financial condition. Based on this examination and on reports by its accountant, Coopers & Lybrand, CBS discovered information causing it to believe that Ziff-Davis's certified financial statements and other financial reports were not prepared according to GAAP and did not fairly depict Ziff-Davis's financial condition.

In a January 31, 1985 letter, CBS wrote Ziff-Davis that, "[b]ased on the information and analysis provided [to it, CBS was] of the view that there [were] material misrepresentations in the financial statements provided [to CBS] by Touche Ross & Co., Goldman, Sachs & Co. and Ziff-Davis." In response to this letter, Ziff-Davis advised CBS by letter dated February 4, 1985 that it "believe[d] that all conditions to the closing...were fulfilled," that "there [was] no merit to the position taken by CBS in its [Jan. 31, 1985] letter" and that the financial statements were properly prepared and fairly presented Ziff-Davis's financial condition. It also warned CBS that, since all conditions to closing were satisfied, closing was required to be held that day, February 4, 1985, and that, if it "should fail to consummate the transactions as provided...Ziff-Davis intend[ed] *to pursue all of its rights and remedies as provided by law.*" (Emphasis added.)

CBS responded to Ziff-Davis's February 4, 1985 letter with its own February 4 letter, which Ziff-Davis accepted and agreed to. In its February 4 letter, CBS acknowledged that "a clear dispute" existed between the parties. It stated that it had decided to proceed with the deal because it had "spent considerable time, effort and money in complying with [its] obligations...and recogniz[ed] that [Ziff-Davis had] considerably more information available." Accordingly, the parties agreed "to close [that day] on a mutual understanding that the decision to close, and the closing, [would] not *constitute a waiver of any rights or defenses either of us may have"* (emphasis added) under the purchase agreement. The deal was consummated on February 4.

CBS then brought this action claiming in its third cause of action that Ziff-Davis had breached the warranties made as to the magazines' profitability. Based on that breach, CBS alleged that "the price bid and the price paid by CBS were in excess of that which would have been bid and paid by CBS had Ziff-Davis not breached its representation and warranties." Supreme Court granted Ziff-Davis's motion to dismiss the breach of warranty cause of action because CBS alleged "it did not believe that the representations set forth in Paragraphs 3.5 and 3.6 of the contract of sale were true" and thus CBS did not satisfy "the law in New York [which] clearly requires that this reliance be alleged in a breach of warranty action." Supreme Court also dismissed CBS's fourth cause of action relating to an alleged breach of condition. The Appellate Division, First Department, unanimously affirmed for reasons stated by Supreme Court. There should be a modification so as to deny the dismissal motion with respect to the third cause of action for breach of warranties.

II

In addressing the central question whether the failure to plead reliance is fatal to CBS's claim for breach of express warranties, it is necessary to examine the exact nature of the missing element of reliance which Ziff-Davis contends is essential. This critical lack of reliance, according to Ziff-Davis, relates to CBS's disbelief in the truth of the warranted financial information which resulted from its investigation *after* the signing of the agreement and *prior to* the date of closing. The reliance in question, it must be emphasized, does not relate to whether CBS relied on the submitted financial information in making its bid or relied on Ziff-Davis's express warranties as to the validity of this information when CBS committed itself to buy the businesses by signing the purchase agreement containing the warranties.

Under Ziff-Davis's theory, the reliance which is a necessary element for a claim of breach of express warranty is essentially that required for a tort action based on fraud or misrepresentation—i.e., a belief in the truth of the representations made in the express warranty and a change of position in reliance on that belief. Thus, because, prior to the closing of the contract on February 4, 1985, CBS demonstrated its lack of belief in the truth of the warranted financial information, it cannot have closed in reliance on it and its breach of warranty claim must fail. This is so, Ziff-Davis maintains, despite its unequivocal rejection of CBS's expressions of its concern that the submitted financial reports contained errors, despite its insistence that the information it had submitted complied with the warranties and that there was "no merit" to CBS's position, and despite its warnings of legal action if CBS did not go ahead with the closing. Ziff-Davis's primary source for the proposition it urges—that a change of position in reliance on the truth of the warranted information is essential for a cause of action for breach of express warranty—is language found in older New York cases....

CBS, on the other hand, maintains that the decisive question is whether it purchased the express warranties as bargained-for contractual terms that were part of the purchase agreement. It alleges that it did so and that, under these circumstances, the warranty provisions amounted to assurances of the existence of facts upon which CBS relied in committing itself to buy the consumer magazines. Ziff-Davis's assurances of these facts, CBS contends, were the equivalent of promises by Ziff-Davis to indemnify CBS if the assurances proved unfounded. Thus, as continuing promises to indemnify, the express contractual warranties did not lose their operative force when, prior to the closing, CBS formed a belief that the warranted financial information was in error. Indeed, CBS claims that it is precisely because of these warranties that it proceeded with the closing, despite its misgivings.

As authority for its position, CBS cites Learned Hand's definition of warranty as "an assurance by one party to a contract of the existence of a fact upon which the other party may rely. It is intended precisely to relieve the promisee of any duty to ascertain the fact for himself; *it amounts to a promise to indemnify the promisee for any loss if the fact warranted proves untrue, for obviously the promisor cannot control what is already in the past.*"

We believe that the analysis of the reliance requirement in actions for breach of express warranties urged by CBS here is correct. The critical question is not whether the buyer believed in the truth of the warranted information, as Ziff-Davis would have it, but whether it believed it was purchasing the seller's promise as to its truth. This view of "reliance"—i.e., as requiring no more than reliance on the express warranty as being a part of the bargain between the parties—reflects the prevailing perception of an action for breach of express warranty as one that is no longer grounded in tort, but essentially in contract. The express warranty is as much a part of the contract as any other term. Once the express warranty is shown to have been relied on as part of the contract, the right to be indemnified in damages for its breach does not depend on proof that the buyer thereafter believed that the assurances of fact made in the warranty would be fulfilled. The right to indemnification depends only on establishing that the warranty was breached.

If, as is allegedly the case here, the buyer has purchased the seller's promise as to the existence of the warranted facts, the seller should not be relieved of responsibility because the buyer, after agreeing to make the purchase, forms doubts as to the existence of those facts. Stated otherwise, the fact that the buyer has questioned the seller's ability to perform as promised should not relieve the seller of his obligations under the express warranties when he thereafter undertakes to render the promised performance....

Viewed as a contract action involving the claimed breach of certain bargained-for express warranties contained in the purchase agreement, the case may be summarized this way. CBS contracted to buy the consumer magazine businesses in consideration, among other things, of the reciprocal promises made by Ziff-Davis concerning the magazines' profitability. These reciprocal promises included the express warranties that the audited reports for the year ending July

31, 1984 made by Touche Ross had been prepared according to GAAP and that the items contained therein were fairly presented, that there had been no adverse material change in the business after July 31, 1984, and that all representations and warranties would "be true and correct as of the time of the closing" and would "survive the closing, notwithstanding any investigation" by CBS.

Unquestionably, the financial information pertaining to the income and expenses of the consumer magazines was relied on by CBS in forming its opinion as to the value of the businesses and in arriving at the amount of its bid; the warranties pertaining to the validity of this financial information were express terms of the bargain and part of what CBS contracted to purchase. CBS was not merely buying identified consumer magazine businesses. It was buying businesses which it believed to be of a certain value based on information furnished by the seller which the seller warranted to be true. The determinative question is this: should Ziff-Davis be relieved from any contractual obligation under these warranties, as it contends that it should, because, prior to the closing, CBS and its accountants questioned the accuracy of the financial information and because CBS, when it closed, did so without *believing in* or *relying on* the truth of the information?

We see no reason why Ziff-Davis should be absolved from its warranty obligations under these circumstances. A holding that it should because CBS questioned the truth of the facts warranted would have the effect of depriving the express warranties of their only value to CBS—i.e., as continuing promises by Ziff-Davis to indemnify CBS if the facts warranted proved to be untrue.[4] Ironically, if Ziff-Davis's position were adopted, it would have succeeded in pressing CBS to close despite CBS's misgivings and, at the same time, would have succeeded in *defeating* CBS's breach of warranties action because CBS harbored these *identical misgivings*.[5] ...

---

a. Understanding "Warranty" and "Representation" after Ziff-Davis

Regardless of the rule prior to *Ziff-Davis*, the majority of states are now in accord with the definition of "warranty" attributed to *Ziff-Davis*.[31] That is,

---

4. In this regard, analogy to the Uniform Commercial Code is "instructive." While acceptance of goods by the buyer precludes rejection of the goods accepted, the acceptance of nonconforming goods does not itself impair any other remedy for nonconformity, including damages for breach of an express warranty.

5. We make but one comment on the dissent: in its statement that our "holding discards reliance as a necessary element to maintain an action for breach of an express warranty" the dissent obviously misses the point of our decision. We do not hold that no reliance is required, but that the required reliance is established if, as here, the express warranties are bargained-for terms of the seller.

31. *See Vigortone AG Prods., Inc. v. PM AG Prods., Inc.*, 316 F.3d 641, 649 (7th Cir. 2002) (explaining that the "general rule" is that "a party to a contract can enforce an express warranty even if he should believe or even does believe that the mishap warranted against will occur" and that Delaware's high court would

most states do not require reliance on the underlying truth of a warranty as an element of proving a breach-of-warranty claim.[32] Implicit in what it means to have a warranty is the right to transfer the risk of the failure of that warranty to the party making the warranty. As the court in *Ziff-Davis* explained, one who obtains a warranty has bought a promise that the warranted statement will be true for the duration of the warranty and the right to damages should that statement prove false.

However, a mere two years after *Ziff-Davis* was decided, the Second Circuit, in *Galli v. Metz*, explained:

> Where a buyer closes on a contract in the full knowledge and acceptance of facts disclosed by the seller which would constitute a breach of warranty under the terms of the contract, the buyer should be foreclosed from later asserting the breach. In that situation, unless the buyer expressly preserves his rights under the warranties (as CBS did in *Ziff-Davis*), we think the buyer has waived the breach.[33]

The court in *Galli* accepted the *Ziff-Davis* definition of "warranty" and that one need not prove reliance on the underlying truth of a warranty in order to prove breach of that warranty. However, the court also narrowed the effect of *Ziff-Davis*, explaining that if a party closes on (i.e., consummates the transaction contemplated by) a contract—presumably when the party is not contractually obligated to close, given the breach—with the full knowledge and acceptance of the falsity of a warranty's underlying facts, then such party will be held to have *waived* the breach of such warranty. Under *Galli*, it is important to ascertain how the party suing for breach of warranty acquired the information that the facts underlying the warranty were untrue. For a party to waive its warranty, the *warranting party* must have disclosed the facts. If the party suing on the warranty acquired such facts elsewhere or as common knowledge, then no waiver will be found.[34] Furthermore, a party could avoid waiver and preserve its

___

subscribe to this rule despite "unthinking" lower court case law in Delaware to the contrary); *Mowbray v. Waste Mgmt. Holdings, Inc.*, 189 F.R.D. 194, 200 (D. Mass. 1999) ("A decisive majority of courts that have considered the issue…have held…that reliance is not an element of a claim for breach of warranty, when the fact that the warranty was created is not in dispute.") (citing cases decided under Illinois, Florida, Pennsylvania, Connecticut, Montana, New York, Indiana, and Massachusetts law). *But see Hendricks v. Callahan*, 972 F.2d 190 (8th Cir. 1992) (Minnesota law); *Land v. Roper Corp.*, 531 F.2d 445, 448 (10th Cir. 1976) (Kansas law).

32. *See supra* note 31.

33. *Galli v. Metz*, 973 F.2d 145, 151 (2d Cir. 1992) (New York law).

34. *See id.; see also Promuto v. Waste Mgmt., Inc.*, 44 F. Supp. 2d 628, 648 (S.D.N.Y. 1999) ("The law is clear that in order to conclude that plaintiffs have waived their right to assert a claim for breach of warranty, we must find that, prior to closing, defendants themselves actively disclosed to plaintiffs facts which would have constituted a breach of the warranties under the terms of the Exchange Agreement."). Presumably, this is because, where the warranting party admits that the warranty is false and a false warranty excuses the non-breaching party from any obligation to close, the non-breaching party's choice to close rather than to exercise its right to refuse to close—and to insist on renegotiating price to reflect the diminished value of the contract due to the breached warranty—evidences a waiver of the warranty and the right to sue for breach. Notice, then, this is different from a situation where a party signs a contract with knowledge that a warranty is untrue. For this warranty to mean anything (and we always try to give

right to bring an action for breach of warranty if the party expressly preserves such a right. This might be accomplished by a provision in the agreement that specifies the exclusive means by which a party may waive a term under the Agreement (e.g., a provision requiring that both parties sign a written waiver).[35] In addition, before closing on an agreement, a party wishing to preserve its warranties under that agreement might insist that a statement of preservation of such warranties be expressly included in the agreement and/or that the warranting party affirmatively state in writing that the facts underlying such warranties remain true. For example, the parties might include a provision in the agreement that states:

> Every warranty set forth in this Agreement and the rights and remedies for any one or more breaches of this Agreement by the Sellers shall not be deemed waived by the Closing and shall be effective regardless of any prior knowledge by or on the part of the Purchaser.[36]

In sum, to bring a breach of warranty action, a plaintiff need not show that she relied on the truth of the warranty but merely that the warranty was breached.[37] A breach of warranty action lies in contract and not tort.[38] As such, punitive damages are ordinarily not available for mere breach of warranty.[39] Unless an agreement provides otherwise, in an action for breach of warranty, one may recover damages generally available for breach of contract, including general and consequential damages.[40] A warranty may be as of a point in time or ongoing into the future, which depends on the nature of the warranty and the language of the contract.[41]

---

meaning to a contractual provision inasmuch as reasonable), we should presume that the receiving party did not intend to "waive" the warranty right by executing the contract with knowledge of the warranty's inaccuracy—indeed, the party did not *have* the right to waive until the contract was executed, and it is nonsensical to think a party intended to gain and waive a right in one fell contractual swoop. Accordingly, *Galli* should be limited to situations after the signing of a contract where a party intentionally acts to waive its contractual warranty right, namely by opting to close and consummate the core transaction contemplated by the agreement in lieu of demanding recompense. (We may also understand *Galli* as a decision in favor of judicial economy, as holding out on closing may be a more efficient, non-judicial means of attaining redress.)

35. *See, e.g., NSA Invs. II LLC v. SeraNova, Inc.*, 227 F. Supp. 2d 200, 205 (D. Mass. 2002) (New York law). However, note that some courts may find such a provision itself to be waivable. For more on this, please see the discussion of implied waiver and no-waiver provisions in Chapter 2.

36. *Pegasus Mgmt. Co. v. Lyssa, Inc.*, 995 F. Supp. 29, 38 (D. Mass. 1998) (internal quotation marks omitted) ("In the instant case, there can be no doubt that the buyers expressly reserved their rights [in accordance with *Ziff-Davis*].")

37. *See, e.g., Bank of Am. Corp. v. Lemgruber*, 385 F. Supp. 2d 200, 229 (S.D.N.Y. 2005).

38. *See, e.g., Shurland v. Bacci Café & Pizzeria on Ogden Inc.*, 259 F.R.D. 151, 163 (N.D. Ill. 2009).

39. *Rosen v. Gupta*, 213 F.3d 626 (2d Cir. 2000) (punitive damages not available for breach of warranty in New York or Texas); *English v. Mentor Corp.*, 67 F.3d 477, 481 (3d Cir. 1995) (punitive damages not available for breach of warranty absent fraud); *Salter v. Al-Hallaq*, No. 02-2406-JWL, 2003 WL 1872991 (D. Kan. Apr. 10, 2003) (punitive damages not available for breach of warranty under U.C.C.).

40. *See, e.g., St. John's Bank & Trust Co. v. Intag, Inc.*, 938 S.W.2d 627, 629 (Mo. App. E.D. 1997).

41. *See, e.g., Marvin Lumber and Cedar Co. v. PPG Indus., Inc.*, 223 F.3d 873, 879 (8th Cir. 2000) (Minnesota law).

In contrast, recall that a representation is a statement of fact as of a point in time usually made to induce reliance. If such a representation proves false, one may bring an action for misrepresentation (which lies in tort) unless an agreement provides otherwise.[42] Misrepresentation may be innocent, negligent, or fraudulent. The major difference between these various flavors is the defendant's state of mind. Innocent misrepresentation is a strict liability offense, negligent misrepresentation only requires that a defendant acted—well—negligently, and fraudulent misrepresentation requires that the defendant knowingly or recklessly made a false representation.[43] An action for misrepresentation requires a showing that the plaintiff reasonably relied on the representation.[44] In addition, the general rule is that an action for misrepresentation may only be based on a statement of present or past fact.[45] As the elements vary across the types of misrepresentation, so too do the available remedies. For example, for fraudulent misrepresentation, punitive damages may be available.[46]

While representations are sometimes oral and sometimes expressly written in a contract, a sophisticated party to an agreement may be unable to demonstrate reliance on an oral representation.[47] Indeed, a *sophisticated* party insists on the express inclusion of representations in a written agreement before relying on such.[48] This, then, demonstrates the importance of commercial players receiving express, written representations and the potential futility of relying on mere oral representations. On the flipside, to avoid responsibility for representations a party wishes not to make, a party may include a provision that expressly states that the party only makes those representations expressly made within the written agreement and that the party has made no other representations related to the subject matter of the agreement. An integration clause

---

42. However, in New York, a party may not bring a tort action for misrepresentation of a statement of *future* intent unless such representations are "collateral and extraneous" to the contract. *See Int'l CableTel Inc. v. Le Groupe Videotron Ltee*, 978 F. Supp. 483, 487 (S.D.N.Y. 1997). An action for misrepresentation based on representations provided by a contract is not "collateral and extraneous" to the contract. *See GBJ Corp. v. E. Ohio Paving Co.*, 139 F.3d 1080, 1088 (6th Cir. 1998) (New York law). This rule does not apply to false statements of present fact. *See Int'l CableTel Inc.*, 978 F. Supp. at 491. Essentially, then, this New York rule forces claims of misrepresentation based on contractual representations of future intent to be stated in terms of contract or, more specifically, warranty, instead of misrepresentation and tort.

43. For innocent misrepresentation, see Restatement (Second) of Torts § 552C (1977). For negligent misrepresentation, see Restatement (Second) of Torts § 552 (1977); *see also Dahlgren v. First Nat'l Bank of Holdrege*, 533 F.3d 681, 693 (8th Cir. 2008) (Nebraska law); *Erickson's Flooring & Supply Co. v. Tembec, Inc.*, 212 F. App'x 558, 563 (6th Cir. 2007) (Michigan law). For fraudulent misrepresentation, see Restatement (Second) of Torts § 525 (1977); *see also Dahlgren*, 533 F.3d at 692; *Erickson's Flooring & Supply Co.*, 212 F. App'x at 562-63.

44. *See supra* note 43.

45. *See, e.g., Siemens Fin. Serv., Inc. v. Robert J. Combs Ins. Agency, Inc.*, 166 F. App'x 612, 617 (3d Cir. 2006); *Showler v. Harper's Magazine Found.*, 222 F. App'x 755, 765 (10th Cir. 2007).

46. *See, e.g., Spreitzer v. Hawkeye State Bank*, 775 N.W.2d 573, 593 (Iowa 2009).

47. *Century Pac., Inc. v. Hilton Hotels Corp.*, 354 F. App'x 496, 498-99 (2d Cir. 2009) (New York law).

48. *Id.* In addition, "reliance on the oral representation by a plaintiff can be utterly unjustified in the face of a clear written contradiction." *Spreitzer*, 775 N.W.2d at 585-86 (citing *Marram v. Kobric Offshore Fund, Ltd.*, 809 N.E.2d 1017, 1031 (Mass. 2004)).

may serve this purpose;[49] however, a prudent party will include a provision that expressly disclaims any extra-contractual representations.[50]

A party under a contract may wish to seek both representations and warranties so as to optimize the party's available causes of action and remedies.[51] If a representation proves false, a party may rescind the contract or seek restitution. If the party can prove fraudulent misrepresentation, then the moving party may be able to obtain punitive damages. However, all forms of misrepresentation require a showing that the plaintiff relied on the truth of the representation, and fraudulent misrepresentation requires a hard-to-prove showing of scienter. One need not make a showing of either reliance or scienter, however, to recover for a breach of warranty, but, for a breach of warranty, punitive damages are unavailable.

Section 9 in the above Agreement addresses representations and warranties. From the perspective of either party, do you consider the representations and warranties in this Agreement to be sufficiently robust? By way of example, is there value in seeking a representation and warranty as to the accuracy and completeness of confidential information exchanged by parties to an agreement? Under what circumstances in particular might this be useful? What other representations and warranties might you consider when negotiating a services agreement?

While parties to a transaction are, of course, free to craft those representations that reflect the facts upon which each party relies and those warranties that reflect the risk each party shall bear, certain representations and warranties are commonplace in the context of certain deals. For instance, a "warranty of non-infringement" is commonly seen in transactions involving intellectual property. This warranty specifies which party shall bear the risk of infringement of the intellectual property rights of others. While the recipient of the warranty may desire a warranty against infringement of intellectual property rights worldwide, a warrantor may be reluctant take on such broad and unknown risk exposure, given the myriad intellectual property regimes the world over. Accordingly, a warrantor of non-infringement is likely to want to limit such warranty of non-infringement of intellectual property rights to the United States.

---

49. *See, e.g., Eastman Kodak Co. v. Teletech Servs. Corp.*, No. 05-CV-6594, 2007 WL 2027843, at *3 (W.D.N.Y. July 11, 2007) ("Because, the terms of a written, integrated and enforceable contract must be given effect over purported extra-contractual representations, I find…that there were no obligations or promises other than those listed in the contract.").

50. *See, e.g., Kronenberg v. Katz*, 872 A.2d 568, 593 (Del. Ch. 2004) ("Stated summarily, for a contract to bar a fraud in the inducement claim, the contract must contain language that, when read together, can be said to add up to a clear anti-reliance clause by which the plaintiff has contractually promised that it did not rely upon statements outside the contract's four corners in deciding to sign the contract. The presence of a standard integration clause alone, which does not contain explicit anti-reliance representations and which is not accompanied by other contractual provisions demonstrating with clarity that the plaintiff had agreed that it was not relying on facts outside the contract, will not suffice to bar fraud claims.").

51. *See* Tina Stark, *Nonbinding Opinion: Another View on Representations and Warranties*, 15 BUS. L. TODAY 8 (Jan./Feb. 2006) (explaining the benefits of obtaining both representations and warranties).

Additionally, it is common to find representations akin to the mutual representation made in the AOL Agreement, that each party has the proper authority in the first place to enter into the agreement itself. If a signatory to an agreement indeed lacks the authority to bind a supposed party to the agreement—and the principal has not ratified the agreement—then the agreement will not bind the principal, regardless of whether the signing agent makes such a representation. However, for what it may be worth, this representation gives the other party an actionable claim against the party stating the false representation.

b. Use of Representations and Warranties in Practice

Practitioners vary in their understanding and use of "representations" and "warranties."[52] Some (often, M&A attorneys) believe there is no meaningful distinction between the terms and no utility to reciting that a party both "represents and warrants."[53] Others point to cases like *Ziff-Davis* and insist that a "representation" is one thing and a "warranty" is another.[54] To reconcile these positions, it is important to differentiate between the *provision* in a contract called a "representation" or a "warranty," on the one hand, and a "representation" that may give rise to a misrepresentation claim or a "warranty" that may give rise to a breach-of-warranty claim, on the other. That is, something called a "warranty" on a piece of paper may also be a statement of fact made to induce reliance on the truth of the statement (i.e., a "representation"), and something called a "representation" may also be a promise that the truth of a statement is guaranteed by a party (i.e., a "warranty").[55] Still, the simplest way to signal to a future reader of a contract (e.g., a judge, an arbitrator) that a contract states *both* a representation (that may give rise to a claim for misrepresentation) and a warranty (that may give rise to a breach of warranty claim) may be to state expressly that a party *both* "represents and warrants."

Some practitioners do not give much weight to the distinction between the two terms (and may opt, for instance, to use only "represents" and not to use "warrants") because, for these practitioners, the rights and remedies intended to follow from the contractual representations are all provided and specified by the contract itself. For example, in an M&A agreement, the parties will generally create contractual termination rights and contractual indemnification rights

---

52. *Compare* Kenneth A. Adams, *A Lesson in Drafting Contracts: What's up with 'Representations and Warranties'?*, 15 Bus. L. Today 32 (Nov./Dec. 2005), *with* Stark, *supra* note 51.

53. *See, e.g.,* Adams, *supra* note 52.

54. See, *e.g.,* Stark, *supra* note 51.

55. *See, e.g.,* U.C.C. §2-313(2) (2003) ("(a) Any affirmation of fact or promise made by the seller which relates to the goods and becomes part of the basis of the bargain creates an express warranty that the goods shall conform to the affirmation or promise. (b) Any description of the goods which is made part of the basis of the bargain creates an express warranty that the goods shall conform to the description."). *See also supra* note 42 and accompanying text.

for the failure of a representation/warranty. In this way, the distinction is largely washed away, where the parties specify in the contract completely and exactly how they desire these things called "representations" and/or "warranties" to operate and what rights and remedies are to follow (i.e., the parties *could* call these things "bananas"—although we do not advise it—so long as the contract provided all that the parties desired to follow from their "banana" rights).

c. Implied Warranties and the Disclaimer Thereof

As we have seen, a contract may provide *express* warranties—warranties that are affirmatively stated by the contract.[56] However, beyond those warranties specifically offered by each party, certain other warranties may be *implied* by law. In Chapter 4, we will return to the topic of implied warranties in the context of Article 2 of the Uniform Commercial Code and sales transactions. For now, know that where a contract involves both goods and services, most jurisdictions look to the "predominate purpose" of the mixed contract to determine whether Article 2 should apply.[57] Accordingly, even with a contract seemingly for "services," a prudent party will plan for the potentiality of Article 2's application.

Article 2 of the U.C.C. imputes implied warranties to be read into a contract for the sale of goods, even if the parties did not expressly include them. The implied warranty of merchantability warrants that goods to be delivered by a merchant are fit for the ordinary purposes for which such goods are used.[58] The implied warranty of fitness for a particular purpose kicks in when a seller has reason to know that a buyer is relying on the seller to select goods for a particular purpose.[59] In such a situation, an implied warranty arises that these goods are so suited.[60]

Outside of Article 2 and contracts for the sale of goods, it is uncommon for a court to find an implied warranty.[61] However, in certain circumstances, courts have done so. For example, the Idaho Supreme Court has "imposed an implied warranty that services will be performed in a workmanlike manner in the context of personal services contracts."[62] Similarly, in contracts for the repair or modification of existing tangible goods or property, Texas has found an implied warranty

---

56. Express warranties may also arise outside a contract, for instance, in a product manual. *See, e.g., Bell Sports, Inc. v. Yarusso*, 759 A.2d 582, 592-93 (Del. 2000).

57. *See Novamedix, Ltd. v. NDM Acquisition Corp.*, 166 F.3d 1177, 1182 (6th Cir. 1999).

58. U.C.C. § 2-314(2) (2003).

59. *Id.* § 2-315.

60. *Id.* In addition, Article 2 is the source of a warranty of title, which promises that the seller has adequate title (i.e., sufficient rights to sell the property to be sold and that will not subject the buyer to a lawsuit to protect the title. *Id.* § 2-312. However, this warranty is not considered "implied" for Article 2 purposes, namely its conspicuous disclaimer requirement. *Id.* § 2-312 cmt. 6. Article 2 also provides that the repeated conduct of a party may give rise to additional implied warranties. *Id.* § 2-314(3).

61. *See, e.g., GMA Accessories, Inc. v. ePartners, Inc.*, No. 07 Civ. 8414(LAK), 2008 WL 781188, at *1 (S.D.N.Y. Mar. 19, 2008) ("[T]here is no claim under New York law for breach of an implied warranty for the performance of professional services in service-oriented contracts.").

62. *Branscum v. 4-J Harvestore, Inc.*, No. 88-3919, 886 F.2d 334, at *3 (9th Cir. 1989) (citing *Hoffman v. Simplot Aviation Inc.*, 539 P.2d 584, 588 (Idaho 1975)).

"that the service will be performed in a good and workmanlike manner."[63] Given that a court may imply warranties beyond that which the parties explicitly provide, how can a commercial party avoid taking on undesirable risk?

Generally, implied warranties may be disclaimed by an agreement. That is, parties to a contract may "opt out" and avoid the application of implied warranties. To be effective, these disclaimers generally must be "conspicuous."[64] To be conspicuous, the disclaimer should be set apart from the contract's other provisions, and the disclaimer's text should appear different from the contract's ordinary text. This is usually accomplished by bolding and/or presenting the text in all caps.[65] Particularly, to disclaim the implied warranty of merchantability, the disclaimer should specifically mention "merchantability."[66] Alternatively, all Article 2 implied warranties may be excluded by specifying that a transaction is "as-is" or "with all faults."[67] Notice that while implied warranties may be disclaimed, most courts are unwilling to give effect to a disclaimer of an *express* warranty.[68] As a matter of prudent drafting, then, while sometimes a contractual provision will state a general rule and then provide exceptions to that general rule, one wishing not to make certain warranties should not provide these warranties in the first place.

7. Force Majeure Provisions and the Doctrine of Excuse

Under the common law, a party may be excused from performing under a contract for a host of reasons. For example, we have already discussed (in Chapter 2) that a party may be excused from—that is suffer no liability from not—performing under a contract if the other party has materially breached that contract. Another basic feature of the common law is that a party is excused from performance if some event (through no fault of that party's) either makes that party's performance impracticable or frustrates that party's principal purpose in undertaking the contract, where the non-occurrence of such event was a basic assumption of the contract.[69] However, like much of contract law, the law of excuse is default law, which means that contractual parties may opt out and strike their own

---

63. *Walker v. Sears, Roebuck & Co.*, 853 F.2d 355, 360-61 (5th Cir. 1988) (citing *Melody Home Mfg. Co. v. Barnes*, 741 S.W.2d 349, 354 (Tex. 1987)).

64. U.C.C. § 2-316(2) (2003) (disclaiming merchantability and fitness); *see Branscum*, 886 F.2d at *3; *GMA Accessories*, 2008 WL 781188, at *1 (rejecting claim for breach of implied warranty of good and workmanlike performance of services agreement partly because the master services agreement contained an express disclaimer of implied warranties). However, note that to disclaim the warranty of title under Article 2, there are not necessarily "any specific requirements that the disclaimer or modification be contained in a record or be conspicuous." U.C.C. § 2-316 cmt. 6 (2003).

65. *See, e.g., Hornberger v. General Motors Corp.*, 929 F. Supp. 884, 889 (E.D. Pa. 1996).

66. U.C.C. § 2-316(2) (2003).

67. *Id.* § 2-316(3).

68. *See, e.g., L.S. Heath & Son, Inc. v. AT&T Info. Sys., Inc.*, 9 F.3d 561, 570-71 (7th Cir. 1993); *Bell Sports, Inc. v. Yarusso*, 759 A.2d 582, 593 (Del. 2000); *see also* U.C.C. § 2-316(1) (2003).

69. *See* Restatement (Second) of Contracts §§ 261, 265 (1981).

accord.[70] This is the basic function of the force majeure provision, a provision commonplace in many agreements and found in § 12.5 of this Agreement.

The force majeure provision will often list several events that excuse a party's performance under the contract. Accordingly, a court need not inquire into what constitutes a "basic assumption" of the contract or what constitutes "impracticable" or "frustration of purpose" under common law doctrines of excuse; the parties may specify in the force majeure provision what constitutes an excuse of a party's performance.[71] What have the Parties specified as excusing events in this Agreement? Under this Agreement, does a party affected by such an event have an incentive to stop all performance, even if she could otherwise partially or fully perform? Notice that section 12.5 conditions excuse for Force Majeure Events on the affected Party taking Commercially Reasonable Efforts to perform still, despite a Force Majeure Event. Does this condition (and the following provisions in § 12.5) apply to the events enumerated in the first sentence of § 12.5? Do you think the Parties intended them to apply? Where in this Agreement might you first look to understand what Commercially Reasonable Efforts means? Does this provide adequate guidance?[72]

Drafting Note: "Including"

Notice that, where § 12.5 lists the several events that constitute Force Majeure Events, the provision states that such Force Majeure Events are those events beyond a Party's reasonable control, "including, without limitation" and then proceeds to enumerate the several events. The word "including" is generally understood to precede an exemplary or illustrative—*but not exhaustive*—list of items.[73] Accordingly, even without the "without limitation" language, a court is unlikely to find the list of events in § 12.5 to be the only potential Force Majeure Events. However, using language like "without limitation" after the word "including" provides additional clarity, expressly instructing a future reader that the following list of items is intended to be non-exhaustive and merely illustrative.

---

70. *See, e.g., Stein v. Paradigm Mirasol, LLC,* 586 F.3d 849, 857 n.6 (11th Cir. 2009) ("It appears to us that force majeure clauses broader than the scope of impossibility are enforceable under Florida law."); *see also* RESTATEMENT (SECOND) OF CONTRACTS §§ 261, 265 (1981) (each providing "unless the language or the circumstances indicate the contrary").

71. *See Wis. Elec. Power Co. v. Union Pac. R.R.,* 557 F.3d 504, 506-07 (7th Cir. 2009) (Wisconsin law). Indeed, while force majeure clauses may commonly provide that an event must be outside the control of a party for such an event to excuse that party, this is up to the parties and not a requirement of law. That is, parties can specify whatever events they like as excusing performance. *See, e.g., PPG Indus., Inc. v. Shell Oil Co.,* 919 F.2d 17 (5th Cir. 1990) (Texas law). However, unless the contract provides otherwise, general doctrines of excuse are available as defenses if the force majeure provision happens not to afford a defense. *See Melford Olsen Honey, Inc. v. Adee,* 452 F.3d 956, 962-64 (8th Cir. 2006) (Minnesota law).

72. Please all see Chapter 4 for further discussion of "commercially reasonable" and performance standards generally.

73. *See, e.g., Cephalon, Inc. v. Johns Hopkins Univ.,* No. 3505-VCP, 2009 WL 4896227, at *8 (Del. Ch. Dec. 18, 2009); *Nextel Wip Lease Corp. v. Saunders,* 666 S.E.2d 317, 322 (Va. 2008); *Alcoa, Inc. v. Whittaker Corp.,* No. V-02-84, 2007 WL 2900591, at *4 (S.D. Tex. Sep. 30, 2007).

Notice what excuse and the Force Majeure Provision do not do. The doctrine of excuse and the Force Majeure Provision free the excused party from liability for failure to perform fully; however, they do not allow the excused party, then, to insist on the continued performance of the other party. The Restatement makes this clear, explaining that despite that a party may be justified in not performing for impracticability or frustration of purpose, that party's failure to perform may still free the other party from performing.[74] The Agreement makes this clear in § 12.5, providing that an unaffected party may terminate affected Services if the Force Majeure event shall occur for more than fifteen consecutive business days and notice is provided. Is a Force Majeure event more likely to affect AOL's or TW's ability to perform under this Agreement?

8. Shifting Risk: Indemnification and Limitation of Liability

Much of the enterprise of contracting involves the allocation of "risk" between private parties. All sorts of contractual provisions allocate risks, some of which we have already discussed. As just one example, something as simple as a notice provision may provide what constitutes effective notice, which in turn may trigger certain obligations under a contract. In specifying when notice is effective (e.g., upon receipt, upon five business days after delivery), a notice clause may specify which party bears what kind of risk for failure of delivery.

Representations and warranties both are tools commonly used to spread risk. A representation puts the risk of inaccurate information on the party making the representation, so long as the receiving party has justifiably relied on such information. A warranty puts the risk of failure of a specified promise on the warrantor. We have also looked at how a party may disclaim certain warranties, putting the risk of such a would-be promise failing on the other party. Force majeure provisions allow a party to avoid the risk of having to perform, despite the occurrence of certain critical events in the future. To understand risk and its contractual allocation, one must first appreciate who would suffer the occurrence of a certain cost, in the absence of a contract providing otherwise. With an understanding of this baseline, one may begin to draft contractual provisions to alter this default arrangement and to place the risk of the occurrence of certain costs on the desired party. For instance, drawing on our discussion of implied warranties, absent a disclaimer of implied warranties, a seller assumes the risk of the breach of an implied warranty: If a seller breaches the implied warranty of merchantability, then the seller is liable for the resulting damages to the buyer. However, if the seller effectively disclaims all implied warranties, then the risk of the seller running afoul of the implied warranty of merchantability falls to the buyer, and the buyer will have no legal

---

74. RESTATEMENT (SECOND) OF CONTRACTS § 267(1) (1981).

recourse for any harm she suffers as a result of such "breach." That is, the buyer is "self-insuring" for this risk; she will bear the burden of her own losses.

Accordingly, with this in mind, let's look at two more of the most commonly used contractual tools for allocating risks between parties: indemnification and limitation of liability.

a. Indemnification

Indemnification clauses act to shift the risk of the occurrence of certain specified events, often third-party claims, to one party (the "indemnitor") by requiring this party to compensate the other party (the "indemnitee") for losses arising from such events.[75] At common law and absent a contract addressing the issue, a party may have an obligation to indemnify a second party for the first party's own wrongdoing, where the second party has been held liable (e.g., on a vicarious-liability theory) for the first party's wrongdoing.[76] However, parties may wish not to rely on these default rights and laws and may instead wish to specify by contract a party's indemnification obligations.

Courts vary in their suspicion of indemnification provisions. While these provisions are generally enforceable, some states have a general policy of distrust of indemnification provisions and will construe them strictly against the interests of the indemnitee.[77] On the other hand, other states subscribe to the "modern rule" that "contracts of indemnity are to be fairly and reasonably construed in order to ascertain the intention of the parties and to effectuate the purpose sought to be accomplished."[78] Futhermore, an indemnification provision will generally not operate to indemnify an indemnitee against the indemnitee's *own negligence*, unless the language of the provision clearly and specifically provides as much.[79] In addition, an indemnification provision will generally not be enforceable to indemnify an indemnitee against the

---

75. *See, e.g., Promuto v. Waste Mgmt., Inc.,* 44 F. Supp. 2d 628, 651 (S.D.N.Y. 1999) (finding an indemnification provision, by its terms, to provide a remedy for breach of a warranty made within that agreement). Indemnification clauses are sometimes referred to as "hold harmless" provisions, and often a provision will include language that a party agrees to "hold harmless" the other party. Indemnification and "hold harmless" language generally will have the same effect. *See* BLACK'S LAW DICTIONARY 837-38 (9th ed. 2009). ("A contractual provision in which one party agrees to answer for any specified or unspecified liability or harm that the other party might incur. — Also termed *hold-harmless clause*."); *see, e.g., Ellis v. Landings Assocs., Ltd.,* No. 1:04CV120LG-RHW, 2006 WL 568706, at *2 n.2 (S.D. Miss. Mar. 7, 2006).

76. *See* RESTATEMENT (THIRD) OF TORTS § 22 (2000); RESTATEMENT (SECOND) OF TORTS § 886B (1979).

77. *See, e.g., Akhenaten v. Najee, LLC,* No. 07 CV 970(RJH), 2010 WL 305309, at *1 (S.D.N.Y. Jan. 26, 2010) ("[U]nder New York law indemnity contracts are narrowly construed.")

78. *See, e.g., MacGlashin v. Dunlop Equip. Co.,* 89 F.3d 932, 940 (1st Cir. 1996) (internal quotation marks and citation omitted) ("The rule that indemnity contracts are to be strictly construed against the indemnitee no longer obtains in Massachusetts.").

79. *See United States v. Seckinger,* 397 U.S. 203, 211 (1970) ("[A] contractual provision should not be construed to permit an indemnitee to recover for his own negligence unless the court is firmly convinced that such an interpretation reflects the intention of the parties. This principle, though variously articulated, is accepted with virtual unanimity among American jurisdictions.").

indemnitee's *intentional* misconduct.[80] (Note that an indemnification provision that is unenforceable with respect to an indemnitee's intentional misconduct may still be valid with respect to the indemnitee's negligent act.[81])

Making Sense of Indemnity Agreements

One of the most common features of both tort and contract liability rules is that their terms are more diverse than one might expect. In dealing with the tort side of matters, commentators often say that negligence is the general rule. But in the next breath, they recognize that the law also incorporates large pockets of strict liability. Take another deep breath, and lo and behold, tort liability in many cases turns on gross negligence or willful neglect. One skeptical view of the tort scene is that the judges or the lawyers, or both, are seeking to juggle too many balls in the air, only to drop them all. But a closer look at the field often suggests that each of these various standards has a peculiar home in which its use makes more sense than any of its rivals.

Linking the different theories of liability to different contexts is what makes for a good lawyer. Here is one partial approximation of how this works on the tort side. Strict liability tends to be the operative norm for harms inflicted against the real property of other individuals, who can scarcely be expected to get out of the way. Negligence, often based on customary care, tends to be the standard of liability in medical malpractice cases, because throwing the risk of adverse events on the physician in difficult cases is too extensive relative to any reasonable fee that could be charged. Recklessness tends to be the standard with athletic injuries because athletes, both professional and amateur, old and young, are all negligent all the time, and the prospect of lawsuits would overwhelm the cooperative venture.

Now note the next move. Of the cases mentioned, only the first is a true tort case. The other two arise out of incompletely defined cooperative arrangements. The variation in their terms reflects the different social setting in which the obligations may be imposed. The object in all cases is to give some protection against misconduct of the other party, without driving them away from the deal altogether. Both sides face the same constraint.

Looking at this complex service arrangement between AOL and TW shows how these same instincts carry over when the requirements of business make deals more formal than they would otherwise be. Some judges look with suspicion on indemnity agreements, thinking that they represent an effort of either, or both,

---

80. *See, e.g., Town of Massena v. Healthcare Underwriters Mut. Ins. Co.*, 779 N.E.2d 167, 171 (N.Y. 2002). *But see Dixon Distrib. Co. v. Hanover Ins. Co.*, 641 N.E.2d 395, 401 (Ill. 1994). In addition, some states will not enforce an indemnification provision with regard to an indemnitee's act of "gross negligence." *Compare Caldwell v. Enyeart*, 72 F.3d 129, at *4 (6th Cir. 1995) ("[W]e conclude that under Michigan law a contract to indemnify a party for liability for its own gross negligence violates public policy."), *with St. Paul Fire and Marine Ins. Co. v. Universal Builders Supply*, 409 F.3d 73, 86 (2d Cir. 2005) (New York law). Also to keep in mind, there may be various federal and state statutes that intersect with and alter the effect of these general rules with regard to certain types of indemnification provisions. *See, e.g., O & G Indus., Inc. v. Nat'l R.R. Passenger Corp.*, 537 F.3d 153, 156-63 (2d Cir. 2008) (explaining how a federal statute preempted a Connecticut state statute, which "prohibit[ed], on public policy grounds, indemnity agreements entered into in connection with construction contracts, if they purport[ed] to shield the indemnitee from liability for its own negligence").

81. *See, e.g., Caldwell*, 72 F.3d at *4.

parties to duck out of serious obligations. But the story does not really hold. Just who is exploiting whom when the obligations are so reciprocal?

Most of these agreements contain mutual covenants between parties whose positions are similar in some respect and different in others. That point is clear with this agreement when the general principle of mutual indemnification does not carry over to IP and Customer Site and Customer Domain Agreements. Looking at this agreement, the first task of the outsider is to figure out why, which is not easily done unless one knows the services that each supplies the other. In this case, the indemnity clause arose in the context of a somewhat unusual transaction, the break-up of the highly public but ill-fated merger of Time-Warner and AOL. It was a classic case in which the supposed synergies of a content provider and an internet service provider did not pan out. At this point, the indemnity is an attempt to make the separation work cleanly, so that AOL has to defend TW on its home turf of IP rights, while TW has to do the same for AOL on its home turf involving distribution matters. It is hard for anyone to think that either party can exploit the other in the first cause, given its reciprocal nature. And once the asymmetrical positions are identified with respect to IP issues, it is easier to understand why these clauses may require each side to protect the other against its own greatest vulnerabilities.

Yet the story is not finished. It doesn't do quite enough in contract contexts to just identify the covered events. The standards of liability have to be established as well. What is notable about these agreements is how parasitic they are in key particulars on many features of the basic contract law. The agreement talks about mutual indemnification in cases of "material breach," which comes straight out of hornbook contract law. The point seems to be that we do not want to invoke the costly machinery of contract to small breaches that tend to cancel each other out anyway, as part of a "live-and-let-live regime."

Next the tort obligations run pretty deep, and they too reflect the full range of liability standards encountered on the tort side of the line. If those distinctions matter in the one context, they surely must matter in the other. Let negligence or misconduct be used in connection with the primary breach, and we know that liability is a likely prospect in at least some cases, given the volume of anticipated business. But when the indemnity is limited, as in Clause 10.4, to actions of negligence, recklessness or intentional misconduct, the standards of care are obviously not symmetrical. To pretend that there are no differences is to mock the agreement. So one has to figure out how this deal is organized. In this regard, it is instructive to note that this agreement parallels the common pattern in liability found in the workers' compensation area, where the strict obligation of the employer is met by a duty on the worker only to avoid willful misconduct. Knowing why is key: here is one hint. In the compensation area a worker is subject to bodily risk and the employer is not. Where would you put most of the legal pressure?

And finally, one way to think about all contractual provisions is as a decision tree. At each point in the life of the contract, a party has to know not only the standard of liability but also the consequences in dollar terms of breach. Why? Well if you can't quantify the liability, how do you know whether the future revenue stream will cover the anticipated losses. So it is again common practice to draft provisions that cap liability, just as in ordinary insurance contracts. This contract has a provision of that sort tied to the total consideration paid between the companies, except in cases of gross negligence or willful breach. Once again, ask why this configuration, and reflect that this dual track damage system is nothing novel. It was in fact part of the Roman law of sale, which limited liability to "direct losses" (e.g. the destruction of a thing) for ordinary breaches, but allowed recovery for "consequential losses"—e.g., lost business opportunities—in the event of willful breach.

In the end, therefore, success in both drafting and interpreting contracts requires a high level of respect for both profession and craft. Unless you know the legal tradition in which you work, you cannot piece together the building blocks needed to assemble your overall agreement. Yet once you know these, you have to be attentive to the needs of the business to determine their proper pattern in an individual case. When drafting agreements, your job is first to get the right distribution of liabilities and benefits, and then to determine the pricing terms that makes the deal go. In litigation, knowing how those business elements work gives you a leg up in understanding and resolving, hopefully short of litigation, the relevant disputes. There is no room for cynicism in working with, and through, the language of the law.

Professor Richard A. Epstein
Laurence A. Tisch Professor of Law
New York University School of Law
Peter and Kirsten Bedford Senior Fellow
The Hoover Institution
Senior Lecturer in Law
The University of Chicago Law School

Sections 10.1 and 10.2 of the AOL Agreement both provide indemnity obligations. As you may have guessed from its caption, section 10.1 specifies indemnification obligations that, on their face, are equally applicable to both Parties. Specifically, section 10.1 provides that should a Third Party bring an action against a Party resulting from the other Party's material breach of this Agreement, then the breaching Party will indemnify the non-breaching party for Losses resulting from that Action. From either Party's perspective, does this indemnification obligation seem fair? Does it seem sufficient—should Losses from Actions based on *non*-material breaches be included, again from the perspective of either party?

Section 10.1 also provides an indemnity for Losses resulting from an Action brought by a Third Party for the Indemnifying Party's (or its various agents') negligence, misconduct, or violation of law in connection with performing this Agreement that caused injury to natural persons (that is, not to business entities) or damages to tangible property. Is this too broad? Is it too narrow? Why should the indemnification be limited to misconduct only related to the performance of this Agreement? What if a Third Party brings suit against a Party for the other Party's illegal act wholly unrelated to this Agreement?

Section 10.2 imposes an indemnification obligation on only AOL for intellectual property infringement and on only Time Warner for various claims relating to Time Warner's Customer Site. If a Third Party brings a claim against a TW Company because AOL's Service infringes that Third Party's intellectual property rights, what are AOL's obligations and rights under this provision? As we briefly discussed in the context of warranties, a party may sometimes give a warranty of non-infringement, and, as we see now, alternatively, a party may promise to indemnify for third-party infringement. Some view the demand for one over the other in practice to turn on a distinction without a difference and to depend mostly on which is listed on the attorney's standard negotiation "checklist." For deeper insight into how practitioners approach and think about this issue, we turned to a couple seasoned practitioners for their perspective.

> ### *A Practitioner Perspective: Warranty vs. Indemnity for IP Infringement*
>
> In the context of a service engagement in which the service provider will potentially (i) utilize pre-existing intellectual property ("IP") owned by the provider, the client and/or a third party, (ii) develop new IP and (iii) include some combination of such pre-existing and newly-developed IP in its deliverables (via grants of ownership or license rights), it is standard practice for the client to negotiate some degree of protection against claims that such activity constitutes IP infringement. Once the general scope of such protection has been defined (e.g., infringement of registered domestic IP rights) and any exceptions thereto have been excluded (e.g., items provided by, on behalf of, or per the specifications of the client; improper usage/modification/combination), the outcome of such negotiation must be documented in a contractual mechanism. Such mechanism typically takes the form of a warranty and/or an indemnity.
>
> There are several key distinctions between the warranty approach and the indemnity approach. Under the indemnity approach, the service provider typically agrees (within the agreed-upon scope and subject to the agreed-upon exceptions) to defend and/or make whole the client if the client faces an infringement claim. In other words, the client seeks protection by causing the service provider to perform an express contractual obligation. Under the warranty approach, the service provider typically warrants (and represents) that there will not be an infringement problem (within the agreed-upon scope and subject to the agreed-upon exceptions). In other words, the client seeks protection by claiming that the service provider committed a breach resulting in a loss. Therefore, at the outset, the warranty approach (i.e., establishing a breach and a related loss) may confront the client with a more difficult burden than the indemnity approach (i.e., demanding performance).
>
> An indemnity-without-warranty approach can offer certain advantages for the service provider (i.e., the indemnitor). For example, it is typical for an

obligation to indemnify to be subject to various procedural preconditions (e.g., the indemnitee must provide prompt notice of a claim for which it seeks indemnification; the indemnitee must surrender control of the defense/settlement thereof; the indemnitee must cooperate in such defense) which can often serve to limit or even effectively eliminate the service provider's exposure, whereas it is not typical to see procedural terms (other than a time limit) barring warranty claims. In addition, although a limitation of liability provision (e.g., a cap on aggregate liability; an exclusion of non-direct damages) or an exclusive remedy provision (e.g., reimbursement of losses; rectification of, replacement of, or license to infringing items; refund of amounts paid for infringing items) is always subject to the risk of being held invalid or unenforceable by a court, such a provision might be even more likely to be held invalid or unenforceable if the party seeking to enforce it committed a breach or otherwise has unclean hands. In other words, such a provision might be more likely to be enforceable under the compliance-with-indemnity approach than under the breach-of-warranty approach. However, despite these apparent benefits of the indemnity approach to the service provider, an inadvertently-overbroad indemnity provision might entitle an indemnitee to recover a loss that might not otherwise be recoverable per a warranty claim (e.g., a loss to which the indemnitee contributed).

Although the client may face a more difficult burden seeking a remedy through a prove-a-warranty-breach mechanism than through an enforce-an-indemnity mechanism, the warranty approach can also offer certain advantages for the client. A demonstration of the client's reliance upon a breached non-infringement warranty may not only form the basis for the client's claims for damages arising from the breach—such reliance may also form the basis for claims regarding the formation of the service contract (e.g., fraud). In addition, a demonstration of the client's reliance upon a non-infringement warranty may assist the client in establishing a defense against an infringement claim by a third party.

For these reasons, the client certainly has reasonable justification for seeking a non-infringement warranty in addition to an infringement indemnity. Conversely, if forced to provide protection against infringement, the service provider will typically prefer to provide a tailored and procedurally-conditioned indemnity without a warranty and subject to a limitation of liability provision and an exclusive remedy provision. A common compromise is a linked warranty-and-indemnity in which the service provider provides a non-infringement warranty and, as an exclusive remedy for breach of such warranty, a limited indemnity for damages arising from such breach. In such a situation, the extent to which the compromise actually holds will depend upon the contract drafting, the factual circumstances and the application of the governing law.

Alan A. D'Ambrosio, Partner
Orrick, Herrington & Sutcliffe LLP

Steven Barnett, Senior Associate
Orrick, Herrington & Sutcliffe LLP

What sections 10.1 and 10.2 giveth, section 10.4 taketh away. Section 10.4 specifically limits the extent of all indemnification obligations provided by the Agreement, providing that a Party's (i.e., the indemnitor's) indemnification obligations are to be reduced to the extent of the other Party's (i.e., the indemnitee's) negligence, recklessness, or intentional misconduct (which, you will notice, is in line with the judicial presumption that an indemnification provision does not operate to indemnify a party for its own negligence). That is, if the indemnitee has contributed to the indemnitor's would-be indemnification obligation (with conduct that is at least negligent), the indemnitor need not indemnify the indemnitee for the amount attributable to this contribution. Does and/or should (and/or could) the Agreement provide clarity as to how this would be measured? Also, notice with this provision that captions do not always capture a provision's entire contents (a lesson for the contract reader, but the lesson for the contract drafter is that captions probably should), as section 10.4 ("Limitation of Indemnity"), in addition to limiting indemnification, also *provides* additional indemnification obligations. As we will soon see, one risks subjecting the scope of a provision to a narrow reading, when one lumps such a provision with other provisions in a section that speaks to a more specific matter.

A Practitioner Perspective: Indemnification Issues in Practice

In contract negotiations, one party frequently seeks to be indemnified against any liabilities and costs that it might incur by virtue of the contractual relationship. The scope of an indemnification provision will thus become a subject of negotiation. At a minimum, any indemnification should be limited to liabilities and costs arising out of the misconduct or negligence of the indemnifying party. Moreover, it should be made reciprocal. In other words, if X is required to indemnify Y against specified developments, Y should be asked to indemnify X against eventualities about which X is concerned. These may, but need not, be the same as those covered by X's indemnifications.

Beyond seeking to minimize the scope of an indemnification and making it reciprocal, it is good practice to avoid giving an indemnification at all. There are two reasons. First, any liability undertaken through an indemnification clause will generally not be covered by the indemnitor's insurance. Thus, if a condition triggering the indemnification arises, the liabilities and costs associated therewith will be the responsibility of the indemnitor—not its insurer. This result can, of course, be devastating if the indemnitor is required to make good on the indemnification.

The risks that an insurance company undertakes are generally limited to negligent and other not-intentionally tortious conduct by the insured. By contrast, indemnification clauses create risks voluntarily undertaken by contract. Underwriters do not factor in such risks in setting premiums. Thus, it is far preferable, if possible, to get the insurance company to add the would-be indemnified party as a named insured to the proposed indemnifier's insurance policy. In this way, the insurer can set premiums based on its valuation of the risk. If the contractual party is added as a named insured, the risk will be on the insurer—not on the contracting party.

The second risk in indemnification clauses is more subtle. Let's say that each party to a contract indemnifies the other against its negligence. Let's say further that something happens that causes injury to a third party. It is foreseeable that each party will take the position that the bad development was the result of the other's negligence—and will seek to be indemnified by the other. The consequence will be a finger-pointing contest that will redound to the benefit of the third party.

The situation can be illustrated by a contract between a hospital and a group of pathologists for the operation of the laboratory at the hospital. Suppose the hospital indemnifies the pathologists against its negligence while the pathology group indemnifies the hospital against its negligence. Now, let's say that a patient suffers an injury allegedly as a result of a laboratory error. There may be a real question as to whether there was any negligence at all. However, if the hospital and the pathology group seek indemnification from the other based on an indemnification against the negligence of the other, they will be rewarded with a huge judgment against each of them.

One final note on indemnification. An indemnification is only as good as the capitalization of the indemnitor. If the indemnitor does not have sufficient assets to cover the indemnification, the indemnified party has bought nothing more than a scrap of paper.

Jack Bierig, Partner
Sidley Austin LLP
Lecturer in Law
The University of Chicago Law School

A classic example of an indemnity agreement is an insurance agreement, as insurance is at its core nothing more than a promise by one party (i.e., the insurer) to pay for the losses of another (i.e., the insured). Contractual parties may sometimes wish to shift the risk of certain losses to a third-party insurer and to obtain an insurance policy to cover this risk. Of course, this insurance is unlikely to come free, and the parties will still have to negotiate about which party (or whether both parties) will pay the cost of this insurance. The viability of third-party insurance as a solution often depends on the specific context, including the type of risk for which insurance is to be obtained, the availability of willing third-party insurers, the type of coverage available, and the cost of obtaining the insurance. On this issue, a seasoned practitioner offers additional insight.

A Practitioner Perspective: Insurance Euphoria

Parties to a contract may feel themselves protected by insurance that they have purchased. However, their sense of security may not be fully justified. This is so for several reasons.

First, insurance policies inevitably contain exclusions. It often happens that an insured party is sued, tenders the claim to the insurer, but finds, to its dismay, that the cause of action asserted against it is excluded by some obscure subparagraph of a multi-page policy. Similarly, sometimes a policy will provide coverage for attorneys' fees but not damages. For these reasons, the exclusions from, and limitations of, any policy need to be clearly understood. It can be disconcerting when the insurer denies coverage—or even when it provides coverage "subject to a reservation of rights."

Second, the insured must be careful to abide by all the conditions of coverage. For example, most policies require prompt reporting of any claim. If the insured does not timely notify the insurer of a threat of litigation, the insured may be deemed to have waived the coverage. In a similar vein, policies generally exclude disputes that existed before the insurance was purchased. If a known dispute was not disclosed in the application form but later ripens into litigation, the company is likely to deny coverage.

Third, almost all policies impose a so-called "retention" or "deductible" threshold. The policyholder must pay all fees and damages until the retention amount is reached. In some policies, the amount can be quite high. It is important to know the retention amount.

Fourth, many policies permit the insurer to designate counsel. This feature can cause difficulties when the insured wants to use lawyers in whom it has confidence but the insurer chooses to assign counsel on its panel. Panel counsel usually have agreed to accept fees significantly lower than those charged by the insured's regular counsel—and may well not have as much experience or skill as counsel that the insured would select. This problem can sometimes be remedied if the insured agrees to pay the difference between the hourly rate of counsel of its choice and that of the insurer's choice. But this solution may not be acceptable to the insurer and, in any event, can result in significant out-of-pocket costs to the insured.

Given these issues in insurance coverage, a party to a contract may want to cap by agreement any liability that it will have to bear arising out of the agreement.

Jack Bierig, Partner
Sidley Austin LLP
Lecturer in Law
The University of Chicago Law School

b. Limitation of Liability

In addition to disclaiming warranties and seeking indemnification, there are several other ways to limit a party's exposure to liability under a contract. Perhaps the simplest way is to place a cap on the dollar amount of a party's liability exposure—such a ceiling may be defined as a stated dollar amount, tied to the purchase price, or defined however else the parties desire. These are commonly referred to as "limitation-of-liability" provisions. Such a provision is found in section 10.9 ("Maximum Liability") of the AOL Agreement. Section 10.9 provides that, regardless of any other provision of the Agreement, each Party's liability for all matters related to the Agreement is limited to the total amount paid by each TW Company to AOL under the Agreement over the course of the prior twelve months. However, notice that this cap does not apply to liability related to (i) acts of gross negligence and willful misconduct, (ii) breaches of confidentiality obligations; (iii) the indemnification obligations found in the Agreement. Why do you suppose the parties removed these things from the cap, leaving these categories of potential liability effectively boundless? To what extent do these "carve-outs" from the cap reduce the cap's overall effectiveness? Taking the perspective of either party, would you argue that anything else should be excluded from—or included under—the cap?

Another common way of limiting a party's exposure to liability under an agreement is to exclude certain *types* of liability. For instance, section 10.8 of this Agreement provides that no Party is liable for several different kinds of damages, including punitive, indirect, and consequential damages. Excepted from this exclusion (that is, carved out from the exclusion) are, again, (i) acts of gross negligence and willful misconduct; (ii) breaches of confidentiality obligations; and (iii) the indemnification obligations. The net of this provision, then, is that no Party shall be liable for certain types of liability (e.g., consequential damages), except for liability related to three circumstances (i.e., gross negligence or willful misconduct, confidentiality, and indemnification), where those types of liability—not available in general—are fair game.

In general, limitation-of-liability clauses are enforced in both services and sale-of-goods contracts between sophisticated parties.[82] Courts will strictly construe provisions that limit a party's liability for the party's own negligence but will enforce them.[83] While contracts generally may not completely exempt a party from liability under that contract, they may limit a party's liability exposure.[84] Still, a

---

82. See *Valhal Corp. v. Sullivan Assocs., Inc.*, 44 F.3d 195, 203-04 (3d Cir. 1995) (Pennsylvania law) (observing that limitation-of-liability clauses are "routinely enforced" in sales contracts between sophisticated parties and in services contracts); *Wartsila NSD N. Am., Inc. v. Hill Int'l, Inc.*, 530 F.3d 269 (3d Cir. 2008) (Maryland law) (excluding consequential damages from the available liability under a contract with a provision explicitly excluding consequential damages). Please see Chapter 4 for further discussion of sale-of-goods contracts.

83. See, e.g., *Anunziatta v. Orkin Exterminating Co.*, 180 F. Supp. 2d 353, 359 (N.D.N.Y. 2001).

84. See, e.g., *Elsken v. Network Multi-Family Sec. Corp.*, 49 F.3d 1470, 1475 (10th Cir. 1995) (Oklahoma law); *Mobile Satellite Commc'ns, Inc. v. Intelsat USA Sales Corp.*, 646 F. Supp. 2d 124, 136 (D.D.C. 2009) (New York law).

limitation of liability generally will not be enforced as to a party's own acts of *gross* negligence or willful misconduct, which explains why this is often a limitation-of-liability "carve-out."[85]

A Practitioner Perspective: Limitations-of-Liability "Carve-Outs" for Services

Limitations of liability in service agreements typically include both (1) an exclusion of consequential, incidental, special and punitive damages, and (2) a cap on the amount of direct damages for which the service provider would be liable. The liability cap may be a specified dollar amount or a dollar limit that is tied in some manner to the amount of fees paid by the customer to the service provider.

The rationale behind limitations of liability is that they reflect both the limited control that the service provider has in managing the risks in a customer's enterprise and the limited reward the service provider stands to gain from assuming the risks of managing that enterprise. The service provider's perspective is that it is performing a service at an efficient price, which does not factor in the cost of insuring the customer against broad business risks. The service provider argues that the customer would have had the same risk if its own employees were performing the services, and that the customer is actually in a better position by virtue of the liability that the service provider will assume, albeit limited. The customer's perspective is that by handing over control of one of its functions to a service provider, the customer becomes dependent on the service provider to properly manage the risk of its performance. The customer further argues that the allocation of risk is essential to maintaining the proper incentive for the service provider, since the financial structure normally creates an adverse incentive by rewarding the service provider with higher profits when it is able to reduce its costs and investments, which can in turn create risks for the customer.

While limitations of liability (including both exclusions and caps) are a staple of service agreements, customers often seek exceptions to these limitations to cover specific risks to which the customer believes the limitations should not apply. The negotiation of these exceptions can be one of the more difficult issues in contracting for services.

Below is a list of exclusions that may be requested by the customer in certain service arrangements.

85.

Three exceptions have been identified where the public interest will render [a limitation of liability] clause unenforceable: (1) when the party protected by the clause intentionally causes harm or engages in acts of reckless, wanton, or gross negligence; (2) when the bargaining power of one party to the contract is so grossly unequal so as to put that party at the mercy of the other's negligence; and (3) when the transaction involves the public interest. *Elsken*, 49 F.3d at 1475; *Hill Int'l*, 530 F.3d at 274 (Maryland law). Under Article 2 of the U.C.C., a contract may disclaim or limit consequential damages; however, this will not be effective as to damages for injury to a person in the context of consumer goods. U.C.C. § 2-719 (2003).

Representative Exceptions

The limitations of liability shall not apply to:

1. *Losses occasioned by the fraud, willful misconduct, or gross negligence of a party.*
2. *Losses occasioned by service provider's refusal to provide services (where "refusal" means the intentional cessation by service provider, in a manner impermissible under this Agreement, of the performance of all or a material portion of the services then required to be provided by service provider under this Agreement).*
3. *Losses occasioned by any breach of a party's representations or warranties under this Agreement.*
4. *Losses that are the subject of indemnification under this Agreement, including:*
(a) *Breach of representations and warranties*
(b) *Death or bodily injury of an agent, employee, business invitee, business visitor or other person or damage, loss or destruction of real or tangible personal property*
(c) *Infringement*
(d) *Compliance with Laws*
(e) *Breach of confidentiality*
(f) *Taxes*
(g) *Employment claims*
(h) *Claims under the Agreement by affiliates and subcontractors*

Analysis and Comment

The selection of the particular exceptions that are appropriate for any service agreement, and the weight of each party's argument in negotiating them, depends heavily on the facts and circumstances of the particular services arrangement. Consider some of the issues that can arise for each of the above exceptions:

1. *Fraud, willful misconduct and gross negligence.* Can a party limit its liability for fraud? If not, then is the exception even necessary, and is conceding it really much of a concession at all? What does *willful misconduct* mean in the selected jurisdiction? That term is not consistently defined and can have very different meanings under different states' laws. For example, in some states willful misconduct includes efficient breaches (i.e., breaches intended only to prevent further economic loss under the contract), while in other states it does not. What does *gross negligence* mean in the applicable jurisdiction? Like willful misconduct, the term gross negligence is not consistently defined under the various state laws. Since gross negligence is a variant of negligence, should it be a complete exception or should it instead only give rise to a higher cap on liability?

2. *Service provider's refusal to provide services.* This exception should only be applicable where the services involve a critical business function of the customer's business. The customer's purpose for having this exception is to ensure that the service provider never has any economic incentive to abandon performance of the services and is never inclined to threaten suspension of mission-critical services as a means of resolving a dispute. Even when

the service involves a mission-critical function, consider whether there are instances where the service provider should or must have the right to with-hold services given the potential harm to the service provider's interest. Could the customer's concern about abandonment be addressed by adequate notice to allow a transition of responsibility? Is there a higher limit of liability that would be adequate to assure customer that the service provider has no incentive to abandon the services, but which still protects the service provider from unlimited liability?

3. *Breach of a party's representations or warranties under this Agreement.* The appropriateness of this exception depends entirely on the content of the representations and warranties. The exception may be appropriate for some representations and warranties, such as compliance with laws, but may be inappropriate for others, such as representations and warranties regarding the quality of the services, which could have the effect of nullifying the limitations of liability by excluding performance failures that result from simple negligence.

4. *Losses that are the subject of indemnification.* The same analysis as above should be applied to the indemnities since the indemnities are another form of allocating risk. For example, which warranties should be subject to an indemnity? What qualifications and exceptions should apply to the infringement indemnity? What laws should be service provider's responsibility and which should be customer's responsibility? Are there any exceptions to service provider's liability for disclosure of customer's confidential information? Are there any exceptions for service provider's responsibility for employment related claims by its employees against the customer? Are there any exceptions where the service provider's affiliates and subcontractors should be entitled to make a direct claim against the customer? Consider also whether the indemnity is limited to third-party claims or if it also includes direct claims by the customer. In service agreements, indemnities are more commonly limited to third-party claims. That is often not the case in other corporate M&A agreements (e.g., stock purchase agreements or asset purchase agreements). Finally, if the service provider has unlimited liability for the indemnities, does the service provider get to control the defense and settlement of the third party claim giving rise to the indemnity?

As noted above, one of the principles of limitations of liability is that the service provider's limited control should result in limited liability. In analyzing undertakings in the contract, consider whether the covenants that can give rise to unlimited liability reflect risks over which the service provider exerts complete control. If not, consider how the covenant can be narrowed to reflect what the service provider can control. For example, a service provider may be able to manage its risk for protecting confidential information by requiring that the customer specify the security protocol that each party must follow with regard to any confidential information supplied to the service provider, with the understanding that service provider's compliance with the protocol will serve as a safe harbor protection, even if unauthorized access was obtained despite its compliance. A similar approach may apply to a compliance with laws covenant.

What makes limitations of liability a difficult issue is that it lends itself both to arguments of fairness and accountability (i.e., "Why shouldn't you (service provider) be responsible for the damages you cause?") and arguments of commercial reasonableness (i.e., "I (service provider) am not your insurance company. I am just an efficient provider who doesn't share in the profits of your company."). Finding the allocation of risk that properly reflects the balance of control, responsibility and reward is a critical component of any transaction. It can also affect the sustainability of the service provider's business model and the willingness of customers to enter into service arrangement for sensitive or critical services. As you consider these issues, bear in mind that there is no simple answer to any of these questions, since they are deal-specific and can vary depending on the subject matter of the contract, the relative position of the parties, industry norms, applicable laws and the general business environment.

Paul Roy, Partner
Mayer Brown LLP

(1) Understanding "Consequential" Damages

As in section 10.8 of the AOL Agreement, services agreements will commonly exclude consequential, special, incidental, punitive, and indirect damages from the potential liability to which one or both (or, more, in the case of a multi-party agreement) parties may be exposed under an agreement. As we explore the distinction between these damages terms, take heart in that even seasoned practitioners may have a hard time explaining the distinction between consequential and general damages as well as the distinction between consequential and special, incidental, punitive, and indirect damages.

(a) Distinguishing General and Consequential Damages

"General" (or "direct") damages refer to those damages that result naturally from a breach of a contract.[86] Such damages act to give the non-breaching party the party's expected value of the contract, as if it were fully performed as contractually provided. That is, a breach occurs when a party does not fully perform in accordance with the contract. This departure from full performance results in the non-breaching party receiving less than that which

---

86. *See Hill Int'l*, 530 F.3d at 277; *TransDulles Ctr., Inc. v. USX Corp.*, 976 F.2d 219, 226 (4th Cir. 1992) (Virginia law) ("Direct damages are those which arise naturally or ordinarily from a breach of contract and which, in the ordinary course of human experience, can be expected to result from the breach.").

the non-breaching party expected to receive as bargained-for consideration under the contract. Accordingly, general contract damages are generally in the amount of this "benefit of the bargain" or "expectation" interest—to compensate the plaintiff for that which she "should" have received under the contract.[87]

In contrast, consequential damages are those damages, beyond general damages, that proximately result as a consequence of a breach of contract.[88] As a general rule of thumb, while general damages are likely to be suffered by any person in the position of the non-breaching party, consequential damages are often peculiar to an individual non-breaching party.[89] To recover consequential damages, a party generally must show that the breach caused the consequential damages and that such damages were foreseeable at the time the parties entered into the contract.[90] In other words, consequential damages are not the same thing as remote or unforeseeable damages. But, whereas consequential damages turn on the occurrence of various events that may *result* from breach, general damages turn on the value of the contract itself, namely the value of the contract unrealized by the non-breaching party due to the other party's breach.[91]

Notice that section 10.8 of the AOL Agreement lists "lost profits" as one of the many things for which no party shall be liable. Are lost profits general or consequential damages? The answer is that they can be both. A party may expect to earn a certain profit *under* a contract: For example, if A expected to pay B ten dollars for a twenty-dollar widget, then A expected to earn a ten-dollar profit under the contract. If B fails to sell the widget to A and if A has not yet paid B, then A's general damages are its lost profits of ten dollars. By contrast, if A planned to use the widgets to make super widgets and, because of B's failure to perform, A claims it missed an opportunity to make a $10,000 profit from selling super widgets, then A may seek to recover such lost profits from B as consequential damages. Accordingly, lost profits may be a loss in the value of the contract as general damages, and lost profits may be a loss resulting from a breach as consequential damages. Some courts have found that, where

---

87. *See New Valley Corp. v. United States*, 72 Fed. Cl. 411, 414 (2006) ("'[G]eneral damages' are damages measured by the loss of the value of the performance promised by the breaching party."); *see also* RESTATEMENT (SECOND) OF CONTRACTS § 347(a) (1981).

88. *See New Valley Corp.*, 72 Fed. Cl. at 414 ("Consequential damages...on the other hand, are those damages that result as a secondary consequence of the defendant's non-performance [and that] arise from the interposition of an additional cause, without which the act done would have produced no harmful result.") (internal citation and quotation marks omitted); *Hill Int'l*, 530 F.3d at 277 ("[D]amages which a plaintiff may recover for breach of contract include...those which may reasonably be supposed to have been in the contemplation of both parties at the time of making of the contract (special damages)."); *see also* RESTATEMENT (SECOND) OF CONTRACTS § 347 cmt. c (1981); U.C.C. § 2-715(2) (2003).

89. *See Hill Int'l*, 530 F.3d at 277.

90. *See id.*

91. *See, e.g., New Valley Corp.*, 72 Fed. Cl. at 414 ("Consequential damages are thus distinguishable from general damages in that rather than being based on the value of the promised performance itself, they are based on the value of some consequence that that performance may produce.").

a contract excludes "lost profits" from liability, as does section 10.8, such a provision refers only to consequential lost profits and "precludes recovery of only those lost profits and lost revenues beyond direct economic loss or ordinary loss of bargain damages."[92]

(b) Distinguishing Consequential and the Litany

As for the other oft-recited types of damages, "special" and "consequential" damages are synonymous.[93] The term "indirect" damages may be used interchangeably with "consequential"[94] or to mean, more broadly, all damages that are not direct damages (e.g., "incidental" damages are not direct damages).[95] Punitive damages refer to damages that seek to punish—that is, to do more than compensate—the breaching party.[96] A fundamental policy of contract law is the principle of "just compensation," which states that contract law's object is to compensate and not to punish.[97] Accordingly, punitive damages are generally not available for a pure breach-of-contract claim.[98] However, because punitive damages may be recovered for tortious conduct,[99] liability-exclusion provisions will still commonly disclaim punitive damages. With certain exceptions, these punitive-damages exclusions have generally been enforced.[100] Finally, inciden-

---

92. *Penncro Assocs., Inc. v. Sprint Corp.*, No. 04-2549-JWL, 2006 WL 416227, at *8 (D. Kan. Feb. 22, 2006) ("The court's conclusion is consistent with other courts that have analyzed similar limitation of damages provisions.") (citing cases decided under California, New York, and Pennsylvania law). The provision in *Penncro* differed from the provision in § 10.8 of the Agreement in that the *Penncro* provision excluded consequential damages and provided that "lost profits" and "lost revenues" were included in the meaning of consequential damages. However, the court in *Penncro* went on to explain that a reading of the provision that excluded damages for both direct and indirect lost profits and revenues would leave a service provider with no recourse in damages if a buyer refused to pay for services rendered and that such "construction is not reasonable." *Id.*

93. *See, e.g., Hill Int'l*, 530 F.3d at 277 n.6 ("The terms 'special damages' and 'consequential damages' usually are viewed as synonymous.").

94. *See, e.g., Cooper v. Meridian Yachts, Ltd.*, 575 F.3d 1151, 1167 (11th Cir. 2009) (using "consequential" and "indirect" interchangeably); *Washington & O.D. Ry. v. Westinghouse Elec. & Mfg. Co.*, 91 S.E. 646 (Va. 1917) (using "consequential" and "indirect" interchangeably).

95. *Compare Wayne Mem'l Hosp., Inc. Wayne Health Corp. v. Elec. Data Sys. Corp.*, No. 87-905-CIV-5-H, 1990 WL 606686, at *9 n.5 (E.D.N.C. Apr. 10, 1990) ("[I]ncidental damages are not direct but rather indirect damages."), *with Mitsui O.S.K. Lines, Ltd. v. Consol. Rail Corp.*, 743 A.2d 362 (N.J. Super. A.D. 2000) (finding "consequential, special, or indirect damages" not to include incidental damages).

96. *See* RESTATEMENT (SECOND) OF CONTRACTS § 355 cmt. a (1981).

97. *See id.; see also* Charles J. Goetz & Robert E. Scott, *Liquidated Damages, Penalties and the Just Compensation Principle: Some Notes on an Enforcement Model and a Theory of Efficient Breach*, 77 COLUM. L. REV. 554 (1977).

98. *See* RESTATEMENT (SECOND) OF CONTRACTS § 355 (1981) ("Punitive damages are not recoverable for a breach of contract unless the conduct constituting the breach is also a tort for which punitive damages are recoverable."); *Pilot Life Ins. Co. v. Dedeaux*, 481 U.S. 41, 49 (1987) ("[T]he Mississippi Supreme Court explained that punitive damages could be available when the breach of contract was attended by some intentional wrong, insult, abuse, or gross negligence, which amounts to an independent tort.") (citation and internal quotation marks omitted).

99. *See supra* note 98.

100. *See, e.g., Sanderson Farms, Inc. v. Gatlin*, 848 So. 2d 828, 854 (Miss. 2003); *Baravati v. Josephthal, Lyon & Ross, Inc.*, 28 F.3d 704, 709 (7th Cir. 1994) ("For that matter, parties to adjudication have considerable power to vary the normal procedures, and surely can stipulate that punitive damages will not be awarded.") (internal citations omitted). However, note that at least one court has refused to enforce a

tal damages are distinct from consequential damages. Incidental damages refer to the expenses reasonably incurred by a non-breaching party in rejecting goods or in attempting to find replacement performance to substitute for the breaching party's less-than-full performance.[101]

(2) The Economic Loss Doctrine, Actions in Tort, and Limitation of Liability

In general, courts limit the availability of recovery in tort actions by a doctrine called the "economic loss doctrine." As the First Circuit explains, "Like 'duty' and 'proximate clause,' the doctrine cabins what could otherwise be open-ended negligence liability to anyone affected by a negligent act."[102] The economic loss doctrine provides that economic losses are not recoverable in a tort action, unless the action is for personal injury or property damage.[103] Under the doctrine, "property damage" does not include mere injury to a property interest but requires some physical damage to property.[104] Some courts have held that the economic loss doctrine only pertains to contracts for the sale of goods under Article 2 of the U.C.C. and not to services contracts.[105]

So what does a doctrine of tort law have to do with contracts? To avoid a contractual limitation of liability, a plaintiff may seek to frame her claim as an action in tort. However, even if the plaintiff has a bona fide tort claim, the economic loss doctrine operates to limit the efficacy of bringing such a claim. This is because, under the doctrine, an action purely for economic loss (i.e., not involving physical harm to property or person) cannot be stated in tort. This may apply, for example, to the tort of misrepresentation discussed earlier in this chapter.[106]

In addition, most courts will not allow a party to "dress" a contract claim as a tort claim by "artful pleading."[107] This doctrine attempts to police the line between tort and contract.[108] "Tort actions lie for breaches of duties imposed by law as a matter of social policy, while contract actions lie only for

---

contractual provision excluding punitive damages as against public policy. *See Ex parte Thicklin*, 824 So. 2d 723 (Ala. 2002), *overruled on other grounds, Patriot Mfg., Inc. v. Jackson*, 929 So. 2d 997 (Ala. 2005).

101. *See* RESTATEMENT (SECOND) OF CONTRACTS § 347 cmt. c (1981); U.C.C. § 2-715(1) (2003).

102. *In re TJX Cos. Retail Sec. Breach Litig.*, 564 F.3d 489, 498 (1st Cir. 2009).

103. *See TJX Cos.*, 564 F.3d at 498; *Irwin Seating Co. v. Int'l Bus. Machs. Corp.*, 306 F. App'x 239, 242-44 (6th Cir. 2009).

104. *See TJX Cos.*, 564 F.3d at 498.

105. *See, e.g., Ins. Co. of N. Am. v. Cease Elec. Inc.*, 688 N.W.2d 462, 467-68 (Wis. 2004) (recognizing a split among jurisdictions as to whether the economic loss doctrine applies to services contracts and declining to extend the doctrine to apply to non-U.C.C. contracts).

106. *See, e.g., Irwin Seating Co.*, 306 F. App'x at 242-44.

107. *See, e.g., Clark Motor Co., v. Mfrs. and Traders Trust Co.*, 360 F. App'x 340, 347 (3d Cir. 2010) (Pennsylvania law); *Spengler v. ADT Sec. Servs., Inc.*, 505 F.3d 456, 457-58 (6th Cir. 2007) (Michigan law); *Lewis v. Methodist Hosp., Inc.*, 326 F.3d 851, 854 (7th Cir. 2003) (Indiana law); *Carolina Cas. Ins. Co. v. Sowell*, 603 F. Supp. 2d 914, 927-28 (N.D. Tex. 2009); *Great Earth Int'l Franchising Corp. v. Milks Dev.*, 311 F. Supp. 2d 419, 428 (S.D.N.Y. 2004) ("[T]he basic rule is that a tort claim cannot be a reiteration of a breach of contract claim.").

108. *See, e.g., Clark Motor Co.*, 360 F. App'x at 347.

breaches of duties imposed by mutual consensus agreements between particular individuals."[109] Accordingly, even if the economic loss doctrine does not apply, a court is likely to preclude a claim that arises out of a duty provided by contract—or that is otherwise not independent of a contract claim—from being brought in tort.[110]

Moreover, contracts between sophisticated parties will often explicitly provide that limitation-of-liability provisions cover all actions whether stated in contract or tort. For an example, see section 10.8 of the AOL Agreement, which disclaims liability for, among other things, consequential damages "whether under theory of contract, tort (including negligence), strict liability or otherwise." In addition, section 10.9 of the AOL Agreement, in broad language, applies a liability cap to "each party's maximum aggregate liability for all matters related to, in connection with, or arising out of, this agreement." In general, courts will respect these provisions and will give effect to a limitation-of-liability provision between sophisticated parties, regardless of whether the action is pled in contract or tort.[111] However, again, these provisions will generally not insulate a party from liability for gross negligence or willful misconduct.[112]

(3) Exclusive Remedies and Failure of Essential Purpose

In addition to disclaiming warranties and otherwise limiting liability, an agreement may provide that only certain remedies are available as the *exclusive* remedies for certain breaches of the contract. In general, courts will give effect to these exclusivity provisions.[113] A classic example is where an agreement provides that the exclusive remedy for breach of warranty is for the seller either to repair or to replace a defective deliverable or good.[114]

However, at least as to contracts governed by Article 2, where exclusively available remedies fail of their essential purpose, then the limitation restricting the buyer to only those remedies will not be enforced.[115] As an illustration, if the seller fails to act in accordance with a repair-or-replace exclusive-remedy provision (i.e., does not repair or replace a good in a timely or sufficient

---

109. *Id.* (quoting *Bash v. Bell Tel. Co.*, 601 A.2d 825, 829 (Pa. Super. Ct. 1992)).

110. *See, e.g., Clark Motor Co.*, 360 F. App'x at 347 (finding that a duty to ensure the accuracy of information arose from the implied duty of good faith between contractual parties and, so, that a claim for breach of this duty must be brought in contract and not tort).

111. *See, e.g., Youtie v. Macy's Retail Holding, Inc.*, 653 F. Supp. 2d 612, 630 (E.D. Pa. 2009) ("Both Missouri and Pennsylvania law enforce limitation of liability clauses between sophisticated parties to the extent that they are reasonable…, regardless of whether the damages are pled in contract or in tort.").

112. *See, e.g., id.; Doty Commc'ns, Inc. v. L.M. Berry & Co.*, 417 F. Supp. 2d 1355, 1358-59 (N.D. Ga. 2006); *Sommer v. Fed. Signal Corp.*, 79 N.Y.2d 540, 554 (1992).

113. *See, e.g., Citadel Group Ltd. v. Washington Reg'l Med. Ctr.*, No. 07-CV-1394, 2009 WL 1329217, at *8 (N.D. Ill. May 13, 2009) (Illinois law); *Carll v. Terminix Int'l Co., L.P.*, 793 A.2d 921, 924 (Pa. Super. 2002); *see also* U.C.C. § 2-719(1)(b).

114. *See, e.g., Mississippi Chem. Corp. v. Dresser-Rand Co.*, 287 F.3d 359, 366 (5th Cir. 2002) (Mississippi law); *Sunny Indus., Inc. v. Rockwell Int'l Corp.*, 175 F.3d 1021, at *9-10 (7th Cir. 1999) (Illinois law).

115. *See, e.g., Sunny Indus., Inc.*, 175 F.3d 1021, at *9-10.

manner), then a court may make other remedies available to the buyer, under the doctrine of failure of essential purpose.[116] While courts have explained that this doctrine is only applicable in the sale-of-goods context,[117] and, so, does not apply specifically to services contracts, the doctrine is still relevant to our concerns in this chapter. Contracts are often for both goods and services. For instance, many a "services" contract will be for the provision of services that are to result in a "deliverable" product. A question then arises as to whether such a "mixed" contract is governed by Article 2 of the U.C.C., as a sale-of-goods contract, or by the common law, as a services contract. Accordingly, the parties to a "services contract" may wish to plan for the possibility that a court may ultimately find the contract to be governed by Article 2.

For instance, as discussed in this chapter's earlier presentation of disclaimer of warranty, Article 2 imputes certain implied warranties into contracts, unless the contract specifically disclaims such. Given that a court may characterize an agreement as a sale-of-goods contract, a seller of services may wish to disclaim Article 2 implied warranties so as to avoid their potential application. Likewise, the doctrine of failure of essential purpose might ultimately apply to a contract ostensibly for services. In addition, while some courts have explicitly explained that failure of essential purpose is a U.C.C. concept, there is no guarantee that a court will not apply the doctrine by analogy to services contracts.[118] Accordingly, where a seller of services does not act in accordance with the terms of the limited remedies it does afford the buyer, the seller runs the risk of causing a failure of essential purpose of such limited remedies and, as a result, making additional remedies available to the buyer.

With this background on failure of essential purpose in mind, we can begin to digest section 10.10 of the AOL Agreement. This section provides that the limitations and exclusions of liability and disclaimers in the Agreement shall survive despite having been found to fail of their essential purpose. Can such a contractual provision trump the failure-of-essential-purpose doctrine? Based on the limited case law on the subject, it appears that these provisions have not been given effect and that the failure-of-essential-purpose doctrine may

---

116. See, e.g., id.

117. See, e.g., *Darby Anesthesia Assocs., Inc. v. Anesthesia Bus. Consultants, LLC*, No. 06-1565, 2008 WL 2845587, at *5 (E.D. Pa. July 23, 2008) ("Plaintiff's reliance on the failure-of-the-essential-purpose doctrine is misplaced because the doctrine is grounded in the Uniform Commercial Code (UCC) and its associated case law and thus, applicable only to contracts for the sale of goods."); *Plymouth Pointe Condo. Ass'n v. Delcor Homes-Plymouth Pointe, Ltd.*, No. 233847, 2003 WL 22439654, at *2 (Mich. App. Oct. 28, 2003); *see also* U.C.C. § 2-719(2) (2003).

118. For example, in *CBS v. Ziff-Davis*, discussed earlier in this chapter, the high court of New York did not decide the case based on the U.C.C. because the sale of a magazine business is unlikely to qualify as a sale of goods. However, nonetheless, the court was heavily influenced by the U.C.C. in its understanding of warranties. *See Rogath v. Siebenmann*, 129 F.3d 261, 264 (2d Cir. 1997) ("*CBS* was not decided on the basis of the UCC, probably because the sale of the magazine business at issue did not constitute the sale of goods. Nevertheless, the court relied heavily on UCC authorities, expressly noting that analogy to the Uniform Commercial Code is instructive.") (internal citations and quotation marks omitted).

still apply when an exclusive remedy fails despite a provision that provides otherwise.[119] Why might a party still wish to include such a provision?

When an exclusive remedy is found to have failed of its essential purpose, should consequential damages then be available, despite a provision excluding consequential damages? While there is a split of authority, it seems that most courts have held that an exclusion-of-consequential-damages provision and a separate exclusive-remedy provision are independent of each other and that the failure of the essential purpose of an exclusive-remedy provision does not invalidate or affect a provision that excludes consequential damages.[120] To help a court find that a certain limitation-of-liability provision is "independent" of an exclusive remedy that may fail, one should be sure to draft the provisions as separate sections in an agreement.[121] In addition, including language that an exclusion of consequential damages "shall be deemed independent of, and shall survive, any failure of the essential purpose of any limited remedy" has assisted in a court's finding that the exclusion provision was independent of an exclusive-remedy provision and insulated from a failure of essential purpose.[122]

(4) The Interaction of Indemnification and Limitation-of-Liability Provisions

While it is clear from the second sentence of section 10.8 and from section 10.9 that the limitation-of-liability provisions therein do not apply to the indemnification obligations otherwise provided in the Agreement, agreements do not always make this explicit. It is not uncommon to find, in the same agreement, a limitation-of-liability provision that purports to limit all liability under that Agreement and an indemnification provision that expressly provides certain payment obligations conditioned on the occurrence of certain events—and for each to make

---

119. *See, e.g., Evans Indus., Inc. v. Int'l Bus. Machs. Co.*, No. Civ.A. 01-0051, 2004 WL 241701, at *8-9 (E.D. La. Feb. 6, 2004) (denying a motion to vacate an arbitration panel's finding, based on Arkansas law, that "[t]he clause which attempts to void the application of the 'failure of essential purpose' theory is against public policy and unenforceable").

120. *See, e.g., McNally Wellman Co. v. New York State Elec. & Gas Corp.*, 63 F.3d 1188, 1197-98 (2d Cir. 1995) ("Under New York law, however, it is well established that the failure of a limited remedy does not render ineffective all other limitations of liability."); *Razor v. Hyundai Motor Am.*, 222 Ill. 2d 75, 93-99 (Ill. 2006) ("This conclusion [that failure of essential purpose does not invalidate exclusion-of-consequential-damages provisions] is buttressed by the fact that a majority of jurisdictions to consider the issue have adopted the independent approach."); *Int'l Fin. Servs., Inc. v. Franz*, 534 N.W.2d 261, 269 (Minn. 1995). *But see, e.g., Murray v. Holiday Rambler, Inc.*, 83 Wis. 2d 406, 430-31 (Wis. 1978) (finding that a failure of essential purpose of a limited warranty makes all remedies available, including consequential damages, notwithstanding that the agreement specifically excluded consequential damages).

121. *See, e.g., Hydraform Prods. Corp. v. Am. Steel & Aluminum Corp.*, 498 A.2d 339, 342 (N.H. 1985) ("However, the fact that the terms were placed together confirms what we believe is the more reasonable interpretation, that the parties were agreeing to eliminate a right to consequential damages for the very reason that replacement or refund would operate as effective remedies. Therefore, we are unable to view this as a case in which the status of the limitation of damages clause should be determined independently of the provision for replacement or refund.").

122. *Sheehan v. Monaco Coach Corp.*, No. 04-C-717, 2006 WL 208689, at *13-14 (E.D. Wis. Jan. 25, 2006).

no mention of, or reference to, the other. Accordingly, with such agreements, it is not clear whether a limitation of liability should apply to an indemnification obligation.

The Fifth Circuit has found that a limitation-of-liability provision, excluding "any punitive, indirect, incidental, special or consequential damages of any kind or nature (including, but not limited to, loss of profits, loss of use, loss of hire, and loss of production)," did not apply to an indemnity obligation, where the contract was silent as to the interaction between the two provisions.[123] The Fifth Circuit explained:

> There is nothing in the third paragraph to suggest that it is a restriction on the indemnity provisions in the preceding paragraphs. It references only liability between the parties to the agreement . . . , and does not reference indemnity or liability to third parties or employees. The types of damages referenced in this paragraph are those traditionally associated with contractual claims, and not the personal injury claims which are the subject of the indemnification provision.[124]

In contrast, the Sixth Circuit has come down the opposite on similar facts, upholding a district court's finding that a limitation-of-liability provision—capping the total liability between the parties to the service fees charged under the contract—limited an indemnity obligation within that same contract, where the contract was silent as to the interaction between the two provisions.[125]

Given this uncertainty, the best way to avoid forcing a court or an arbitrator to undergo an inquiry into the parties' intent is to draft with clarity. To this end, a contract should explicitly specify whether (and how) provisions that limit liability—either to a certain amount or by excluding certain types of damages—under the contract, limit an indemnity obligation under the same contract.[126] Note that section 10.4, the second sentence of section 10.8, and section 10.9 of the AOL Agreement specifically explain whether the Agreement's limitation-of-liability provisions apply to the Agreement's indemnity provisions.

---

123. *Becker v. Tidewater, Inc.*, 586 F.3d 358, 369 (5th Cir. 2009) (Louisiana law); *see also Howard P. Foley Co. v. Cox*, 679 S.W.2d 58, 63 (Tex. App. 1984) ("[T]he word 'indemnity' is not even included in the clause. We refuse to find that the contract foreclosed Braun's indemnity claim."); *see also Martin v. Midwest Exp. Holdings, Inc.*, No. 07-55063, 2009 WL 306216, at *1 (9th Cir. Feb. 9, 2006).

124. *Becker*, 586 F.3d at 369.

125. *Moore & Assocs. Inc. v. Jones & Carter Inc.*, 217 F. App'x 430 (6th Cir. 2007) (Texas law).

126. Indeed, a contract may specify that an exclusion of liability applies *only* to indemnification and not to other liability. For example, the Tenth Circuit refused to vacate an arbitrator's decision that a provision that excluded from an indemnification obligation "any direct, indirect, incidental, consequential, special or other damages . . . resulting from loss of actual or anticipated revenues or profits, or loss of business, customers, or goodwill" did not apply to the parties' liability to each other for breach of contract more generally. *Dominion Video Satellite, Inc. v. Echostar Satellite LLC*, 430 F.3d 1269, 1277 (10th Cir. 2005).

Drafting Note: "Herein" and Broadly Worded Limitations of Liability

Take a moment to reflect on the lack of clarity in section 10.8. The first sentence says, "Except as expressly provided herein, AOL shall not be liable...for any claims arising out of or related to this Agreement...." For one, to what does "herein" refer? According to Black's Law Dictionary, "herein" means, "In this thing (such as a document, section, or paragraph)."[127] As Black's proceeds to explain, "This term is inherently ambiguous."[128] Are we to read the first sentence except as expressly provided in this *section* or in this *agreement*? Unless the parties would like to leave it up to a court or arbitrator to parse the entire document for uses of "herein," to perhaps look to extrinsic evidence should they find the document ambiguous on its face, and to decide ultimately on the parties' intentions, this provision should lose the "herein" in favor of either "in this section 10.8" or "in this Agreement."

Putting "herein" to the side and assuming it refers to this Agreement, this sentence provides that AOL is not liable for *any claims related to this Agreement,* unless the Agreement *expressly* provides to the contrary. Read literally, this provision essentially says that AOL is liable for nothing, except where the Agreement *expressly* provides that AOL is so liable. Other than AOL's express indemnity obligations, where does the Agreement expressly provide that AOL is liable for anything? Does the Agreement, for example, anywhere expressly provide that AOL is liable for basic general damages for breach of the contract? How does the second sentence in section 10.8 comport with the first? For instance, the second sentence excepts breaches of confidentiality obligations from the sentence's liability limitations. Does the Agreement ever expressly provide that AOL shall be liable for breaching its confidentiality obligations? If not, does the first sentence swallow the provisions of the second sentence as applied to AOL?

While it may have been the intent of the Parties strongly to limit AOL's liability exposure under this Agreement, could they have done so with greater clarity to avoid the second-guessing of a judge? (And could they limit AOL's liability *so* strongly?) It is also important to realize that sometimes a party might strategically push for vague or ambiguous aspects in a contract in order to leave certain arguments for litigation or because the party believes that a clear provision would only serve to reduce the party's potential rights under the agreement; however, a litigated result might prove less advantageous than what the party may have been able to achieve in negotiations (not to mention that litigating issues can be expensive). Please consider these issues in the context of the *Mobil* case below.

A drafter of contracts must appreciate her audience and how her contracts will be read. Please consider this in the context of the following case—and

---

127. BLACK'S LAW DICTIONARY 795 (9th ed. 2009).
128. *Id.*

please consider the following case in the context of our discussion of limitation of liability, indemnification, and clarity as well as the importance of understanding provisions within a contract together as part of an entire agreement.

Mobil Chem. Co. v. Blount Bros. Corp.
United States Court of Appeals, Fifth Circuit, 1987.
809 F.2d 1175.

GEE, Circuit Judge:

The parties to this action somehow built a chemical plant. They have been trying to figure out who should pay for it ever since. Both the owner and the general contractor have tried to escape all liability, although neither disputes that the subcontractors ended up about $4 million underpaid. We agree with the district court that both are liable. On this and other issues too numerous to summarize here, we affirm in large part, reverse in part, and remand for further proceedings.

A. Facts and Prior Proceedings

This case arises out of a $37 million contract for the construction of a chemical plant. Mobil Chemical is the owner, Blount Brothers the general contractor, and the other parties are subcontractors. Blount Brothers acted as construction manager; it did none of the actual construction. The general contract was for a fixed-price and called for "best efforts" to complete the project by January 1983.

Work began in the fall of 1981. The early phases of the project were significantly delayed by Mobil's failure to provide foundations and to have various components in place at times specified by the contract. Construction fell behind schedule. Blount's planning and scheduling tasks grew more complicated when Mobil failed to meet deadlines for delivery of components. Moreover, Blount's first project manager was not capable of managing such a large and complex construction job. Also, Blount's first construction schedule was prepared by an employee innocent of the ability to prepare such a schedule for a complex project, and Blount did not assign a competent full-time scheduler to the project site until December 1981. The work of the different crafts went uncoordinated, and construction proceeded chaotically and behind schedule.

In the fall of 1982, Mobil and Blount made a joint decision to push the subcontractors to meet the January 1983 completion date by overmanning and acceleration. Mobil knew that the project would not be finished until some months later and told Blount that a later completion would be acceptable. Both Blount and Mobil, however, maintained a united position toward the subcontractors that completion by January was crucial. Mobil threatened to black-ball several subcontractors if they did not add workers and make up time. Mobil's motive for rushing the project is obvious: it wanted a producing plant as soon as possible. Blount's motive is less clear, but apparently its costs as project manager were increased little by acceleration. Indeed, an early completion date would reduce its total overhead costs for managing the project, thereby increasing its profit on the fixed-price contract.

The project was completed in April 1983. Blount submitted claims to Mobil for additional compensation for itself and on behalf of its subcontractors Sauer Industrial Contracting, Inc.; Newtron, Inc.; Andreco Refractory Services, Inc.; B & B Insulation, Inc.; and Riggers and Constructors, Inc. In response, Mobil launched a preemptive strike: it sued Blount and the subcontractors in the Eastern District of Texas for a declaratory judgment that it owed nothing to any of them, and, in the alternative, that it was contractually indemnified by Blount for any amounts it owed Blount and the subcontractors. Blount and the subcontractors filed counterclaims against Mobil and each other.

Shortly before trial, Mobil settled with Sauer, Newtron, B & B, and Riggers. These settlements took the form of "Mary Carter" agreements. The subcontractors accepted payments from Mobil, agreeing to pursue their claims against Blount and to pay Mobil any amount received from Blount up to the amount of Mobil's payment. Excess amounts were to be split fifty-fifty. Only Andreco did not settle with Mobil.

The case was tried to the bench. The district court concluded that the general contract was governed by New York law and that the subcontracts were governed by Texas law. Holding that contract breaches by Mobil and Blount and their negligent joint decision to accelerate were equal causes of the subcontractors' acceleration costs, the court ordered Mobil to release the final $2 million retainage to Blount, awarded the subcontractors virtually all of their claimed damages to be paid by Blount and Mobil in equal shares, and settled several other minor disputes. Both Blount and Mobil appeal.

B. *Divvying Up Liability Between Blount and Mobil*

The district court found that the subcontractors' acceleration damages were due equally to negligence and contract breaches by Blount and Mobil. Because "the district court's account of the evidence is plausible in light of the record viewed in its entirety," we may not reverse even were we inclined to disagree. And, after reviewing the record, we are not even inclined to disagree.

This case is a paradigm of the inadequacy of legal rules and legal institutions for parsing the messy stuff of life into precise categories. Only God knows to what exact extent the various strategic choices and mistakes of all those concerned in this case eventually caused the damages at stake. And that is exactly why the "clearly erroneous" rule is an appropriate standard of review. It shifts educated guess-work and intuitive justice to the trial court, to the person who was immersed in and who looked most carefully at the mess, from the best vantage point.

No party directly challenges the findings of the district court. Instead, both Blount and Mobil seek to absolve themselves of liability in the face of the facts found by the district court. We take up their arguments in turn....

2. Mobil's Attempted Escape: The Indemnity Clause

The contract between Mobil and Blount contains a section entitled "Article 12-Insurance." There are four paragraphs in Article 12. In paragraphs one and two, Mobil assumes the risk of all loss or damage to the plant, materials, and equipment, including those in transit to the construction site. In the third, Blount agrees to maintain insurance for workmen's compensation, comprehensive liability, and automobile liability. The fourth paragraph of Article 12 is an indemnity provision:

> 12.4 CONTRACTOR shall defend, indemnify and hold COMPANY, Mobil Oil Corporation and its subsidiaries and affiliates harmless from and against all losses, expenses, liens, claims, demands and cuases [sic] of action of every kind and character (including those of the parties, their agents and employees) for death, personal injury, property damage *or any other liability,* damages, fines or penalties (except where reimbursement of fines and penalties is prohibited by applicable laws) including costs, attorneys [sic] fees and settlements *arising out of or in any way connected with the WORK whether claimed by (a) CONTRACTOR,* its employees or agents or (b) *any of CONTRACTOR's subcontractors,* its employees or agents or (c) any other contractor, its employees or agents or (d) any third party *and whether resulting from or contributed to by (i) the negligence in any form except sole negligence* of COMPANY, Mobil Oil Corporation and its subsidiaries and affiliates and their agents, employees or independent third parties directly responsible to COMPANY or (ii) any defect in, or condition of the premises on which the WORK is to be performed or any equipment thereon or any materials furnished by COMPANY.

(Emphasis added.) Mobil argues that the "any other liability" indemnity provision covers any and all of its breaches of the contract. Mobil urges, in the alternative, that even if the clause does not cover contract breaches, it covers Mobil's negligent decision to accelerate because the acceleration was not the result of its "sole negligence."

The language of the provision is so broad that it might be read to indemnify Mobil against every liability related to the work except for "sole negligence." But New York law disapproves of indemnity provisions, so Mobil must make a powerful showing:

> Because it is unnatural that one would agree to indemnify another when otherwise under no such legal obligation, indemnity clauses are strictly construed. In construing such clauses, the court must determine whether "the intention to indemnify can be clearly implied from the language and purposes of the entire agreement, and the surrounding facts and circumstances." Further, the court must consider whether the agreement reflects an unmistakable intent to indemnify.

We must decide if the indemnity clause relied on by Mobil "clearly implies" the intention to indemnify or shows an "unmistakable intent" to make Blount liable for all harms done by Mobil other than "sole negligence."

The district court held: "It is inconceivable that Blount would have agreed to indemnify Mobil for damages resulting from its [Mobil's] own breaches of contract." We agree. Mobil's interpretation is completely artificial in the context of the entire contract. First, the location of the indemnity provision in "Article 12-Insurance" following provisions requiring Blount to maintain liability insurance shows that it was meant to apply to run-of-the-mill tort claims for injury, property damage, and death. It was not intended to alter fundamentally the meaning of the entire contract. Second, in "Article 25-Consequential Damages," the parties explicitly agree that neither should be liable to the other for any indirect or consequential damages. This Article is meaningless if Blount must indemnify Mobil for both direct and indirect damages to Blount itself and everyone else in the world. Finally, if the indemnity provision is given the meaning advanced by Mobil, no contract was formed at all. Under Mobil's reading, the contract would be void for lack of mutuality. Mobil would have no obligations under the contract; it could breach the contract in any way and to any extent and Blount would be liable to itself! This interpretation is ridiculous.

Mobil tries to rescue the argument from the lack of mutuality objection by urging that even if the indemnity provision does not cover its own breaches of contract, it does cover the joint *negligent* decision to accelerate. It is not clear to us why we should treat a negligent breach of contract differently from a deliberate one; but even if we were willing to grant that distinction, the argument

---

6. Mobil does not attempt to justify its interpretation by pointing to similar contractual language or similar facts in any New York cases. Instead, it cites two of our cases that apply *Texas* law: *Leonard v. Aluminum Co. of Am.*, 767 F.2d 134 (5th Cir. 1985), and *Gulf Oil Corp. v. Burlington N. R.R.*, 751 F.2d 746 (5th Cir.1985). These cases do not help Mobil's cause.

In *Leonard*, the plaintiff was injured by an exploding soft drink bottle cap. He sued ALCOA, the manufacturer of the capping machine. ALCOA sought indemnity from the bottling company that installed the cap. The district court held that under Texas law a blanket indemnity clause in the contract between the bottler and ALCOA was not to ALCOA's avail. ALCOA was found liable at trial for negligent failure to warn about the risks "that bottle caps might suddenly take flight." Our court reversed. We held that ALCOA was not liable for negligent failure to warn under Texas law. Furthermore, we held that the clause required the bottler to pay ALCOA its costs and attorneys' fees in the suit; negligence was no longer an issue, so it was now immaterial that the indemnity clause did not meet the tough Texas standard for clauses indemnifying one party for its own *negligent* acts. The entire decision in *Leonard* has since been vacated and remanded. *Leonard* relied on *Alm v. Aluminum Co. of America*, which was reversed by the Texas Supreme Court.

In *Gulf Oil*, our court enforced an indemnity provision in a lease of a railroad spur. Cars on the spur had rolled onto the main track and hit a train, damaging property of both the lessor and lessee. The lessor railroad's employees were found negligent in the way they had parked the lessee's cars. We held that a clause indemnifying the railroad for "loss or destruction of or damage to property whatsoever, in any manner caused by, resulting from or incident to storage of private cars on said track" satisfied the Texas requirement that the obligation be expressed in "clear and unequivocal" terms. We relied on a line of Texas cases holding that contracts making one party fully responsible for an "instrumentality, operation, or premises" satisfy the "clear and unequivocal" requirement. Obviously, neither case helps Mobil meet its burden under New York law.

will not fly. Either the indemnity clause covers both negligent and non-negligent breach of contract or neither. Negligent acceleration damages must be indemnified, if at all, under a literal reading of the same all-inclusive phrase ("any other liability") that would indemnify breach of contract claims as well. That phrase simply does not support the distinction that Mobil urges.[6]

Although we are lawyers, and although we spend too much of our professional lives listening to this sort of argument, we are nevertheless human beings of average intelligence and average common sense. It is inconceivable that a few words buried in the fourth section of the "Insurance" provisions of the general contract were intended to supersede the normal operation of tort and contract law for the entire agreement, to shift all risks arising out of the contract to Blount, to alter essentially the relationship between the parties. We hold that Mobil is liable for the damages that it caused....

Comments

The court in *Mobil v. Blount* explains that if Mobil were to have no obligations under its contract, then the contract would necessarily fail for lack of mutuality. Most courts now understand the requirement of mutuality as calling for nothing more than consideration.[129] Indeed, as the Restatement of Contracts explains, "If the requirement of consideration is met, there is no additional requirement of...'mutuality of obligation.'"[130] Accordingly, inasmuch as a contract is supported by consideration, most courts will not inquire further as to whether obligations under a contract or provision flow both ways.[131]

---

129. *See, e.g., Structural Polymer Group, Ltd. v. Zoltek Corp.*, 543 F.3d 987, 992 (8th Cir. 2008) (Missouri law); *Riner v. Allstate Life Ins. Co.*, 131 F.3d 530, 536 (5th Cir. 1997) (Texas law); *see also* 3 WILLISTON ON CONTRACTS § 7:14 (4th ed.) (clarifying the confusion associated with the "supposed requirement of mutuality of obligation" and explaining that such is not required for a contract to have binding effect).

130. RESTATEMENT (SECOND) OF CONTRACTS § 79 (1981).

131. *See supra* note 129. For further discussion of the requirement of consideration and that this does not always require mutual obligations within a contract, please see the discussion of consideration in Chapter 1 in the context of non-disclosure agreements.

· CHAPTER FOUR ·

AGREEMENTS FOR THE SALE OF GOODS

Having determined that Florida law applies, we need not decide whether the agreement is a contract for the sale of goods or for services. Though the provisions of the Florida Uniform Commercial Code ("UCC") would apply only if the contract were deemed a sale of goods, the limitation of liability provision governs to bar Meridian's third-party claims regardless of whether the UCC or general Florida contract law applies.

Cooper v. Meridian Yachts, Ltd., 575 F.3d 1151, 1166 (11th Cir. 2009).

In the previous chapter, we began the discussion of how contractual parties may plan for the application of Article 2, even in contracts ostensibly for "services." In this chapter, we continue this discussion. As the above excerpt demonstrates, a prudent drafter can be sure to draft a contract so as to achieve certain results whether Article 2 applies or not and, in this chapter, we further examine the ways in which a drafter may do so. (Indeed, the above excerpt demonstrates the utility of limitation-of-liability provisions, which we discussed in Chapter 3.)

What do we mean by "sale of goods"? What are the important contractual terms applicable to a sale of goods? In the event a contract is silent on one or more of these terms, is there applicable law establishing the rights and obligations of the parties? What role does the Uniform Commercial Code play in this regard? Are parties free to contract around or against particular provisions of the U.C.C.? These are just a few of the questions one encounters when negotiating contracts for the sale of goods.

We turn our attention in this chapter to these and numerous other questions. From dog food to doughnuts, televisions to teapots, toasters to transformers, these are the goods that move commerce.

Many of these goods are often the subject of purchase orders and form contracts; others—particularly those of a unique or bespoke nature—often form the basis of heavily negotiated standalone agreements. In most cases, these contracts rely upon and showcase the building blocks of many commercial contracts, namely: term and termination, price and payment, warranty, and liability. How these component terms best serve each party's interests—and the degree of leverage each party brings to the negotiation table—informs the art of commercial negotiation.

We begin our analysis with a discussion of the scope of Article 2 of the U.C.C. and the sometimes unclear meaning of "goods" and the "transactions" therein.

A. THE SCOPE OF ARTICLE TWO OF THE UNIFORM COMMERCIAL CODE

1. Some Background on the U.C.C.

We already have encountered Article 2 of the Uniform Commercial Code in Chapter 3, with our discussion of services contracts. There, we discussed that Article 2 ostensibly applies only to contracts for the sale of goods[1] but that a prudent party will always plan for the possibility that Article 2 may apply. Here, before we look at this chapter's agreement and the various issues that arise therein, we delve further into the world of the Uniform Commercial Code.

Though we have discussed the U.C.C. some throughout this book, we should take a moment to explore the background and nature of the Uniform Commercial Code. The U.C.C. is a joint collaboration between the American Law Institute ("ALI") and the National Conference of Commissioners on Uniform State Laws ("NCCUSL"). An overarching purpose of the U.C.C. is to harmonize commercial law throughout the United States.[2] Accordingly, the U.C.C. is a uniform, model act, which does not have the effect of law in any given state until that state adopts the U.C.C. by statute. A state legislature may adopt the U.C.C. wholesale or make various substantive changes before passing the uniform code as state law (or, as in the case of Louisiana and Article 2 of the U.C.C., the state may decline to adopt the uniform code altogether). The Uniform Commercial Code contains nine primary articles, addressing ten areas of commercial law: Article 2 (sales), Article 2A (leases), Article 3 (negotiable instruments), Article 4 (bank deposits), Article 4A (fund

---

1. Some courts find that Article 2 applies not merely to sales but more broadly to "transactions" in goods, as we discuss below.
2. *See* U.C.C. § 1-103(a)(3) (2003) ("[The Uniform Commercial Code] must be liberally construed and applied to promote its underlying purposes and policies, which [include] . . . to make uniform the law among the various jurisdictions.").

transfers), Article 5 (letters of credit), Article 6 (bulk transfers), Article 7 (warehouse receipts, bills of lading, and other documents of title), Article 8 (investment securities), and Article 9 (secured transactions). Article 1 of the U.C.C. contains "general provisions," which apply generally to the other articles that comprise the U.C.C. In addition to Article 1, we discuss Article 2 (primarily in this chapter) inasmuch as it applies to the transactions and agreements in this book.

A fundamental policy underlying the U.C.C. is freedom of contract between commercial parties. Consistent with this policy, Article 2 is deferential to the contractual arrangements of private parties. Frequently, a provision within Article 2 will state that the provision applies "unless otherwise agreed" by contract and the like. Moreover, the U.C.C. expressly provides that, even where a provision of the U.C.C. is silent as to whether it may be altered by contract, parties may generally alter the effect of the statutory provision by agreement.[3] This means that most of the U.C.C. is "default" law as opposed to "mandatory" law. Default laws may be altered; they are the stand-in rules unless the parties agree otherwise. In contrast, mandatory laws may not be altered by private arrangement. For example, Article 1 explains, "The obligations of good faith, diligence, reasonableness, and care prescribed by [the Uniform Commercial Code] may not be disclaimed by agreement."[4] In addition, as we will discuss later in this chapter, whenever the U.C.C. "requires an action to be taken within a reasonable time, a time that is not manifestly unreasonable may be fixed by agreement."[5] Accordingly, the U.C.C. gives the parties the freedom to stipulate what constitutes a "reasonable time" but reserves a mandatory rule that a contractually specified reasonable time that is manifestly unreasonable is not sufficient to satisfy a U.C.C. reasonable-time requirement.

The ALI and NCCUSL adopted Revised Article 2 in 2003. While the revisions did not mark a complete overhaul of the previous version, there are some substantive and meaningful departures. Because, as of this publication, states have not yet widely adopted Revised Article 2, we address both versions. In this book, when we refer to Article 2 without providing further specification, we are referring to the revised version of Article 2. When we discuss a matter on which the two versions meaningfully diverge, we will discuss both the pre-revised and the revised versions. Accordingly, when we speak of Article 2 generally, without further adieu, you can assume that we are speaking of the revised version of Article 2 and that both versions are in at least basic accord on the matter.

---

3. *Id.* §§ 1-302(a) & (c).
4. *Id.* § 1-302(b).
5. *Id.*

An International Focus with Domestic Implications: The United Nations Convention on Contracts for the International Sale of Goods

As of January 1, 1988 and the United States' adoption of the United Nations Convention on Contracts for the International Sale of Goods ("CISG"), the CISG is *domestic* American contracts law—no less than the U.C.C. or the common law.[6] Indeed, in some respects, it is *more*. As a ratified treaty, the CISG is U.S. federal law that preempts state law (e.g., the U.C.C. as adopted by state legislatures and state common law) where the CISG applies.[7] So, where does the CISG apply? And, what substantive law does the CISG provide?

For starters, as with the U.C.C. generally, the CISG applies only to the sale of goods and adopts a predominate-purpose test to address mixed contracts.[8] Furthermore, the CISG applies only to transactions between parties with places of business in *different* signatory countries (i.e., countries that have adopted the CISG as law). If a party has more than one place of business, then the party's place of business with the "closest relationship to the contract and its performance" is its place of business for the purposes of the CISG and its application.[9] The CISG expressly excludes many types of transactions from its scope, including sales of goods for personal or household use, sales by auction, sales of investment securities or negotiable instruments, sales of ships or aircraft, and sales of electricity.[10] In addition, parties may "opt out" of the CISG entirely (as evident in the AOL Agreement in Chapter 3);[11] however, merely designating that "domestic" law governs is insufficient to avoid the CISG's application because the CISG *is* domestic law where adopted.[12] Accordingly, contractual parties can be sure to avoid the CISG by *expressly* saying so in their contract. Do you think the CISG is likely to govern the agreement in this chapter?

---

6. United Nations Convention on Contracts for the International Sale of Goods, *reprinted in* 15 U.S.C.A. App. (West. Supp. 1995), *available at* http://www.uncitral.org/pdf/english/texts/sales/cisg/CISG.pdf [hereinafter "CISG"]. The U.S. Senate ratified the CISG in 1986. *See BP Oil Int'l, Ltd. v. Empresa Estatal Petoleos de Ecuador*, 332 F.3d 333, 336 n.6 (5th Cir. 2003).

7. *See, e.g., Caterpillar, Inc. v. Usinor Industeel*, 393 F. Supp. 2d 659, 673 (N.D. Ill. 2005). Note, however, that the CISG does not apply to claims against persons not party to an agreement that falls within the scope of the CISG. *Id.* at 676. In addition, the CISG does not apply to non-contract claims, such as promissory estoppel or misrepresentation. *See, e.g., Miami Valley Paper, LLC v. Lebbing Eng'g & Consulting GmbH*, No. 1:05-CV-00702, 2006 WL 2924779, at *3 (S.D. Ohio Oct. 10, 2006) ("[T]he CISG does not prevent Plaintiff from pleading negligent misrepresentation and fraudulent inducement."); *Caterpillar*, 393 F. Supp. 2d at 676 ("[T]he court declines to extend the preemptive force of the CISG to state law claims for promissory estoppel.").

8. CISG, *supra* note 6, at art. 3.

9. CISG, *supra* note 6, at art. 10(a) (considering the "circumstances known to or contemplated by the parties at any time before or at the conclusion of the contract" when determining the place of business).

10. CISG, *supra* note 6, at art. 2.

11. CISG, *supra* note 6, at art. 6 ("The parties may exclude the application of this Convention or…derogate from or vary the effect of any of its provisions.").

12. *See, e.g., BP Oil Int'l, Ltd. v. Empresa Estatal Petoleos de Ecuador*, 332 F.3d 333, 337 (5th Cir. 2003) ("Given that the CISG is Ecuadorian law, a choice of law provision designating Ecuadorian law merely confirms that the treaty governs the transaction.") (emphasis in original).

The CISG deals much with contract *formation*, a topic that is not a focus of this book. In short, the CISG adopts rules that differ from the much feared "battle of the forms" found in pre-revised U.C.C. § 2-207 and that are closer to the U.S. common law and its "mirror image" rule.[13] In addition, the CISG does away with the "statute of frauds" by not requiring that any contract be in writing, so long as its existence may be proved.[14] Like the U.C.C., the CISG departs from U.S. common law by giving real effect to no-oral-modification clauses, providing parties may not orally modify contracts that contain such clauses but that the clauses may still be waived.[15]

The CISG also contains implied warranty provisions similar to those found in the U.C.C., including implied warranties that goods are fit for their ordinary purpose ("merchantability," in U.C.C. parlance) and that goods are fit for a particular purpose made known to the seller, where the buyer reasonably relied on the seller's skill and judgment (i.e., "fitness").[16] However, unlike the U.C.C. and the common law (at least after *Ziff-Davis*), the CISG will not enforce a "breach of warranty" (note that the CISG does not use this terminology) where the buyer knew or should have known of the "breach" at the time of the conclusion of the contract.[17] Also unlike the U.C.C., the CISG does not require conspicuous disclaimers or "magic words" to disclaim implied warranties effectively—although, the CISG may be less concerned with consumer protection, as personal and household goods are excluded from its scope.

These are just a sampling of the variations between the CISG and the U.C.C. We proceed to focus our discussion on the implications of the U.C.C. and this chapter's agreement, between two companies with their places of business in the U.S.

2. The Scope of Article Two

To determine when Article 2 does and does not apply, we look first to Article 2 itself, which defines its own scope in § 2-102:

> Unless the context otherwise requires, this Article applies to transactions in goods; it does not apply to any transaction which although in the form of an unconditional contract to sell or present sale is intended to operate only as a security transaction nor does this Article impair or repeal any statute regulating sales to consumers, farmers or other specified classes of buyers.

Right from the start, we know that Article 2 applies to "transactions in goods."

---

13. CISG, *supra* note 6, at art. 19.
14. CISG, *supra* note 6, at art. 11.
15. CISG, *supra* note 6, at art. 29(2).
16. CISG, *supra* note 6, at art. 35(2).
17. CISG, *supra* note 6, at art. 35(3).

a. What Is a "Good"?

The definition of "goods" under Article 2 turns on whether the subject of a transaction is a movable thing.[18] Examples of such movable things that have been found to meet the definition of a good under Article 2 include: animals,[19] cars,[20] trees,[21] equipment,[22] and ships.[23] Courts have split as to whether utilities such as electricity[24] and water[25] are goods. In addition, courts have generally found software to fall within the meaning of "goods" under Article 2 and accordingly have found Article 2 to govern transactions in software.[26]

18.
> "Goods" means all things that are movable at the time of identification to a contract for sale. The term includes future goods, specially manufactured goods, the unborn young of animals, growing crops, and other identified things attached to realty as described in Section 2-107. The term does not include information, the money in which the price is to be paid, investment securities under Article 8, the subject matter of foreign exchange transactions, or choses in action.

U.C.C. § 2-103(k) (2003). The pre-revised version of Article 2 defines "goods" similarly but does not expressly state that the "term does not include information."

19. *See, e.g., Flanagan v. Consol. Nutrition*, 627 N.W.2d 573, 577 (Iowa Ct. App. 2001) (holding that pigs were "goods" within the meaning of Article 2); *Trad Indus., Ltd. v. Brogan*, 805 P.2d 54, 58 (Mont. 1991) (holding that elk were "goods" under Article 2).

20. *See, e.g., Hodges v. Johnson*, 199 P.3d 1251, 1259 (Kan. 2009).

21. *See, e.g., Kaitz v. Landscape Creations, Inc.*, No. 1271, 2000 WL 694274, at *2 (Mass. App. Div. May 24, 2000) (finding that "trees, shrubs and plants provided by the defendant are 'goods' within the meaning of the U.C.C." because they were grown in a nursery for the purpose of replanting on a third party's property).

22. *See, e.g., Boyle v. Douglas Dynamics, LLC*, 292 F. Supp. 2d 198, 211 (D. Mass. 2003).

23. *See, e.g., Benetic v. Alexander*, No. CV 00-06845 ABC (EX), 2001 WL 1843781, at *3 (C.D. Cal. Aug. 13, 2001).

24. *Compare New Balance Athletic Shoe, Inc. v. Boston Edison Co.*, No. 95-5321-E, 1996 WL 406673, at *2 (Mass. Super. Ct. Mar. 26, 1996) ("The decision to expose public utilities to liability for their 'products' is best left in the capable hands of the legislative body that is charged with regulating those utilities. Accordingly, this court finds that electricity is not a 'good' as defined in the Uniform Commercial Code."), *with Helvey v. Wabash County REMC*, 278 N.E.2d 608, 610 (Ind. Ct. App. 1972) (finding electricity to be a "good" within the meaning of the U.C.C.).

25. *Compare Mattoon v. City of Pittsfield*, 775 N.E.2d 770, 784 (Mass. App. Ct. 2002) (finding water sold by a city not to be a "good" within the meaning of the U.C.C.), *with Zepp v. Mayor of Athens*, 348 S.E.2d 673, 677-78 (Ga. Ct. App. 1986) (finding water sold by a city to be a "good" within the meaning of the U.C.C.).

26. *See, e.g., Micro Data Base Sys., Inc. v. Dharma Sys., Inc.*, 148 F.3d 649, 654 (7th Cir. 1998) ("we can think of no reason why the UCC is not suitable to govern disputes arising from the sale of custom software") (internal citations omitted); *Advent Sys. Ltd. v. Unisys Corp.*, 925 F.2d 670, 676 (3d Cir. 1991); *SoftMan Prods. Co. v. Adobe Sys., Inc.*, 171 F. Supp. 2d 1075, 1084 (C.D. Cal. 2001) ("A number of courts have held that the sale of software is the sale of a good within the meaning of Uniform Commercial Code"). *But see, e.g., Conwell v. Gray Loon Outdoor Mktg. Group, Inc.*, 906 N.E.2d 805, 812 (Ind. 2009) ("On the surface, these cases might suggest that customized software is a service while pre-made software is a good, but when courts try to pour new wine into old legal bottles, we sometimes miss the nuances. It would be a mistake, for instance, to treat software as a good simply because it was contained in a tangible medium that fits within that category.") (citing *Olcott Int'l & Co., Inc. v. Micro Data Base Sys., Inc.*, 793 N.E.2d 1063, 1071 (Ind. Ct. App. 2003); *Data Processing Servs., Inc. v. L.H. Smith Oil Corp.*, 492 N.E.2d 314, 318-20 (Ind. Ct. App. 1986); *Liberty Fin. Mgmt. Corp. v. Beneficial Data Processing Corp.*, 670 S.W.2d 40, 49 (Mo. Ct. App. 1984)) (holding that a sale of custom software is not a transaction in goods within the meaning of Article 2).

b. *What Is a "Transaction in Goods"?*

Courts subscribe to one of two schools of thought with regard to the meaning of "transaction" under Article 2. First, all jurisdictions agree that Article 2 applies to the sale of goods. Under Article 2, a "sale" occurs upon "the passing of title from the seller to the buyer for a price."[27] And, "[u]nless otherwise explicitly agreed title passes to the buyer at the time and place at which the seller completes performance with reference to the delivery of the goods...."[28] We further discuss the concept of "title" along with "risk of loss" and delivery later in this chapter, but, for our purposes, an Article 2 "sale" occurs when the seller, in exchange for a price, satisfies its obligations to deliver goods. A seller's delivery obligations are generally set by contract; for example, a contract may require the seller to deliver the goods to the buyer's location or not to deliver the goods at all.

Some courts have held that Article 2 may apply to transactions in goods other than pure sales. These courts justify their position by making some combination of two arguments: (1) that the word "transaction" is plainly broader than the word "sale"; and (2) that transactions similar to sales should be treated as sales by analogy.[29] In contradistinction, other courts have noticed that Article 2 defines "goods" as movable things subject to a contract for *sale* and have held, then, that a "transaction in goods" requires an actual sale of goods.[30] Even where a transaction takes the form of a non-sale transaction, a court may characterize the transaction, based on its economic substance, as a sale.[31] Accordingly, whether Article 2 governs a particular non-sale transaction in

---

27. U.C.C. § 2-106(1) (2003).

28. *Id.* § 2-401(2).

29. *See, e.g., Imaging Fin. Serv., Inc. v. Lettergraphics/Detroit, Inc.*, No. 97-1930, 1999 WL 115473, at *5 (6th Cir. Feb. 9, 1999) ("The use of the term transaction rather than sale in U.C.C. §2-102 is significant in that it makes clear that the reach of Article 2 goes beyond those transactions where there is a transfer of title. Thus, Article 2 sections have been applied in decisions involving transactions that are not sales, but which are used as substitutes for a sale or which have attributes analogous to a sale, such as leases, bailments, or construction contracts.") (quoting *Wells v. 10-X Mfg. Co.*, 609 F.2d 248, 254 n.3 (6th Cir. 1979)); *Embryo Progeny Assocs. v. Lovana Farms*, 416 S.E.2d 833, 835 (Ga. Ct. App. 1992) ("'[T]ransactions in goods' to which the sales article of the Uniform Commercial Code applies, has been given a broader meaning than the sale of goods."); *Xerox Corp. v. Hawkes*, 475 A.2d 7, 9 (N.H. 1984) ("Although a 'lease' and not a 'sale' was contemplated by the parties to the service agreements, the Uniform Commercial Code still applies to the warranty provisions of the two service agreements. [U.C.C. § 2-102] does not refer to 'sales,' but instead to 'transactions in goods.'").

30. *See, e.g., Neuhoff v. Marvin Lumber and Cedar Co.*, 370 F.3d 197, 205 (1st Cir. 2004) ("Article 2 of the U.C.C. applies to all 'transactions in goods.' Typically, the U.C.C. only implies warranties in connection with goods that are involved in a 'sale.' In contrast, gifts do not receive implied warranties under Article 2.") (internal citations omitted); *Computer Servicenters, Inc. v. Beacon Mfg. Co.*, 328 F. Supp. 653, 654-55 (D.S.C. 1970) ("'Goods' as used in the section means 'all things (including specially manufactured goods) which are movable at the time of identification to the contract for sale....' That definition is indeed broad, however, it must be noted that the article deals with, and the definition of goods is cast in terms of, the contract for sale.") (internal citations omitted).

31. *See, e.g., Neilson Bus. Equip. Ctr., Inc. v. Italo V. Monteleone, M.D., P.A.*, 524 A.2d 1172, 1175 (Del. 1987) ("Here, the parties cast their agreement in terms of a lease with an option...to purchase the computer system later. Although structured as a lease, it is clear that the parties intended to enter into the equivalent of a purchase and sale.... Though structured as a lease, the substance of the transaction was a sale....").

goods largely depends on the jurisdiction, a court's willingness to read Article 2 broadly, and the economic substance of a transaction.

For example, software publishers usually characterize the exchange of software for cash consideration as a "license" and not as a "sale."[32] These license agreements often take the form of so-called "shrink-wrap" or "click-wrap" license agreements. "Shrink-wrap" license agreements require a user to agree to license terms before tearing open the shrink-wrap plastic that covers a software box, and "click-wrap" license agreements require a user to click a dialog box on a computer screen indicating the user's assent to certain license terms before the user may access the software. Courts generally enforce these agreements.[33] However, enforceability notwithstanding, some courts will look past an agreement's self-identification as a "license" to find the transaction to be a "sale" for Article 2 purposes.[34] Even without recasting the parties' transaction as a sale, many courts have been willing—if begrudgingly—to apply Article 2 to software license transactions.[35] In so doing, some courts have found comfort in precedent for a broad reading of "transaction in goods," while others have applied Article 2 for lack of a better alternative.[36]

In fact, the National Conference of Commissioners on Uniform State Laws proposed, in 1999, that a uniform act be added to the Uniform Commercial Code, as Article 2B. The proposal for U.C.C. Article 2B called for a more comprehensive and tailored approach to addressing computer information transactions generally, software licenses especially. However, this proposal was met with meaningful opposition, and the American Law Institute refused to cast its necessary vote in favor of creating the proposed Article 2B. The NCCUSL went on to release the model act on its own as the Uniform Computer

---

32. A major reason software publishers license, instead of sell, their software is to avoid the so-called "first sale doctrine," which gives the first purchaser of certain intellectual property (most notably, copyrighted works) the right to resell the work without risk of infringement.

33. *See, e.g., ProCD, Inc. v. Zeidenberg*, 86 F.3d 1447, 1449 (7th Cir. 1996) ("Shrinkwrap licenses are enforceable unless their terms are objectionable on grounds applicable to contracts in general.").

34. *See, e.g., Sagent Tech., Inc. v. Micros Sys., Inc.*, 276 F. Supp. 2d 464, 467 n.1 (D. Md. 2003) ("[T]he U.C.C. should apply to a transaction that, although labeled a license, is for all practical purposes a sale of computer software.").

35. *See, e.g., i.Lan Sys., Inc. v. Netscout Serv. Level Corp.*, 183 F. Supp. 2d 328, 332 (D. Mass. 2002) ("For the time being, Article 2's familiar provisions—which are the inspiration for UCITA—better fulfill those expectations than would the common law. Article 2 technically does not, and certainly will not in the future, govern software licenses, but for the time being, the Court will assume it does."); *Colonial Life Ins. Co. of Am. v. Elec. Data Sys. Corp.*, 817 F. Supp. 235, 239 (D.N.H. 1993) ("The Court holds that the Uniform Commercial Code, as adopted in New Hampshire, applies to the contract between EDS and Chubb, the principal object of which was to provide for a license to use computer software."); *Schroders, Inc. v. Hogan Sys., Inc.*, 522 N.Y.S.2d 404, 406 (N.Y. App. Div. 1987) ("Although the parties' agreement in the instant matter did not involve sale of computer hardware, but simply a licensure of software, the arrangement should nevertheless be construed to fall within the provisions of UCC Article 2."). *See also Cytyc Corp. v. DEKA Prod. Ltd. P'ship*, 439 F.3d 27, 35-36 (1st Cir. 2006) ("Indeed, it is hopelessly unclear whether this provision, which appears in New Hampshire's version of Article 2 of the Uniform Commercial Code, governs agreements to license patented intellectual property."); *Arbitron, Inc. v. Tralyn Broad., Inc.*, 400 F.3d 130, 138 (2d Cir. 2005) ("It is not clear whether, under New York law, a license agreement of the sort at issue in this case [of copyrighted radio listener data] constitutes a contract for the sale of goods, or is otherwise governed by the U.C.C.").

36. *See supra* note 35.

Information Transactions Act ("UCITA"). Accordingly, while not a part of the Uniform Commercial Code, UCITA has gone on to become statutory law in two states: Virginia and Maryland.[37]

The next event in this saga occurred in 2010, when the ALI published the Principles of the Law of Software Contracts, the purpose of which is to present "legal principles to guide courts in deciding disputes involving transactions in software and to guide those drafting software contracts."[38] Accordingly, the Principles do not represent a model code or uniform act, along the lines of the U.C.C. or UCITA, to be adopted by state legislatures as statutory law. Rather, the Principles are similar to the Restatements of the Law (which, incidentally, the ALI also promulgates), a body of "soft law" published to influence and guide common law courts—in the case of the Principles, in deciding contract matters involving software. What level of prominence and influence the Principles of the Law of Software Contracts attains remains to be seen.

c. "Mixed" Contracts for Both Goods and Services

The real world features a variety of worthwhile business transactions that happen not to fit the sort of tidy boxes that sometimes preoccupy the minds of lawyers. The reality is that sometimes transactions are for goods, sometimes they are for services, and sometimes they are for both goods and services. For example, as we see in this chapter's agreement, a buyer of computer-related products may wish to purchase not only the products but also, as part of the same transaction, any services necessary to use, support, and maintain the products. Certainly you can relate: When was the last time you bought a computer or television (or just about anything) without a sales associate trying to sell you additional support services? Other examples abound: If a buyer commissions a painter to produce a painting, is the buyer purchasing the painter's services or the resulting painting? If a buyer pays a carpeting manufacturer to install carpeting in the buyer's building, is the buyer purchasing the manufacturer's carpeting or the manufacturer's installation services? The answer is both; the question is whether and how Article 2 applies to these contracts for both goods and services.

---

37. MD. CODE ANN., COM. LAW I § 22-101 (West 2000); VA. CODE. ANN. § 59.1-501.1 (Michie 2001). In response to the passage of UCITA, several states passed "bomb shelter" acts that void a choice of law and/or forum provision that would result in the application of UCITA. *See, e.g.,* IOWA CODE § 554D.104 (2000); IOWA CODE § 554D.125 (2005); N.C. GEN. STAT. § 66-329 (2001); VT. STAT. ANN. tit. 9, § 2463a (2003); W. VA. CODE § 55-8-15 (2001).

38. The American Law Institute, Principles of the Law of Software Contracts, http://www.ali. org/index.cfm? fuseaction=projects.proj_ip&projectid=9 (last visited July 23, 2010); *see also* The American Law Institute, Principles of the Law of Software Contracts, http://www.ali.org/index. cfm?fuseaction=publications.ppage&node_id =121 (last visited July 23, 2010).

The majority of states answer this question by applying what is called the "predominate-factor" test.[39] Under the predominate-factor test, "the court determines whether [the parties'] predominant factor, their thrust, their purpose, reasonably stated, is the rendition of service, with goods incidentally involved (e.g., contract with artist for painting) or is a transaction of sale, with labor incidentally involved (e.g., installation of a water heater in a bathroom)."[40] In determining the primary purpose of a contract, courts will look to the contract's language, the parties' purpose for entering the contract (i.e., to produce goods or services), the relative costs of the goods and services involved, whether the contract charges separately for goods and services, and, if so, the relative contract price of the goods and services.[41] A drafter can help guide a court's framing and understanding of a contract by prominently (e.g., in the title of the contract) and consistently specifying throughout a contract that the contract is really about the sale of goods or really about the provision of services, as the case may be.[42]

Under the majority "predominate-factor" test, the court determines whether the contract is predominately about goods or not. If the contract is predominately about goods, then the court applies Article 2 to the whole contract; if not, then Article 2 does not apply at all.[43] In general, this is an all-or-nothing endeavor. However, where a contract is "divisible," some courts have applied Article 2 to the goods portion of a contract and the common law to the non-goods portion.[44] A willingness to "bifurcate" contracts and to apply Article 2

---

39. *See BMC Indus. v. Barth Indus.*, 160 F.3d 1322, 1329 (11th Cir. 1998) ("Most courts follow the 'predominant factor' test to determine whether such hybrid contracts are transactions in goods, and therefore covered by the UCC, or transactions in services, and therefore excluded.").

40. *BMC Indus.*, 160 F.3d at 1330.

41. *See, e.g., Paramount Aviation Corp. v. Agusta*, 288 F.3d 67, 72 (3d Cir. 2002) (New Jersey law); *BMC Indus.*, 160 F.3d at 1330.

42. *See, e.g., Old Country Toyota Corp. v. Toyota Motor Distribs., Inc.*, 966 F. Supp. 167, 169 (E.D.N.Y. 1997) ("The prominence of the word 'sales' and its location in the Agreement's title...are revealing."); *Conopco, Inc. v. McCreadie*, 826 F. Supp. 855, 868 (D.N.J. 1993) ("The initial engagement letter...unmistakably contemplates a services agreement, referring in its opening to 'the management consulting services you requested' and indicating elsewhere that 'we will serve as facilitators and implementors.'").

43. *See, e.g., United States v. City of Twin Falls*, 806 F.2d 862, 871 (9th Cir. 1986), *cert denied*, 482 U.S. 914 (1987); *Wheeler Peak, LLC v. L.C.I.2, Inc.*, No. CIV 07-1117 JB/WDS, 2009 WL 1329115, at *3 (D.N.M. Apr. 13, 2009); *Respect, Inc. v. Comm. on Status of Women*, 781 F. Supp. 1358, 1364 (N.D. Ill. 1992).

44. *See BMC Indus.*, 160 F.3d at 1329 n.13 ("A few courts do not categorize hybrid contracts as either transactions in goods or services, but rather apply the UCC only to the sale of goods elements of the contract.") (citing *Foster v. Colorado Radio Corp.*, 381 F.2d 222, 226 (10th Cir. 1967)); *TK Power, Inc. v. Textron, Inc.*, 443 F. Supp. 2d 1058, 1064 (N.D. Cal. 2006) ("A number of courts have held that where a transaction involves a mix of "goods" covered by the UCC and non-goods such as service or real estate, the court may apply non-UCC law to that portion of the contract that does not involve 'goods.'"). In *TK Power*, the court explained that whether or not a contract is "divisible" for Article 2 purposes turned on three factors:
   1. Whether the non-goods aspect of the transaction is clearly distinct and easily separable from the goods aspect....
   2. Whether the alleged performance or non-performance pertains solely to the non-goods aspect of the transaction.
   3. Whether it makes sense to apply the UCC to the non-goods aspect of the transaction and whether applying non-UCC law accords with the parties' intent.

only to a portion of a contract has been attributed to a "minority" position; however, it seems even "predominate-factor" courts have found occasion to divide contracts and to apply Article 2 only to its goods-related parts.[45] Warranties present a prominent example of this. As Article 2 is the source of certain implied warranties that may not otherwise be available, plaintiffs often argue for Article 2's broad application so as to support a claim for breach of warranty. Some courts have refused to extend Article 2 warranties to the services component of a contract predominately for the sale of goods.[46]

As we turn our attention to this chapter's agreement, please consider whether or not Article 2 is likely to apply. Is this agreement for goods? Is this agreement for services? If it is for both, is a court applying the predominate-factor test likely to find the agreement to be within the scope of Article 2? As we began to discuss in Chapter 3, a prudent drafter will plan for the possibility that a court may find Article 2 to govern his contract.

B. MASTER PURCHASE AGREEMENT

The following Master Purchase Agreement contains the terms pursuant to which Dell Products L.P. and Dell Computer Corporation's other subsidiaries and affiliates (collectively, "Dell") will purchase products from Adaptec, Inc., the manufacturer of a range of products for data centers and cloud computing environments.

Things to Consider...

As you read through the following agreement, please consider these items. You will want to return to the agreement, as you study the substantive discussion that follows.

> **Price.** What price or pricing mechanism have the parties agreed to for the goods to be sold under this agreement? Is price determined as of this agreement? If not, have the parties agreed as to how price will be determined?

> **Quantity.** How many goods are to be sold under this agreement? Is this determined as of this agreement? Does the agreement impose any obligations on the parties with respect to the quantity of goods to be sold, or at least with respect to the determination of the quantity of goods to be sold under this agreement?

---

433 F. Supp. 2d at 1064. The court went on to find, "All three factors are present here. Under these circumstances, even if it is assumed that there was a larger agreement of which the prototype development was only a part, applying the common law to this segregable portion of the transaction comports with the purposes of the UCC...." *Id.* at 1064-65.

45. *See, e.g., TK Power*, 433 F. Supp. 2d at 1062-65 (reciting the predominate-factor test and then proceeding to apply the common law to the non-Article-2 portion of an arguably larger contract).

46. *See, e.g., Lemley v. J & B Tire Co.*, 426 F. Supp. 1378, 1379 (W.D. Pa. 1977).

> **Acceptance.** How does this agreement provide that the buyer may accept or reject goods that the seller delivers to the buyer? Are there certain restrictions (e.g., time period) on what constitutes effective acceptance or rejection under this agreement? What rights of the buyer are triggered (and what rights of the buyer are lost) by the buyer's acceptance of goods?

[Note that a footnote to the following agreement as published on EDGAR states: "Confidential treatment requested: Certain portions of this agreement have been omitted pursuant to a request for confidential treatment and, where applicable, have been marked with an asterisk to denote where omissions have been made. The confidential material has been filed separately with the Securities and Exchange Commission."[47] In the following agreement, these omissions generally relate to specific business terms, and the authors have generally edited this agreement around these omissions.]

DELL SUPPLIER
MASTER PURCHASE AGREEMENT[48]

This Master Purchase Agreement by and between Adaptec, Inc. ("SUPPLIER"), a corporation registered in Delaware and located for the purposes of this Agreement at 691 S. Milpitas Boulevard, Milpitas, California 95035 and Dell Products L.P., a Texas limited partnership located at One Dell Way, Round Rock, Texas 78682, is effective as of September 27, 2002 ("Effective Date"). This Master Purchase Agreement and its Schedules, Addenda, Exhibits and Attachments, as so identified, will be hereinafter collectively referred to as the "Agreement."

1.0 Introduction

This Agreement sets forth the only terms and conditions under which Dell Products L.P. and Dell Computer Corporation's other subsidiaries and affiliates (collectively, "Dell") will purchase products from SUPPLIER. The terms and conditions of this Agreement will apply to all products purchased by Dell from SUPPLIER. For the purpose of this Agreement, products include required service, and any software and/or documentation that accompany the products (collectively, "Products"). Unless specifically stated otherwise, all references to Product will include, without limitation, all services and spare parts necessary for SUPPLIER to meet the terms of this Agreement. The terms and conditions of this Agreement will apply to all purchase orders ("Dell PO(s)") issued by Dell for the purchase of Products.

---

47. Adaptec Inc, Dell Supplier Master Purchase Agreement (Form 8-K), at Exhibit 99.1 (Jan. 24, 2003), *available at* http://www.sec.gov/Archives/edgar/data/709804/000104746903002474/a2100825zex-99_1.htm.

48. *Id.*

2.0 Term and Termination

The initial term of this Agreement will be three (3) years beginning on the Effective Date. This Agreement will automatically renew for additional successive one-year terms unless one party informs the other of its intent to let the Agreement expire one hundred and eighty (180) days before the end of the then-current term. Either party may terminate this Agreement based on the material breach of the other party, provided that the party alleged to be in material breach receives written notice stating the cause and sixty (60) days to cure.

3.0 Price

3.1 SUPPLIER agrees to work with Dell to develop a mutually agreed-upon pricing model for each Product no less than ninety (90) days prior to planned first shipment that meets Dell's price/performance objectives and provides an agreed-upon level of return for SUPPLIER. The unit price for each Product may be reviewed on a quarterly basis or as otherwise required by Dell. . . . Worldwide prices will be negotiated between SUPPLIER and Dell Worldwide Procurement at Dell's corporate headquarters in Austin, Texas.

3.2 Dell expects material cost reductions to be worked aggressively by SUPPLIER. . . . SUPPLIER will review with Dell, on an ongoing basis [details omitted]. All prices will be in United States dollars and are exclusive of applicable sales taxes, but are inclusive of all other charges including any charges for freight, freight insurance, labeling, packing and crating, any finishing or inspecting fees, any applicable royalties, duties and all other taxes. Dell will have no liability for any tax for which it has an appropriate exemption.

3.3 . . . SUPPLIER agrees to provide service spare part pricing on a monthly basis as requested by Dell Service. Dell shall have the right, but not the obligation, to have the pricing audited by a mutually agreed independent third party upon five (5) days notice to SUPPLIER. Dell agrees that the exclusive remedy of Dell and sole liability of SUPPLIER for any failure by SUPPLIER to comply with this Section 3.3 shall be the right of Dell to receive the payment, if any, determined by such audit to be owed to Dell and/or the right of Dell to terminate this Agreement.

4.0 Payment

4.1 Unless otherwise agreed in writing, all payments will be stated (and payments made) in United States dollars and are exclusive of applicable sales, use or similar taxes for which Dell will be obligated to pay SUPPLIER. All invoices for Products received by Dell will be accumulated, upon receipt, for a period from the 16th day of a month to the 15th day of the following month (the "Accumulation Period"). Dell will pay invoices received during the Accumulation Period net [x] days from the end of such Accumulation Period . . . . No invoice can be dated prior to the date the Products reflected in such invoice are received or in the case of products shipped directly to Dell factories, the date of such shipment.

4.2 SUPPLIER acknowledges and agrees that Dell has the right to withhold any applicable taxes from any royalties or other payments due under this Agreement if required by any government authority.

5.0 Delivery of Products

5.1 The parties recognize that Products may be provided to Dell in two ways: (i) from an approved Supplier Logistics Center ("SLC"), or (ii) directly to Dell without use of an SLC. The parties recognize that some terms and conditions will be the same in both situations and others terms may vary depending on the method by which Dell receives the Products. The parties, therefore, agree that the applicable provisions will be as follows:

5.2 Provisions applicable to Products whether or not an SLC is used:

5.2.1 SUPPLIER will exert commercially reasonable efforts to meet scheduled delivery dates. Subject to the provisions of Section 5.2.4, SUPPLIER agrees to fill all Dell POs and will use commercially reasonable efforts to reduce the lead-time during the term of this Agreement. SUPPLIER will not ship Products to Dell that were manufactured in locations not approved in advance and in writing by Dell.

5.2.2 SUPPLIER will handle, pack, mark and ship the Products in accordance with Dell's packaging and labeling specifications (P/N's 11500 and 13190, respectively). SUPPLIER will meet additional packaging and labeling requirements of Dell Service, as stated in Dell Document #40.09.SQ.0055. Upon request, Dell will provide a copy of these specifications and requirements to SUPPLIER.

5.2.3 All Products are subject to inspection and acceptance at destination, notwithstanding any prior payments or inspection. This inspection and acceptance process may include the following, without limitation:

(a) Dell may perform those tests it deems necessary to determine if the Products are acceptable. If, upon inspection, Dell reasonably determines that the Products are defective or otherwise fail to comply with SUPPLIER'S Product specifications, Dell may reject an entire lot based upon a sampling or inspect all units of the lot. Any such lot may be returned to SUPPLIER for one hundred percent (100%) retesting within forty-eight (48) hours at SUPPLIER'S cost. After the retesting, the lot may be reinspected by Dell.

(b) Dell's acceptance of any Products will in no way be construed as a representation by Dell that Dell has completely tested the Products or that such Products comply with their specifications or conform to any other warranties made by SUPPLIER under this Agreement. Dell's acceptance of any Product will in no way negate any warranty provided under this Agreement or affect any other provision of this Agreement. Acceptance is only to be used to determine whether SUPPLIER is entitled to receive payment for the Products.

(c) Dell will be deemed to have accepted the Products only in the event that Dell: (i) fails to accept or reject the Products within two (2) days of delivery to Dell, (ii) explicitly accepts the Products in writing, (iii) uses the Products in Dell's manufacturing process and the Products successfully complete final test, or (iv) delivers the Products to any customer.

5.2.4 On approximately a monthly basis, Dell will provide rolling six (6) month forecasts of projected purchases of Products for AMF, NCC, EMF, APCC, CCC, BCC and potentially other delivery locations, but any such forecasts provided by Dell are for planning purposes only and do not constitute a commitment of any type by Dell. No later than three (3) days after receipt of the Dell six (6) month forecast, SUPPLIER shall advise Dell whether or not it can confirm supply for the rolling six (6) month period (current month plus five) and if not, SUPPLIER shall advise Dell of the supply to which it can commit. Confirmation of the forecast by SUPPLIER shall constitute a commitment by SUPPLIER to provide the forecasted quantities to Dell, if ordered by Dell.

5.2.5 Dell will transmit Dell PO(s) by facsimile or other agreed upon means to cover Dell's forecasted requirements for the next two (2) months. Such Dell PO(s) will be continually updated to reflect Dell's next two (2) month forecast. SUPPLIER will send Dell an acknowledgement within two (2) business days of receipt of the Dell PO confirming the quantity, delivery date and delivery location(s)....Upon Dell's request, SUPPLIER will execute a monthly reconciliation of open Dell POs. SUPPLIER will perform this reconciliation within three (3) business days of Dell's request.

5.2.6 Except as expressly set forth in this Agreement, any expenditures or commitments by SUPPLIER in anticipation of Dell's requirements will be at SUPPLIER'S sole risk and expense.

5.3 Delivery to Dell using an SLC:

5.3.1 Unless Dell specifically requests that Product be delivered directly to Dell, all Product delivered under this Agreement to Dell for manufacturing and service will come from inventory held by SUPPLIER at an approved SLC ("Revolver Inventory"). SUPPLIER agrees to maintain an SLC for American Manufacturing Facility ("AMF") in Austin, Texas, Nashville Customer Center ("NCC") in Nashville, Tennessee, and the European Manufacturing Facility ("EMF") in Limerick, Ireland. As reasonably requested by Dell, SUPPLIER agrees to maintain an SLC for Asia Pacific Customer Center ("APCC") in Penang, Malaysia, China Configuration Center in Xiamen, China ("CCC"), Brazil Customer Center ("BCC") in Eldorado do Sul, Brazil and, any other major delivery locations reasonably requested by Dell. If the Product volume in a particular region does not warrant the use of an SLC, Dell may provide SUPPLIER with a written waiver relieving the SUPPLIER of its revolver obligations for that particular region until such time as the volumes warrant reinstatement or implementation of an SLC.

5.3.2 SUPPLIER agrees to maintain Revolver Inventory at each SLC in quantities equal to Dell's most recent two (2) week forecasted demand requirements for the applicable Dell location unless otherwise agreed to in writing by the applicable Dell region. After four weeks of operation, the two (2) week inventory will be calculated as follows: one (1) week based on the average of Dell PO(s) for the preceding four weeks and the second week based on the most recent Dell forecast. The parties will work together to determine the appropriate Revolver Inventory required for End of Life ("EOL") situations. SUPPLIER agrees to replenish the Revolver Inventory as necessary to ensure the required Revolver Inventory is on hand at all times. Dell and SUPPLIER will meet periodically for an inventory pipeline assessment. At this meeting, inventory status at both Dell and SUPPLIER will be reviewed, along with any changes in Dell demand.

5.3.3 Dell's transmission of a Pull Order is SUPPLIER'S only authorization to deliver Products to Dell and invoice Dell for the part numbers and quantities set forth in the Pull Order. Title and risk of loss will not pass to Dell until the Products are pulled from the SLC and Dell takes physical possession and control of the Products at the applicable Dell manufacturing facility....

5.3.4 In the event that Dell requests that SUPPLIER utilize used or repaired parts to meet the needs of Dell Service, such used or repaired parts will be clearly marked as used and will be segregated from new Product inventory.

5.4 Delivery directly to Dell without using an SLC:

5.4.1 If Dell authorizes SUPPLIER to deliver Product directly from SUPPLIER to Dell without using a SLC, the following terms will apply. SUPPLIER will schedule delivery of each Product to the delivery location on the delivery date listed in the Dell PO. Delivery will not be deemed to be complete until all Products have been actually delivered to the applicable delivery location. SUPPLIER will not make deliveries more than three (3) days earlier than the delivery date. If Products are delivered more than three (3) days early, Dell may: (i) refuse to take possession of all or some of the Products in which case Products that are returned will be redelivered only upon Dell's instructions or (ii) store the Products at SUPPLIER'S risk and expense and delay processing the corresponding invoice until the agreed to delivery date. SUPPLIER will inform Dell immediately if late deliveries become likely in which case SUPPLIER will ship the Products by air-freight or other expedited routing, at SUPPLIER'S expense. Dell reserves the right to cancel deliveries on Dell PO(s) that are at least [x days] past-due unless delayed shipment is mutually agreed in advance. If only a portion of the Products are available for shipment to meet the delivery date, SUPPLIER will notify Dell and ship the available Products unless otherwise directed by Dell. Dell may return any unauthorized under-shipment or any over-shipment or any portions thereof, at SUPPLIER'S expense and without charge to Dell. If a complete delivery is not made after Dell receives confirmation of the shipment, SUPPLIER will pay to Dell the sum of $ (to be discussed) for each unit not delivered.

5.4.2 Dell's transmission of a Dell PO is SUPPLIER'S only authorization to deliver Products to Dell and invoice Dell for the part numbers and quantities set forth in the Dell PO. Title and risk of loss will not pass to Dell until Dell takes physical possession and control of the Products at the applicable Dell manufacturing facility. . . .

6.0 Acceleration . . . and Cancellation
6.1 Acceleration:

6.1.1 Dell may, without cost or liability, increase the pull quantities scheduled to be delivered to Dell, over and above its confirmed six (6) month rolling forecast as follows:

Days From Planned delivery to Dell	Acceleration Amount
0–10	15%
11–30	30%
31–60	75%
61+	100%

(By way of example, if on January 1 Dell wanted to increase the quantities scheduled to be delivered on January 20, SUPPLIER agrees to increase the originally scheduled delivery quantity by up to 30%.)

6.1.2 In order to ensure that SUPPLIER can meet the upside requirements, SUPPLIER will maintain a safety stock for certain Product components, which will include without limitation any Dell unique components, as follows:

Component	Weeks of Supply
ALL OF IOPs MEMORY, AND CONTROLLERS, AND ANY OTHER COMPONENTS EXPERIENCING INCREASING LEAD-IMES OR INDUSTRY ALLOCATION	8

6.2 [omitted]

6.3 Cancellation:

6.3.1 Dell may, without cost or liability, cancel Dell PO(s) as follows:

[Schedule of Dell's Cancellation Rights and Obligations Omitted]

To be entitled to consideration under this Agreement, SUPPLIER must meet the following conditions: (i) provide documentation of its actual incurred costs as a result of Dell's cancellation, (ii) limit such costs to Dell-unique components that cannot be utilized by other customers, and (iii) use commercially reasonable efforts to mitigate Dell's liability.

6.3.2 If SUPPLIER'S quality does not meet the agreed-upon quality metrics set forth in the applicable Schedule, Dell may terminate (in whole or in part) any or all outstanding Dell PO(s) without liability or charge.

6.3.3 SUPPLIER acknowledges and agrees that the remedies set forth in this Section 6.3 represent the sole and exclusive remedies of SUPPLIER, and Dell's sole liability for, cancellation of Dell PO(s).

7.0 Documentation, Software and Trademarks

7.1 Documentation. SUPPLIER agrees to provide Dell with clear and accurate Product documentation ("Documentation"). The structure and content of the Documentation will be as specified by the applicable Dell commodity STR (Shared Technology Resource) [DEFINE]. The Documentation will be provided in hard copy, PDF and HTML formats unless otherwise requested by Dell. Dell may reproduce and distribute the Documentation in hard copy or softcopy form as well as in electronic form (e.g., on Dell's website).

SUPPLIER agrees to provide such national language versions as are required by Dell. Supplier agrees to comply with Dell's Supplier E Docs (HTML) and Double-byte Language Testing Requirement.

7.2 **Software.** For all device drivers, firmware, and all necessary software for the proper operation and support of the Product (collectively "Software"), Dell is granted a non-exclusive, non-transferable...worldwide right and license to use, reproduce, and distribute the Software solely in connection with Dell's distribution and support of the Products including without limitation distribution in electronic form (e.g., via Dell's website). Dell may not prepare derivative works of Software accept as authorized by SUPPLIER in writing. SUPPLIER agrees to provide all updates to the Software to Dell during the term of this Agreement.

7.3 **Trademarks.** SUPPLIER hereby grants Dell a non-exclusive, non-transferable...worldwide right and license to utilize the SUPPLIER Trademarks in connection with advertising, promotion, and sale of Products. "SUPPLIER Trademarks" will mean those trademarks, trade names, service marks, slogans, designs, distinctive advertising, labels, logos, and other trade-identifying symbols as are or have been developed and used by SUPPLIER or any of its subsidiaries or affiliate companies anywhere in the world. Dell shall use the SUPPLIER Trademarks only in strict accordance with SUPPLIER's trademark and logo use guidelines as outlined in Schedule C. SUPPLIER shall provide Dell with notice prior to modifications to the SUPPLIER'S trademark and logo use guidelines. Dell agrees to implement such modifications into any materials created and distributed after receipt of such notice. Dell shall properly attribute the SUPPLIER Trademarks to SUPPLIER in any materials that reference or contain a SUPPLIER Trademark.

8.0 Product Withdrawal

SUPPLIER will provide Dell with at least [x days] written notice prior to the last date of manufacture of any Product. SUPPLIER will provide Product sufficient to meet Dell's forecasted pulls that SUPPLIER has confirmed before the last day of manufacture. SUPPLIER will provide Dell a one time, non-cancelable last time buy opportunity...prior to the last day of manufacture. SUPPLIER agrees to inventory last time buy quantities in an SLC for a period not to exceed [x days] from the last day of manufacture. All Product not pulled by the end of the [specified time period] will be shipped to Dell and invoiced at the PO price, subject to the parties' joint good faith efforts to otherwise dispose of the Products. Additionally, SUPPLIER will retain spare parts for the Products...from the last date of manufacture. If spares or repairs are not available, SUPPLIER will use reasonable efforts to provide similar product with equivalent or better functionality, subject to approval by Dell. SUPPLIER will allow Dell to make a final purchase in order to provide support for such Products. Dell may assign its rights to warranty replacement parts or end of life parts to a third party.

9.0 Warranties

9.1 SUPPLIER represents and warrants on an ongoing basis that:

(a) Dell will acquire good and marketable title to the Products, and that all Products will be free and clear of all liens, claims, encumbrances and other restrictions;

(b) All Products will be new and unused and will not contain used or repaired parts unless requested by Dell in writing, in which case such Products will be clearly labeled as refurbished;

(c) all Products will be free from defects in design, materials and workmanship, including but not limited to, cosmetic defects, and will conform to SUPPLIER'S Product specifications and specifications provided by Dell...from the Product manufacturing date code. SUPPLIER agrees to use a first-in/first-out inventory method for finished goods, and further agrees that the Product manufacturing date code will not be more than [x days] prior to shipment to Dell;

(d) Notwithstanding the foregoing, Batteries provided to Dell by SUPPLIER for use with SUPPLIER's Products will be free from defects in design, materials and workmanship, including but not limited to, cosmetic defects, and will conform to SUPPLIER'S Product specifications and specifications provided by Dell for thirteen (13) months from the Product manufacturing date code.

(e) it has all the rights and licenses in the Products necessary to allow Dell to distribute and resell Products without restriction or additional charge; and

(f) SUPPLIER will pass through warranty coverage from its suppliers, whenever allowable by (c) suppliers, upon the request of Dell Service.

9.2 SUPPLIER is responsible for reasonable out of pocket liability, cost and expense...with respect to defects in design, manufacturing process or material that constitute epidemic defects ("Epidemic Defects"). A defect is an Epidemic Defect when found in [x] or more of the units delivered during any three (3) month period.

9.3 Return Product. SUPPLIER agrees to fulfill the following terms and conditions.

9.3.1 The following provisions are applicable to return Product, whether returned from Dell manufacturing facilities or from the customer installed-base (field):

(a) At SUPPLIER's expense, Dell or Dell's designated service provider will return Product to a commercially reasonable location designated by SUPPLIER. Dell, at its sole option, will declare a credit (or demand a refund) equal to the last purchase price of the returned Product, which credit will be applied no later than five (5) days after Dell's notice of Product return. Dell may, at its sole option, apply such credit to the purchase of new Product, or repaired or replacement Product.

(b) In support of Dell's manufacturing and service organizations and to facilitate return of Products to SUPPLIER for credit or exchange, SUPPLIER will issue Return Material Authorization numbers ("RMA") in rolling blocks of up to fifty (50) for each Dell manufacturing facility and Dell Service organization. Dell or Dell's designated service provider will notify SUPPLIER when they have fifteen (15) pre-approved RMAs remaining and SUPPLIER will provide another block of fifty (50) pre-approved RMAs within two (2) business days of such request. If the additional RMAs are not provided within two business days, and no block RMAs remain, Dell will ship return Product to SUPPLIER without an RMA at SUPPLIER's expense. For each return shipment from Dell Service, a pre-shipment notification form will be provided to SUPPLIER communicating the Return PO number, part number, quantity, price, and extended value of that shipment. No additional information will be provided to return in-warranty Products to the SUPPLIER.

(c) SUPPLIER will establish and maintain an extended testing process for returned Products. This testing process will be subject to audit and approval by Dell's worldwide Supplier Quality Engineer. SUPPLIER will provide an initial failure analysis of the returned Product within forty-eight (48) hours of its receipt, and a failure analysis to the component level within ten (10) days of receipt. SUPPLIER will segregate and separately report returns by region.

9.3.2 The following provisions are applicable to Product returned from Dell's manufacturing facility:

(a) SUPPLIER will validate each returned Product, and will report the results of its testing to Dell on a weekly basis. This weekly report will reflect, by Product type and part number, the number of units returned, number of CND Manufacturing Products (as defined below), and number and type of defective parts. Additionally, SUPPLIER will validate that returned Product is not a result of a production test escape. For purposes of this Agreement, "CND Manufacturing Product" will refer to returned Product that has not yet been shipped to a Dell customer, for which SUPPLIER is unable to duplicate reported failures after thorough testing.

(b) Dell may (at its sole option) repurchase such CND Manufacturing Product for use in new product manufacturing, provided that such CND Manufacturing Product has completed extended testing. SUPPLIER will ensure that CND Manufacturing Product to be returned to Dell has completed such testing, and meets the latest Product revision and BIOS levels. SUPPLIER will warrant such returned Product in accordance with the terms of the full new Product warranty outlined above in this Section 9.0

9.3.3 The following provisions are applicable to Product returned from the customer installed-base (the field):

(a) If Dell Service determines that a Product that has been shipped to a Dell customer must be returned to SUPPLIER, Dell or Dell's designated service provider will return such Product, untested, directly to the location designated by the SUPPLIER, documenting the transaction with a Dell return purchase order ("Return PO"). Dell Service will return all such Products to the SUPPLIER at SUPPLIER's expense, and will debit SUPPLIER's worldwide account in an amount equal to the last purchase price of the Product at the time of shipment from Dell or Dell's designated service provider. SUPPLIER agrees to provide to Dell these Return for Credit terms ("RFC", as further described below in this Section 9.3.3) on all Products returned from the field unless otherwise mutually agreed in writing. Dell will not be required to repurchase the returned Product.

(b) For purposes of this Section, Product for which SUPPLIER cannot duplicate failures after thorough testing will be referred to as "CND Field Product". Dell may (at its sole option) repurchase CND Field Product (if any) for use by Dell Service, provided that such CND Field Product has completed extended testing. SUPPLIER will ensure that CND Field Product to be returned to Dell meets the latest Product revision and BIOS levels prior to being returned for Dell Service inventory. CND Field Product will be covered by the longer of (i) the remainder of the original warranty (as described in Section 9.1 above), or (ii) one hundred eighty (180) days. SUPPLIER will validate each returned Product, and will report the results of its testing to Dell on a weekly basis. This weekly report will reflect, by Product type and part number, the number of units returned, number of CND Field Products, and number and type of defective parts.

9.3.4 The following provisions are applicable to Product returned for repair using Dell Service's Exchange Process:

(a) Product that will be returned to SUPPLIER for repair will be referred to as "Return for Repair" or "RFR" Product. SUPPLIER will exchange all RFR Product with new or repaired Product within twenty-four (24) hours of receipt at SUPPLIER's facility. This mechanism will be referred to as the "Return for Exchange" or "RFE" Process.

(b) To support this RFE Process, SUPPLIER will SUPPLIER [sic] establish and maintain a finished goods exchange inventory ("FG Inventory") based on Dell Service's forecast. SUPPLIER will ensure that Product to be returned to Dell through the RFE Process has completed, thorough testing, and meets the latest Product revision and BIOS levels.

(c) SUPPLIER will perform all repairs within three (3) to five (5) business days of receipt of RFR Product. As the repaired Product is completed, it will be used to replenish the FG Inventory at the SUPPLIER'S facility. If at any point the required FG Inventory falls below seventy five percent (75%) of the inventory target (based on Dell Service's forecast and the RFE Process), SUPPLIER will meet the FG Inventory target requirements with new Product, at SUPPLIER's expense.

(d) All repaired or replacement Product being returned by SUPPLIER to Dell Service will be shipped at the expense of Dell Service. . . .

(e) To facilitate tracking and control of RFR Product return, Dell will debit SUPPLIER's worldwide account by means of a Return PO. This debit will reflect amounts consistent with the most recent purchase price of the Product, at the time of RFR Product shipment from Dell or Dell's designated service provider. Upon shipment by SUPPLIER of the repaired Product to Dell (for use by Dell Service), SUPPLIER will re-invoice Dell for the quantity and price specified on the applicable Return PO.

(f) At Dell's request, SUPPLIER will use Dell Service's capacity management process. If SUPPLIER'S repair capacity is insufficient to meet the requirements of this Section 9.3.4, SUPPLIER agrees to work diligently with Dell Service to certify a third-party repair center acceptable to Dell and agrees to authorize such center to perform in-warranty repair of Products on SUPPLIER'S behalf and expense.

(g) SUPPLIER will continue to support the RFE Process throughout the Product life cycle (i.e., while the Product is in-production, at end of production and during end of life).

9.4 SUPPLIER will provide [a certain type of] service to Dell at commercially reasonable prices for a period of [x days] after the last date of manufacture of a Dell system containing the Product. SUPPLIER agrees to provide three (3) to five (5) day turn around time (TAT) on all [such] repair unless instructed otherwise by Dell Service. Supplier will use commercially reasonable efforts to reduce the total cost of [such] service, while meeting Dell Service quality requirements.

10.0 Indemnification

10.1 SUPPLIER agrees to defend, indemnify and hold harmless Dell, Dell Computer Corporation, and all their respective directors, officers, employees agents and OEM distributors from and against any and all claims, actions, demands, legal proceedings, liabilities, damages, losses, judgments, authorized settlements, costs and expenses, including without limitation attorney's fees, arising out of or in connection with any alleged or actual:

(i) infringement by SUPPLIER and/or a Product(s), alone or in combination with SUPPLIER authorized hardware or software, of a copyright, patent, trademark, trade secret or other intellectual property right of any third party;

(ii) claim that a Product provided under this Agreement has caused bodily injury (including death) or has damaged real or tangible personal property;

(iii) claim arising out of or relating to SUPPLIER'S provision of repaired Products that contain used or refurbished parts that are not clearly and conspicuously labeled as such;

(iv) any violation by SUPPLIER of any governmental laws, rules, ordinances or regulations; and/or

(v) claim by or on behalf of SUPPLIER'S subcontractors, materialmen, providers, employees or agents.

10.2 SUPPLIER will provide the above indemnity even if losses are due, or alleged to be due, in part to Dell's concurrent negligence or other fault, breach of contract or warranty, violation of the Texas Deceptive Trade Practices Act, or strict liability without regard to fault; provided, however, that SUPPLIER'S contractual obligation of indemnification will not extend to the percentage of the third party claimant's damages or injuries or the settlement amount attributable to Dell's negligence or other fault, breach of contract or warranty, or breach of the Texas Deceptive Trade Practices Act, or to strict liability imposed upon Dell as a matter of law.

10.3 In the event of any such claims, Dell will: (i) promptly notify SUPPLIER, (ii) cooperate with SUPPLIER in the defense thereof and (iii) not settle any such claims without SUPPLIER'S consent, which SUPPLIER agrees not to unreasonably withhold.

10.4 In addition to SUPPLIER'S obligations and liabilities above, if an infringement claim is made or appears likely to be made about a Product, SUPPLIER will, at SUPPLIER'S option, either procure for Dell the right to continue to market the Product, modify the Product so that it is no longer infringing or replace it with a non-infringing Product. If the parties determine that none of these alternatives is commercially reasonable, Dell will return any Products in inventory freight-collect to SUPPLIER'S designated location for a credit or refund of the purchase price.

11.0 Liability

11.1 EXCEPT AS SET FORTH BELOW in Sections 11.2 and 11.3, NEITHER PARTY WILL BE LIABLE FOR ANY LOST PROFITS, LOST SAVINGS OR ANY OTHER INCIDENTAL, INDIRECT, PUNITIVE, SPECIAL, OR CONSEQUENTIAL DAMAGES UNDER ANY PART OF THIS AGREEMENT EVEN IF ADVISED OR AWARE OF THE POSSIBILITY OF SUCH DAMAGES.

11.2 SUPPLIER'S entire cumulative liability to Dell arising out of or in connection with or relating to this Agreement, the sale of Products, license of software, and the use, performance, receipt or disposition of such Products or software, from any cause whatsoever, whether based upon warranty, contract, tort, statute, or otherwise, shall not exceed all sums paid by Dell to SUPPLIER in the twelve (12) month period preceding the date of claim.

11.3 Notwithstanding the foregoing, the limitation set forth in Section 11.1 and 11.2 above will not apply to SUPPLIER'S obligations and liabilities under section 10.1(i) (Indemnification) and 18.4 (Confidentiality). SUPPLIER'S entire liability for each claim or cause of action for section 10.1(i) (Indemnification) and 18.4 (Confidentiality) shall not exceed the greater of all sums paid by Dell to SUPPLIER in the twelve (12) month period proceeding [sic] the date of claim . . . .

12.0 Quality, Product Safety, Regulatory Compliance and Engineering Changes

12.1 SUPPLIER agrees to meet or exceed the quality requirements set forth in the Schedule B.

12.2 In the event either SUPPLIER or Dell becomes aware of any information that reasonably supports a conclusion that a hazard may exist in any Product and the defect could cause death or bodily injury to any person or property damage (a "Hazard"), the party becoming aware of this information will notify the other of the potential Hazard. Whenever possible, notification to the other party will precede notice to any governmental agency, unless required by law. SUPPLIER and Dell will promptly exchange all relevant data and then, if practical, as promptly as possible, meet to review and discuss the information, tests, and conclusions relating to the alleged Hazard. At this meeting the parties will discuss the bases for any action, including a recall, and the origin or causation of the alleged Hazard. SUPPLIER will be responsible for the costs of effecting a recall including, but not limited to, the reasonable out-of-pocket costs to Dell directly related to the recall Each party will, on request, provide to the other reasonable assistance in (i) determining how best to deal with the Hazard; and (ii) preparing for and making any presentation before any governmental agency which may have jurisdiction over Hazards involving Products.

12.3 SUPPLIER is responsible for obtaining and maintaining all necessary U.S. and foreign regulatory approvals for the Product(s). Additionally, SUPPLIER will assist Dell in addressing problems with its Products that contribute to a Dell system's failure to meet any regulatory requirement due to SUPPLIER Products being integrated into the Dell system. Notwithstanding the foregoing, to the extent SUPPLIER provides sufficient detail to Dell that the Hazard is due to the interoperability of the Product with a Dell system, Dell agrees to meet with SUPPLIER to mutually agree on the cost allocation, between the parties, to execute a recall.

12.4 SUPPLIER may issue "Mandatory Changes," which are changes required to satisfy governmental standards or for safety. SUPPLIER will provide Dell with prior written notice of Mandatory Changes prior to implementing such changes. SUPPLIER will provide, at SUPPLIER'S expense, all necessary materials, reasonable labor and instructions if Mandatory Changes must be installed on Products already delivered to Dell. SUPPLIER will also provide ninety (90) days prior written notice of changes that affect any Product's (including Software or drivers) form, fit or function to allow Dell to evaluate such changes. . . . SUPPLIER agrees to supply Dell for evaluation purposes with up to twenty-five (25) samples of Product that incorporate the agreed-to ECO.

13.0 Compliance

13.1 Dell is an Affirmative Action/Equal Opportunity Employer. Since Dell transacts business with the United States Government, the Equal Opportunity Clauses at 41 CFR sections 60-1.4(a), 60-250.5(a) and 60-741.5(a) are hereby incorporated and SUPPLIER will, if applicable, comply with FAR 52.212-3, Offer or Representations and Certifications-Commercial Items, and FAR 52-219-8, Utilization of Small Business Concerns.

13.2 SUPPLIER agrees to give full consideration to use minority and women owned businesses to provide components to SUPPLIER for subsequent integration into Product sold to Dell.

14.0 Import/Export Requirements

14.1 SUPPLIER acknowledges that the Products licensed or sold under this Agreement, and the transaction contemplated by this agreement, which may include technology and software, are subject to the customs and export control laws and regulations of the United States ("U.S.") and may also be subject to the customs and export laws and regulations of the country in which the Products are manufactured and/or received. SUPPLIER agrees to abide by those laws and regulations. Further, under U.S. law, the Products may not be sold, leased or otherwise transferred to restricted end-users or to restricted countries. In addition, the Products may not be sold, leased or otherwise transferred to, or utilized by an end-user engaged in activities related to weapons of mass destruction, including without limitation, activities related to the design, development, production or use of nuclear weapons, materials, or facilities, missiles or the support of missile projects, and chemical or biological weapons.

14.2 SUPPLIER agrees not to provide any written regulatory certifications or notifications on behalf of Dell without first seeking prior written approval from Dell's Export Compliance Representative. When applicable and necessary, Dell will provide SUPPLIER with all U.S. export licenses, license designations, National Defense Authorization Act ("NDAA") authorizations and commodity classifications unless otherwise agreed to in writing by SUPPLIER and Dell and unless SUPPLIER is obligated to obtain the license under U.S. law.

14.3 SUPPLIER is prohibited from diverting any Dell shipment without first securing written approval from Dell's Export Compliance Representative. SUPPLIER agrees not to support or engage in any boycott related transaction and/or requests in order to execute a transaction on behalf of Dell.

14.4 In addition, SUPPLIER agrees to indemnify, defend and hold Dell harmless from any loss, expense, penalty or claim against Dell due to SUPPLIER'S violation or alleged violation of any such applicable laws and regulations.

14.5 Further, regarding processing Shippers Export Declarations (SED) or the Automated Export System (AES), Dell will retain the right to name its own Freight Forwarder in all transactions. Dell may, at its sole discretion, permit the SUPPLIER to name its own Freight Forwarder for the purpose of clearing outbound Customs from the United States. In such cases, SUPPLIER must provide the name, address, contact person, telephone number, and email address of that Freight Forwarder and must indicate in the order that it has authorized its Freight Forwarder to prepare to prepare and file the Shipper's Export Declaration (SED) with the Bureau of the Census. In no circumstances will Dell rely upon the Freight Forwarder of SUPPLIERS to obtain export licenses from the United States Government even if the SUPPLIER has authorized its Freight Forwarder to act as the exporter for purposes of the Export Administration regulations. Instead, Dell will obtain the necessary export license with reliance upon the transaction information that the SUPPLIER has made available to Dell.

14.6 Neither SUPPLIER, nor Dell shall, directly or indirectly, export, re-export or transship Products in violation of any applicable

U.S. export control laws and regulations or any other applicable export control laws promulgated and administered by the government of any country having jurisdiction over the parties or the transactions contemplated herein. In accordance with the US Export Administration Regulations, SUPPLIER will provide required classification information by completing the Global Export Compliance Questionnaire attached hereto as Schedule ____.

15.0 Continuity of Supply

15.1 SUPPLIER shall within sixty (60) calendar days from the Effective Date of this Agreement identify an escrow custodian ("Escrow Custodian") acceptable to both parties and contract with such Escrow Custodian ("Escrow Agreement") for the pre-arranged holding and releasing of materials required to produce or have produced the Products ("Escrow Material"). Escrow Material shall include, but is not limited to, all materials, specifications, and other items necessary to enable Dell, or a third party designated by Dell, to manufacture, support, distribute, license, and sell the Products. Within thirty (30) calendar days after the execution of the Escrow Agreement, SUPPLIER shall deposit with the Escrow Custodian the most current production level of the Escrow Material, as defined in the Escrow Agreement. Thereafter, SUPPLIER shall within ten (10) days after the release of an update to a Product, deposit updated Escrow Material with the Escrow Custodian. SUPPLIER agrees to bear the cost of establishing and maintaining the escrow account for the Products and the costs associated with its compliance with this Section, including without limitation the costs of any and all document preparation necessary to meet the requirements of this Section and the Escrow Agreement. If due to the occurrence of any of the following events SUPPLIER is unable to or fails to provide Products for Dell: (a) any bankruptcy, reorganization, or other case or proceeding under any bankruptcy or insolvency law or any dissolution or liquidation proceeding is commenced by or against SUPPLIER, and if such case or proceeding is not commenced by SUPPLIER, it is acquiesced in or remains undismissed for ninety (90) days; or (b) SUPPLIER ceases active operation of its business for any reason; or (c) SUPPLIER applies for or consents to the appointment of a trustee, receiver or other custodian for SUPPLIER or makes a general assignment for the benefit of its creditors; or (d) SUPPLIER does not remedy any supply issue within ninety (90) days of receipt of notice from Dell that a supply issue exists, then Dell shall have the right to receive possession of the Escrow Materials pursuant to the provisions of the Escrow Agreement and SUPPLIER agrees that it authorizes Dell to use the Escrow Material to produce or have produced the Products by sources other than SUPPLIER. Such authorization consists of a worldwide, non-exclusive manufacturing rights license to make or have made the Products only for use consistent with the terms of this Agreement. Such license shall be in force until such time as SUPPLIER is able to resume manufacturing of the Products; provided, however, that if Dell has commenced manufacturing the Products, it shall be entitled to continue manufacturing the Products despite SUPPLIER's ability to resume doing so, for [x days] after SUPPLIER is able to resume manufacturing the Products. Dell may not sell, lease, or otherwise distribute Products other than as intended in this Agreement. Following the Escrow License Period, Dell shall return all of SUPPLIER's Escrowed Material and documentation to SUPPLIER or its successor or trustee within thirty (30) calendar days.

15.2 In the event that Dell has the Products manufactured directly for Dell in accordance with Subsections 15.1, SUPPLIER will be liable to Dell under Section 10.0 "Indemnification" for such Products. Not withstanding [sic] the foregoing, SUPPLIER will be liable to Dell for design defects under Section 9.1 (c) and Section 9.2. SUPPLIER will also provide Dell with a list of those Manufacturers used by SUPPLIER for custom components. SUPPLIER agrees that Dell may use such component Manufacturers as well as any SUPPLIER-owned or -unique tooling used by such Manufacturer. In addition, SUPPLIER will provide an on-site expert engineer at Dell, at no charge, to assist Dell in the manufacturing, design and validation of the Product.

15.3 If SUPPLIER reasonably anticipates that Section 15.1 will be invoked and SUPPLIER does not manufacture the Products itself, SUPPLIER will make best efforts to execute written agreements with each Manufacturer naming Dell as a third party beneficiary. SUPPLIER will provide copies of such agreement to Dell. Such agreements) will contain provisions that:

(a) obligate the Manufacturer to provide the applicable Products to Dell at the same price that the Manufacturer charges SUPPLIER in the event that Section 15.1 is invoked;

(b) grant the Manufacturer a license to manufacture and sell the Products directly to Dell in the event that Section 15.1 is invoked;

(c) allow Dell to use any SUPPLIER-owned or -unique tooling used by the Manufacturer to manufacture the Products in the event that Section 15.1 is invoked;

(d) require the Manufacturer to comply with Sections 5.0, 6.0, 9.0, 10.0, 11.0, 12.0, 13.0, 14.0, 15.0, 17.0, 18.0 and Schedule B of this Agreement.

16.0 Capacity Constraints

SUPPLIER shall reasonably inform Dell on an ongoing basis of any negative impact on SUPPLIER'S production capacity as a result of large orders SUPPLIER receives from third parties. SUPPLIER will make best efforts to ensure Dell that such additional sales will in no way impact SUPPLIER'S ability to provide to Dell the quantities of the applicable Product set forth in Dell's six (6) month forecast for such Product.

17.0 New Products

17.1 During the term of this Agreement or for a period of three (3) years, whichever is greater, SUPPLIER agrees to offer to sell to Dell all products developed, manufactured, distributed or sold by SUPPLIER. If Dell agrees to purchase such products, such sale will be pursuant to the terms and conditions of this Agreement at a price equivalent to or lower than the price paid by other customers purchasing similar quantities. The terms of this Subsection 17.1 will survive any termination of this Agreement.

17.2 Prior to offering for sale any new standard SUPPLIER product (hereafter "new product"), SUPPLIER will first consult with Dell and allow Dell to place Dell PO(s) for such new product no later than when SUPPLIER extended a similar offer to any other customer. Prior to the addition of a new product to a Schedule, the parties will mutually agree on a new product program schedule which will include the appointment of business and technical contacts for each party to monitor compatibility issues and product release issues with Dell systems. SUPPLIER agrees that Dell will receive limited quantities of pre-release versions of all new products that are added to this Agreement.

17.3 Prior to the general availability of Dell's systems containing any new SUPPLIER product, SUPPLIER will provide mutually agreed-upon training to Dell for its sales, customer support and technical support organizations. Following Dell's award of business to SUPPLIER with respect to a new product, SUPPLIER will obtain Microsoft's certification for the products to the applicable current PC specification and WHQL standards and all other government and regulatory certifications required by Dell.

17.4 SUPPLIER will provide Dell with detailed silicon and board ramp-up plans. Dell will be entitled to participate in hardware and software design reviews for all new products. Dell will be entitled to participate in the formulation and direction of SUPPLIER'S future product and technology roadmaps.

17.5 Following Dell's award of new product business to SUPPLIER, SUPPLIER will provide manufacturing, customer and field diagnostics, as agreed, to Dell for testing and evaluation at least ninety (90) days prior to Dell's shipment of a new Product. These diagnostics must comply with the Dell Diagnostics specification.

17.6 Upon Dell's award of new product business to SUPPLIER, SUPPLIER will provide Dell with a minimum of one hundred (100) samples of new Products for Dell's validation, compatibility, and test processes. Such Products will be delivered to Dell as directed by the Dell Strategic Commodity Manager. If a new product does not meet Dell's requirements, Dell may return some or all of the new product samples for a credit of the price paid.

17.7 SUPPLIER agrees to support Dell Service's requirements with respect to spare parts availability. SUPPLIER will provide new Product information reasonably requested by Dell at least ninety (90) days in advance of Dell's shipment of new Product, and will stock Revolver Inventory of spare parts as requested by Dell at least fifteen (15) days prior to Dell's shipment of new Product.

18.0 General

18.1 Before initiating a lawsuit against the other relating to this Agreement, the parties agree to work in good faith to resolve between them all disputes and claims arising out of or relating to this Agreement. To this end, either party may request that each party designate an officer or other management employee with authority to bind the party to meet to resolve the dispute. During their discussions, each party will honor the other's reasonable requests for non-privileged and relevant information. This paragraph will not apply if: (i) the expiration of the statute of limitations for a cause of action is imminent, or (ii) injunctive or other equitable relief is necessary to mitigate damages.

18.2 The provisions of Sections 9.0, 10.0, 11.0 and 18.0 will survive any termination or expiration of this Agreement and will continue to bind the parties and their permitted successors and assigns.

18.3 SUPPLIER will not use the name of Dell nor any Dell trademarks, trade names, service marks, or quote the opinion of any Dell employee in any advertising or otherwise without first obtaining the prior written consent of Dell.

18.4 Any confidential information that will be disclosed by either party related to this Agreement will be pursuant to the terms and conditions of the (9/21/98) (date) Non-disclosure Agreement between Dell and Adaptec. The terms and conditions of this Agreement will be deemed to be confidential information. Notwithstanding the terms of the Non-disclosure Agreement, SUPPLIER agrees that Dell may provide information related to SUPPLIER'S Product roadmaps and other related information to certain Dell customers provided such Dell customers have executed a non-disclosure agreement with Dell that requires the customer not to disclose the information to a third party. SUPPLIER may not publicly release any information relating to this Agreement, including the existence of this Agreement, or use the Dell name or names of Dell officials, without first receiving the prior written approval of Dell's

Corporate Communications department. No other department within Dell is authorized to consent to public releases of information.

18.5 SUPPLIER will maintain accurate and legible records for a period of three (3) years records of its quality programs, test documentation and any other documents related that pertain to this Agreement. SUPPLIER will grant Dell reasonable access to and copies of such records.

18.6 Except as may be otherwise provided in this Agreement, the rights or remedies of the parties hereunder are not exclusive, and either party will be entitled alternatively or cumulatively, subject to the other provisions of this Agreement, to damages for breach, to an order requiring specific performance, or to any other remedy available at law or in equity.

18.7 The parties are independent contractors and neither party is an agent, servant, representative, partner, joint venturer or employee of the other or has any authority to assume or create any obligation or liability of any kind on behalf of the other.

18.8 No waiver of any term or condition is valid unless in writing and signed by authorized representatives of both parties, and will be limited to the specific situation for which it is given. No amendment or modification to this Agreement will be valid unless set forth in writing and signed by authorized representatives of both parties. No other action or failure to act (including inspection, failure to inspect, acceptance' of late deliveries, or acceptance of or payment for any Products) will constitute a waiver of any rights.

18.9 This Agreement may not be assigned by SUPPLIER in whole or in part, even by operation of law in a merger or stock or asset sale, without the express written permission of Dell. Such consent will not be unreasonably withheld. Any attempt to do so will be null and void.

18.10 This Agreement will be governed and construed in accordance with the laws of the State of New York, U.S.A., exclusive of any provisions of the United Nations Convention on the International Sale of Goods and without regard to its principles of conflicts of law. SUPPLIER hereby irrevocably submits to the jurisdiction of the federal and state courts of the State of Texas U.S.A. and hereby agrees that any such court will be a proper forum for the determination of any dispute arising hereunder.

18.11 Any notice required or permitted by this Agreement will be in writing in English and delivered by certified or registered mail, return receipt requested, postage prepaid and addressed as follows or to such other addresses as may be designated by notice from one party to the other, all such notices being effective on the date received or, if mailed as set forth above, three (3) days after the date of mailing:

[Notice Information Omitted]

18.12 Whenever possible, each provision of this Agreement will be interpreted in such a manner as to be effective and valid under applicable law, but if any provision of this Agreement is found to violate a law, it will be severed from the rest of the Agreement and ignored and a new provision deemed added to this Agreement to accomplish to the extent possible the intent of the parties as evidenced by the provision so severed. The headings used in this Agreement have no legal effect.

18.13 Dell will have full freedom and flexibility in its decisions concerning the distribution and marketing of the Product(s), including without limitation the decision of whether or not to distribute or discontinue distribution of the Product(s). Dell does not guarantee that its marketing, if any, of the Product(s) will be successful. . . .

18.14 Nothing in this Agreement will require Dell to purchase from SUPPLIER a minimum quantity or any or all of its requirements for products that are the same or similar to the Products. Dell may also purchase similar or identical products from others. Furthermore, SUPPLIER agrees to cooperate and work with Dell and any other providers that Dell may engage in connection with the provision of Products.

18.15 With the exception of the ROMB software letter agreement dated 3/15/2001 and attachment A to that agreement dated 6/26/01, and with the exception of the Indirect Purchase agreement dated October 16, 2000, This Agreement, and its attached Addenda, Exhibits, Attachments and Schedules, as so designated, set forth the entire agreement and understanding of the parties relating to the subject matter contained herein, and merges all prior discussions and agreements, both oral and written, between the parties. Each party agrees that use of pre-printed forms, such as purchase orders or acknowledgments, is for convenience only and all terms and conditions stated thereon, except as specifically set forth in this Agreement, are void and of no effect. Unless otherwise expressly set forth in an Addendum, Exhibit, Attachment or Schedule, as so designated, in the event of a conflict between this Master Purchase Agreement and any Addenda, Exhibit, Attachment or Schedule, the terms of this Master Purchase Agreement will prevail.

18.16 SUPPLIER agrees that for the term of this Agreement and any extensions thereof it will not seek orders in any legal or administrative proceeding that would prevent Dell from shipping any Dell or third party products.

18.17 Orders issued by Dell pursuant to this Agreement are placed with the expectation of potential acquisition of credit for current and/or anticipated future offset obligations of Dell, Dell Computer Corporation or Dell Computer Corporation's subsidiaries or affiliates, or their designated assignees to various governments around the world. Supplier agrees to reasonably assist Dell, Dell Computer Corporation or Dell Computer Corporation's subsidiaries or affiliates, or their designated assignees in their efforts to secure offset credit from these governments in an amount equal to the value of the applicable in-country content of the orders placed under this Agreement.

18.18 Throughout this Agreement, any reference to "days" means calendar days unless otherwise specified.

18.19 SUPPLIER will ensure that all specifications, prints and other documentation will be provided to Dell in the English language.

[Signature Page Omitted]

How "balanced" is the preceding Master Purchase Agreement? If you were counsel to Adaptec, what would you tell your client about the Agreement? Would you draw a line between identifying risk issues and advising your client whether to sign the Agreement? If so, how and where would you draw this line?

Assume for our purposes that you are an attorney in Adaptec's General Counsel's Office and your business leaders ask you to identify the risk issues in the Agreement. What would you say? To what extent would business considerations inform your analysis? How closely would your findings come to those in the following fictitious risk memorandum?

RISK MEMORANDUM (FICTIONAL)

DATE: September 20, 2002
TO: Adaptec Management
FROM: Adaptec Office Of General Counsel
SUBJECT: Dell Supplier Master Purchase Agreement — Risk Assessment

We have reviewed Dell's proposal for a Master Purchase Agreement pursuant to which Dell Products L.P. and unspecified other subsidiaries and affiliates of Dell Computer Corporation (collectively, "Dell") would purchase Adaptec's products through issuance of purchase orders. The Agreement appears to be a

Dell form document and, accordingly, is heavily weighted in favor of Dell. In particular, we have the following concerns, viz.:

(i) The agreement imposes upon Adaptec burdens typically associated with a requirements contract (e.g., Adaptec has obligations with respect to meeting Dell's possibly changing needs for products) without any of the benefits (e.g., Dell's commitment to purchase a minimum quantity or any or all of its requirements for the same or similar products);

(ii) The agreement requires Adaptec to be aggressive in delivering material reductions in its pricing and appears to require "most favored nations" pricing.

We address these and other concerns in the balance of this memorandum. For ease of reference and to facilitate discussions with Dell, our analysis proceeds sequentially through the 18 sections of the agreement.

Section 1.0 — Introduction

The agreement contemplates the sale of Adaptec products to Dell Products L.P. and unnamed other subsidiaries and affiliates of Dell Computer Corporation. Greater clarity around the subsidiaries and affiliates would be helpful for purposes of understanding the particular Dell entities against which Adaptec will have recourse to enforce payment and other contractual obligations and to plan product development and inventory.

Beyond this, the particular services, software, and documentation subsumed in the definition of "Products" should be specified and, as necessary, priced.

Section 2.0 — Term and Termination

The initial three-year term of the Agreement automatically renews for additional successive one-year terms absent 180 days' notice of either party prior to end of the then-current term. We recommend the addition of a mechanism providing for price increases (perhaps tied to the Consumer Price Index).

Section 3.0 — Price

The agreement contains an "agreement to agree" upon a "pricing model" for each Product meeting "Dell's price/performance objectives" and providing for "an agreed-upon level of return" to Adaptec. This is at best vague and is likely to lead to misunderstandings. (Insofar as Dell has the unfettered right to distribute or discontinue distribution of the Products, we caution against any pricing model that is tied to distribution. See subsection 18.13.)

We recommend against sharing margin information with Dell to meet the level-of-return approach.

Additionally, subsections 3.2 and 3.3 require, among other things, "material cost reductions" and pricing audits—the latter, we suspect, in connection with a most-favored-nations clause. (Portions of the text have been omitted for our review.)

Lastly, subsection 3.3 makes reference to "Dell Service"; the precise corporate entity, state of incorporation, and principal place of business should be specified.

Section 4.0 — Payment

We recommend the inclusion of an interest provision to serve as a disincentive to late payment. Also, the approach of accumulating invoices for payment will have the effect of increasing the terms of invoices received prior to the last day of the "Accumulation Period."

Section 5.0 — Delivery of Products

Dell's rights around acceptance are broad and have the potential to lead to delayed or withholding of payments to Adaptec. Beyond this, Dell has the right to dictate the locations at which Products are produced; this strikes us as overreaching and may have cost implications. Lastly, the Agreement imposes stringent inventory requirements upon Adaptec (in this regard, see subsection 5.3.2).

Section 6.0 — Acceleration and Cancellation

Dell's ability to increase quantities of Product upon limited notice will have inventory and cost implications for Adaptec. Additionally, the Agreement imposes stringent mitigation requirements upon Adaptec as a precondition to receiving payment for cancelled Products and limits Dell's liability to Adaptec to payment of still-to-be-determined cancellation sums.

Section 7.0 — Documentation, Software and Trademarks

The Agreement grants various IP rights to Dell without regard to restrictions (nonpayment, etc.); at a minimum, rights should be tied to payment.

Section 8.0 — Product Withdrawal

Adaptec is required to maintain inventories of cancelled products and spare parts for a period still to be determined. Beyond this, we strongly recommend against permitting Dell to assign to third parties its rights to warranty replacement and end-of-life parts, given the costs associated with meeting these warranty obligations.

Section 9.0 — Warranties

We recommend against offering warranties associated with cosmetic defects. We also recommend against warranting batteries against noncompliance with specifications for 13 months from the Product manufacturing date code. This period seems excessive, and there may be factors outside of Adaptec's control that bear upon compliance.

We believe Dell should be required to specify the reasons for return of in-warranty Products; the Agreement does not currently require this.

The testing process for returned Products seems unnecessarily burdensome.

We recommend that the Agreement make clear that Adaptec's satisfaction of its warranty obligations constitutes Dell's exclusive remedy in connection with deficient Products. (See also subsection 18.6.)

Section 10.0 — Indemnification

Adaptec's indemnity obligations appear to extend to unnamed Dell subsidiaries and affiliates (given the use of the defined "Dell"); this universe of potential claimants needs to be limited.

Section 11.0 — Liability

To the extent possible, we recommend seeking to limit liability for Adaptec's indemnification obligations. Also, Dell should agree that the liability limitations of the Agreement apply in the aggregate to its subsidiaries and affiliates, and Dell should indemnify Adaptec for any damages Adaptec sustains in excess of this amount. In addition, the last sentence of section 11.3, which limits Adaptec's liability for certain matters, is unclear and appears to be incomplete.

Section 12.0 — Quality, Product Safety, Regulatory Compliance and Engineering Changes

Adaptec's obligation to obtain Product approvals should be limited to approvals necessary only through the time the Products leave Adaptec's control; Dell should bear responsibility for obtaining any approvals that may be necessary in connection with Dell's use of the Products.

Section 13.0 — Compliance

The cost of compliance with all governmental requirements must be factored into pricing.

Section 14.0 — Import/Export Requirements

Dell should acknowledge and agree to abide by all applicable import and export laws and regulations applicable to its use of the Products.

Section 15.0 — Continuity of Supply

Dell should bear the costs associated with maintaining Escrow Material. The "best efforts" requirement in subsection 15.3 is unacceptable; we recommend substituting a "commercially reasonable" standard in its place.

Section 16.0 — Capacity Constraints

Likewise, the "best efforts" standard (to ensure that sales to third parties will not impact Adaptec's ability to provide Dell with Product) is unduly burdensome; we should replace this with a "commercially reasonable" standard. Moreover, we question why Adaptec should agree to capacity constraints absent Dell's agreement to purchase minimum quantities of the Products.

Section 17.0 — New Products

Similarly, we question why Adaptec should agree to "most favored nations" pricing of new products, absent Dell's minimum purchase of new products or agreement to other favorable commercial terms. Beyond this, we recommend that all costs associated with the undertakings of section 17.0 be carefully considered.

Section 18.0 — General

We recommend eliminating subsection 18.14 (which confirms, for the avoidance of doubt, that Dell is not required to purchase any minimum quantities or requirements), and, instead, imposing minimum purchase requirements upon Dell.

We recommend seeking clarification from Dell as to its reasons for requiring agreement to subsection 18.16 (preventing Adaptec from seeking orders in legal or administrative proceedings that prevent Dell from shipping any Dell or third-party products).

Likewise, we recommend seeking clarification as to the expectation language in subsection 18.17 (Dell's orders are placed with the expectation of potential acquisition of credit and/or anticipated future offset obligations of Dell for Dell's acquisition of credit and/or anticipated future offset obligations), and the reasons for requiring Adaptec's reasonable assistance to Dell to secure offset credit. (Among other concerns, what is meant by "reasonable"?) Certainly, Adaptec should not be exposed to the consequences of Dell's failure to obtain such offset credit.

1. Familiarity Breeds Fluency: A Review

While prior to reading this chapter you may not have seen or read an agreement for the sale of goods, hopefully you found this Agreement's structure and many of its terms to be familiar.

- To review, does this Agreement contain a definitions section? How does this Agreement define its terms? What are the benefits and drawbacks of the method this Agreement has adopted? (See Chapter 3.)

- According to § 18.11 of this Agreement, what is required for notice to be effective? Who bears the risk of the failure of delivery? That is, if notice is sent but not received, will such notice be considered "effective" so as to constitute the notice required or contemplated by various terms of the Agreement? (See Chapter 3.)

- Consider the structure of this sale-of-goods agreement. Section 1.0 of this Agreement contemplates, "The terms and conditions of this Agreement will apply to all purchase orders ('Dell PO(s)') issued by Dell for the purchase of Products." How might the parties wish to be sure that the terms of this Agreement do indeed govern future Dell purchase orders? (See Chapter 3.)

- According to § 18.15 of the Agreement, if there is a conflict between the Master Agreement and any Addendum, Exhibits, Attachments, or Schedules, the terms of which document will prevail? What is the effect and the limits of such order-of-precedence provisions? (See Chapter 3.)

- Section 9.1 presents various representations and warranties made by SUPPLIER. Review the difference between representations and warranties. How would it affect the warranty presented in § 9.1(a) if, before entering into the Agreement, Dell had knowledge that Products would necessarily be encumbered? Do these representations and warranties seem to favor SUPPLIER or Dell? Taking the perspective of SUPPLIER's counsel, what representations and/or warranties would you advise your client not to make? What, if anything, would you ask that Dell represent and/or warrant? Taking the perspective of Dell's counsel, for what, if anything, would you advise your client to negotiate in addition to the representations and/or warranties already made? (See Chapter 3.)

- Sections 10.0 and 14.4 specify the indemnity obligations provided by the Agreement. For what does SUPPLIER indemnify Dell? For what does Dell indemnify SUPPLIER? From the perspective of each party, do these indemnification obligations appear overly broad or narrow? Are these indemnity obligations broader or narrower than the indemnity obligations found in the AOL Agreement in Chapter 3? Is either party taking on "too much" risk? (See Chapter 3.)

- Sections 11.1 and 11.2 of the Agreement act to limit the liability of the parties. What types of damages and other liability are excluded from each party's potential liability? Is the total liability of each party capped at a certain maximum amount? If so, how is that maximum amount figured? As provided by § 11.3, what are excluded from these limitation-of-liability provisions? We have discussed that it may be unclear whether a limitation-of-liability provision applies to limit indemnification obligations under the same Agreement. Can you discern from this Agreement whether or not such limitations of liability are intended to apply to the Agreement's indemnity obligations? Are all of these indemnity obligations unbounded? (See Chapter 3.)

2. Revisiting No-Oral-Modification Provisions under Article Two

Notice that § 18.8 of the Agreement provides that no amendment or modification to the Agreement will be valid unless it is in writing and signed by both parties. In Chapter 2, we explored the issues of "no-oral-modification" provisions. There we discussed that the general rule has been that a contract cannot prevent or govern its own modification. However, Chapter 2 also discussed significant limitations on this general rule. Namely, by statute, several states (e.g., New York, California) have given no-oral-modification provisions some bite.[49]

Article 2 presents yet another important exception to the general rule regarding no-oral-modification provisions. The U.C.C. provides, "An agreement in a signed record which excludes modification or rescission except by a signed record may not be otherwise modified or rescinded...."[50] Accordingly, unlike the rule for contracts generally (and similar to the New York and California rules), a contract for the sale of goods may indeed effectively prevent its own oral modification.[51]

Also of note is another departure Article 2 makes from the common law of contracts: A modification to a contract for the sale of goods need not be supported by additional consideration to be effective. Under the common law, a modification must be supported by consideration to create contractual rights and obligations, and, under the common law's pre-existing duty rule, rights and obligations already owed under an original contract do not constitute consideration for a subsequent modification.[52] Article 2 summarily does away with this, expressly providing, "An agreement modifying a contract within this Article needs no consideration to be binding."[53] Accordingly, parties may modify their contracts for the sale of goods in a subsequent agreement, without so much as a consideration for—well—consideration.

Accordingly, because § 18.8 requires it and Article 2 likely governs, a modification to this Agreement will need to be in writing—but will not need consideration—in order to be of effect.

---

49. *See* CAL. CIV. CODE § 1698 (West 1985); N.Y. GEN. OBLIG. LAW § 15-301 (Consol. 2001).

50. U.C.C. § 2-209(2) (2003).

51. However, consider that the U.C.C. explicitly provides that a no-oral-modification provision does not operate to prevent a finding that a party later waived a right under the contract. U.C.C. § 2-209(4). The official comment to Section 2-209(4) states, "Subsection (4) is intended, despite the provisions of subsections (2) and (3), to prevent contractual [no-oral-modification] provisions... from limiting in other respects the legal effect of the parties' actual later conduct." *Id.* § 2-209(4) cmt. 4. For more on the topic of no-oral-modification provisions, please see Chapter 2; for more on the topic of waiver, please also see Chapter 2.

52. *See* RESTATEMENT (SECOND) OF CONTRACTS § 73 cmt. c (1981).

53. U.C.C. §2-209(1) (2003).

3. Conditions

We have already encountered several "conditions" throughout the agreements explored thus far throughout this book. A "condition" generally refers to something that must happen (or happen to be the case) in order to trigger a party's rights or obligations.[54] This type of condition is also commonly called a "condition precedent," as it precedes the activation of certain rights. A "condition subsequent," on the other hand, refers to an event that terminates or discharges a contractual right or a duty.[55] In other words, a condition precedent states a logical relationship where the condition is generally necessary (although, not necessarily sufficient) to activate the rights that follow the condition—in the case of a condition subsequent, to terminate the rights that precede the condition.[56] For instance, a condition might require one party to perform some act before the other party will be obligated to perform certain obligations. Likewise, a condition may require certain circumstances to be true or certain events to occur before a party's obligations will "kick in." Conditions may be conditions precedent to the entire agreement, or they may be conditions precedent to certain specific obligations within the agreement.[57] Accordingly, agreements may contain (i) conditions nestled within provisions and/or (ii) entire conditions sections, providing that all (or certain) obligations under the agreement are premised on certain conditions enumerated within the section. A condition precedent to an entire agreement generally must be satisfied before the contract itself comes into existence.[58]

Drafting Note: The Language of Conditions

Courts will find conditions to exist where the parties so intended: "the inclusion of words such as 'if,' 'provided,' 'on condition that,' or some similar phrase of conditional language indicate that the parties intended there to be a condition

---

54. *See* RESTATEMENT (SECOND) OF CONTRACTS § 224 (1981) ("A condition is an event, not certain to occur, which must occur, unless its non-occurrence is excused, before performance under a contract becomes due.").

55. *Id.* § 224 cmt. e.

56. *Id.* § 224 cmt. d ("A duty may be subject to any number of conditions, which may be related to each other in various ways. They may be cumulative so that performance will not become due unless all of them occur. They may be alternative so that performance may become due if any one of them occurs. Or some may be cumulative and some alternative. Furthermore, a condition may qualify the duties of both parties.").

57. *See, e.g., John M. Floyd & Assocs. Inc. v. Star Fin. Bank*, 489 F.3d 852, 855 (7th Cir. 2007) (Indiana law) ("We recognize, however, that the term 'condition precedent' carries multiple meanings, and can refer to a condition precedent to the formation of a contract, or a condition precedent to an obligation that arises under an already existing contract.").

58. *Id.*

precedent."[59] However, courts often will err on the side of construing a provision as a promise (that is, an ordinary covenant) rather than as a condition, where there is any uncertainty.[60] Accordingly, a prudent drafter will take care to create conditions expressly and clearly, for instance, by calling a provision a "condition."

For examples of conditions, we need turn no further than this chapter's Agreement. Section 2.0 essentially provides that the Agreement will endure indefinitely, *unless* one party provides 180-day notice of termination for a given year. Accordingly, "unless" signals that effective notice is a condition of the Agreement's not automatically renewing (i.e., a party's termination right). Section 4.2 provides that Dell has the right to withhold certain taxes, *if* required by a governmental authority. "If" signals that governmental authority is sufficient to give Dell the right to withhold certain taxes. While governmental authority may not be the exclusive source of such a right, the "if" clause operates to state a condition upon which Dell's rights arising out of § 4.2 depend. (That is, Dell may find the right to withhold taxes outside of § 4.2, and, so, we do not know that satisfaction of the "if" clause is *necessary* for Dell to withhold taxes. However, the "if" clause found in § 4.2 restricts Dell's ability to access *§ 4.2 rights* to the if-clause's satisfaction.) In order to state a right that a party will have upon, but *only* upon, the satisfaction of a condition, "if" should be replaced with "if and only if." If § 4.2 provided that "Dell has the right to withhold any applicable taxes, if and only if required by any government authority," then § 4.2 would not only provide Dell with a source for its right to withhold taxes but it also would restrict Dell to look only to § 4.2 for such a right. As a final illustration, section 6.3.1 contains a list of several so-named "conditions," providing that SUPPLIER "must" satisfy such conditions in order for SUPPLIER to be entitled to payment in the event of cancellation (within the meaning of section 6.2). Perhaps there is no clearer way to signal a condition than expressly to label a provision a "condition" and to specify that for certain rights to be available, a party "must" satisfy these "conditions."

Notice that conditions differ from covenants and warranties. Both covenants and warranties impose obligations on the party making them. A covenant states an obligation of a party to act. A warranty states a party's promise that a statement is true and to provide a remedy for any breach of the warranty. By contrast, a condition is not framed as an *obligation* of a party; rather, a condition states what *is necessary to trigger* an obligation under the contract. A condition—inasmuch as it turns on the behavior of one party—poses a "take it or leave it" scenario. Imagine that party B's obligation to sell 100 widgets to party

---

59. *Cedyco Corp. v. PetroQuest Energy, LLC*, 497 F.3d 485, 488 (5th Cir. 2007).

60. *See, e.g., Sahadi v. Contiental Illinois Nat. Bank and Trust Co. of Chicago*, 706 F.2d 193, 198 (7th Cir. 1983) ("In general, contractual terms are presumed to represent independent promises rather than conditions.").

A is conditioned on party A producing a third-party audit report detailing party A's financial condition. Party A has a choice: He may cause the report's production and satisfy a necessary precursor to party B's obligation to sell the widgets, or party A may opt not to have the report produced and to lose the right to purchase the widgets. While conditions are framed as options and covenants and warranties are framed as obligations, notice that in the end all contractual obligations are in some sense "options." A party may choose to perform its contractual obligations, or a party may choose not to perform its contractual obligations and, instead, to pay the damages that result from this breaching non-performance. The difference here is that *within* the contractual arrangement, both covenants and warranties impose obligations, *the non-performance of which amounts to a breach of that contract*, whereas the non-performance of a condition does not result in a breach of contract but leaves certain rights and obligations on the table un-triggered.[61]

Subject to certain exceptions, generally one must *precisely* meet an express condition in order to unlock any rights and obligations that flow from the satisfaction of the condition.[62] As one well-known commentator has explained: "The promisor can only be held liable according to the terms of the promise which he or she makes.... [I]f he or she makes a promise to do an act on condition that he or she receives $5.01, the promisor cannot be required to perform on being paid $5.00."[63] In contrast, recall from Chapter 2 that contractual *obligations* need not be precisely performed in order to bind the other party to his contractual obligations. If a party, in good faith, fails to perform his contractual obligations fully but still performs substantially, then the non-breaching party may sue for damages but is not excused from performing his obligations under the contract. Conditions, then, are different. If party A's obligations to perform under a contract are conditioned on party B's use of Reading brand pipes and party B uses a different but equal brand of pipe, then party B will have failed to have satisfied the condition.[64] Accordingly, any rights and obligations that were premised on such condition's satisfaction remain dormant. A pushback on this general rule requiring strict satisfaction of conditions is that a court may be unwilling to cause a party to forfeit rights under a contract,

---

61. *See, e.g., Frost Constr. Co. v. Lobo, Inc.,* 951 P.2d 390, 397 (Wyo. 1998) ("The assertion that the nonperformance of a condition precedent constitutes a breach of the agreement is incorrect. A breach of contract is the nonperformance of some duty created by a promise.").

62. *See, e.g., In re Krueger,* 192 F.3d 733, 738 (7th Cir. 1999) ("In Illinois, courts generally demand strict compliance with the requirement that a condition precedent be satisfied.").

63. RICHARD A. LORD, 13 WILLISTON ON CONTRACTS § 38:6 (4th ed. 2009).

64. This is a play on the famous case of *Jacob & Youngs, Inc. v. Kent,* 230 N.Y. 239 (1921), where a contractor agreed to build a house according to certain specifications, including that all pipes in the house were to be Reading brand pipe. The contractor built the house but mistakenly—neither fraudulently nor willfully—failed to use Reading pipe and instead used a pipe identical in all but its name. The defendant refused to pay the contractor the remaining, unpaid balance of the price. The contractor sued to recover this amount. Then Judge Cardozo found that the contractor had substantially performed his obligations and, so, had not forfeited his right to payment under the contract.

where a condition has fallen short of complete satisfaction.[65] Courts generally disfavor the forfeiture of rights so as to avoid unjust results.[66] As the Fifth Circuit has explained:

> Texas courts excuse non-performance of a condition precedent if the condition's requirement (a) will involve extreme forfeiture or penalty, and (b) its existence or occurrence forms no essential part of the exchange for the promisor's performance.[67]

This is necessarily a soft standard that leaves much discretion to the court.[68] Courts have been more willing to enforce a condition by its strict terms, despite a resulting forfeiture of rights, where the condition is part of a contract negotiated between sophisticated parties.[69]

4. Open Price Terms

Section 3.0 is the portion of this Agreement devoted to price. Having reviewed the section, can you determine how much Dell must pay for the Products it receives under this Agreement? The answer, of course, is "no," and this is not because *this* information has been redacted for confidentiality reasons. Because this is a master agreement, where Dell plans to purchase various Products from the SUPPLIER under separate purchase orders (i.e., Dell POs), the parties lack the knowledge necessary to designate in the master contract the price of these Products to be purchased in the future. Accordingly, the price of each such Product is to be agreed upon by the parties and presumably specified in the corresponding Dell PO. As we discussed in Chapter 3, this is the nature of a master agreement, which provides the global terms governing a relationship to involve the future purchase of services and/or goods by a work order. Indeed, Article 2 of the U.C.C. anticipates commercial contracts with open price terms, providing in § 2-305, "The parties if they so intend may conclude a contract for sale even if the price is not settled."[70]

---

65. *See* RESTATEMENT (SECOND) OF CONTRACTS § 229 (1981) ("To the extent that the non-occurrence of a condition would cause disproportionate forfeiture, a court may excuse the non-occurrence of that condition unless its occurrence was a material part of the agreed exchange.").

66. *See, e.g., Klipsch, Inc. v. WWR Tech., Inc.,* 127 F.3d 729, 737 (8th Cir. 1997) ("Indiana law generally disfavors forfeitures; however, forfeiture may be appropriate under circumstances in which it is found to be consonant with notions of fairness and justice under the law.") (internal citations and quotation marks omitted); *Varel v. Banc One Capital Partners, Inc.,* 55 F.3d 1016, 1018 (5th Cir. 1995) ("Texas courts disfavor forfeitures.").

67. *Varel,* 55 F.3d at 1018 (internal citations and quotation marks omitted).

68. *See* RESTATEMENT (SECOND) OF CONTRACTS § 229 cmt. b (1981) ("The rule stated in the present Section is, of necessity, a flexible one, and its application is within the sound discretion of the court.").

69. *See, e.g., Klipsch,* 127 F.3d at 737 ("Forfeiture based on the facts of this case is in keeping with the concepts of fairness and justice. In negotiating the License Agreement, [the relevant parties] were all represented by counsel and freely agreed to the clear and unambiguous language contained in the termination provision.").

70. U.C.C. § 2-305(1) (2003).

In this Agreement, SUPPLIER agrees to work with Dell to develop a mutually agreeable price for each Product. What if the parties fail to agree on a price? Article 2 not only contemplates that commercial arrangements may include open price terms but also provides for what happens if the parties later fail to agree on an open price term. Article 2 resolves the situation where "the price is left to be agreed by the parties and they fail to agree," by providing that "the price is a reasonable price at the time for delivery."[71] Article 2 often plays a gap-filling role, providing substantive terms where parties otherwise neglect to do so. Under this Agreement, if the parties fail to agree on a price, must SUPPLIER still fill Dell POs? Does SUPPLIER have any protection or recourse other than whatever confidence may be attained from a right to receive a "reasonable" price?

Parties will sometimes agree — either within a larger contract or as the subject of an entire document — to agree in the future to certain terms. These so-called "agreements to agree" occur when parties have not yet come to agreement on the issue in question as of the time of the contract but do agree that they *will* come to an agreement on the issue in the future. As of the contracting time, the parties may not have sufficient information or the desire to overcomplicate the present contract negotiations so as to come to agreement on the additional issue. Courts routinely hold that these agreements to agree in the future are *not* enforceable contractual obligations.[72] Accordingly, in general, the failure of parties to agree, despite an agreement to do so, does not constitute a breach of contract.[73] However, courts have generally found that attaching a performance standard (which we discuss in further detail below) to negotiate an agreement (e.g., in good faith) *can* create an enforceable obligation to negotiate in conformance with that standard. To illustrate, some courts have found an agreement to negotiate in "good faith" or with "best efforts" creates an enforceable obligation to negotiate — although not necessarily to agree — accordingly.[74] As the Seventh Circuit has explained:

> The obligation to negotiate in good faith has been generally described as preventing one party from, renouncing the deal, abandoning the negotiations, or insisting on conditions that do not conform to the preliminary agreement. For instance, a party might breach its obligation to bargain in good faith by unreasonably insisting on a condition outside the scope of the parties' preliminary agreement, especially where such insistence is a thinly disguised pretext for scotching the deal because of an unfavorable change in market conditions.

---

71. *Id.* § 2-305(1).

72. *See, e.g., Diamond Elec. Inc. v. Pace Pac. Corp.,* 346 F. App'x 186, 187 (9th Cir. 2009) (Nevada law); *Specialized Transp. of Tampa Bay, Inc. v. Nestle Waters N. Am., Inc.,* No. 09-12807, 2009 WL 3601606, at *7 (11th Cir. Nov. 3, 2009) (Florida law); *Tractebel Energy Mktg., Inc. v. AEP Power Mktg., Inc.,* 487 F.3d 89, 95 (2d Cir. 2007) ("'[A] mere agreement to agree, in which a material term is left for future negotiations, is unenforceable.'") (quoting *Joseph Martin, Jr., Delicatessen, Inc. v. Schumacher,* 417 N.E.2d 541, 543 (N.Y. 1981)) (alteration in original).

73. *See supra* note 72.

74. *See, e.g., Dual, Inc. v. Symvionics, Inc.,* No. 97-1228, 1997 WL 565663, at *4 (4th Cir. Sept. 12, 1997).

The full extent of a party's duty to negotiate in good faith can only be determined, however, from the terms of the letter of intent itself.[75]

Still, some courts have held that an agreement to negotiate in good faith or with best efforts, while perhaps creating a contractual obligation *in theory*, does not result in an obligation that courts can practically enforce, "[u]nless the parties delineate in the contract objective standards by which their efforts are to be measured."[76] This is because "the very nature of contract negotiations renders it impossible to determine whether the parties have used their 'best' efforts."[77] If parties wish, then, to create an enforceable obligation to negotiate, at least according to these courts, they should consider imposing definite obligations: "For instance, the parties could agree in the contract that 'best efforts' means that they would not negotiate with others for a specific period of time or that one party has the right to match any offer received from another."[78]

Accordingly, the work of Article 2 here is to address a particular instance of "agreements to agree" — agreements to agree to a price term in the future. A failure to agree to price in accordance with an agreement's provision does not cause the contract to fail nor does it amount to a breach of contract; Article 2 merely fills the gap with a "reasonable" price.

5. Most-Favored-Nations Clauses

Often department stores will pay customers if a reduction in price occurs after a certain number of days after the purchase of an item. While it is unlikely that the customer came upon this right through active negotiations with the store, the store is concerned that the customer may be less willing to buy something now — and may become dissatisfied later — given the possibility that the item may go down in price in the future. Certainly, from the vantage point of the buyer, one can appreciate the value of such a right — it can only mean a better price (although perhaps it creates some incentive for the store not to offer cheaper prices in the future). Similarly, a commercial buyer of goods benefits

---

75. *A/S Apothekernes Laboratorium for Specialpraeparater v. I.M.C. Chem. Group, Inc.*, 873 F.2d 155, 158 (7th Cir. 1989) (internal citations and quotation marks omitted).

76. *Pinnacle Books, Inc. v. Harlequin Enters., Ltd.*, 519 F. Supp. 118, 122 (S.D.N.Y. 1981); *see also Precision Indus., Inc. v. Tyson Foods, Inc.*, No. 8:09CV195, 2009 WL 4377558, at *4 (D. Neb. Nov. 25, 2009) ("It is particularly difficult to enforce this provision as there is no way to measure the breach, if any, or to give a particular remedy."). As the Seventh Circuit has explained:

> [W]e are mindful of the powerful argument that the parties' undertakings were too vague to be judicially enforceable.... This is the approach taken in some states. But interpreting Illinois law, we have held that agreements to negotiate toward the formation of a contract are themselves enforceable as contracts if the parties intended to be legally bound.

Venture Assocs. Corp. v. Zenith Data Sys. Corp., 96 F.3d 275, 277 (7th Cir. 1996) (internal citations and quotation marks omitted).

77. *Pinnacle Books*, 519 F. Supp. at 122.

78. *Id.* at 122 n.4.

from a provision that entitles the buyer to a price reduction, if the seller ever makes a better price available to another buyer. These provisions are commonly called "most-favored-nations" clauses and can be found not only in agreements for the sale of goods but also in almost any type of commercial agreement, where one party has the right to float its "deal" to the level of the best terms made available by the other party.

From the language in §§ 3.2 and 3.3 of the Agreement, it appears that Dell has the right to cause SUPPLIER to review prices on an ongoing basis. We do not know the details to inform these reviews and the associated reductions in price, but, if Dell's prices are to be reduced to match the price offerings made to others for similar products, then we have here a most-favored-nations provision. Indeed, the party wishing to enforce a most-favored-nations provision needs access to information regarding what terms the other party has given to third parties in order to know if the party's most-favored-nations provision has been implicated. Including an auditing mechanism along with the most-favored-nations provision in the agreement is one means of causing the production of such information and, so, of facilitating the enforcement of a most-favored-nations provision. Section 17.0 of the Agreement presents a variation on most-favored-nations terms, providing that SUPPLIER must make available to Dell any products sold by SUPPLIER to a third party "at a price equivalent to or lower than the price paid by other customers purchasing similar quantities." Accordingly, § 17.0 differs from a standard most-favored-nations provision in that § 17.0 addresses Dell's pricing rights not for products already the subject of a Dell PO but, rather, those products that Dell has not yet ordered and that SUPPLIER has made available to another customer.

As a brief aside, notice further that, while § 17.0 addresses the *advent* of *new* Products, § 8.0 of the Agreement provides Dell with certain rights upon SUPPLIER's *cessation* of production of *old* Products. Among these, SUPPLIER must give Dell notice before the last date of manufacture and continue to supply Dell with the quantity of Products that SUPPLIER has committed to supply to meet Dell's forecasted needs as provided by § 5.2.4.[79] Before discontinuing a Product, SUPPLIER must give Dell a single opportunity to order the Product and must warehouse these quantities. In exchange, Dell must pay for all such Product at the price specified in the associated purchase order, provided that both parties make a good faith effort otherwise to sell the Product.[80]

Returning to most favored nations, a primary concern with such provisions is the scope of third-party transactions that may trigger adjustment rights under the provision. That is, a contract for the purchase of apples is unlikely to include a most-favored-nations clause that gives the buyer the right to purchase apples for the price at which the seller sells oranges to a third-party

---

79. Please see the discussion of quantity below.
80. For more on "good faith," please see the discussion of the implied covenant of good faith and fair dealing below.

customer. A major point of negotiations, then, is defining what types of transactions are "similar" enough to the transaction at hand so as to be within the scope of a most-favored-nations clause and to cause adjustments to price and, perhaps, other terms. A buyer (or, borrower, or whatever party stands to benefit from a most-favored-nations provision) will want to define what constitutes a triggering transaction broadly because the buyer will want to cast a wide net around what may allow him to reduce prices. Of course, then, in contrast, a seller (or, again, whatever party must offer the better deal in the event that a most-favored-nations provision is triggered) will want to define the scope of a most-favored-nations provision narrowly so as to minimize the types of deals that will cause the seller to reduce the price of goods. Looking to the Agreement, as we mention above, § 17.1 provides a variation of a most-favored-nations clause. What is the scope of this provision? Why is the concern, as discussed in this paragraph, for what constitutes a "similar" transaction not at play here? From the language found in § 17.1, what limits the types of transactions that may trigger Dell's pricing rights? Which party — SUPPLIER or Dell — does the inclusion of this limitation benefit? Is this limitation vague or well defined in the text of § 17.1? Which party does such vagueness or definiteness benefit?

6. Quantity: Output and Requirements Contracts

Along with price, quantity is some of the basic information a contract for the sale of goods might include. There are a number of ways for contracts to address quantity. Straightforwardly, sale-of-goods contracts may simply state the number of goods to be sold under the contract. Alternatively, a contract may be for all the goods that the buyer requires or, as another example, all the goods that the seller produces. The former is commonly called a "requirements" contract and the latter, an "output" contract. As these are common modes of doing business, Article 2 contemplates their use and offers its own gloss for their interpretation. The U.C.C. provides that where a contract defines the quantity of goods to be sold as the seller's output or the buyer's requirements, this quantity term "means such actual output or requirements as may occur in good faith."[81] What does it mean for output or requirements quantities to occur in "good faith"? As the Fourth Circuit has explained:

> Although there is no established standard for determining whether a buyer acted in good faith, courts focus on whether the buyer's reduction of its requirements stemmed from second thoughts about the terms of the contract and the desire to get out of it. Thus, if the buyer had a legitimate business reason for

---

81. U.C.C. § 2-306(1) (2003). We discuss below the implied covenant of good faith, which permeates all contractual relationships.

eliminating its requirements, as opposed to a desire to avoid its contract, the buyer acts in good faith.[82]

The Fourth Circuit went on to find that a buyer that closed its plant facility "as part of its overall restructuring" and "because of its low profitability" and, thus, eliminated its requirements under a requirements contract did so based on "a legitimate business decision" and in good faith.[83] In addition, the U.C.C. expresses concern for the situation where the quantity (i.e., the amount required or the amount produced) is "unreasonably disproportionate" to the parties' stated estimate or—if no estimate is stated—"to any normal or otherwise comparable prior output or requirements."[84] Despite an output or requirements quantity provision, in these cases where a "disproportionate" quantity results from the goods required or produced, such a quantity will not be forced upon, say, a buyer (by a seller in an output contract) or a seller (by a buyer in a requirements contract). Many courts have held that this concern for disproportionately is asymmetrical—that it only applies when the quantity term would be disproportionately *greater* than an estimated or reasonable amount and that good faith *reductions* that result in disproportionately low quantities do not violate Article 2.[85]

Does this Agreement contemplate a requirements or output arrangement? In other words: Must SUPPLIER supply all the Products that Dell requires, or must Dell purchase all the Products that SUPPLER produces? Subsection 5.2.4 speaks to the quantity of Products that SUPPLIER will supply Dell, stating that Dell will give SUPPLIER notice of a six-month-advance quantity amount and that SUPPLIER will respond, in kind, with whether or not SUPPLIER will meet the forecasted quantity. Subsection 5.2.4 further specifies that it is SUPPLIER's confirmation of its commitment to meet Dell's forecasted quantity that will bind SUPPLIER to do so. Subsection 5.2.1 provides, "Subject to the provisions of Section 5.2.4, SUPPLIER agrees to fill all Dell POs...." In addition, notice that § 18.14 provides explicitly that the Agreement itself imposes no obligation on Dell to purchase any minimum quantity from SUPPLIER. Accordingly, SUPPLIER is not obligated to supply all of Dell's requirements, and Dell is not obligated to purchase all of SUPPLIER's output. Rather, this Agreement provides specific mechanisms by which Dell and

---

82. *Brewster of Lynchburg, Inc. v. Dial Corp.*, 33 F.3d 355, 365-66 (4th Cir. 1994) (internal citations and quotation marks omitted).

83. *Id.* at 366.

84. U.C.C. § 2-306(1) (2003).

85. *See, e.g., Brewster*, 33 F.3d at 365 ("[U]nder Arizona law, a requirements contract allows a buyer to reduce the quantity demanded to any amount, including zero, so long as it does so in good faith. If the seller wishes to reallocate some of the inherent risks in such a contract, it may specify some minimum requirement."); *Empire Gas Corp. v. Am. Bakeries Co.*, 840 F.2d 1333, 1339 (7th Cir. 1988). *But see Simcala, Inc. v. Am. Coal Trade, Inc.*, 821 So.2d 197 (Ala. 2001) ("We conclude that the interpretation supported by the plain meaning of the language of the statute and by the official comments is that [U.C.C. § 2-306(1)] prohibits unreasonably disproportionate decreases made in good faith.").

SUPPLIER may agree to the purchase and supply of certain quantities of goods.

Section 2-201 is the U.C.C. version of the statute of frauds and requires that a contract for the sale of goods over $5,000 contain a quantity term in order to be enforceable.[86] If the Agreement does not require Dell to purchase and/or SUPPLIER to sell any certain quantity of goods, does this Agreement run afoul of the statute of frauds? Does it matter that a purchase order (presumably incorporating the Agreement by reference) is likely to include a specific quantity term? The official comments to § 2-201 provide some guidance:

> A term indicating the manner by which the quantity is determined is sufficient. Thus, for example, a term indicating that the quantity is based on the output of the seller or the requirements of the buyer satisfies the requirement. The same reasoning can be extended to a term that indicates that the contract is similar to, but does not qualify as, an output or requirement contract. Similarly, a term that refers to a master contract that provides a basis for determining a quantity satisfies this requirement.[87]

Please consider this official comment along with the case excerpted below in determining whether you think the Agreement is likely to be enforceable under the U.C.C.

Advent Sys. Ltd. v. Unisys Corp.
United States Court of Appeals, Third Circuit, 1991.
925 F.2d 670.

WEIS, Circuit Judge.

...Plaintiff, Advent Systems Limited, is engaged primarily in the production of software for computers. As a result of its research and development efforts, by 1986 the company had developed an electronic document management system (EDMS), a process for transforming engineering drawings and similar documents into a computer data base.

Unisys Corporation manufactures a variety of computers. As a result of information gained by its wholly-owned United Kingdom subsidiary during 1986, Unisys decided to market the document management system in the United States. In June 1987 Advent and Unisys signed two documents, one labeled "Heads of Agreement" (in British parlance "an outline of agreement") and, the other "Distribution Agreement."

In these documents, Advent agreed to provide the software and hardware making up the document systems to be sold by Unisys in the United States. Advent was obligated to provide sales and marketing material and manpower

---

86. U.C.C. § 2-201(1) (2003). Note the pre-revised version of section 2-201 sets the threshold at $500, which the revised version increased to $5,000.

87. *Id.* § 2-201 cmt. 1 (internal citations omitted).

as well as technical personnel to work with Unisys employees in building and installing the document systems. The agreement was to continue for two years, subject to automatic renewal or termination on notice.

During the summer of 1987, Unisys attempted to sell the document system to Arco, a large oil company, but was unsuccessful. Nevertheless, progress on the sales and training programs in the United States was satisfactory, and negotiations for a contract between Unisys (UK) and Advent were underway.

The relationship, however, soon came to an end. Unisys, in the throes of restructuring, decided it would be better served by developing its own document system and in December 1987 told Advent their arrangement had ended. Unisys also advised its UK subsidiary of those developments and, as a result, negotiations there were terminated.

Advent filed a complaint in the district court alleging, *inter alia,* breach of contract, fraud, and tortious interference with contractual relations....

On appeal Advent argues that the Distribution Agreement prohibited Unisys from pressuring its UK subsidiary to terminate negotiations on a corollary contract. Unisys contends that the relationship between it and Advent was one for the sale of goods and hence subject to the terms of statute of frauds in the Uniform Commercial Code. Because the agreements lacked an express provision on quantity, Unisys insists that the statute of frauds bans enforcement....

III. THE STATUTE OF FRAUDS

This brings us to the Unisys contention that the U.C.C. statute of frauds bars enforcement of the agreement because the writings do not contain a quantity term.

Section 2-201(a) provides that a contract for the sale of goods of $500 or more is not enforceable unless in writing. "[A] contract...is not enforceable...unless there is some writing sufficient to indicate that a contract for sale has been made....A writing is not insufficient because it omits ... a term agreed upon but the contract is not enforceable...beyond the quantity of goods shown in such writing." The comment to this section states that although the "required writing need not contain all the material terms" there are "three definite and invariable requirements as to the memorandum," one of which is that "it must specify a quantity."

The statute of frauds has been frequently criticized as a means for creating rather than preventing fraud, and there have been calls for its total repeal. Serious considerations therefore counsel courts to be careful in construing its provisions so that undesirable rigidity does not result in injustice.

The limited scope of section 2-201 should not be overlooked. "It is also clear that a sufficient writing merely satisfies the statute of frauds under the Code, i.e., it does not, in itself, prove the terms of the contract."

Moreover, compliance with the statute of frauds must be distinguished from enforcement of a remedy. At this point we focus on the statute of frauds, reserving for discussion enforcement under § 2-204.

Courts have generally found that a quantity term must be stated for compliance with the Code, and commentators have agreed.

A contrary view, however, has been advanced. In her article *The Weed and the Web: Section 2-201's Corruption of The U.C.C.'s Substantive Provisions—The Quantity Problem*, Professor Bruckel argues that the quantity section of the statute of frauds should be construed so that the contract is not enforceable beyond the quantity shown in the writing—if a quantity is specified. If no quantity is mentioned, the omission should not be fatal.

Respected scholars concede some force to this argument. As White and Summers state, "All commentators say the memo must state a quantity term. However, a close reading of section 2-201 indicates that all commentators may be wrong. An alternative explanation is that only if the writing states a quantity term is that term determinative."

This liberal approach found an interested audience in *Riegel Fiber Corp. v. Anderson Gin Co.*, 512 F.2d 784 (5th Cir. 1975), where the Court described that reasoning as "plausible," noting that the quantity term offers little aid in the primary purpose of the statute of frauds. Once a party alleges that the agreement took place and proves a signed writing, "surely he is no more likely to lie about the agreed quantity term than about price, time of performance, or any other material term." A Pennsylvania court also struck a sympathetic chord in discussing the effect of a memorandum that refers to an oral agreement.

The circumstances here do not require us to adopt an open-ended reading of the statute but permit us to apply a narrower holding. Nothing in the Code commands us to ignore the practicality of commercial arrangements in construing the statute of frauds. Indeed, the Code's rule of construction states that the language "shall be liberally construed and applied to promote its underlying purposes and policies." As noted earlier, Comment 1 to that section observes that the Code promotes flexibility in providing "machinery for expansion of commercial practices." Following this guidance, we look to the realities of the arrangement between the parties.

In the distribution agreement, Unisys agreed to engage in the business of selling identified document systems during the two-year term of the contract and to buy from Advent on stated terms the specified products necessary to engage in that venture. The detailed nature of the document, including as it does, such provisions as those for notice of breach, opportunity for cure, and termination leaves no doubt that the parties intended to create a contract.

The parties were obviously aware that they were entering a new, speculative market and some uncertainty was inevitable in the amount of sales Unisys could make and the orders it would place with Advent. Consequently, quantity was not stated in absolute terms. In effect, the parties arrived at a nonexclusive requirements contract, a commercially useful device. We do not consider that in the circumstances here the arrangement raises the statute of frauds bar.

The Code recognizes exclusive requirements contracts in section 2-306, and imposes on the parties to such agreements a duty of good faith. For present purposes, the salient factor is that exclusive requirements contracts satisfy the quantity requirements of the statute of frauds, albeit no specific amount is stated.

The reasons for excepting exclusive requirements contracts from the strictures of the statute of frauds are strong. The purchasing party, perhaps unable to anticipate its precise needs, nevertheless wishes to have assurances of supply and fixed price. The seller, on the other hand, finds an advantage in having a steady customer. Such arrangements have commercial value. To deny enforceability through a rigid reading of the quantity term in the statute of frauds would run contrary to the basic thrust of the Code—to conform the law to business reality and practices.

By holding that exclusive requirements contracts comply with the statute of frauds, courts have decided that indefiniteness in the quantity term is acceptable. If the agreement here does not satisfy the statute of frauds because of indefiniteness of a quantity term, then neither does an exclusive requirements contract. We find no reason in logic or policy to differentiate in the statute of frauds construction between the contract here and an exclusive requirements arrangement.

The same reasons that led courts to dispense with a specific and certain quantity term in the exclusive requirements context apply equally when a continuing relationship is non-exclusive. The same regulating factor—good faith performance by the parties—applies and prevents the contracts from being illusory. The writings here demonstrate that the parties did not articulate a series of distinct, unrelated, simple buy and sell arrangements but contemplated what resembles in some respects a joint venture or a distributorship.

A construction of the statute of frauds that does not recognize the quite substantial difference between a simple buy and sell agreement and what occurred here is unduly restrictive. Section 2-306 in recognizing exclusive requirements and output contracts does not purport to treat them as the only permissible types of open quantity agreements. We do not read section 2-306 as an exclusionary measure, but rather as one capable of enlargement so as to serve the purposes of the Code.

We emphasize once again that our focus has been on a technical requirement of the statute of frauds whose *raison d'etre* is dubious. We have not yet considered the importance of evidence to support a remedy, an issue we consider to be addressed by section 2-204 rather than being comprehensively covered by the statute of frauds.

The separation of the concepts advanced by the statute of frauds and section 2-204 has a very practical significance. If the statute of frauds was not satisfied, this case would be dismissed on the complaint, but by surmounting that threshold, the litigation proceeds to a point where the terms of the contract and its enforcement may be determined. This disposition comports with the goals of the Code and gives due recognition to legitimate business practices.

In sum, we hold that the writings here satisfy the statute of frauds....

Comments

The official comments to revised § 2-201 cite *PMC Corp. v. Houston Wire & Cable Co.*[88] In that case, the Supreme Court of New Hampshire found that an agreement for the sale of goods did not fail the statute of frauds because the agreement "was not totally silent as to quantity because it referred to [a party's] expectation to purchase a 'major share'" of its products from the other party.[89] The comments also cite *Riegel Fiber Corp. v. Anderson Gin Co.*[90] There, the court focused its inquiry on whether commercial buyers and sellers in the relevant industry would view the approach to the agreement's determination of quantity to be acceptable.[91] Accordingly, the court found a master contract for the sale of cotton with an undefined quantity term to be enforceable because the approach to contracting conformed to "acceptable practices in the cotton trade."[92] How do these cases inform your understanding of the Dell Agreement and its enforceability under § 2-201 of the U.C.C.?

7. Delivery, Transfer of Title, and Risk of Loss

"Title" refers to "the legal right to control and dispose of property."[93] "Risk of loss" refers to "[t]he danger or possibility of damage to, destruction of, or misplacement of goods or other property."[94] While title and risk of loss often move together from a seller to a buyer, the transfer of one does not always coincide with the other.[95] Understanding how and when risk of loss passes is important: The party bearing the risk of loss for certain goods at a given moment suffers any harm that befalls those goods through no fault of either party. For example, if the risk of loss has already transferred from the seller to

---

88. 797 A.2d 125 (N.H. 2002).

89. *Id.* at 129.

90. 512 F.2d 784 (5th Cir. 1975).

91. *Id.* at 790.

92. *Id.* at 792.

93. Black's Law Dictionary 1622 (9th ed. 2009).

94. *Id.* at 1443.

95. *See, e.g., Commonwealth Propane Co. v. Petrosol Int'l, Inc.*, 818 F.2d 522, 526-27 (6th Cir. 1987); *see also* U.C.C. § 2-509 cmt. 1 (2003) ("The underlying theory of this section on risk of loss is in conformity with common commercial and insurance practice, to base the risk of loss on the physical location of the goods and not by shifting of the risk with the 'property' in the goods.").

the buyer when goods are damaged, then the buyer must still pay for the goods, as agreed upon in the contract. If the seller still holds the risk of loss when goods are damaged and the seller is unable to deliver conforming goods as required by the contract, then the seller is liable to the buyer for failure to deliver conforming goods.

For how and when risk of loss passes from a buyer to a seller, we first look to Article 2. And Article 2 makes it clear that the first step is to look at what the parties to the contract specified.[96] If the contract provides specific terms for how and when risk of loss is transferred, then, as we discuss below, this governs. Absent the parties' so providing, Article 2 fills this gap with a host of its own rules. As an illustration, if the contract provides for delivery by a common carrier, then the risk of loss transfers to the buyer upon the seller's completion of its delivery obligations.[97] Either party's breach of contract may change when the risk of loss passes from the seller to the buyer. In short, the seller retains the risk of loss if the seller has not satisfied all conditions necessary for the seller to obligate the buyer to accept the goods (e.g., the seller has not delivered conforming goods).[98] If the buyer has breached the contract, the buyer is liable to the seller for any damage to the goods beyond what the seller's insurance covers.[99] To be clear, if a party causes damage to the other party's goods, the aggrieved party has the same rights it always does to seek to recover in contract or tort from the party causing such damage.[100] "Risk of loss" refers to the risk of loss or damage that occurs through no fault of either party.

If you found the above paragraph dizzying (or, if not, feel free to review U.C.C. § 2-509 in further detail), take heed of the wondrous power of contracts to alter "default" law. As with much of contract law, the U.C.C. provides default risk-of-loss terms that designate how and when the risk of loss passes from the seller to the buyer in the absence of contractual provisions providing otherwise.[101] Parties to a contract for the sale of goods may specify in that contract how the risk of loss may (or may not) pass from the seller to the buyer.[102] Accordingly, to understand when Dell assumes the risk of damage befalling Products, Article 2 instructs us first to look to the Agreement itself.

---

96. U.C.C. § 2-509(4) (2003).

97. *Id.* § 2-509(1) (2003). Note that the 2003 revisions of Article 2 altered some of the default risk-of-loss rules under Article 2.

98. *Id.* § 2-510(1).

99. *Id.* § 2-510(3).

100. As we discussed in Chapter 3, the contract may seek to insulate a party from such liability. Please see the discussion in Chapter 3 on indemnification and limitation-of-liability provisions.

101. *See, e.g.,* U.C.C. §§ 2-509, 2-510 & 2-327 (2003).

102. *See supra* note 101. For example, § 2-509(4) provides, "The provisions of this section are subject to contrary agreement of the parties...."

Subsections 5.3.3 and 5.4.2 explain how risk of loss may pass under two mutually exclusive scenarios. As § 5.1 explains, SUPPLIER may deliver Products to Dell in either of two ways: (i) from certain Supplier Logistic Centers (SLCs); or (ii) directly to Dell. As § 5.3.1 clarifies, SUPPLIER will provide all Products from an SLC, unless Dell specifically requests direct delivery. Subsection 5.3.3 addresses risk of loss in the context of delivery from an SLC, and § 5.4.2 provides the risk-of-loss rules for direct delivery. For delivery from an SLC, SUPPLIER is only "authorized" to deliver Products to Dell, once Dell has given Supplier a "Pull Order." (Notice that the Agreement nowhere provides a definition of "Pull Order.") Absent a Pull Order, risk of loss cannot pass for any Products to be delivered from an SLC. If Dell issues a Pull Order, then the risk of loss passes once Dell takes physical possession and control of the Products at a Dell facility. Similarly, with regard to Products to be delivered directly to Dell, the risk of loss does not pass until Dell takes physical possession and control of the Products at a Dell facility. In addition, recall that Products, under this Agreement, do not attain "direct delivery" status (and so § 5.4.2 does not apply) unless Dell specifically authorizes SUPPLIER to deliver the Products directly. Test yourself: If Dell has transmitted a Pull Order for the Product but has not specifically requested direct delivery and a Product is damaged while en route to Dell (through no fault or doing of either party), which party bears this loss? Is it Dell or SUPPLIER who bears the costs of the damaged goods?

Understanding Terms of Delivery: Pre-Revised Article Two and "Incoterms"

Revised Article 2 did away with §§ 2-319 through 2-324, which provided various terms and rules for the delivery of goods. Under the pre-revised Article 2, § 2-319 addresses "F.O.B" (free on board) and "F.A.S" (free alongside) terms, and § 2-320 addresses "C.I.F." (cost, insurance, and freight) and "C. & F." (cost and freight) terms. For example, under pre-revised § 2-319, when a contract specifies that goods are to be delivered F.O.B. place of shipment, then the seller must deliver the goods to a common carrier and arrange for their shipment to the buyer. When a contract specifies that goods are to be delivered F.O.B. place of destination, then the seller must deliver the goods to this specified destination. Under the pre-revised Article 2, the parties are free to vary the meaning and obligations associated with these terms as used in their contract. Absent such variation, pre-revised Article 2 steps in to specify delivery obligations and the transfer of risk of loss, when the parties specify one of these delivery terms of art.

The revised version of Article 2 does not provide particular meaning or rules for the use of these delivery terms, but the use of terms, such as "F.O.B" or "F.A.S.," in a contract governed by Revised Article 2 will be interpreted as any other term. If the parties do not define the terms within their contract, the course of performance between the parties under that contract, the course of dealing between the parties under previous contracts, and the usage of trade by those in the relevant industry may inform the interpretation of these terms.[103]

In addition, the International Chamber of Commerce ("ICC") has promulgated International Commercial Terms (or "Incoterms") for the delivery of goods within the international commercial community.[104] Contractual parties may signal their intention to subscribe to the rights and responsibilities (e.g., delivery obligations, insurance obligations, transfer of risk of loss) afforded to certain Incoterms by expressly incorporating "Incoterms" by reference into their contract. As the ICC releases updated versions of Incoterms (e.g., "Incoterms 2010"), parties should specify the year of the Incoterms they wish to incorporate. As with Article 2 delivery terms, the parties may alter or change the incorporated meaning of Incoterms by so providing in their contract.

8. Acceptance and Rejection: Triggering Payment and Warranties

As with the risk-of-loss rules described above, the rules for acceptance and rejection are largely default law, which means that the parties may alter them by contract.[105] However, some rules are mandatory, namely that a buyer generally have a "reasonable time" to inspect the goods before having accepted them.

The default rules of rejection under Article 2 are as follows. In general, when a buyer receives goods from a seller that "fail in any respect to conform" to contractual specifications, the buyer has the right (i) to reject all of the goods, (ii) to accept all of the goods, or (iii) to accept some of the goods, rejecting the rest.[106] This is commonly called the "perfect-tender" rule, as the buyer has the right to reject the whole delivery for any nonconformity whatsoever. However, the perfect-tender rule does not apply to "installment contracts."[107] An installment contract is defined broadly as a contract for multiple goods that allows

---

103. U.C.C. § 1-303 (2003).
104. *See generally* Incoterms, http://www.iccwbo.org/incoterms/ (last visited Aug. 15, 2010).
105. *See* U.C.C. § 1-302 (2003).
106. *Id.* § 2-601.
107. *Id.*

for delivery in separate groups, each of which is to be separately accepted.[108] Indeed, even if such a contract contains language that each delivery constitutes its own contract, the entire contract will still be treated as an "installment contract" for the purposes of Article 2.[109] As follows, this chapter's Agreement is likely to be treated as an installment contract. With installment contracts, "The buyer may reject any installment that is nonconforming if the nonconformity substantially impairs the value of that installment to the buyer...."[110] Accordingly, an installment contract allows a buyer to reject goods for nonconformity only where the nonconformity constitutes a "substantial impairment," whereas any nonconformance of goods whatsoever is sufficient grounds for rejection under a non-installment contract (under the perfect-tender rule and subject to the seller's assurance of cure).

Assuming that a buyer has a right to reject, in order to effect such a rejection, the buyer must "seasonably" notify the seller of the rejection and such rejection must be within a reasonable time after delivery.[111] An action occurs "seasonably" if it occurs within a contractually specified time; if the contract does not so specify, an action occurs "seasonably" if it occurs within a "reasonable time."[112] What constitutes a "reasonable time" depends on the "nature, purpose, and circumstances" of the particular context.[113] Parties may fix a "reasonable time" by contract; however, a contractually agreed upon "reasonable time" that is "manifestly unreasonable" is not a "reasonable time" under the U.C.C., notwithstanding the agreement to the contrary.[114] If the buyer effectively rejects the goods, the seller under certain circumstances may still have the right to cure any nonconformity; this means the seller is allowed to fix any problems with the goods and re-deliver them to the buyer for acceptance but may still be liable to the buyer for any reasonable expenses caused by the breach and delayed performance.[115]

The buyer's alternative to rejecting goods is to accept them. Under Article 2, acceptance occurs in one of three ways: (1) the buyer notifies the seller, after a reasonable opportunity to inspect them, that the goods are conforming or that the buyer will take them despite their nonconformity; (2) the buyer fails to

---

108. *Id.* § 2-612(1); *see also Midwest Mobile Diagnostic Imaging v. Dynamic Corp. of Am.*, No. 97-1673, 1998 WL 537592, at *2 (6th Cir. Aug. 7, 1998) (Michigan law) ("An installment sale is a contract for multiple items that permits delivery in separate groups and at different times.").

109. U.C.C. § 2-612(1) (2003) (A contract is an installment contract "even if the contract contains a clause 'each delivery is a separate contract' or its equivalent.").

110. *Id.* § 2-612(2). Note that a "defect in the required documents" (e.g., required insurance documents, a bill of lading) is also a sufficient basis to reject any installment. *Id.* However, if a seller gives adequate assurance that the seller will cure the defect (i.e., nonconformity constituting substantial impairment of value, defect in the required documents), then the buyer must accept the installment, unless the nonconformity substantially impairs the value of the *whole* contract. *Id.* § 2-612(2) & (3).

111. *Id.* § 2-602(1).

112. *Id.* § 1-205(b).

113. *Id.* § 1-205(a).

114. *Id.* § 1-302(b).

115. *Id.* § 2-508.

reject the goods and the buyer has had a reasonable opportunity to inspect the goods; or (3) the buyer acts in any way inconsistent with the seller's owning the goods.[116] Note that payment alone is generally not conclusive of acceptance.[117]

Two competing concerns are at play regarding what constitutes a "reasonable time" in the context of acceptance and rejection: (1) the buyer's right to have a reasonable opportunity to inspect the goods before accepting them; and (2) the seller's right to have rejection occur, if it is to occur, within a reasonable time. The easy cases are when the buyer expressly accepts the goods or expressly rejects the goods right away. The more difficult cases are when the buyer does not expressly reject the goods immediately, and it becomes a question of fact whether a reasonable time for rejection has passed and whether the buyer has had a reasonable chance to inspect the goods, such that a failure to reject is a deemed acceptance. Again, as with the "reasonable time" that sets the outer bound for a timely rejection, what constitutes a reasonable time for a buyer's inspection may be fixed by contract, unless the contractual time limit has left the buyer with a "manifestly unreasonable" opportunity to inspect.[118] This is one place where a contract generally cannot completely alter a party's rights under Article 2, as the official comments explain: "However, no agreement by the parties can displace the entire right of inspection except where the contract is simply for the sale of 'this thing.'"[119] For example, the Eighth Circuit has held that a requirement that a notice of rejection be provided within five days after delivery did not prevent a later rejection because the buyer could not know within the contractual time period of the nonconformity.[120] In that case, the buyer of a tower received a warped base plate, which the seller assured would not affect the performance of the tower, and the buyer could not discover that the warped base plate affected the tower's conformance to specifications until after the buyer had erected the tower.[121]

In addition, even if a buyer has accepted goods, the buyer may still be able to "revoke" the acceptance. Revocation gives the buyer the same rights the buyer would have had if the buyer had rejected the goods in the first place.[122] A buyer may revoke an acceptance of goods when a "nonconformity substantially impairs [the goods'] value" to the buyer.[123] In addition, revocation requires that the buyer has accepted the goods "on the reasonable

---

116. *Id.* § 2-606(1); *see also id.* § 2-513(1).

117. *Id.* § 2-606 cmt. 3.

118. *See, e.g., Northwest Airlines, Inc. v. Aeroservice, Inc.,* 168 F. Supp. 2d 1052, 1054-55 (D. Minn. 2001) ("The reasonable inspection time is here defined by the contract: ten days. Aeroservice did not notify Northwest of any possible lack of conformance of the goods until *at least* eleven days after delivery of the second shipment. Thus, as a matter of law, Aeroservice accepted the goods—conforming or not—and yet has not fully performed its obligations under the contract.") (emphasis in original).

119. U.C.C. § 2-513 cmt. 1 (2003).

120. *Trinity Prods., Inc. v. Burgess Steel, LLC,* 486 F.3d 325, 332 (8th Cir. 2007) (Missouri law).

121. *Id.* at 331.

122. U.C.C. § 2-608(3) (2003).

123. *Id.* § 2-608(1).

assumption that its nonconformity would be cured and it has not been seasonably cured" or "without discovery of the nonconformity," in the latter case such acceptance being "reasonably induced either by the difficulty of discovery before acceptance or by the seller's assurances."[124] Note that wrongful rejection or revocation of goods is a breach of contract that leaves the seller with the full panoply of remedies available as with any breach of contract.[125]

What is the meaning of all this talk of rejection and acceptance (and, then, revocation still)? Rejection and revocation are important because they generally allow the buyer to return the goods to the seller without liability or having to pay.[126] Moreover, as discussed above, absent a contract to the contrary, the seller retains the risk of loss for certain goods if the buyer has a right to reject such goods.[127] In addition, absent a contract to the contrary, acceptance triggers the buyer's payment obligations.[128] Indeed, this Agreement provides as much: Subsection 5.2.3(b) provides that acceptance triggers SUPPLIER's right to payment for delivered Products. Acceptance forecloses rejection (although, revocation may be available) of goods for nonconformity,[129] but acceptance generally triggers or, at least preserves, the buyer's right to sue for breach of warranty for the nonconformity of goods. Under subsection 5.2.3(b) of the Agreement, acceptance preserves Dell's warranty rights, as the provision makes clear that Dell's acceptance of the Products in no way waives a claim for breach of warranty or an argument that Products comport with specifications or warranties. To preserve a remedy for breach of warranty the buyer must generally notify the seller of the breach within a reasonable time of discovery.[130] Indeed, parties may contractually agree that the buyer will have waived all remedies for a nonconformity, where the notice of such is not given within a contractually stipulated number of days, and this contractual waiver will be enforced so long as the stipulated number of days reasonably allows for the buyer to discover the defect.[131]

What constitutes acceptance and rejection under this Agreement? Recall that the U.C.C. generally defers to a contract, except where the U.C.C. provides otherwise.[132] Also, recall that one example of the U.C.C. "providing otherwise" is with regard to a "reasonable time" to inspect goods before

---

124. *Id.* § 2-608(1); *see, e.g., Trinity,* 486 F.3d at 331-32.

125. U.C.C. § 2-703(1) (2003); *see also id.* § 2-602(3) (citing U.C.C. § 2-703 for remedies generally available to the seller).

126. *Id.* § 2-602(2)(c).

127. *See id.* § 2-510(1).

128. *Id.* § 2-607(1) ("The buyer must pay at the contract rate for any goods accepted.").

129. *Id.* § 2-607(2).

130. *Id.* § 2-607(3)(a). Under pre-revised Article 2, failure to notify within a reasonable time for a breach of warranty bars any remedy, whereas under Revised Article 2 failure to notify within a reasonable time bars the buyer from a remedy if the seller is prejudiced by the failure.

131. *See, e.g., Traffic Safety Devices, Inc. v. Safety Barriers, Inc.,* No. 3:02-CV-636, 2006 WL 2709229 (E.D. Tenn. Sept. 20, 2006). See Chapter 3 for more on notice-requirement provisions and contractual "statute of limitations" provisions.

132. *See* U.C.C. § 1-205(a) (2003).

acceptance. As Article 2 requires, then, § 5.2.3 of the Agreement affords the buyer, Dell, an opportunity to inspect the Products before accepting them. Subsection 5.2.3(c) specifies how acceptance may occur under this Agreement. Recall that acceptance may occur under Article 2 upon the buyer's giving notice of acceptance to the seller.[133] This is the easy instance of acceptance, and § 5.2.3(c)(ii) of the Agreement provides that Dell may explicitly accept the Products in writing. The more difficult scenario turns on the question of when "silence" amounts to acceptance. Section 2-606(1)(b) of the Revised U.C.C. tells us that a buyer will be deemed to have accepted goods when the buyer fails to make an effective rejection and has had a reasonable opportunity to inspect the goods. And we know from § 2-602(1) that the buyer must "seasonably notify" (recall, parties may set by contract what constitutes a "seasonable" duration of time) the seller of the rejection for it to be effective. If the buyer has not "seasonably notified" the seller of rejection and the buyer has had a reasonable opportunity to inspect the goods, then the buyer will be deemed to have accepted the goods. Subsection 5.2.3(c)(i) provides that if Dell does not reject the Products within two days of delivery, then Dell will be deemed to have accepted the Products. As long as this provides Dell with a reasonable opportunity to inspect, then such deemed acceptance will be effective. (However, Dell still would retain the right to revoke its acceptance, if the requirements for such, as discussed above, are satisfied.) The last two methods of acceptance under § 5.2.3(c) of the Agreement are consistent with U.C.C. § 2-606(1)(c), as Dell's use of the Products in its manufacturing process or delivering of such Products to a customer each likely constitutes an "act inconsistent with seller's ownership."[134]

9. Revisiting Warranties and Disclaimers Under Article Two

We have already discussed warranties at length in Chapter 3. In the context of goods sold, warranties often speak to the quality or nature of the goods and are promises that such goods will meet certain specifications. Warranties may be express or implied, and Article 2 is a source of implied warranties. We first explore the requirements for the creation of express warranties under Article 2, and then we reexamine the implied warranties Article 2 imputes into a contract for the sale of goods, absent an effective disclaimer.

a. Express Warranties

Under Article 2, a seller makes an express "warranty" to a buyer when the seller makes a promise, which relates to the goods and which "becomes part of

---

133. *Id.* § 2-606(1)(a).
134. *Id.* § 2-606(1)(c).

the basis of the bargain."[135] The official comments explain that this requirement dispenses with the requirement of reliance.[136] The question, then, is similar to that posed by the court in *Ziff-Davis*: Did the buyer purchase the warranty as part of the bargain? A seller's description of goods in a written agreement is likely to steer a court to find the description of fact to be a basis of the bargain.[137] Another question is whether such warranty is as of a point in time or ongoing into the future. Courts will generally look to the nature of the promise, usually requiring some explicit statement extending the warranty to future performance in order to find a warranty of future performance.[138] Accordingly, § 9.1 provides express warranties from SUPPLIER to Dell, the breach of which occurs if such warranties prove untrue. Notice that § 9.1 removes doubt that such warranties are "ongoing" and speak not only to the state of the goods at the point of delivery but also going forward into the future. What warranties does SUPPLIER provide?

b. Implied Warranties

Recall that Article 2 is the source of two types of implied warranties: merchantability and fitness. Article 2 supplies implied warranties as "gap fillers," as warranties that will attend any sale of goods unless the parties otherwise provide. As to the implied warranty of merchantability, which applies if the seller is a "merchant,"[139] Article 2 provides:

Goods to be merchantable must be at least such as:

(a) pass without objection in the trade under the contract description;

---

135. *Id.* § 2-313(2).

136. *Id.* § 2-313 cmt. 5 ("In actual practice affirmations of fact and promises made by the seller about the goods during a bargain are regarded as part of the description of those goods; hence no particular reliance on these statements need be shown in order to weave them into the fabric of the agreement."). Please see Chapter 3 for further discussion of the requirement of reliance in the context of breach of warranty actions. Note that some courts still require some showing of reliance to make out a claim for breach of warranty. *See, e.g., McManus v. Fleetwood Enters.*, 320 F.3d 545, 550 (5th Cir. 2003) (Texas law)

137. *See, e.g., Martin v. Am. Med. Sys., Inc.*, 115 F.3d 102, 105 (4th Cir. 1997) ("Any description of the goods, other than the seller's mere opinion about the product, constitutes part of the basis of the bargain and is therefore an express warranty."); *see also* U.C.C. § 2-313 cmt. 8 (2003) ("In general, the presumption is that...any affirmation of fact...is intended to become a basis of the bargain.").

138. *See, e.g., Marvin Lumber and Cedar Co. v. PPG Indus., Inc.*, 223 F.3d 873, 879 (8th Cir. 2000) (Minnesota law) ("Moreover, an express warranty of the present condition of goods without a specific reference to the future is not an explicit warranty of future performance, even if the description implies that the goods will perform a certain way in the future.").

139. Under Article 2:

"Merchant" means a person that deals in goods of the kind or otherwise holds itself out by occupation as having knowledge or skill peculiar to the practices or goods involved in the transaction or to which the knowledge or skill may be attributed by the person's employment of an agent or broker or other intermediary that holds itself out by occupation as having the knowledge or skill.

U.C.C. § 2-104(1) (2003). Is SUPPLIER likely to be found a merchant?

(b) in the case of fungible goods, are of fair average quality within the description;

(c) are fit for the ordinary purposes for which goods of that description are used;

(d) run, within the variations permitted by the agreement, of even kind, quality and quantity within each unit and among all units involved;

(e) are adequately contained, packaged, and labeled as the agreement may require; and

(f) conform to the promise or affirmations of fact made on the container or label if any.[140]

Accordingly, merchantability generally warrants that the goods will be what they are supposed to be—that they will be fit for the ordinary purpose for which such goods are used. As for the implied warranty of fitness for a particular purpose, Article 2 provides:

Where the seller at the time of contracting has reason to know any particular purpose for which the goods are required and that the buyer is relying on the seller's skill or judgment to select or furnish suitable goods, there is unless excluded or modified under [§ 2-316] an implied warranty that the goods shall be fit for such purpose.[141]

Do you think that the warranty of fitness is likely to apply to the Agreement? What additional information might be helpful in drawing this conclusion?

When we last visited these concepts (in Chapter 3) we discussed that these implied warranties may be disclaimed by contract. Again, implied warranties mark another instance of Article 2 acting as a friendly filler of contractual gaps: If a contract effectively tells Article 2 "thanks, but no thanks," Article 2 will happily defer and refrain from imputing implied warranties. Still, to be sure the parties so intended, Article 2 requires that such disclaimers meet certain criteria in order to be effective.[142] Indeed, in Chapter 3, we saw an example of a contract's conspicuous—and likely effective—disclaimer of Article 2's implied warranties. Does this chapter's Agreement disclaim any of these implied warranties? If so, is such disclaimer effective?

---

140. *Id.* § 2-314(2).

141. *Id.* § 2-315.

142. U.C.C. § 2-316 explains what makes for an effective exclusion of Article 2 implied warranties. Note that the warranty of title is not considered an "implied warranty," at least with respect to disclaimer. U.C.C. § 2-312(3) cmt. 5 (2003). For further discussion of this, please see Chapter 3. Please also see Chapter 3 for a discussion of exclusive remedies and the failure of essential purpose, both concepts that arise under Article 2.

10. Licensing Intellectual Property

Sections 7.2 and 7.3 of the Agreement grant Dell, respectively: (i) a license to use, reproduce, and distribute Software (a defined term) solely in connection with Dell's distribution and support of Products; and (ii) a license to use SUPPLER Trademarks (again, as defined) in connection with advertising, promotion, and sale of Products. In the context of intellectual property, a license grants the licensee the right to do certain specified things with the licensor's intellectual property. Here, the license grants Dell the right to engage in certain activities (with respect to Software: to use, to reproduce, and to distribute; with respect to SUPPLIER Trademarks: to use) and limits the scope of such permissible activities to Dell's promotion and sale of the Products. In addition, both licenses are non-exclusive, meaning Dell has no right to exclude, or to expect the exclusion of, others (including SUPPLIER) from engaging in the same activities with respect to Software and SUPPLIER Trademarks, and both licenses are non-transferable, meaning that Dell may not sell, assign, or otherwise convey the rights granted to Dell under the license to another party.[143] That both licenses are "worldwide" is perhaps self-explanatory: Dell may exercise its rights under the license anywhere in the world. It is also common for such license provisions to specify the term and revocability of the license. The term of the license may be perpetual or fixed in length, and the license may be revocable or irrevocable, which speaks to the licensor's right to terminate the license and, so, the licensee's right to engage in the licensed activities. For illustration, a license may be perpetual but subject to the licensor's right to revoke the license, or, as another example, a license may be fixed in length but not subject to a right of the licensor to revoke.

Accordingly, here, SUPPLIER has given Dell limited permission to use SUPPLIER's intellectual property by granting Dell non-exclusive license rights to exploit such intellectual property in connection with the sale and distribution of Products. This serves both parties' interests, as both SUPPLIER and Dell have a financial stake in Dell's reselling of the Products. Dell may be better positioned to make sales if Dell has permission to use SUPPLIER's Trademarks in the advertising, promotion, and sale of the Products and to use and pass along the software necessary to the proper operation and support of the Products. Absent such license rights, Dell risks infringing SUPPLIER's intellectual property rights and potential future lawsuits, despite that litigation may seem unrealistic at the time of contracting. If nothing else, without a license, Dell would be treading in uncertain waters in its use of another's property, left to argue that it had an implied license or rights under fair use to use the property.[144] Accordingly, when feasible, a prudent party will obtain express

---

143. For more on the transfer, assignment, and the delegation of rights and duties, please see Chapter 1.
144. "Fair use" refers to a doctrine found in both copyright and trademark and that allows persons to use (or otherwise exploit) the copyright or trademark of another without permission in certain narrow and "fair" manners, such that this use does not constitute infringement of the intellectual property.

license rights to use another party's intellectual property. For more on the licensing of intellectual property, we turn the floor over to a couple seasoned practitioners.

A Practitioner Perspective: Intellectual Property License Agreements

In many ways, intellectual property license agreements are similar to other commercial contracts and include many of the same provisions (e.g., representations and warranties, term and termination provisions, limitations of liability, and dispute resolution provisions). They are unique, though, because they also include licenses to one or more of the four main types of intellectual property: patents, trademarks, copyrights, and trade secrets. Under a license, the licensor agrees that it will not sue the licensee for certain activities that would otherwise be prohibited due to the licensor's ownership of certain intellectual property.

Licenses can be granted or limited in many different ways, including: (a) geographically (e.g., a license for the United States but not Australia, or for Chicago but not New York); (b) temporally (e.g., a license for 10 years or a perpetual license); (c) by field of use (e.g., a license for veterinary but not human medical purposes); or (d) numerically (e.g., a license to make 5,000 widgets per year). The ways in which intellectual property rights can be subdivided, especially with respect to fields of use, are limited only by your imagination. In a license we handled for the movie rights to a comic book character, the field-of-use provisions went on for pages—which party had rights to coloring books, lunch boxes, toys accompanying children's fast-food meals, computer games, and much more.

Unlike public M&A agreements and syndicated loan agreements, the terms of which are often driven significantly by market conditions, the terms of license agreements are typically not public, tend to be unique and are highly dependent on the facts and circumstances of each transaction, especially the relative bargaining power of the licensor and licensee. A lawyer who works on a license agreement should find out first what the business dynamics of the transaction are. Who needs the transaction less? That party will likely have the upper hand when difficult issues arise.

License agreements often mix state and federal law. Rights in a patent or copyright arise under federal law, and trademark rights can arise under both state and federal law. Only trade secrets are solely based on state law. In each case, though, state law governs the general interpretation and enforcement of the license. State law, however, can be preempted by federal law if the application of state law would run counter to the purposes of federal intellectual property laws. For example, under most states' contract law, if a contract is silent as to whether or not it can be assigned, the contract is freely assignable without the consent of the other party. However, for patent, copyright, and trademark licenses, the default rule is the opposite (i.e., absent an express provision permitting assignment, the contract cannot be assigned without the licensor's consent).

A license may contain royalty provisions, pursuant to which the licensee agrees to make ongoing payments to the licensor based on what the licensee makes or sells using or under the intellectual property. When drafting royalty provisions, the lawyer should pay careful consideration to the way royalties will be measured (e.g., what deductions from gross sales will be included before the royalty is applied), when and how royalties will be paid, and how the calculation of the royalties will be verified by the licensor. If there is ambiguity as to which products are covered by a royalty provision and which are not, or as to which costs of sale may be deducted from gross sales before the royalty is applied, the client may find itself in a dispute down the road.

Trademark and trade secret licenses require special provisions. A trademark license agreement must contain quality control provisions that give the licensor a meaningful way to monitor and control the quality of products and services sold under its trademark. Without those provisions, the licensor risks the abandonment of the mark. A trade secret license must require the licensee to maintain the trade secret in confidence. Since a trade secret is only protectable as long as the owner is using appropriate means to keep it secret, providing the trade secret to a third party without an obligation to keep it confidential could cost the owner its right to prevent others from using it.

A licensor often indemnifies its licensee against infringement claims arising from the licensee's use of the licensed intellectual property. In other words, if a third party sues the licensee for the use of material provided by the licensor, the licensor will pay all of the attorneys' fees, court costs, and damages resulting from such suit, and often assume the defense of the suit as well. In certain circumstances, a licensee may indemnify the licensor for claims arising from the licensee's use of the licensed intellectual property. These indemnities are often among the most heavily negotiated provisions in a license. Again, the scope of each indemnity is highly dependent on the dynamics of the transaction.

The best licensing lawyers understand the technology they are licensing, and they use that knowledge to advance their clients' interests. A Ph.D. is not necessary, but a licensing lawyer must understand the nature of the technology, how it was developed, how it is made and used, and how it interrelates with other technology. A lawyer should not be shy about asking questions. It is usually not hard to find a scientist or engineer at the client company who will be delighted to teach. This detailed knowledge will enable the lawyer to think through how each provision of the agreement needs to be customized to fit the client's needs, and it will give the lawyer the background to develop practical and creative ways to resolve the issues that will arise during negotiations.

Jeffrey S. Rothstein, Partner
Sidley Austin LLP

Timothy M. Swan, Associate
Sidley Austin LLP

11. The "Ipso Facto" Clause: Anticipating Bankruptcy

Provisions that terminate or alter a party's interests in certain property, as triggered by the occurrence of a bankruptcy case, the party's insolvency, or the appointment of a custodian (before bankruptcy) or trustee (in bankruptcy), are often called "ipso facto" clauses.[145] As a matter of federal law (i.e., the Bankruptcy Code), these provisions are generally of no effect.[146] Accordingly, why are these provisions so commonly included in contracts, if they are not enforceable?

Part of the answer is found in a theme that runs throughout this book: While a provision may be unlikely to have legal effect in court, a party may still wish to include the provision if to do so is virtually costless. In other words, the answer is essentially another question: "Why not?" In addition, there are specific exceptions where an ipso facto clause may be enforceable (if still redundant as Professor Baird explains below); for example, the Bankruptcy Code allows a creditor to enforce an ipso facto clause (e.g., to accelerate payment under a loan agreement upon bankruptcy) in "a contract to make a loan, or extend other debt financing or financial accommodations, to or for the benefit of the debtor."[147]

Understanding the "Ipso Facto" Clause

Contracts of every sort commonly contain what is known as an "ipso facto" clause. It provides that the mere fact of filing a bankruptcy petition constitutes a default that terminates the contractual relationship.

A party to a contract may want such a clause for entirely defensive reasons. If the other a party files for bankruptcy, one wants to be able to come into court and assert one's rights, even if no obligations are then owing. If you make a long-term loan, you do not want to be left helpless while other creditors whose loans are overdue go after whatever assets are available.

Ipso facto clauses also serve an offensive purpose. Even if the other side is not behind on any obligations, the bankruptcy filing signals information. The operations of a business often suffer when someone is in financial distress. At the very least, it raises doubts about the business's long-term viability. News of a bankruptcy filing wakes everyone up and makes them take stock. It is useful to have the ability to bail out if, on investigation, the warning signal proves justified.

---

145. *See* 11 U.S.C.A. § 365(e)(1) (West Supp. 2005); 11 U.S.C.A. § 541(c)(1)(B) (West Supp. 2010).

146. *See supra* note 145.

147. *See* 11 U.S.C.A. § 365(e)(2)(B) (West Supp. 2005); *see also, e.g., Mims v. Fidelity Funding, Inc.*, 307 B.R. 849, 858 (N.D. Tex. 2002) ("[I]t is clear that the Bankruptcy Code's invalidation of *ipso facto* clauses does not apply in this situation involving a contract to make a loan for the benefit of the debtor.").

Notwithstanding their logic, ipso facto clauses present something of a mystery, as they represent parts of a contract that do no work. Ipso facto clauses are either redundant or unenforceable. They could disappear from a contract and the legal rights of the parties would be entirely unaffected.

A defensive ipso facto clause is part of the background rules built into every contract. Under bankruptcy law, the filing of a bankruptcy petition automatically accelerates obligations, regardless whether the contract provides for it. A creditor whose loan is due in ten years time is treated the same as someone whose loan is due today.

Moreover, the Bankruptcy Code prohibits the offensive use of an ipso facto clause. The rules governing the treatment of executory contracts are among the most complicated in all of bankruptcy. A debtor in bankruptcy may or may not be able to assume an executory contract. The debtor in some cases can even reinstate loans. But the debtor's ability to do so exists independently of whether the contract contains an ipso facto clause. This idea is one of the few that are clear.

The pervasiveness of ipso facto clauses likely exists for a combination of reasons. Path dependence explains much. These clauses were generally enforceable before a dramatic revision of the bankruptcy law in 1978. Though they have long ceased to do any work, they do no harm either. There is no evolutionary pressure to eliminate them, especially as they often appear in conjunction with other language—such as a reference to state insolvency proceedings—which might still be effective.

There is one qualification to all of this, however. While the inclusion of an ipso facto clause for offensive purposes is wholly ineffective, their defensive use may bring a small benefit at the margin. The concept that the filing of a petition constitutes a default that accelerates the obligations owing under a contract is imminent in the structure of the Bankruptcy Code, but it is not stated in so many words. Ever cautious, lawyers do not want to take the chance that some judge might misunderstand. The chance that a judge would do so is low, but the costs of including the clause in a contract are lower still.

Professor Douglas Baird
Harry A. Bigelow Distinguished
Service Professor of Law
The University of Chicago Law School

12. The Implied Covenant of Good Faith and Fair Dealing

Last but certainly not least, is an important concept that affects every contract in this book — and every contract outside this book. We have spoken a bit about implied warranties, and, so, the concept of implied contractual terms should be familiar to you by now. An "implied" term is one that is not expressly written in a contract but that is nonetheless found to be a part of the contract's terms. Warranties are not the only type of contractual provisions impliedly found in an agreement. Indeed, courts also impute a special covenant: the "implied covenant of good faith and fair dealing." While implied warranties are not frequently found outside contracts governed by the U.C.C., the implied covenant of good faith and fair dealing is ubiquitous, found in every contractual agreement, including those between sophisticated parties.[148] As the Restatement explains: "Every contract imposes upon each party a duty of good faith and fair dealing in its performance and its enforcement."[149] The U.C.C. echoes the Restatement: "Every contract or duty within [the Uniform Commercial Code] imposes an obligation of good faith in its performance and enforcement."[150]

We have already encountered the concept of "good faith" a few times. Earlier in this chapter we discussed output and requirements contracts and that a quantity term tied to the seller's output production or the buyer's requirements requires that the seller produce its output or that the buyer determine its requirements in "good faith." Indeed, as discussed by the court in *Advent Systems*, the implied covenant of good faith and fair dealing works to impose this duty of good faith even in *non-exclusive* "output" and "requirements" contracts.[151] We also discussed "good faith" earlier in this chapter in the context of "agreements to agree," specifically with regard to agreements to negotiate in good faith.

What is this omnipresent covenant to act in good faith and to deal fairly? The official comments to the Restatement explain:

> Subterfuges and evasions violate the obligation of good faith in performance even though the actor believes his conduct to be justified. But the obligation goes further: bad faith may be overt or may consist of inaction, and fair dealing may require more than honesty. A complete catalogue of types of bad faith is impossible, but the following types are among those which have been recognized in judicial decisions: evasion of the spirit of the bargain, lack of diligence and slacking off, willful rendering of imperfect performance, abuse of

---

148. *See, e.g., Anthony's Pier Four, Inc. v. HBC Assocs.*, 583 N.E.2d 806, 821 (Mass. 1991) ("Anthony's asks us to hold that, in contracts between sophisticated businesspeople, no covenant of good faith and fair dealing is implied. We decline so to hold....Indeed, the rule is clear in Massachusetts that every contract is subject to an implied covenant of good faith and fair dealing.").

149. RESTATEMENT (SECOND) OF CONTRACTS § 205 (1981); *see O'Tool v. Genmar Holdings, Inc.*, 387 F.3d 1188, 1195 (10th Cir. 2004) ("Under Delaware law, an implied covenant of good faith and fair dealing inheres in every contract.") (citation omitted); *see also In re Ocwen Loan Servicing, LLC*, 491 F.3d 638, 645 (7th Cir. 2007) ("Most state laws impose a duty of good faith performance of contracts, meaning that a party to a contract cannot engage in opportunistic behavior.").

150. U.C.C. § 1-304 (2003).

151. *Advent Sys. Ltd. v. Unisys Corp.*, 925 F. 670, 680-81 (3d Cir. 1991). Query what it means to have a "non-exclusive" output or requirements contract. Under a non-exclusive output contract, the seller must sell and the buyer must buy some of the seller's output but not all of its output—to require the seller to sell all of its output to the buyer would amount to requiring the seller to deal exclusively with the buyer. Under a non-exclusive requirements contract, the buyer must purchase and the seller must sell some of the buyer's requirements but not all of its requirements—to require the buyer to buy all of its requirements from the seller would amount to requiring the buyer to deal exclusively with the seller. Is there any difference between such an arrangement and just a regular agreement to buy or sell an undetermined amount?

a power to specify terms, and interference with or failure to cooperate in the other party's performance.[152]

The implied covenant is a duty to perform the express provisions of the contract in consonance with the spirit of the agreement. In this way, the implied covenant of good faith and fair dealing offers a thick understanding of contractual provisions: The implied covenant tells us to understand contractual duties to perform not as reduced to their barest terms. Accordingly, the implied covenant suggests that parties enter contracts with an expectation of good-faith performance.

a. The Implied "Fruits" of Express Provisions

The implied covenant of good faith and fair dealing only operates when attached to, or rooted in, an express provision.[153] A breach of the implied covenant occurs when one party deprives the other of the "fruits" of the express provisions of an agreement.[154] This comports with our earlier discussion of the essential nature of the implied covenant, which imposes a duty on parties to perform in good faith their already existing contractual duties. Accordingly, the covenant does not impose independent substantive duties beyond those expressly provided in a contract but, rather, provides a standard for how parties are to perform such duties.[155]

In deciding how to impute the implied covenant, courts sometimes will ask whether the parties would have provided as much in their contract had they contemplated the question at issue.[156] Indeed, courts will not find the *implied* covenant to contravene the *express* provisions of a contract.[157] Accordingly, parties may wish to provide expressly in their contract what is and is not expected of a party in performing its contractual duties. Otherwise, if the contract ends up in litigation or arbitration, a court or arbitrator will have to discern the contours of what constitutes appropriate party behavior.

For example, in *O'Tool v. Genmar Holdings, Inc.*,[158] the Tenth Circuit found that a reasonable finder of fact could find that a company, acquiring another com-

---

152. RESTATEMENT (SECOND) OF CONTRACTS § 205 cmt. d (1981).

153. *See, e.g., Metro. Life Ins. Co. v. NJR Nabisco*, 716 F. Supp. 1504, 1519 (S.D.N.Y. 1989).

154. *See id.* at 1518 ("The appropriate analysis, then, is first to examine the indentures to determine 'the fruits of the agreement' between the parties, and then to decide whether those 'fruits' have been spoiled—which is to say, whether plaintiffs' contractual rights have been violated by defendants."); *Warner Ins. Co. v. Comm'r of Ins.*, 548 N.E.2d 188, 471 (Mass. 1991).

155. *See, e.g.,* U.C.C. § 1-304 cmt. 1 (2003). Please see above for the discussion of "good faith" in the context of "agreements to negotiate in good faith," as part of the earlier discussion of "agreements to agree."

156. *See, e.g., Third Story Music, Inc. v. Waits*, 48 Cal. Rptr. 2d 747, 750 (Cal. Ct. App. 1995); *Fashion Fabrics of Iowa, Inc. v. Retail Investors Corp.*, 266 N.W.2d 22, 28 (Iowa 1978); *O'Tool*, 387 F.3d at 1197.

157. *See, e.g., Uno Rests., Inc. v. Boston Kenmore Realty Corp.*, 805 N.E.2d 957, 964 (Mass. 2004); *Dalton v. Educ. Testing Serv.*, 663 N.E.2d 289, 291-92 (N.Y. 1995) ("The duty of good faith and fair dealing, however, is not without limits, and no obligation can be implied that would be inconsistent with other terms of the contractual relationship.") (internal citations and quotation marks omitted).

158. 387 F.3d 1188 (10th Cir. 2004) (Delaware law).

pany, violated the implied covenant of good faith and fair dealing when it made decisions that minimized the payment under an "earn-out" provision. An earn-out provision provides a way for owners of an acquired company to earn additional consideration for the acquisition of the company. An earn-out provision is generally tied to some earnings metric (e.g., revenue, net income) of the acquired line of business. In *O'Tool*, a large boat-manufacturing company, Genmar, acquired another boat-manufacturing company, Horizon, in exchange for: (i) cash consideration of $2.3 million; and (ii) an earn-out with the potential to pay $5.3 million over five years based on the annual gross revenues from the sale of Horizon (or any successor) brand boats and boats manufactured in Horizon's plant facility. However, after the acquisition, Genmar immediately changed the name of the Horizon-line boats to Nova, saddled the Horizon facility with the production of a new and expensive-to-produce line of boats, and implemented a policy giving production priority to non-Horizon/Nova-line boats. Genmar also eventually caused its dealers to change from selling Horizon/Nova-brand boats to other Genmar brands, stopped the manufacture of Horizon/Nova-brand boats, and closed the Horizon plant facility. All of these acts hampered the gross revenues from the sale of Horizon/Nova-line boats and from the boats manufactured in the Horizon plant facility, reducing payment available under the earn-out provision. The acquisition agreement between Genmar and Horizon neither authorized nor prohibited any of these acts. The Tenth Circuit explained:

> [W]e conclude that a reasonable finder of fact could have concluded the parties (had they actually thought about it) would not have simultaneously included within the agreement provisions expressly allowing Genmar to: (1) immediately change the brand name of the boats designed and produced by GMK [the subsidiary that acquired Horizon]; (2) set production schedules or priorities that effectively reduced the maximum earn-out consideration available to Pepper [an owner of Horizon, whom Genmar hired as president of GMK]; (3) impose significant design and production costs upon GMK for other Genmar brands of boats...; or (4) "flip" Horizon dealers to other brands of Genmar boats.[159]

b. Performance Standards: "Commercially Reasonable" and "Best Efforts"

Quoting a commentator, the court in *Advent Systems* explained that even when a contract does not have a "best efforts" clause, the law implies that a party must act in good faith and that, in the context of an (exclusive or non-exclusive) requirements contract that does not expressly speak to the purchaser's obligation to sell or otherwise to maintain minimum requirements, a purchaser must "do more than the bare minimum to comply with a contract;

---

159. *Id.* at 1197 (citing *Katz v. Oak Indus., Inc.*, 508 A.2d 873, 880 (Del. Ch. 1986)).

[the purchaser] must really make some attempt to sell."[160] Accordingly, absent some contractually provided standard for the performance of a party's duties, the implied covenant of good faith and fair dealing steps in to provide a "reasonableness" standard.[161] Parties desiring to lower or to heighten (or to be confident in) a standard of performance may wish to specify in the contract the standard by which one must perform his obligations.

Examples of performance standards commonly found in agreements include "commercially reasonable" and "best efforts." That is, a contract may require that one perform some obligation in a "commercially reasonable" manner or that one use "best efforts" in so performing.

What meaning do these standards have? "Best efforts" intuitively calls for something more than a "commercially reasonable" performance—but how *much* more? How can we give measure to these necessarily vague concepts? Are these standards too amorphous to impose enforceable obligations?[162] In general, courts will enforce "best efforts" and "commercially reasonable" standards for performance,[163] but what does this mean? These are necessarily imprecise, "facts-and-circumstances" standards and do not lend themselves to precise definition.

A "best efforts" standard does not require efforts of Herculean proportions,[164] nor does it require that a party disregard his own interests.[165] Indeed, at least one court has equated "best efforts" with the level of performance required by the implied covenant of good faith.[166] Still, a party agreeing to perform his "best efforts" should take note that courts have often required something more than mere good faith.[167] In addition, many practitioners representing the performing party will seek to avoid a "best efforts" standard at all costs.

In contrast, courts have seemed not to require anything more of a "commercially reasonable" standard than what is required by the implied covenant of good faith.[168]

---

160. The court in *Advent Systems* quoted and cited THEODORE BANKS, DISTRIBUTION LAW, 226-62 (1990) for this proposition. *Advent Sys. Ltd. v. Unisys Corp.*, 925 F.2d 670, 680 (3d Cir. 1991).

161. *See* RESTATEMENT (SECOND) OF CONTRACTS § 205 cmt. 1 (1981).

162. See this chapter's earlier discussion of agreements to negotiate in good faith and that some courts have found these agreements to be enforceable in the abstract but too imprecise to allow for enforcement in practice.

163. *See, e.g., NBC Capital Mkts. Group, Inc. v. First Bank*, 25 F. App'x 363, 365 (6th Cir. 2002).

164. *See, e.g., Triple-A Baseball Club Assocs. v. Ne. Baseball, Inc.*, 832 F.2d 214, 228 (1st Cir. 1987) (Maine law) ("We have found no cases, and none have been cited, holding that 'best efforts' means every conceivable effort.").

165. *See, e.g., Baron Fin. Corp. v. Natanzon*, 509 F. Supp. 2d 501, 514 (D. Md. 2007).

166. *See, e.g., Triple-A Baseball*, 832 F.2d at 225 (1st Cir. 1987) (Maine law) ("We have been unable to find any case in which a court found, as here, that a party acted in good faith but did not use its best efforts.").

167. *See, e.g., Nat'l Data Payment Sys., Inc. v. Meridian Bank*, 212 F.3d 849, 854 (3d Cir. 2000); *Olympia Hotels Corp. v. Johnson Wax Dev.*, 908 F.2d 1363, 1373 (7th Cir. 1990).

168. *See, e.g., Subaru Distrib. Corp. v. Subaru of Am., Inc.*, 47 F. Supp. 2d 451, 462 (S.D.N.Y. 1999); *Wilson v. Amerada Hess Corp.*, 168 A.2d 1121, 1131 (N.J. 2001).

Even if parties have agreed to a performance standard requiring no more than the implied covenant of good faith, a prudent party may still wish to write a performance standard into the contract. As judges or arbitrators may be uneasy and reluctant to use a legal rule of implication to impose a standard of duty on contractual parties,[169] stating the standard expressly instructs the reader that the parties entered into their contract having contemplated and with the expectation that a party's performance would meet at least *some* level or standard.

Notice that §§ 5.2.1, 6.3.1, 9.3.1(a), 9.4, and 10.4 of the Agreement each use a "commercially reasonable" standard, whereas §§ 15.3 and 16.0 impose a potentially more stringent "best efforts" standard. Look back to each of these sections and seek to determine which party would benefit from switching a "commercially reasonable" standard to a "best efforts" standard (or vice versa, in the cases of §§ 15.3 and 16.0)?

---

169. *See Fashion Fabrics*, 266 N.W.2d at 27 ("Courts are slow to find implied covenants.").

· INDEX ·